This book is dedicated to my dad.
--JPP

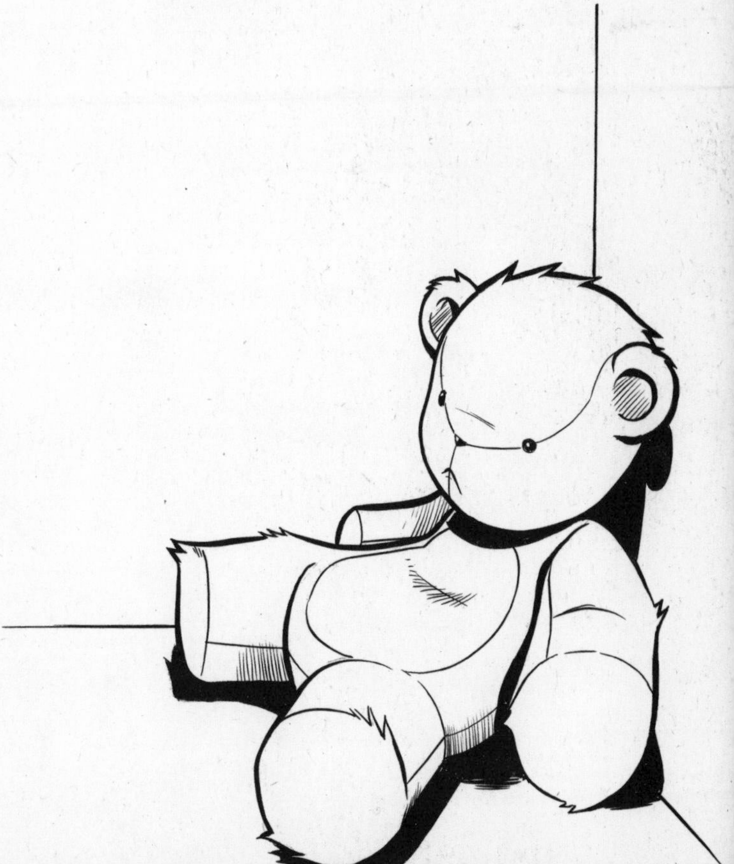

Undertown Vol.1
Written by Jim Pascoe
Illustrated by Jake Myler

Lettering - Lucas Rivera
Cover Design - Jake Myler & James Lee

Editor - Paul Morrissey
Digital Imaging Manager - Chris Buford
Pre-Production Supervisor - Erika Terriquez
Art Director - Anne Marie Horne
Production Manager - Elisabeth Brizzi
VP of Production - Ron Klamert
Editor-in-Chief - Rob Tokar
Publisher - Mike Kiley
President and C.O.O. - John Parker
C.E.O. and Chief Creative Officer - Stuart Levy

A **TOKYOPOP** Manga

TOKYOPOP and 👁 are trademarks or registered trademarks of TOKYOPOP Inc.

TOKYOPOP Inc.
5900 Wilshire Blvd. Suite 2000
Los Angeles, CA 90036

E-mail: info@TOKYOPOP.com
Come visit us online at www.TOKYOPOP.com

ISBN: 978-1-4278-0782-3

First TOKYOPOP printing: July 2007
10 9 8 7 6 5 4 3 2 1
Printed in the USA

UNDERTOWN

VOLUME 1

WRITTEN BY JIM PASCOE
ILLUSTRATED BY JAKE MYLER

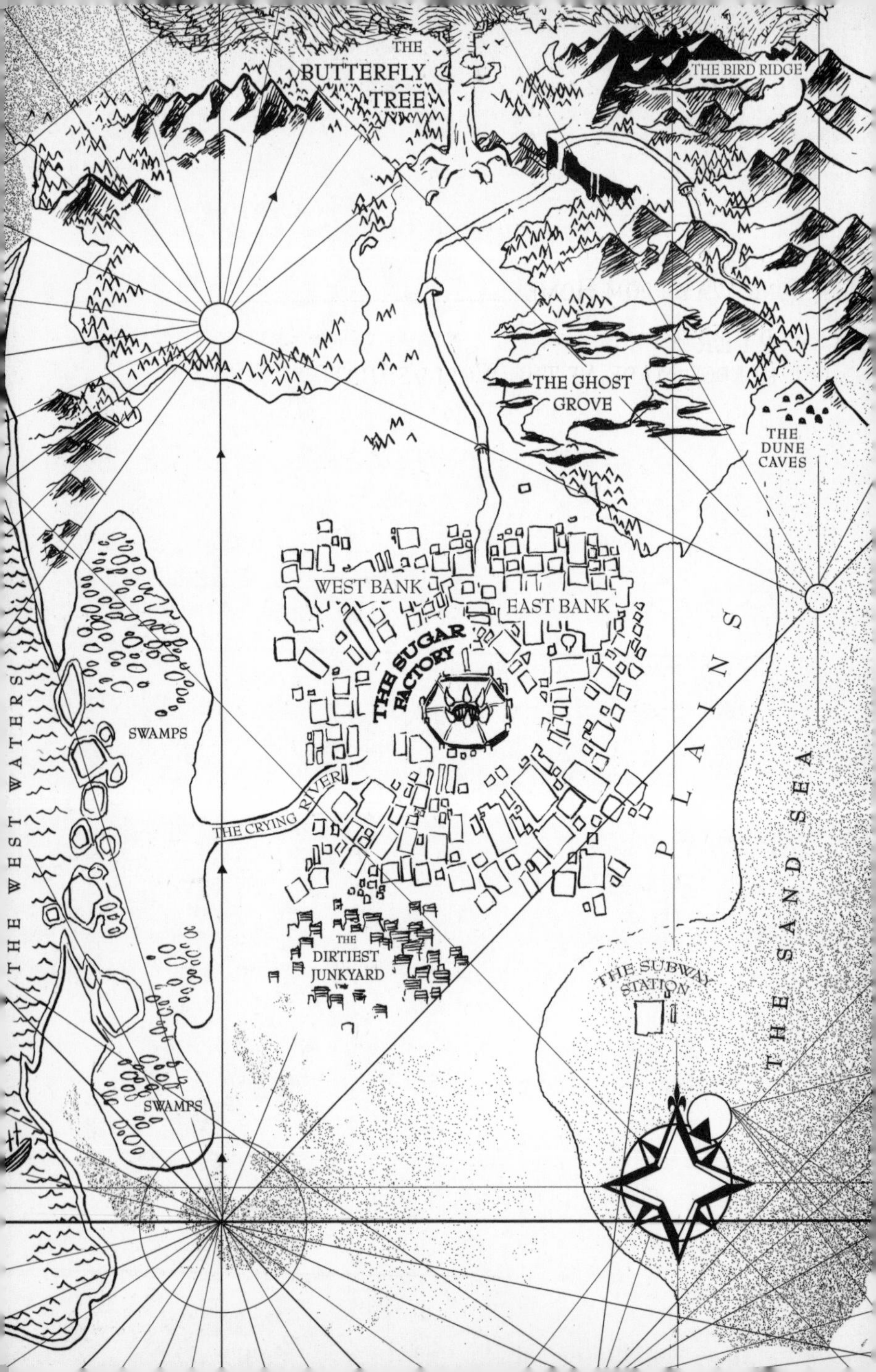
THE BUTTERFLY TREE
THE BIRD RIDGE
THE GHOST GROVE
THE DUNE CAVES
WEST BANK
EAST BANK
THE SUGAR FACTORY
PLAINS
THE SAND SEA
THE WEST WATERS
SWAMPS
THE CRYING RIVER
THE DIRTIEST JUNKYARD
THE SUBWAY STATION
SWAMPS

TABLE OF CONTENTS

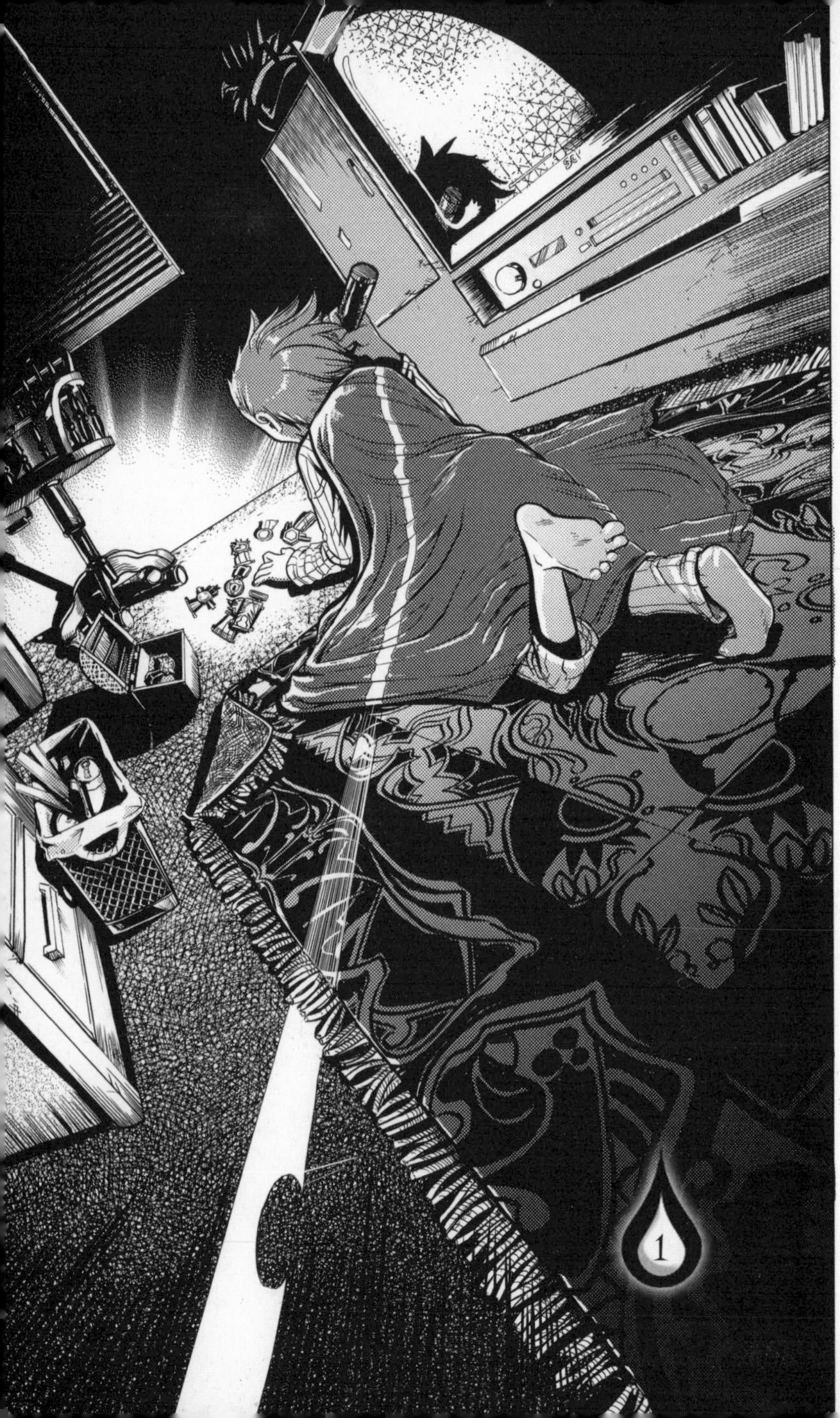
1

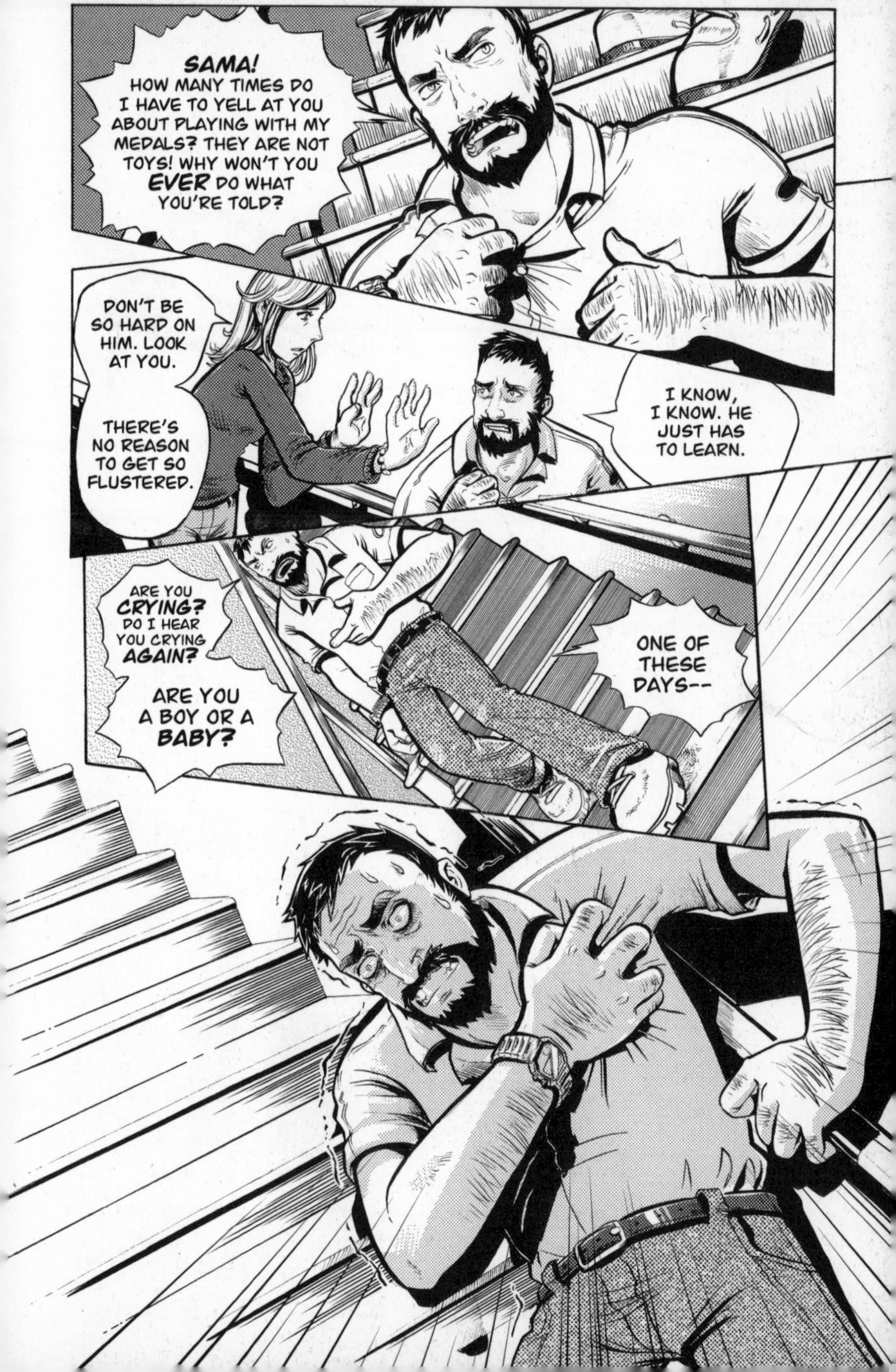
SAMA! HOW MANY TIMES DO I HAVE TO YELL AT YOU ABOUT PLAYING WITH MY MEDALS? THEY ARE NOT TOYS! WHY WON'T YOU EVER DO WHAT YOU'RE TOLD?
DON'T BE SO HARD ON HIM. LOOK AT YOU.
THERE'S NO REASON TO GET SO FLUSTERED.
I KNOW, I KNOW. HE JUST HAS TO LEARN.
ARE YOU CRYING? DO I HEAR YOU CRYING AGAIN?
ARE YOU A BOY OR A BABY?
ONE OF THESE DAYS--

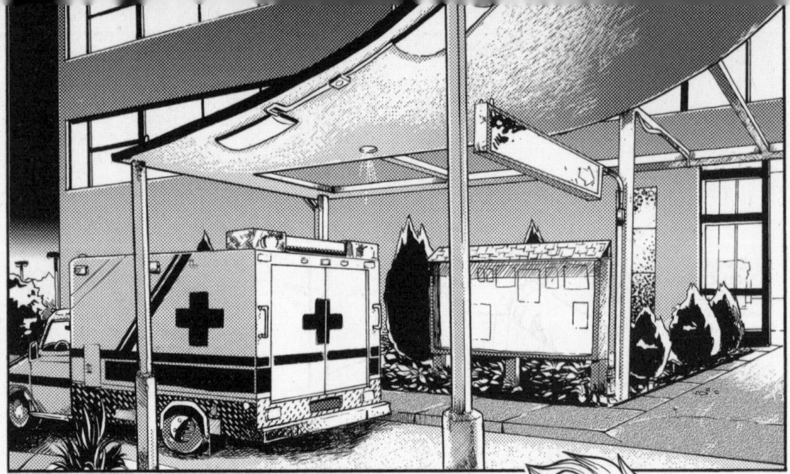

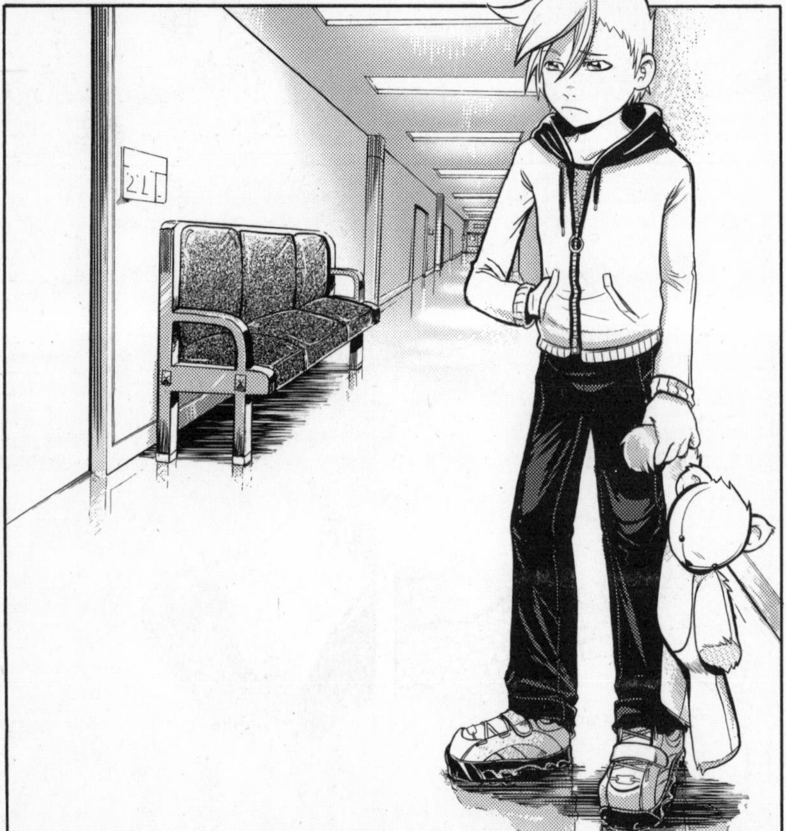

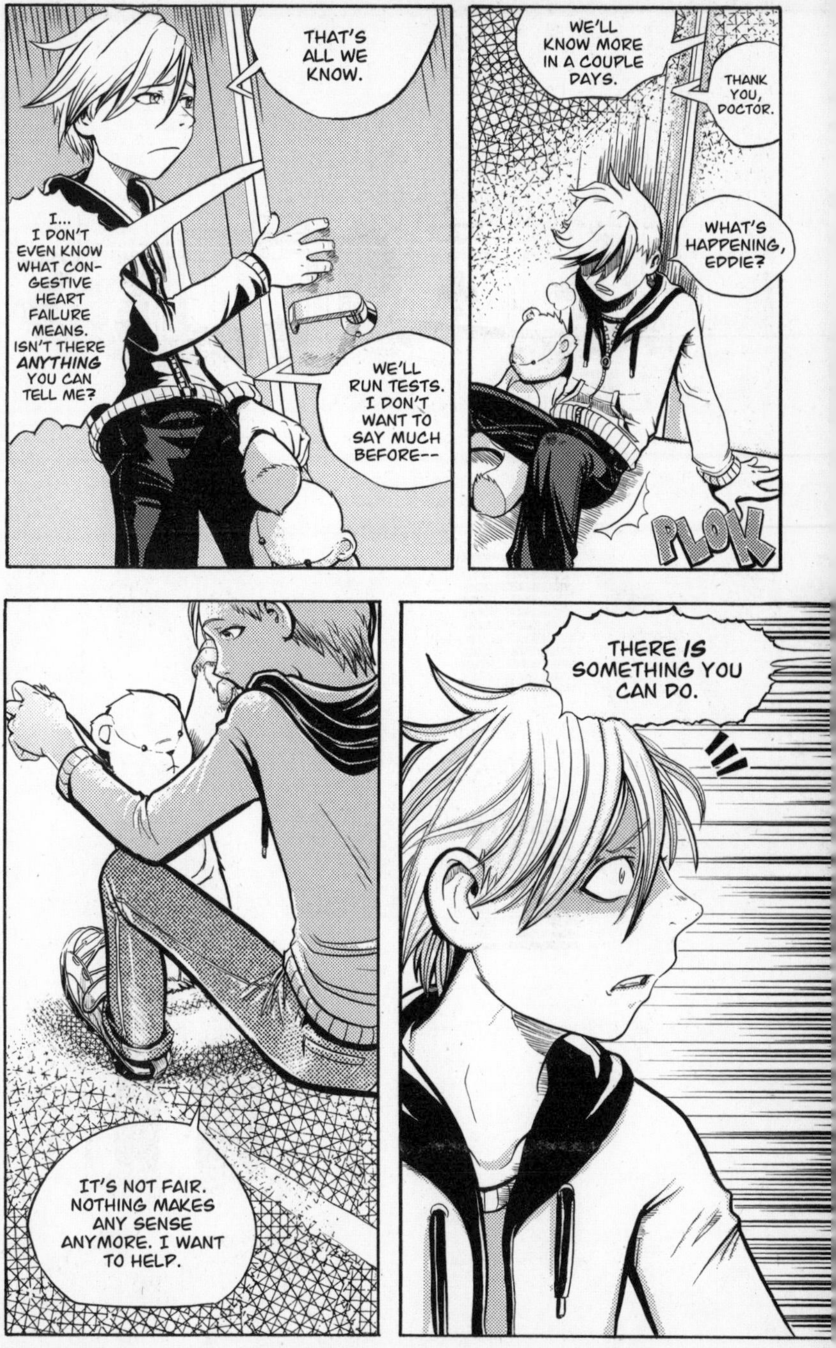
THAT'S ALL WE KNOW.
I... I DON'T EVEN KNOW WHAT CON-GESTIVE HEART FAILURE MEANS. ISN'T THERE ANYTHING YOU CAN TELL ME?
WE'LL RUN TESTS. I DON'T WANT TO SAY MUCH BEFORE--
WE'LL KNOW MORE IN A COUPLE DAYS.
THANK YOU, DOCTOR.
WHAT'S HAPPENING, EDDIE?
PLOK
IT'S NOT FAIR. NOTHING MAKES ANY SENSE ANYMORE. I WANT TO HELP.
THERE IS SOMETHING YOU CAN DO.

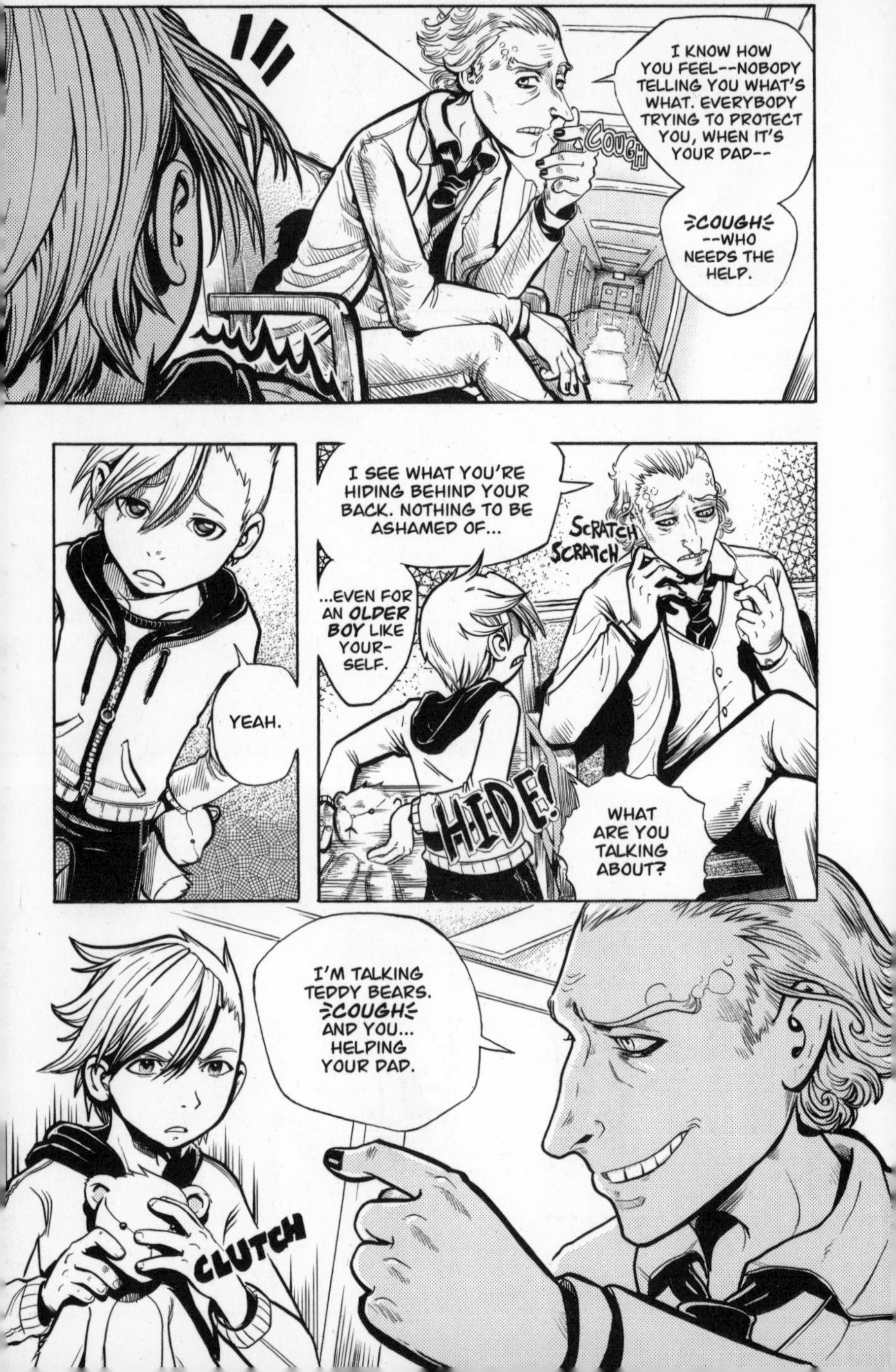
I KNOW HOW YOU FEEL--NOBODY TELLING YOU WHAT'S WHAT. EVERYBODY TRYING TO PROTECT YOU, WHEN IT'S YOUR DAD--
COUGH
≡COUGH≡ --WHO NEEDS THE HELP.
YEAH.
I SEE WHAT YOU'RE HIDING BEHIND YOUR BACK. NOTHING TO BE ASHAMED OF...
SCRATCH SCRATCH
...EVEN FOR AN OLDER BOY LIKE YOUR-SELF.
HIDE!
WHAT ARE YOU TALKING ABOUT?
I'M TALKING TEDDY BEARS. ≡COUGH≡ AND YOU... HELPING YOUR DAD.
CLUTCH

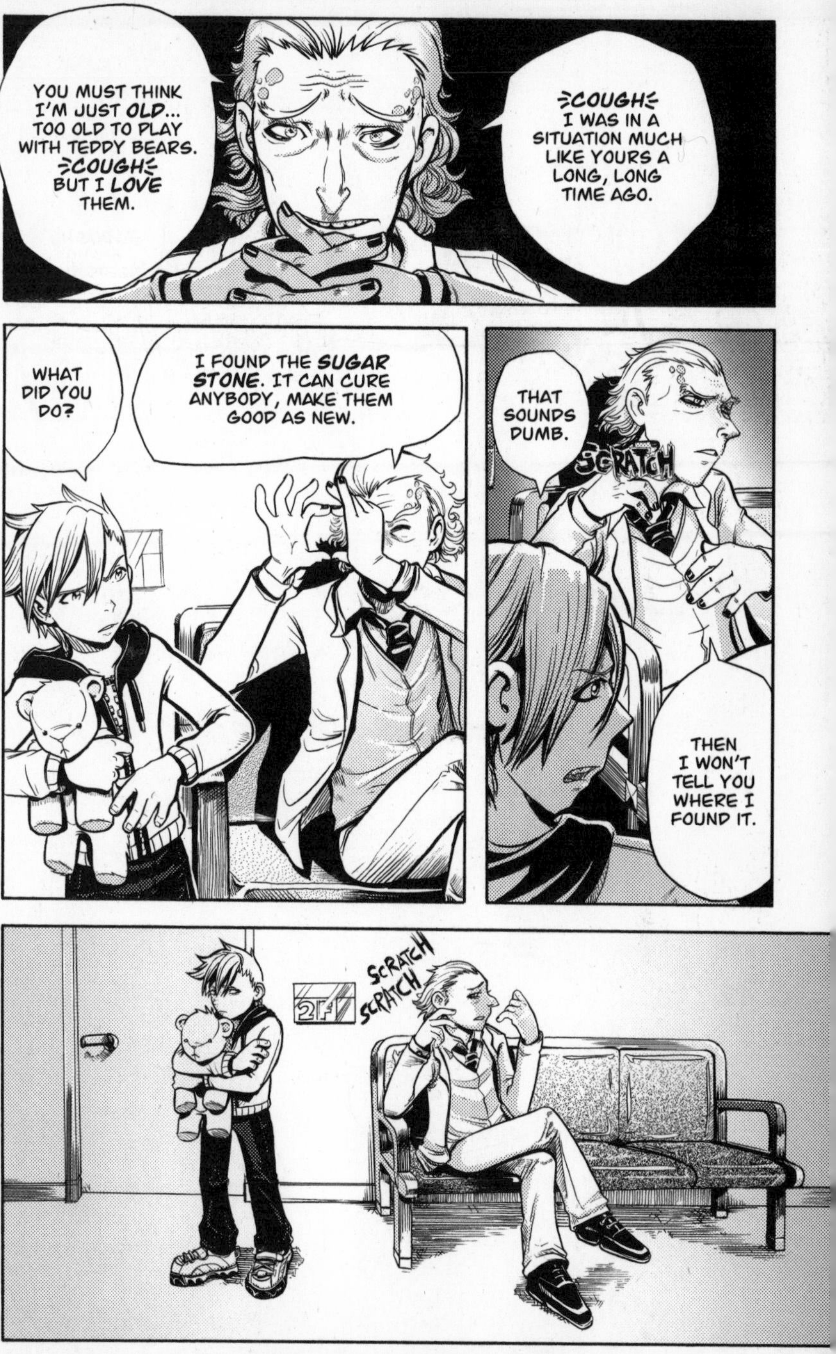
YOU MUST THINK I'M JUST OLD... TOO OLD TO PLAY WITH TEDDY BEARS. COUGH BUT I LOVE THEM.
COUGH I WAS IN A SITUATION MUCH LIKE YOURS A LONG, LONG TIME AGO.
WHAT DID YOU DO?
I FOUND THE SUGAR STONE. IT CAN CURE ANYBODY, MAKE THEM GOOD AS NEW.
THAT SOUNDS DUMB.
SCRATCH
THEN I WON'T TELL YOU WHERE I FOUND IT.
2F
SCRATCH SCRATCH

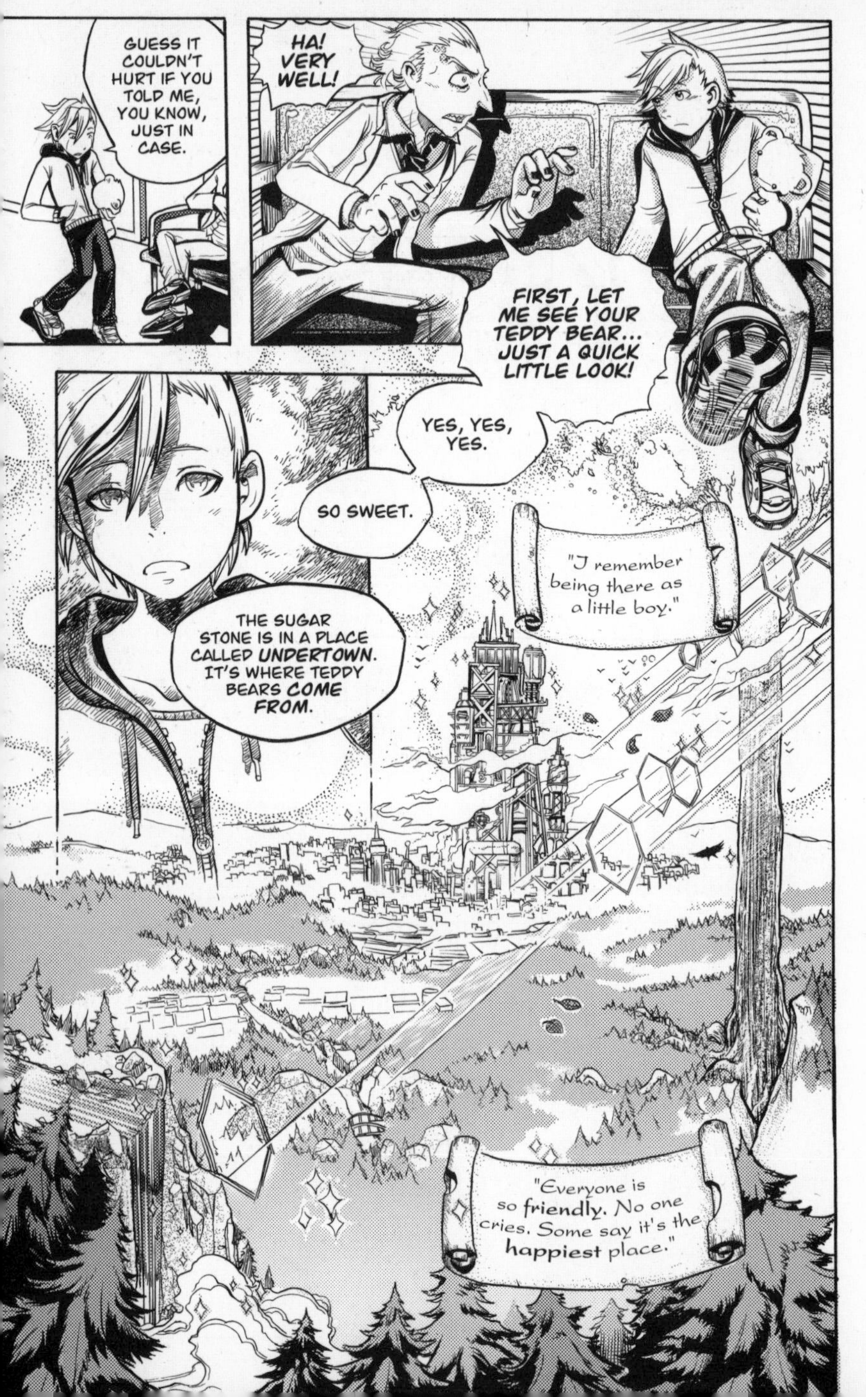
GUESS IT COULDN'T HURT IF YOU TOLD ME, YOU KNOW, JUST IN CASE.
HA! VERY WELL!
FIRST, LET ME SEE YOUR TEDDY BEAR... JUST A QUICK LITTLE LOOK!
YES, YES, YES.
SO SWEET.
THE SUGAR STONE IS IN A PLACE CALLED UNDERTOWN. IT'S WHERE TEDDY BEARS COME FROM.
"I remember being there as a little boy."
"Everyone is so friendly. No one cries. Some say it's the happiest place."

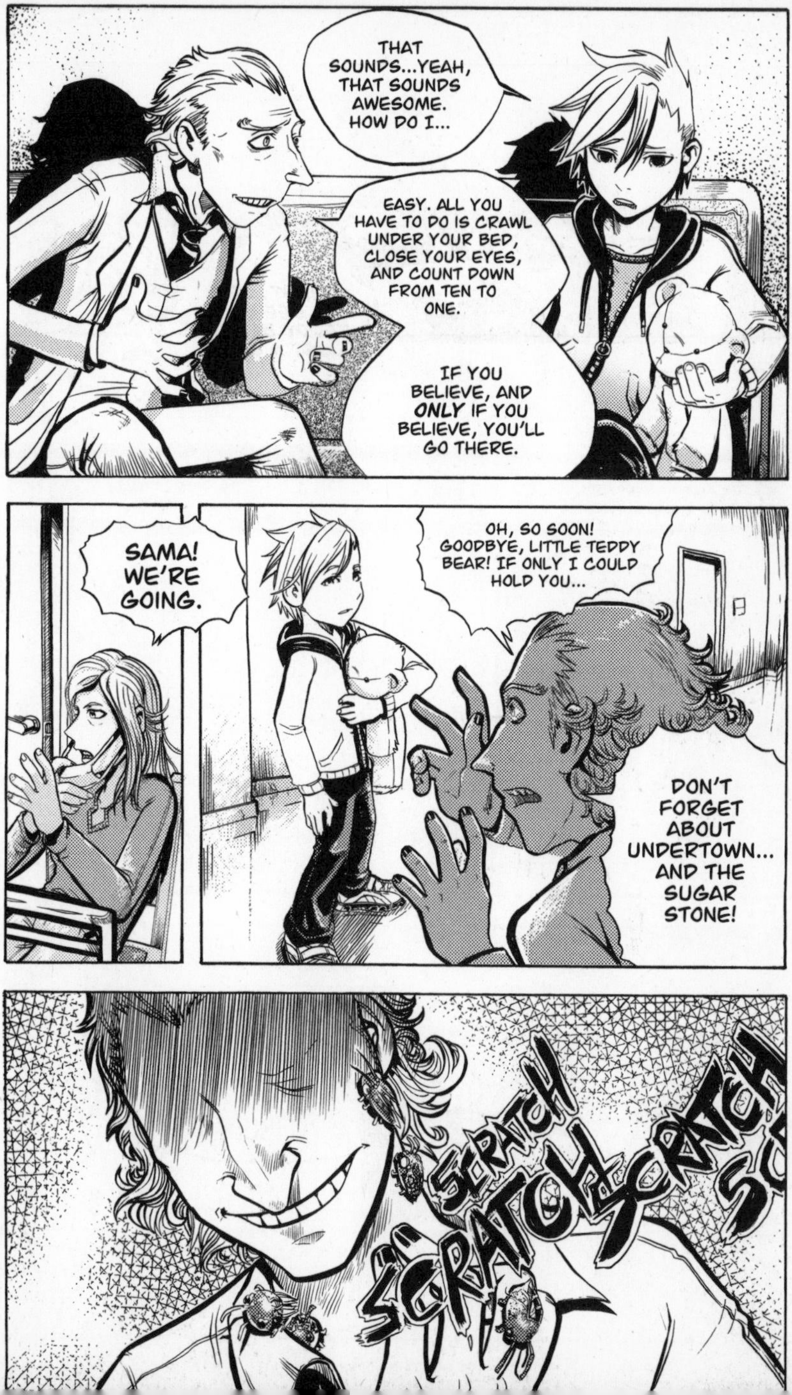
THAT SOUNDS...YEAH, THAT SOUNDS AWESOME. HOW DO I...
EASY. ALL YOU HAVE TO DO IS CRAWL UNDER YOUR BED, CLOSE YOUR EYES, AND COUNT DOWN FROM TEN TO ONE.
IF YOU BELIEVE, AND *ONLY* IF YOU BELIEVE, YOU'LL GO THERE.
SAMA! WE'RE GOING.
OH, SO SOON! GOODBYE, LITTLE TEDDY BEAR! IF ONLY I COULD HOLD YOU...
DON'T FORGET ABOUT UNDERTOWN... AND THE SUGAR STONE!
SCRATCH
SCRATCH
SCRATCH
SCRATCH

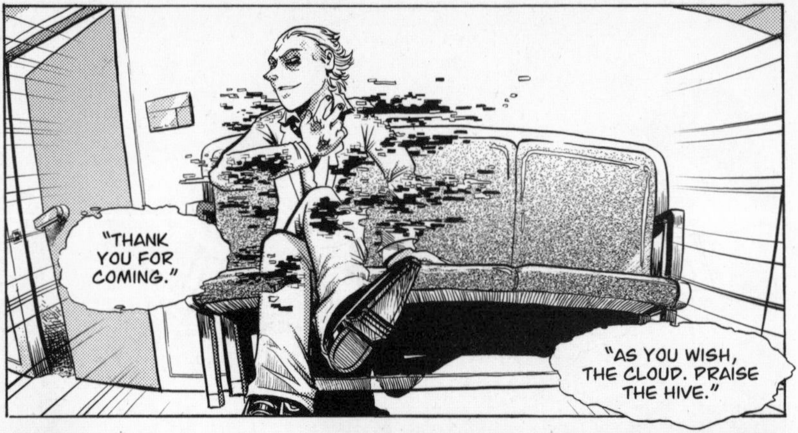
"THANK YOU FOR COMING."
"AS YOU WISH, THE CLOUD. PRAISE THE HIVE."

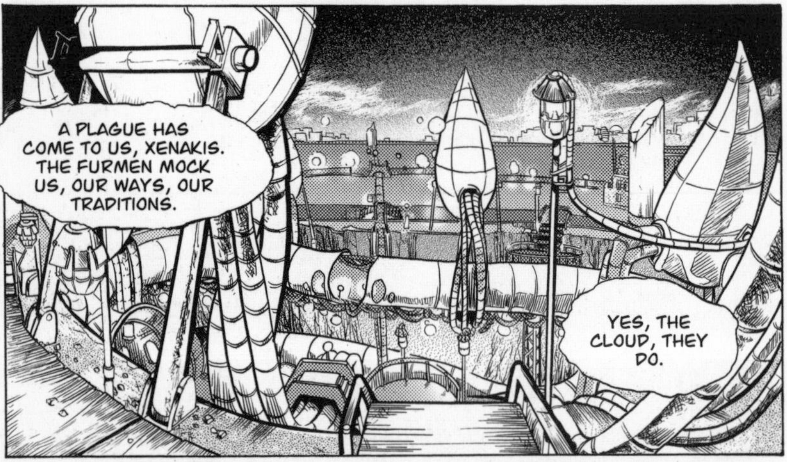
A PLAGUE HAS COME TO US, XENAKIS. THE FURMEN MOCK US, OUR WAYS, OUR TRADITIONS.
YES, THE CLOUD, THEY DO.

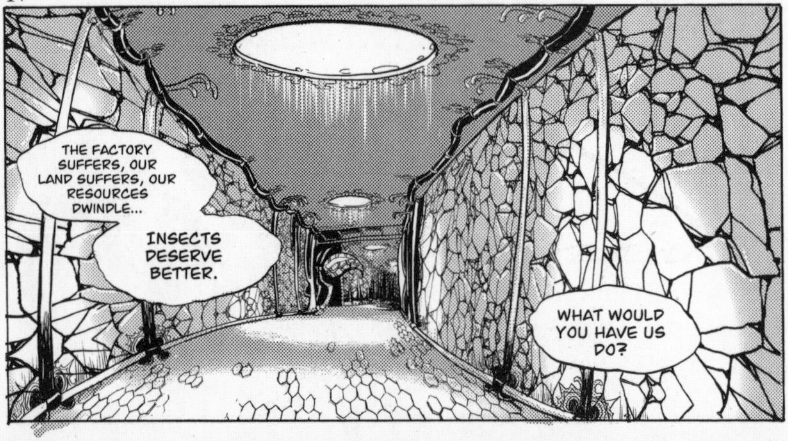
THE FACTORY SUFFERS, OUR LAND SUFFERS, OUR RESOURCES DWINDLE...
INSECTS DESERVE BETTER.
WHAT WOULD YOU HAVE US DO?

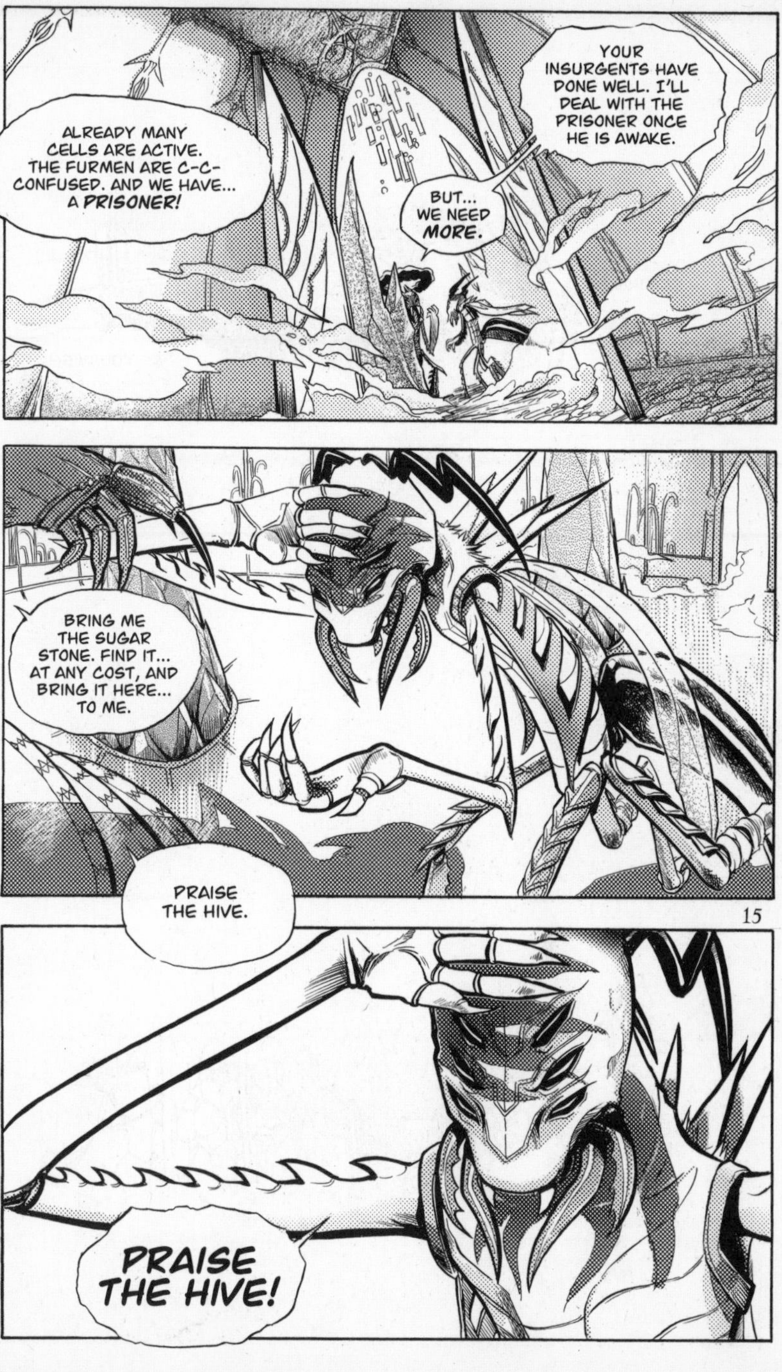
ALREADY MANY CELLS ARE ACTIVE. THE FURMEN ARE C-C-CONFUSED. AND WE HAVE... A PRISONER!
YOUR INSURGENTS HAVE DONE WELL. I'LL DEAL WITH THE PRISONER ONCE HE IS AWAKE.
BUT... WE NEED MORE.
BRING ME THE SUGAR STONE. FIND IT... AT ANY COST, AND BRING IT HERE... TO ME.
PRAISE THE HIVE.
PRAISE THE HIVE!

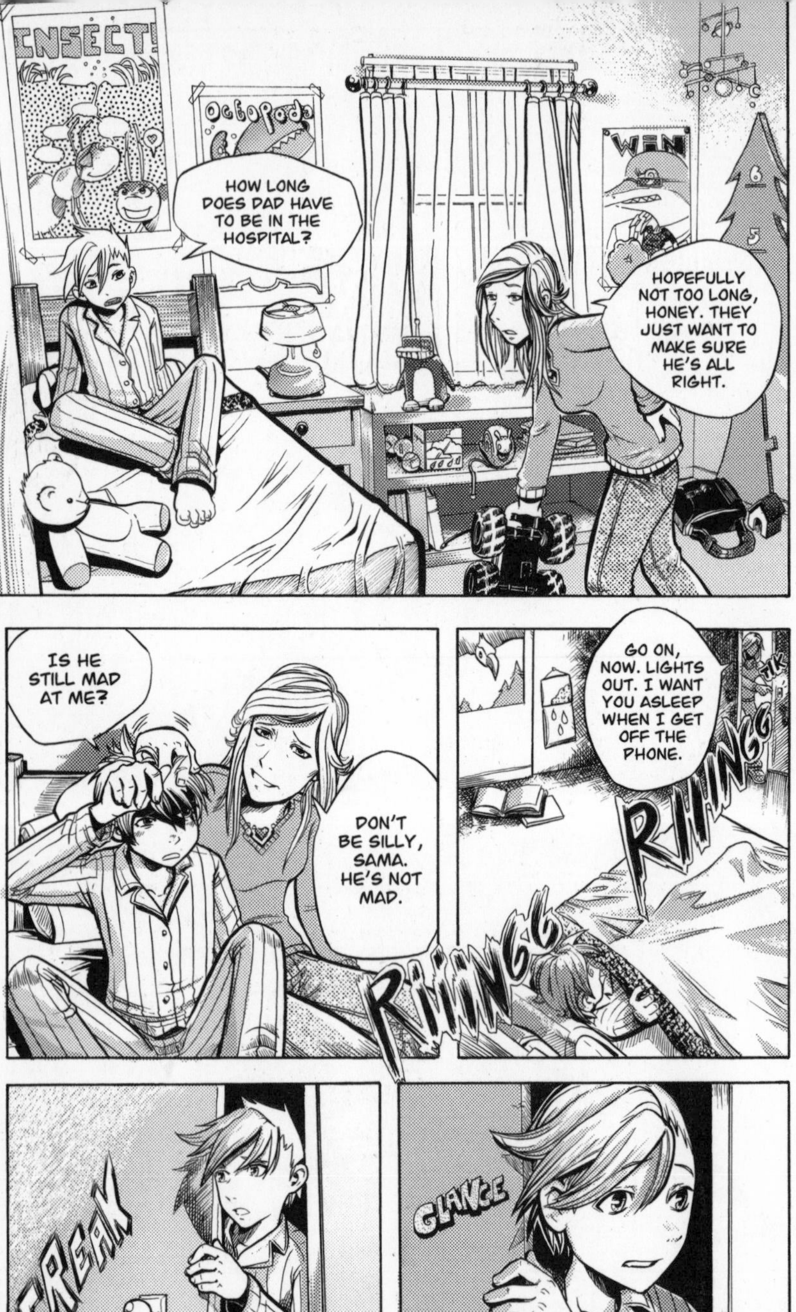
INSECT!
HOW LONG DOES DAD HAVE TO BE IN THE HOSPITAL?
HOPEFULLY NOT TOO LONG, HONEY. THEY JUST WANT TO MAKE SURE HE'S ALL RIGHT.
IS HE STILL MAD AT ME?
DON'T BE SILLY, SAMA. HE'S NOT MAD.
RIIINGG
GO ON, NOW. LIGHTS OUT. I WANT YOU ASLEEP WHEN I GET OFF THE PHONE.
RIIINGG
CREAK
GLANCE

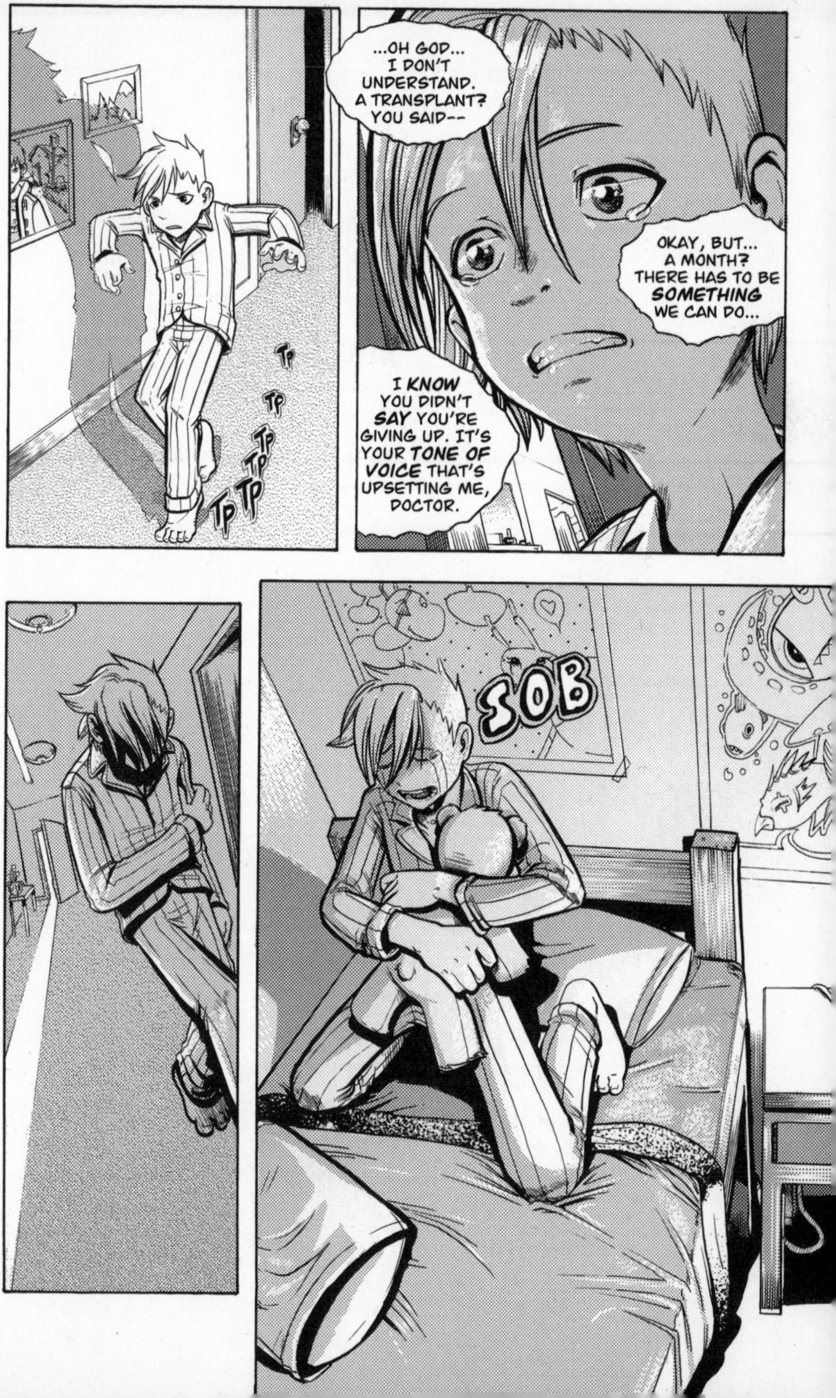
Tp Tp Tp Tp Tp Tp
...OH GOD... I DON'T UNDERSTAND. A TRANSPLANT? YOU SAID--
OKAY, BUT... A MONTH? THERE HAS TO BE SOMETHING WE CAN DO...
I KNOW YOU DIDN'T SAY YOU'RE GIVING UP. IT'S YOUR TONE OF VOICE THAT'S UPSETTING ME, DOCTOR.
SOB

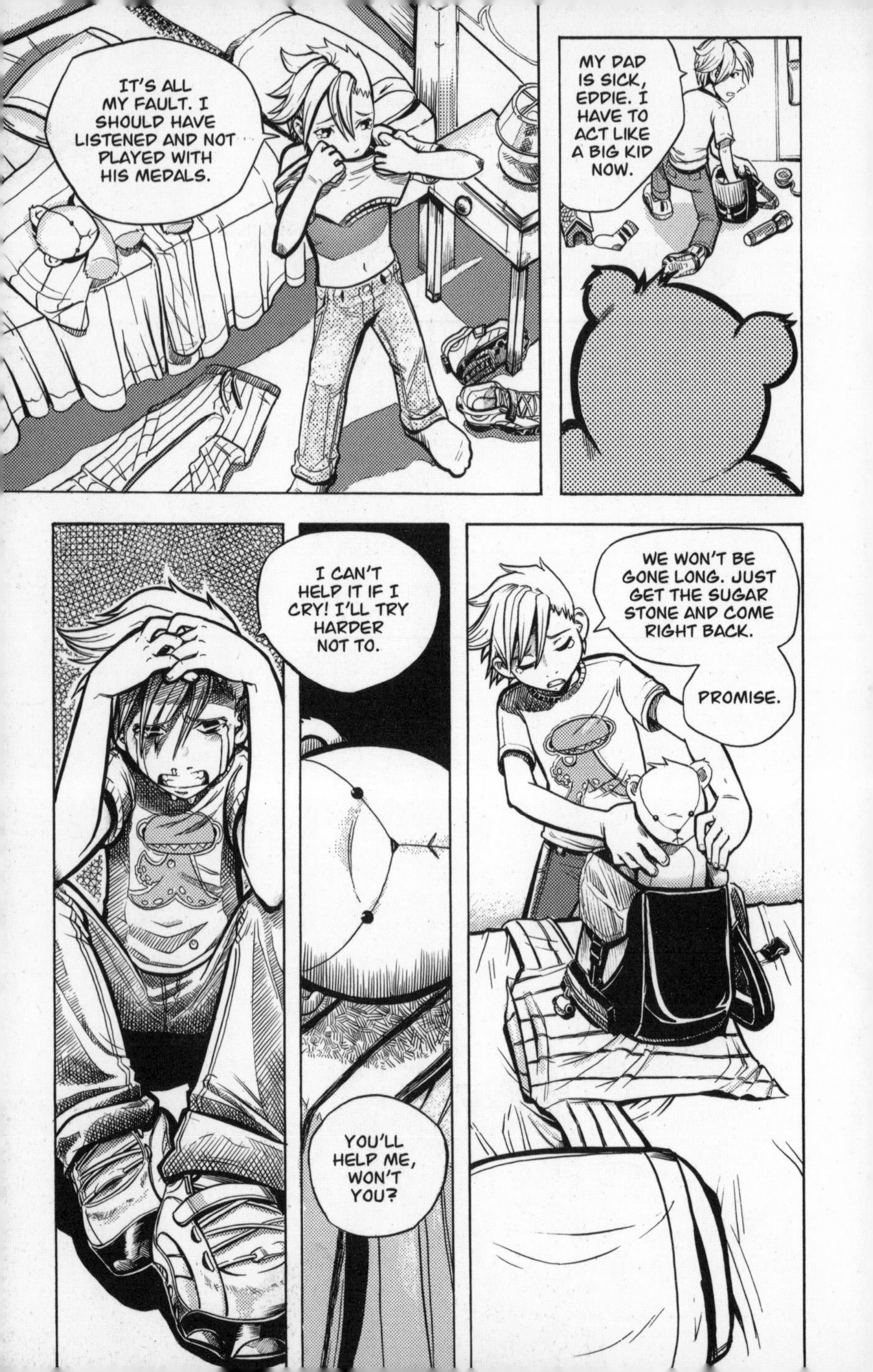
IT'S ALL MY FAULT. I SHOULD HAVE LISTENED AND NOT PLAYED WITH HIS MEDALS.
MY DAD IS SICK, EDDIE. I HAVE TO ACT LIKE A BIG KID NOW.
I CAN'T HELP IT IF I CRY! I'LL TRY HARDER NOT TO.
YOU'LL HELP ME, WON'T YOU?
WE WON'T BE GONE LONG. JUST GET THE SUGAR STONE AND COME RIGHT BACK.
PROMISE.

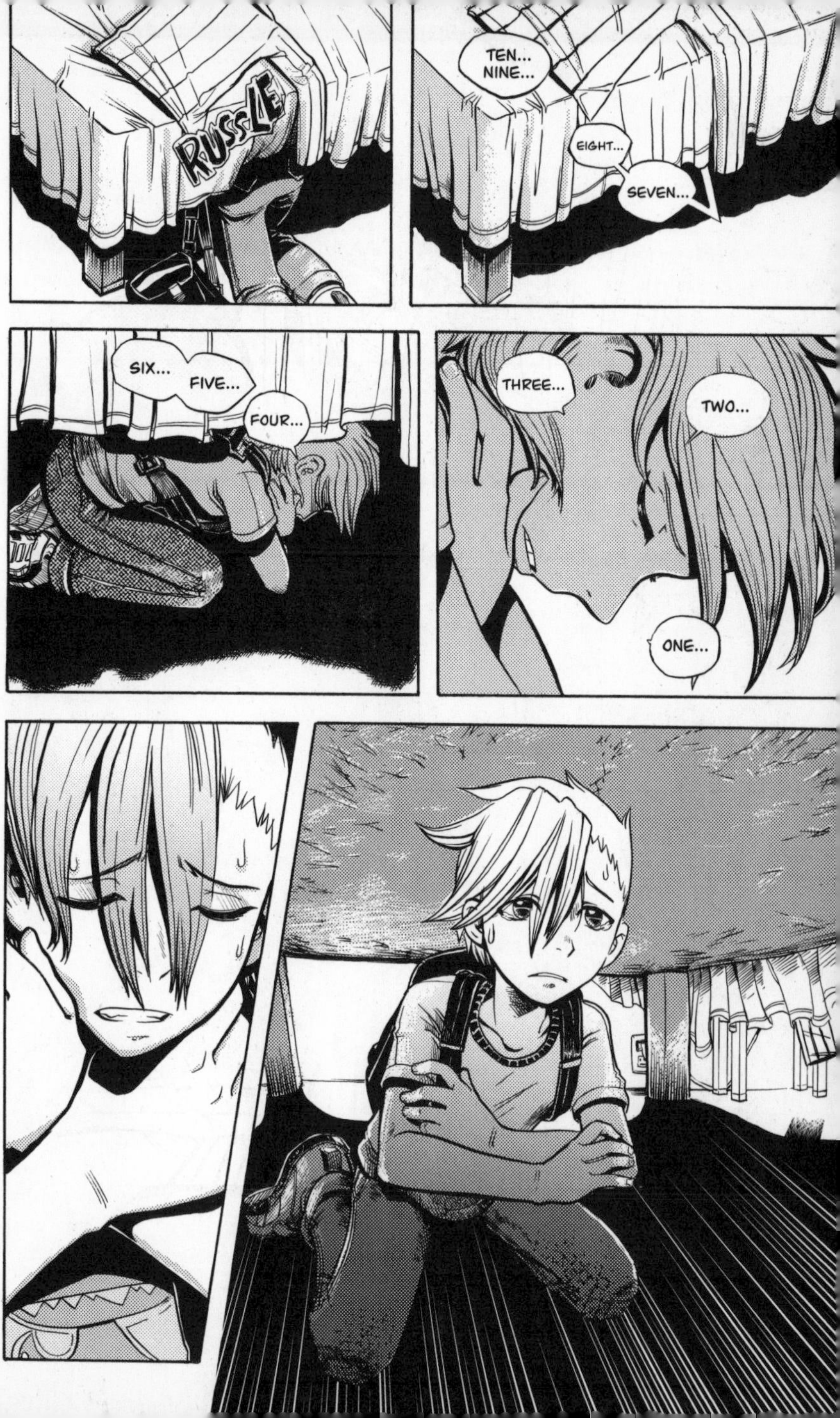
RUSSLE
TEN... NINE...
EIGHT...
SEVEN...
SIX...
FIVE...
FOUR...
THREE...
TWO...
ONE...

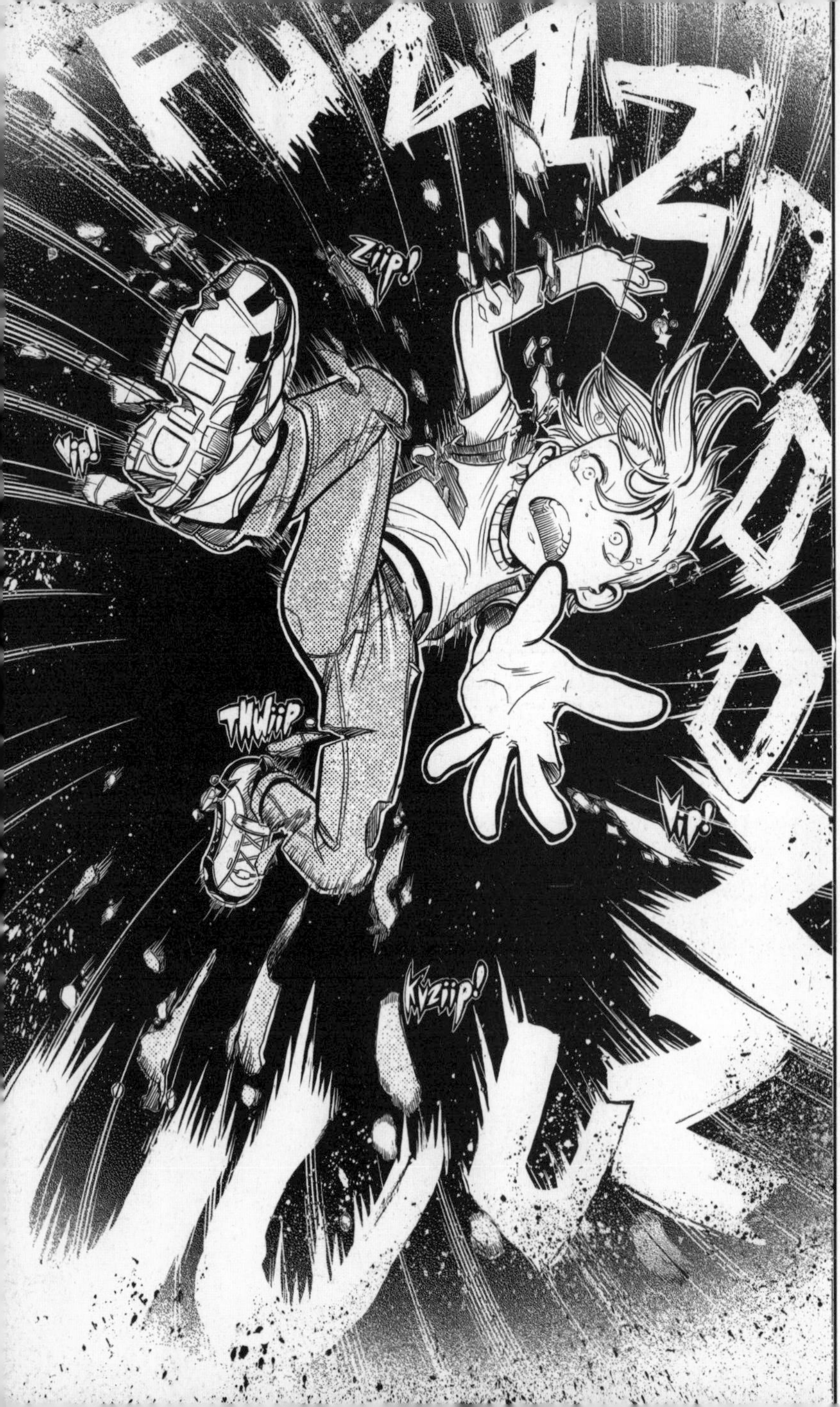
Ziip!
Vip!
THWiip
Vip!
Kvziip!

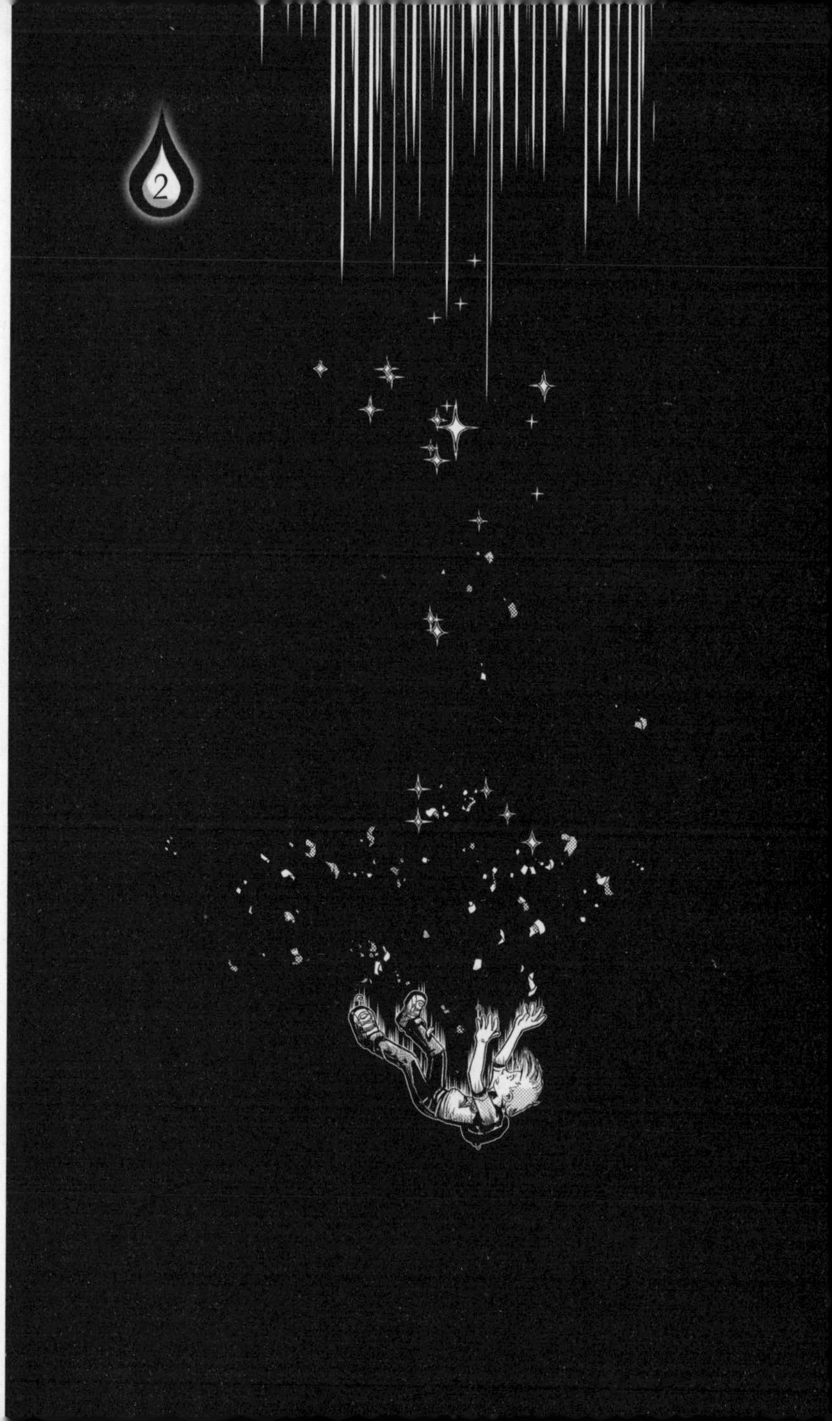
2

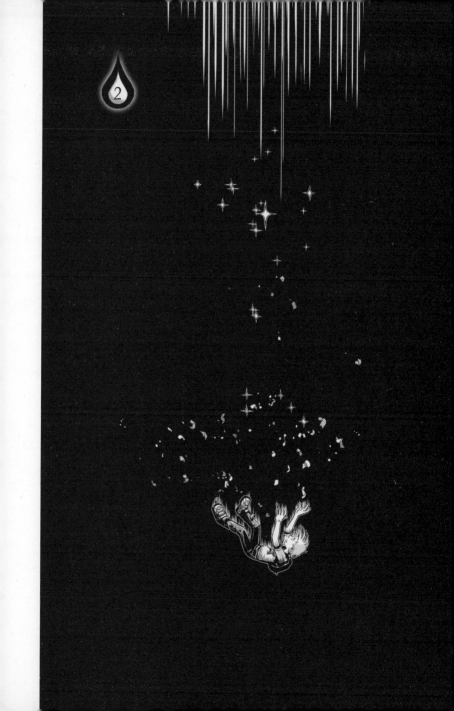

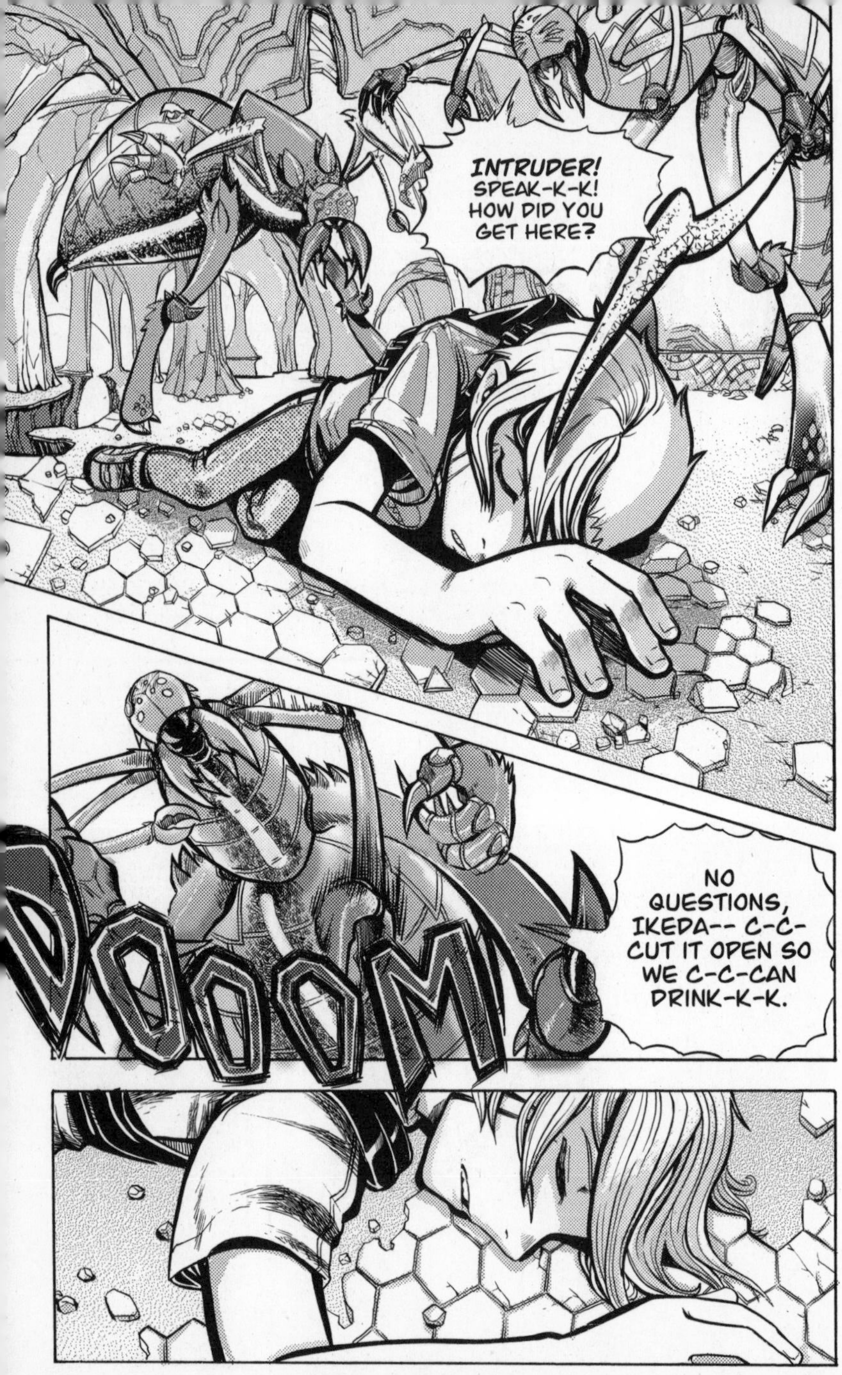
INTRUDER! SPEAK-K-K! HOW DID YOU GET HERE?
DOOOOM
NO QUESTIONS, IKEDA-- C-C-CUT IT OPEN SO WE C-C-CAN DRINK-K-K.

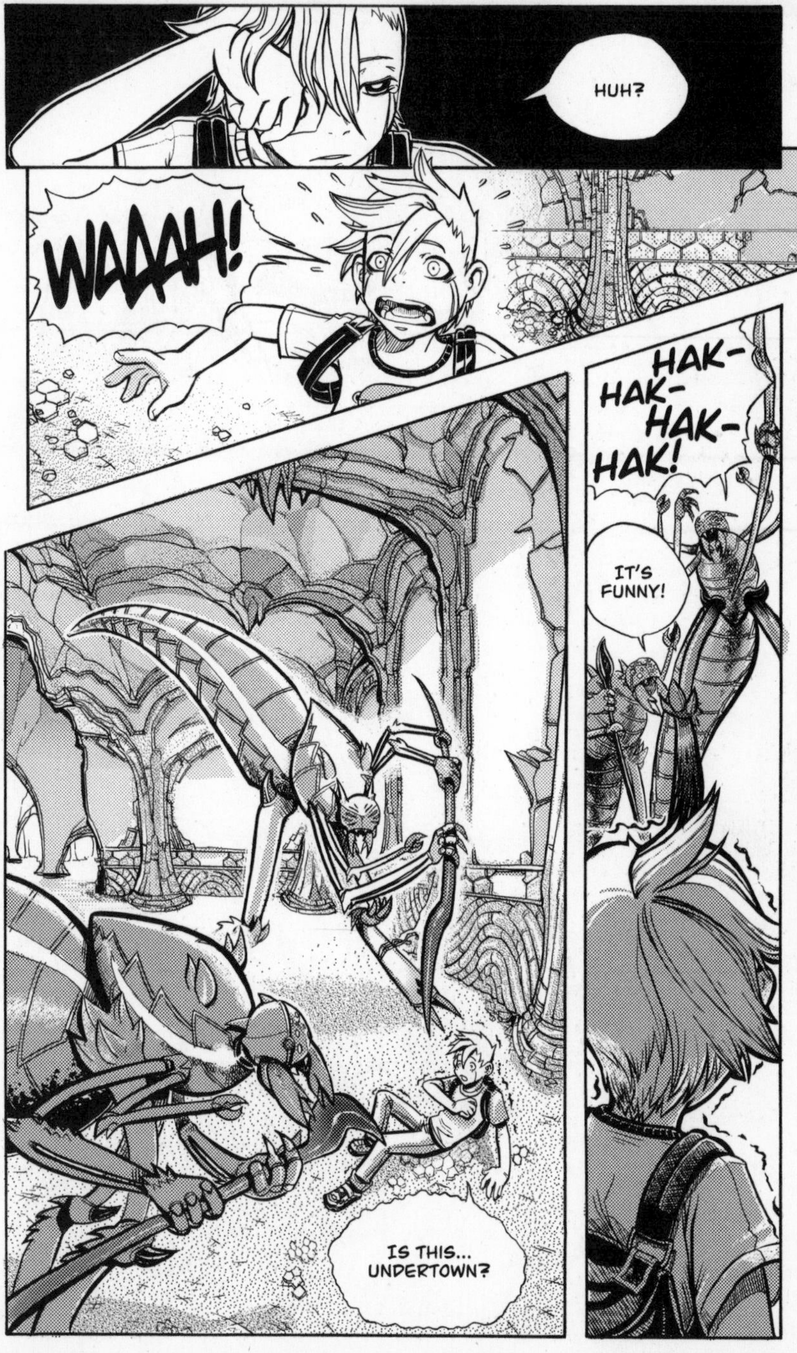
HUH?
WAAAH!
IS THIS... UNDERTOWN?
HAK-HAK-HAK-HAK!
IT'S FUNNY!

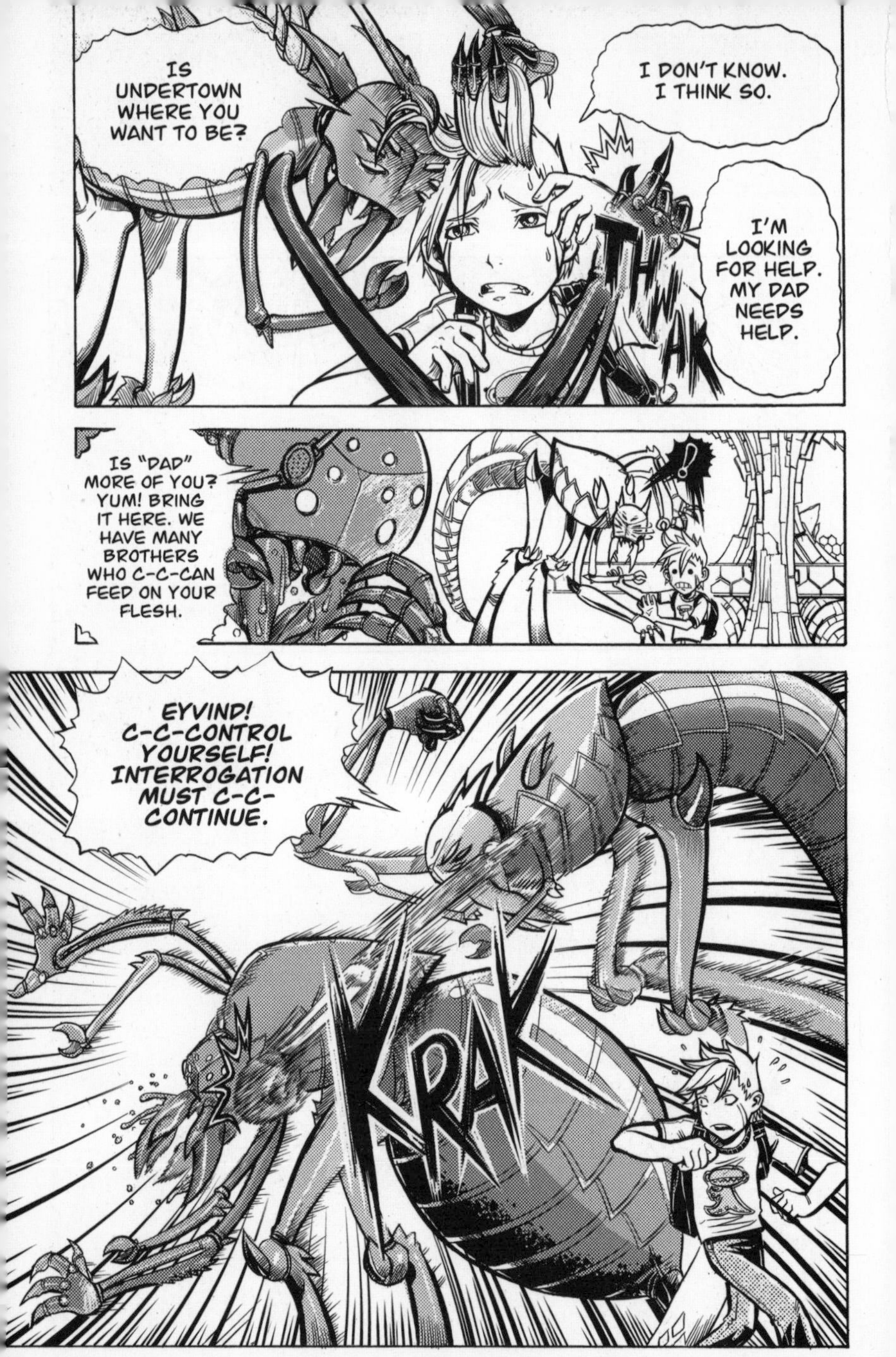
IS UNDERTOWN WHERE YOU WANT TO BE?
I DON'T KNOW. I THINK SO.
I'M LOOKING FOR HELP. MY DAD NEEDS HELP.
IS "DAD" MORE OF YOU? YUM! BRING IT HERE. WE HAVE MANY BROTHERS WHO C-C-CAN FEED ON YOUR FLESH.
!
EYVIND! C-C-CONTROL YOURSELF! INTERROGATION MUST C-C-CONTINUE.
KRAK

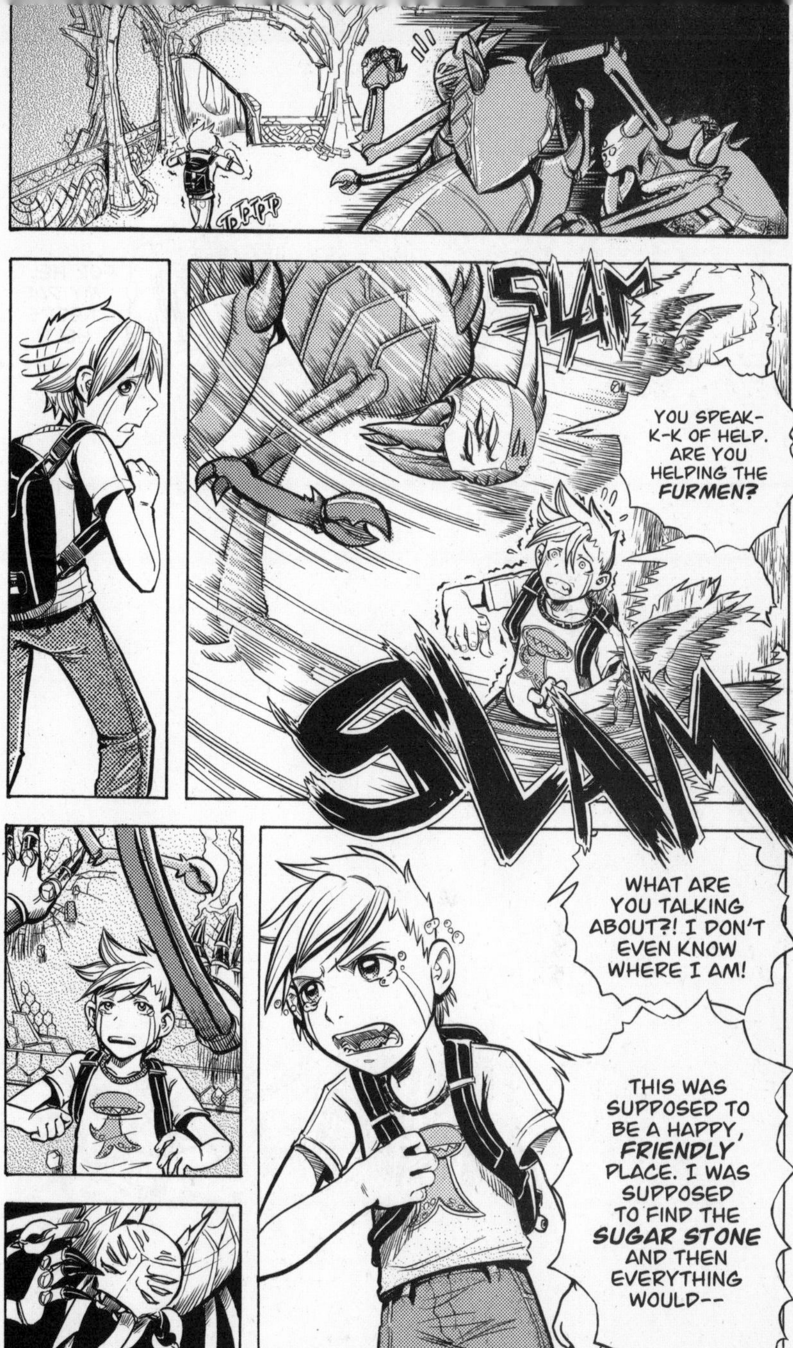
TPTPTPTP
SLAM
YOU SPEAK-K-K OF HELP. ARE YOU HELPING THE FURMEN?
SLAM
WHAT ARE YOU TALKING ABOUT?! I DON'T EVEN KNOW WHERE I AM!
THIS WAS SUPPOSED TO BE A HAPPY, FRIENDLY PLACE. I WAS SUPPOSED TO FIND THE SUGAR STONE AND THEN EVERYTHING WOULD--

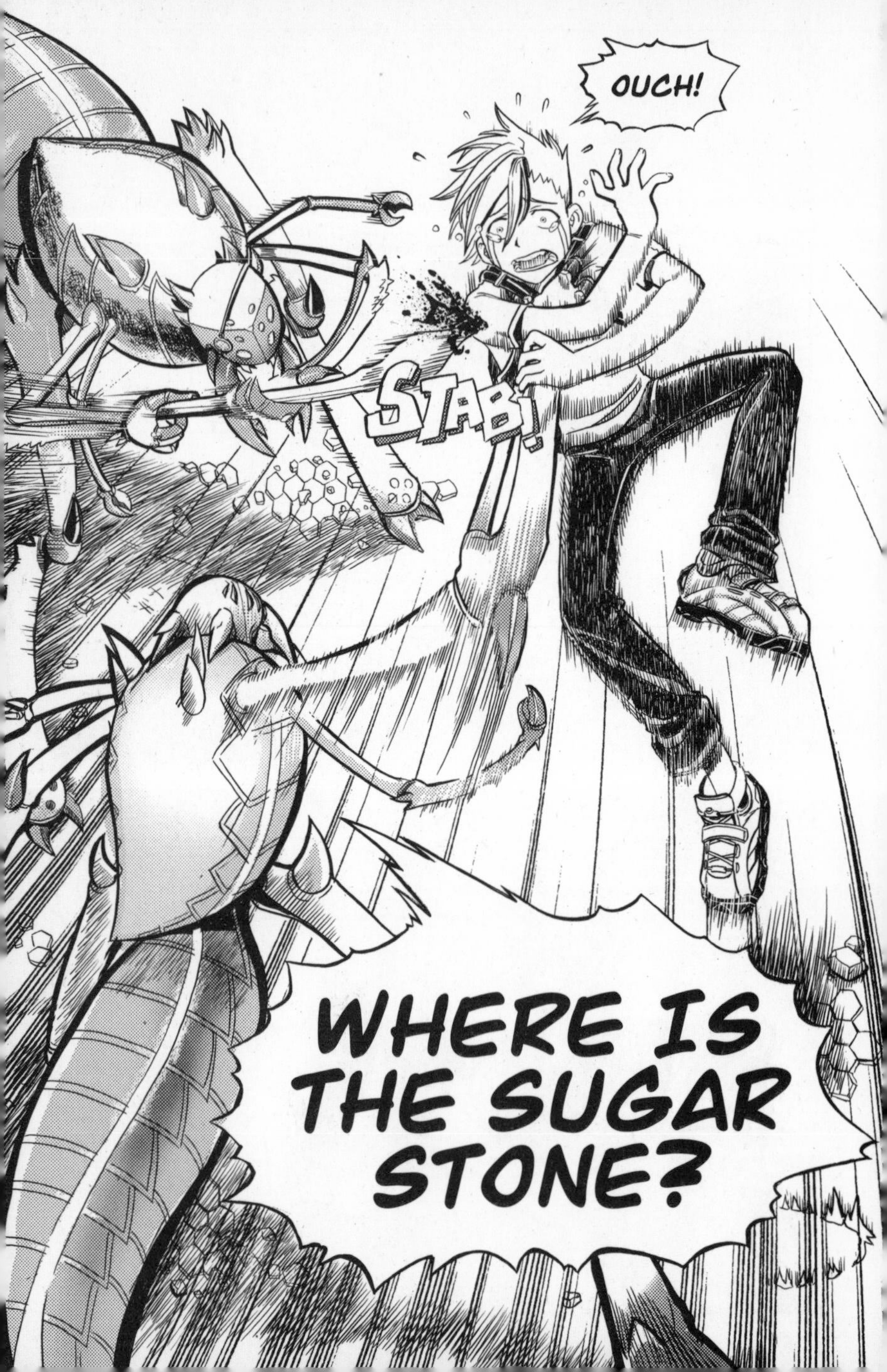
OUCH!
STAB!
WHERE IS THE SUGAR STONE?

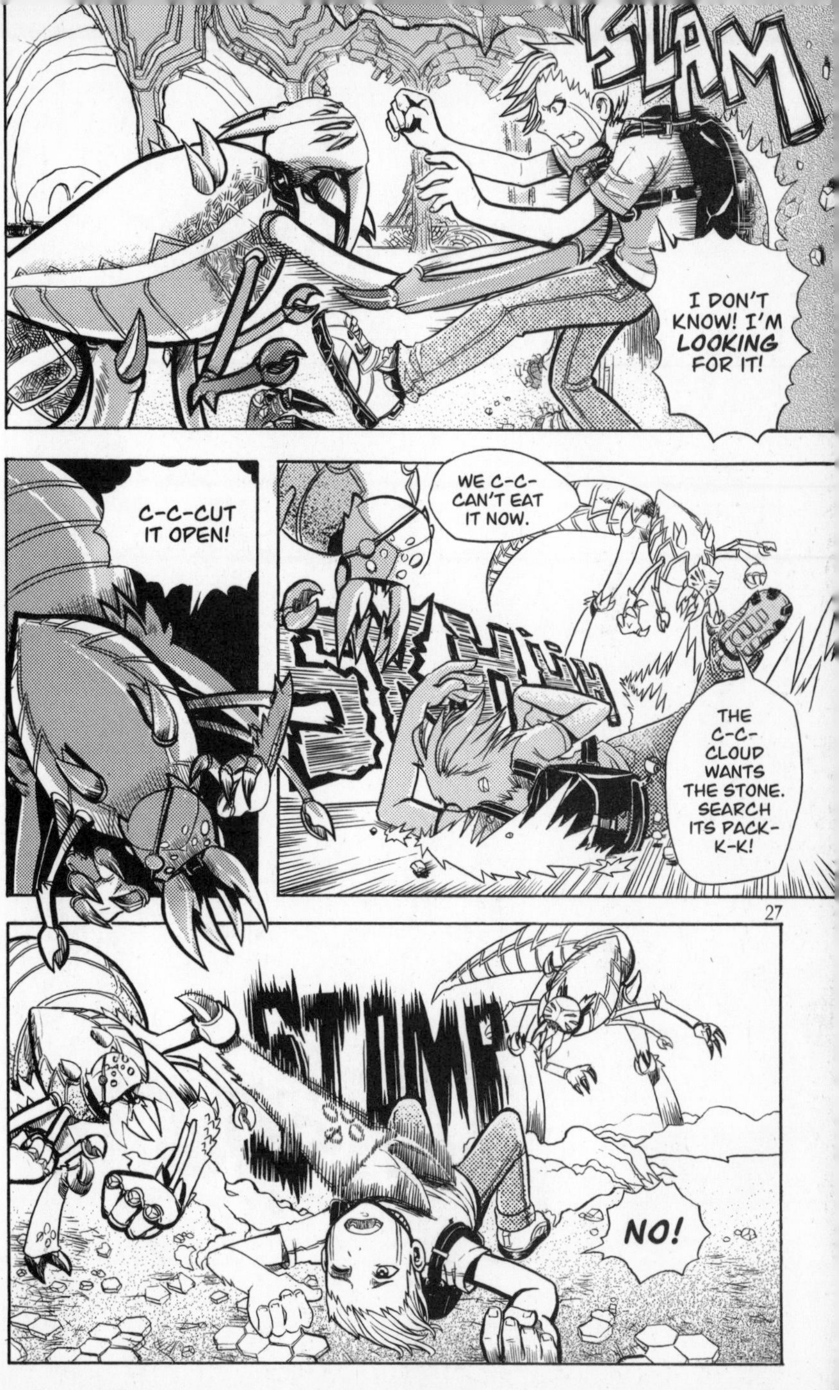
SLAM
I DON'T KNOW! I'M LOOKING FOR IT!
C-C-CUT IT OPEN!
WE C-C-CAN'T EAT IT NOW.
THE C-C-CLOUD WANTS THE STONE. SEARCH ITS PACK-K-K!
STOMP
NO!

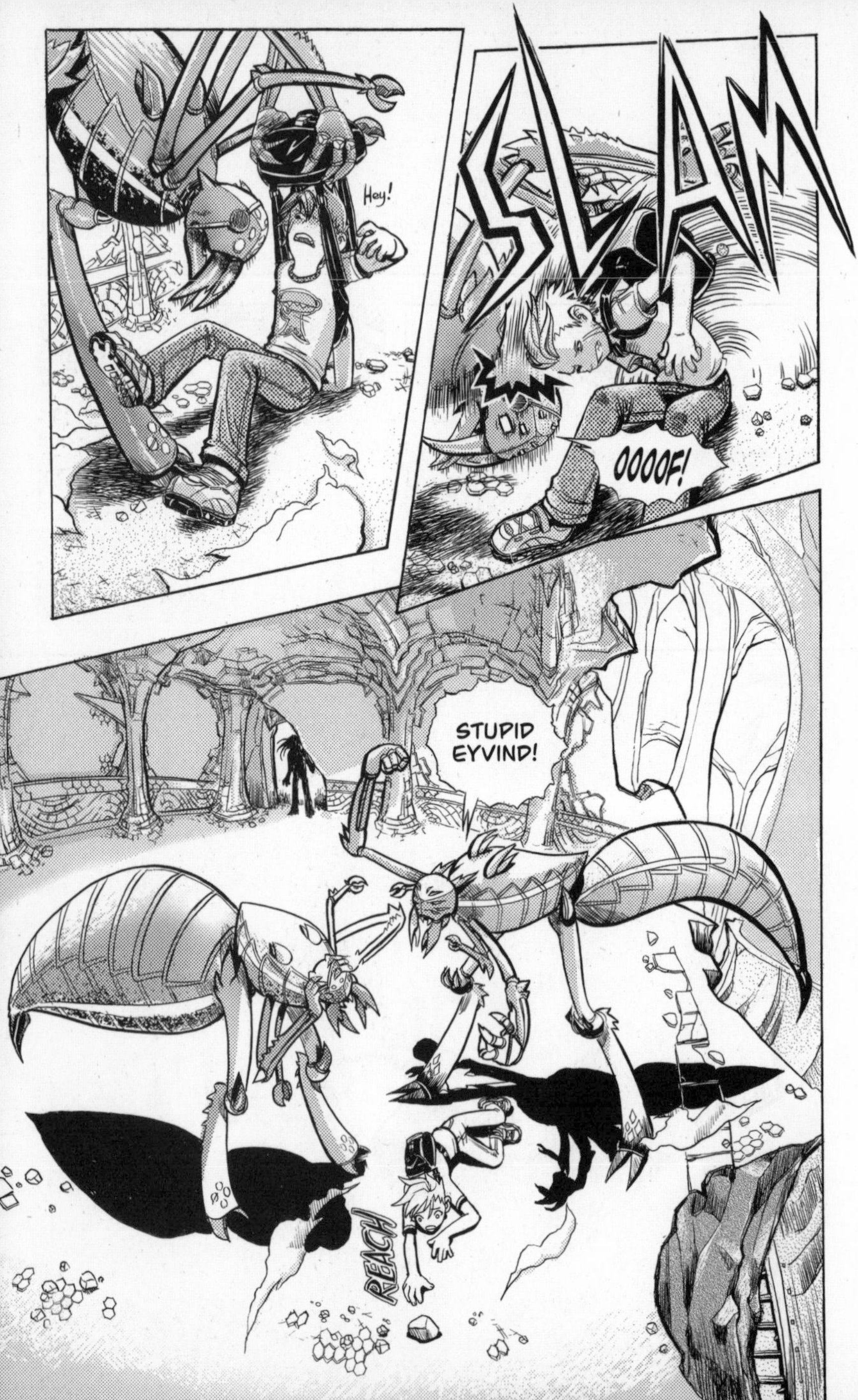
Hey!
SLAM
OOOOF!
STUPID EYVIND!
REACH

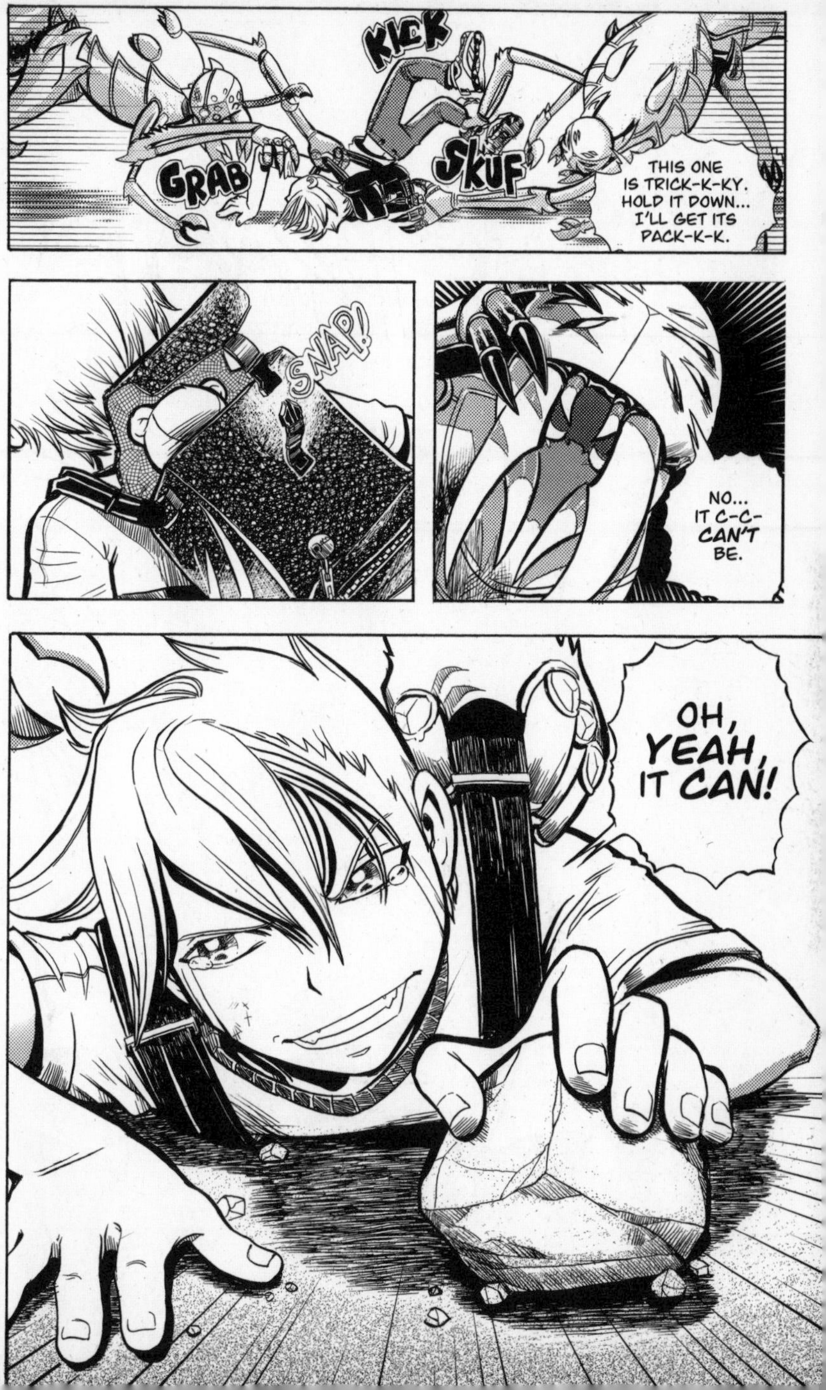
KICK
GRAB
SKUF
THIS ONE IS TRICK-K-KY. HOLD IT DOWN... I'LL GET ITS PACK-K-K.
SNAP!
NO... IT C-C-CAN'T BE.
OH, YEAH, IT CAN!

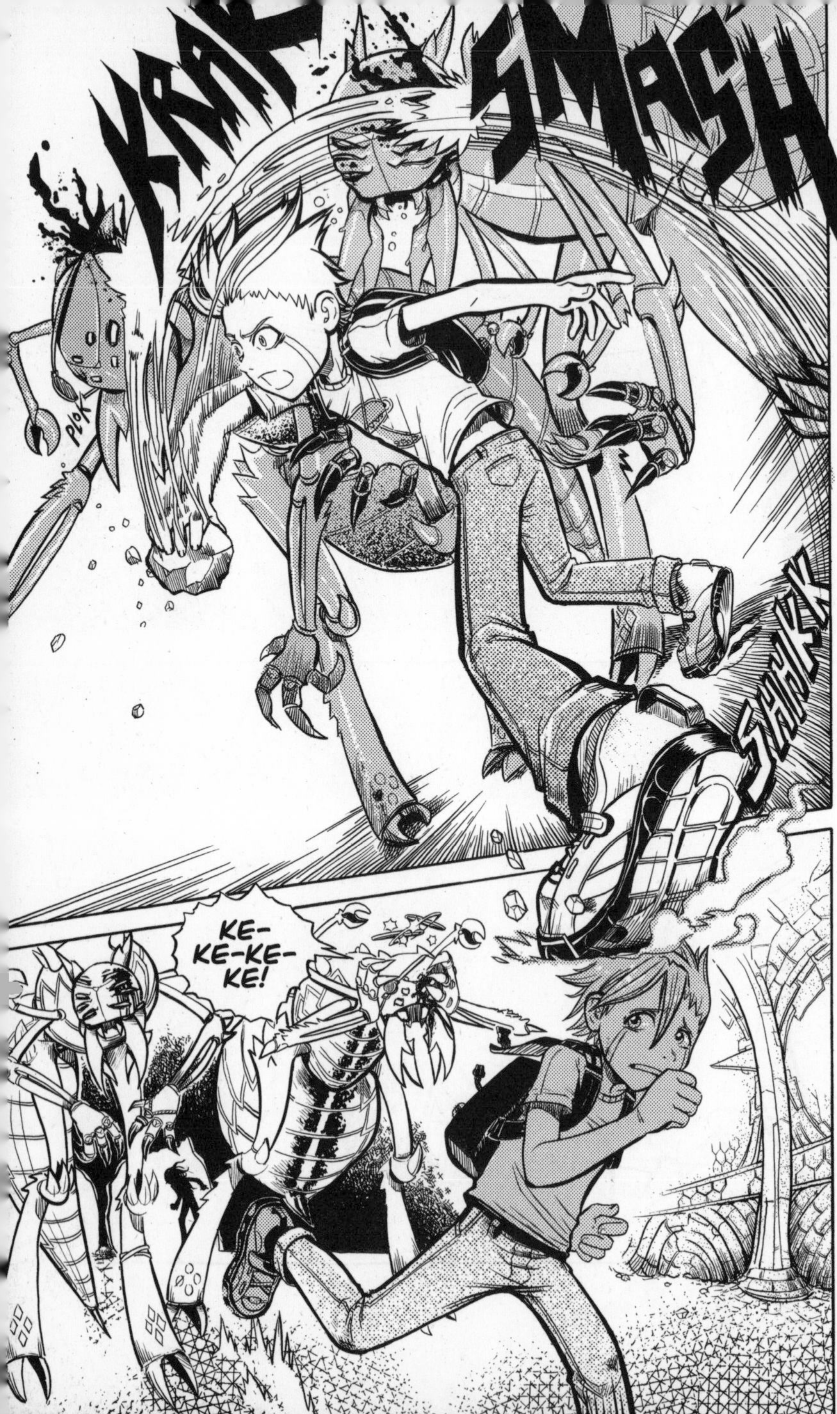
KRAK
SMASH
PLOK
SHHKK
KE-KE-KE-KE!

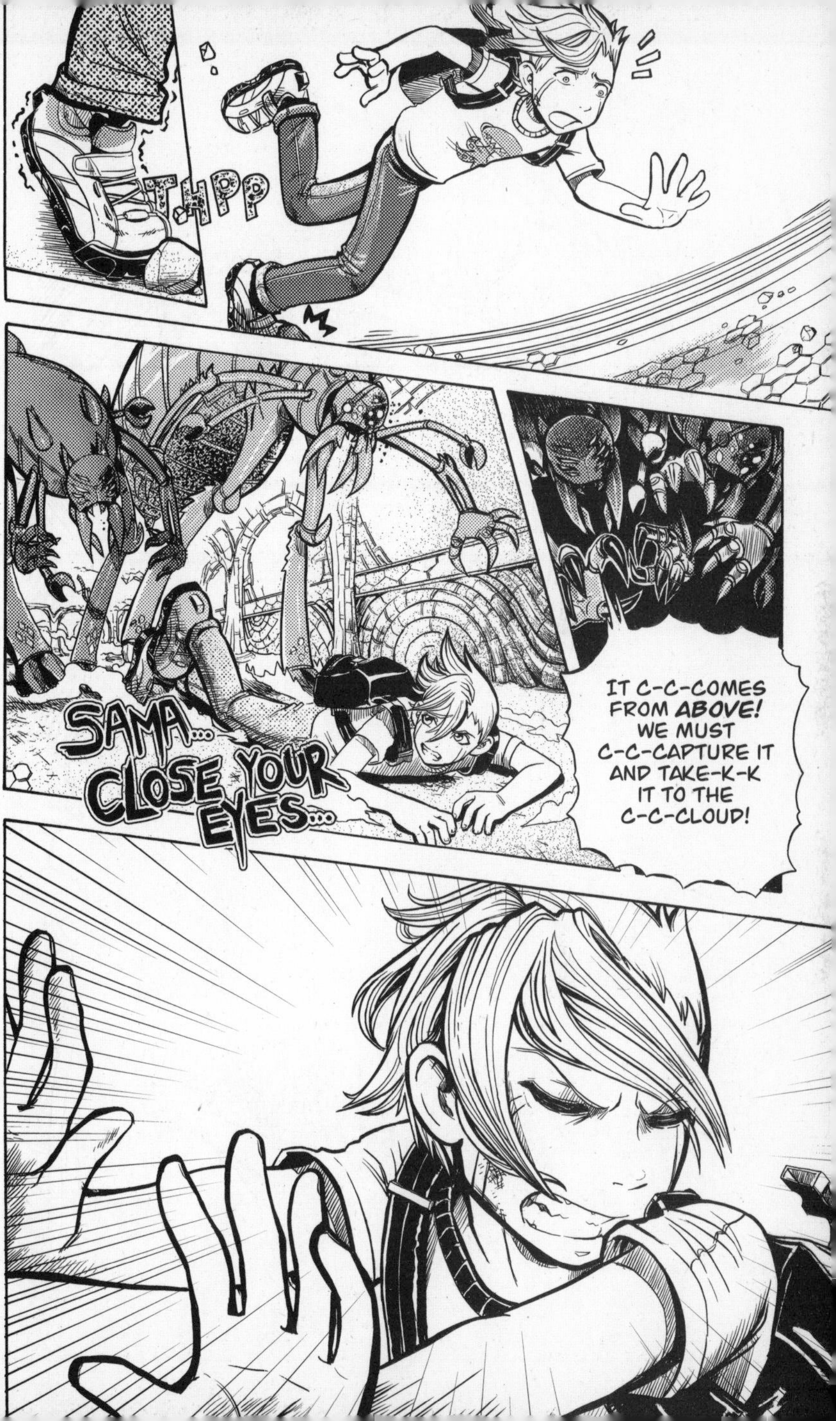
THPP
SAMA... CLOSE YOUR EYES...
IT C-C-COMES FROM ABOVE! WE MUST C-C-CAPTURE IT AND TAKE-K-K IT TO THE C-C-CLOUD!

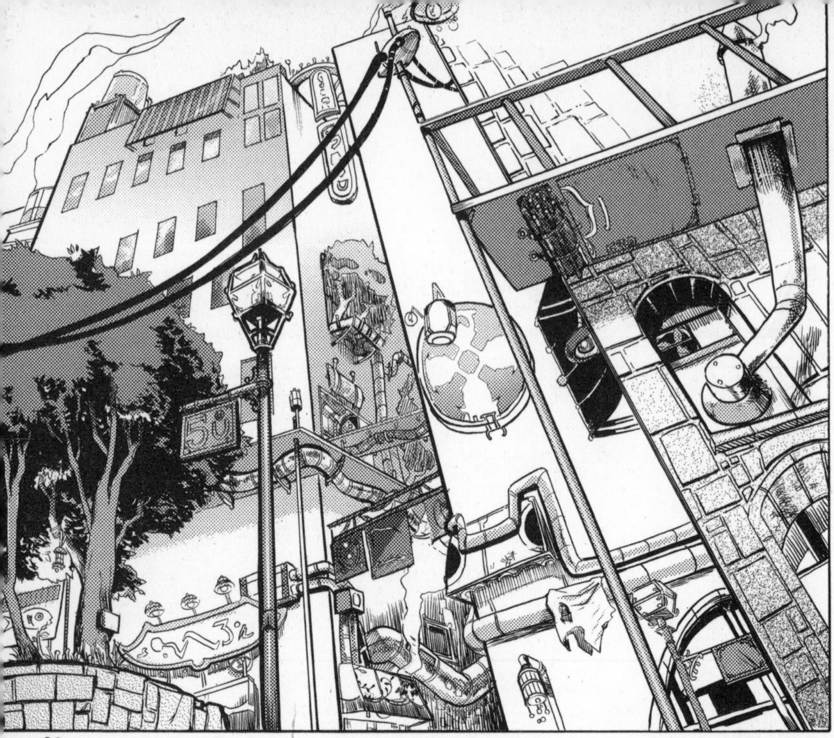
50

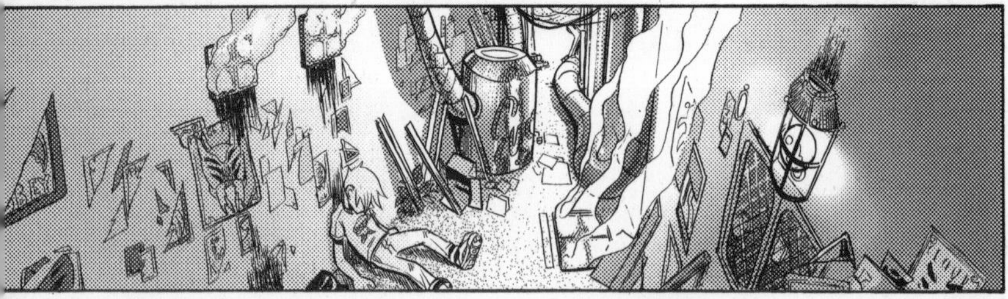

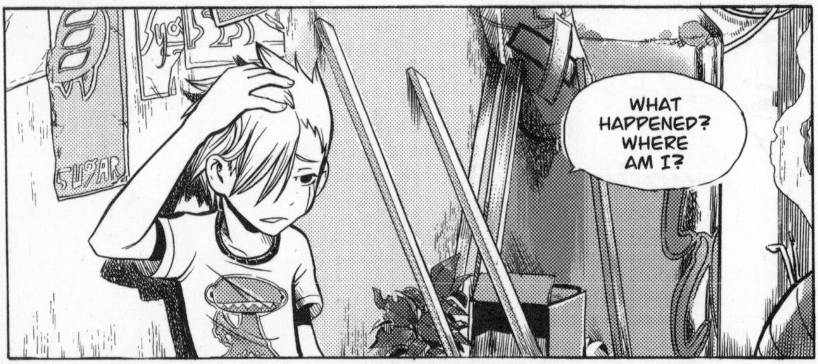
WHAT HAPPENED? WHERE AM I?

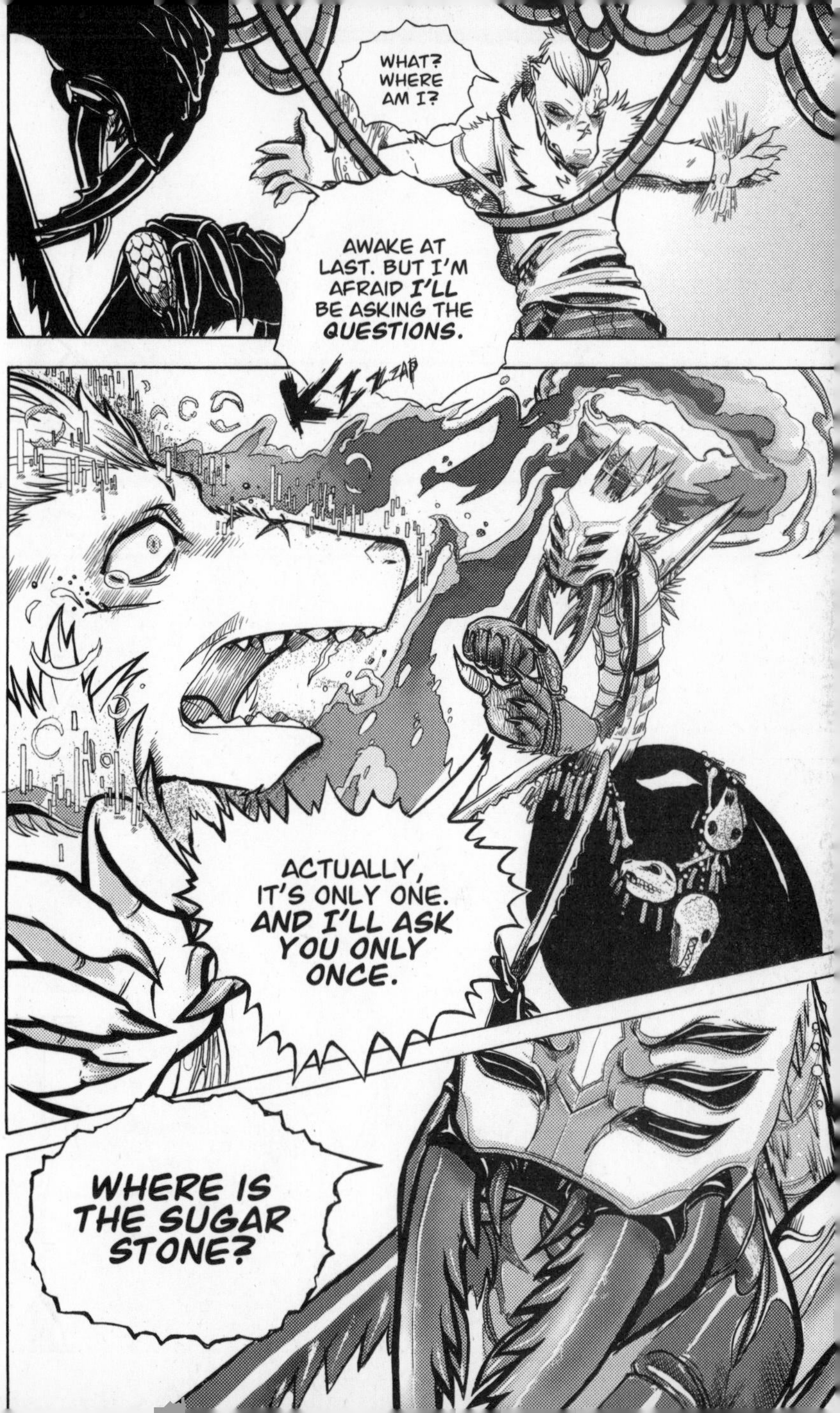
WHAT? WHERE AM I?
AWAKE AT LAST. BUT I'M AFRAID I'LL BE ASKING THE QUESTIONS.
ZZZAP
ACTUALLY, IT'S ONLY ONE. AND I'LL ASK YOU ONLY ONCE.
WHERE IS THE SUGAR STONE?

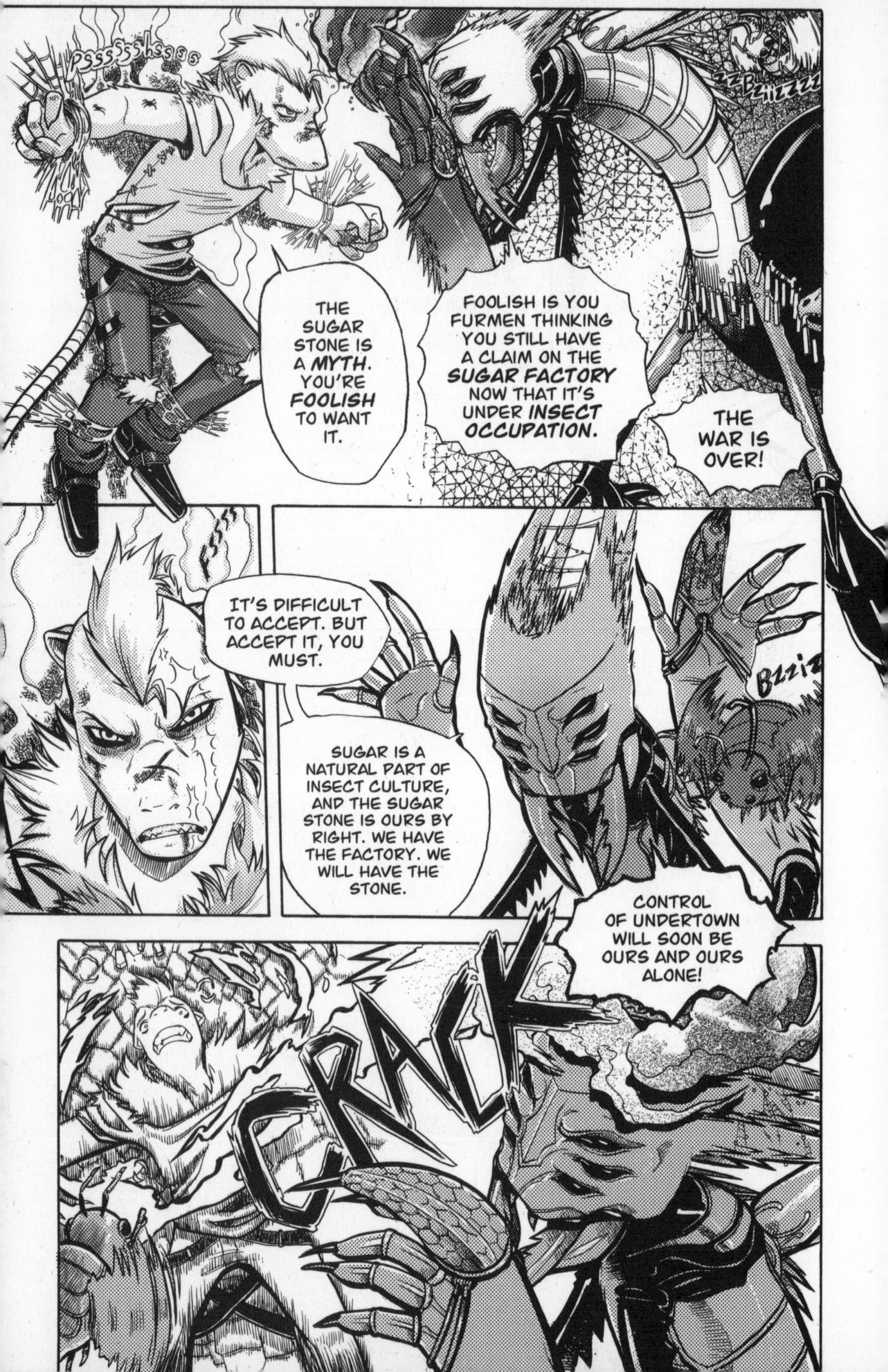
PSSSSSSHSSSS
ZZBZIIZZZZ
THE SUGAR STONE IS A MYTH. YOU'RE FOOLISH TO WANT IT.
FOOLISH IS YOU FURMEN THINKING YOU STILL HAVE A CLAIM ON THE SUGAR FACTORY NOW THAT IT'S UNDER INSECT OCCUPATION.
THE WAR IS OVER!
FSSSS
IT'S DIFFICULT TO ACCEPT. BUT ACCEPT IT, YOU MUST.
SUGAR IS A NATURAL PART OF INSECT CULTURE, AND THE SUGAR STONE IS OURS BY RIGHT. WE HAVE THE FACTORY. WE WILL HAVE THE STONE.
BZZIZ
CONTROL OF UNDERTOWN WILL SOON BE OURS AND OURS ALONE!
CRACK

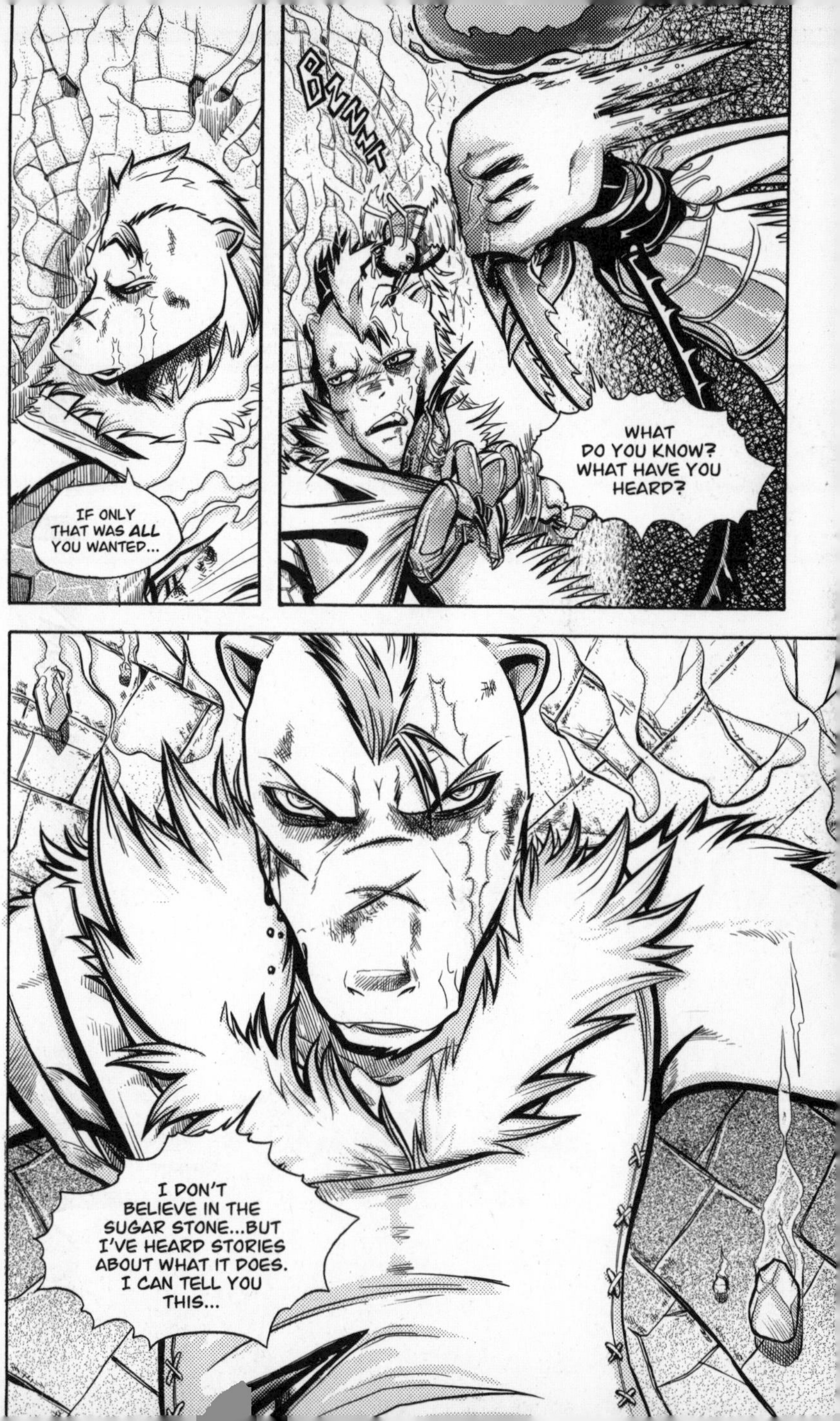
IF ONLY THAT WAS ALL YOU WANTED...
BANNNK
WHAT DO YOU KNOW? WHAT HAVE YOU HEARD?
I DON'T BELIEVE IN THE SUGAR STONE...BUT I'VE HEARD STORIES ABOUT WHAT IT DOES. I CAN TELL YOU THIS...

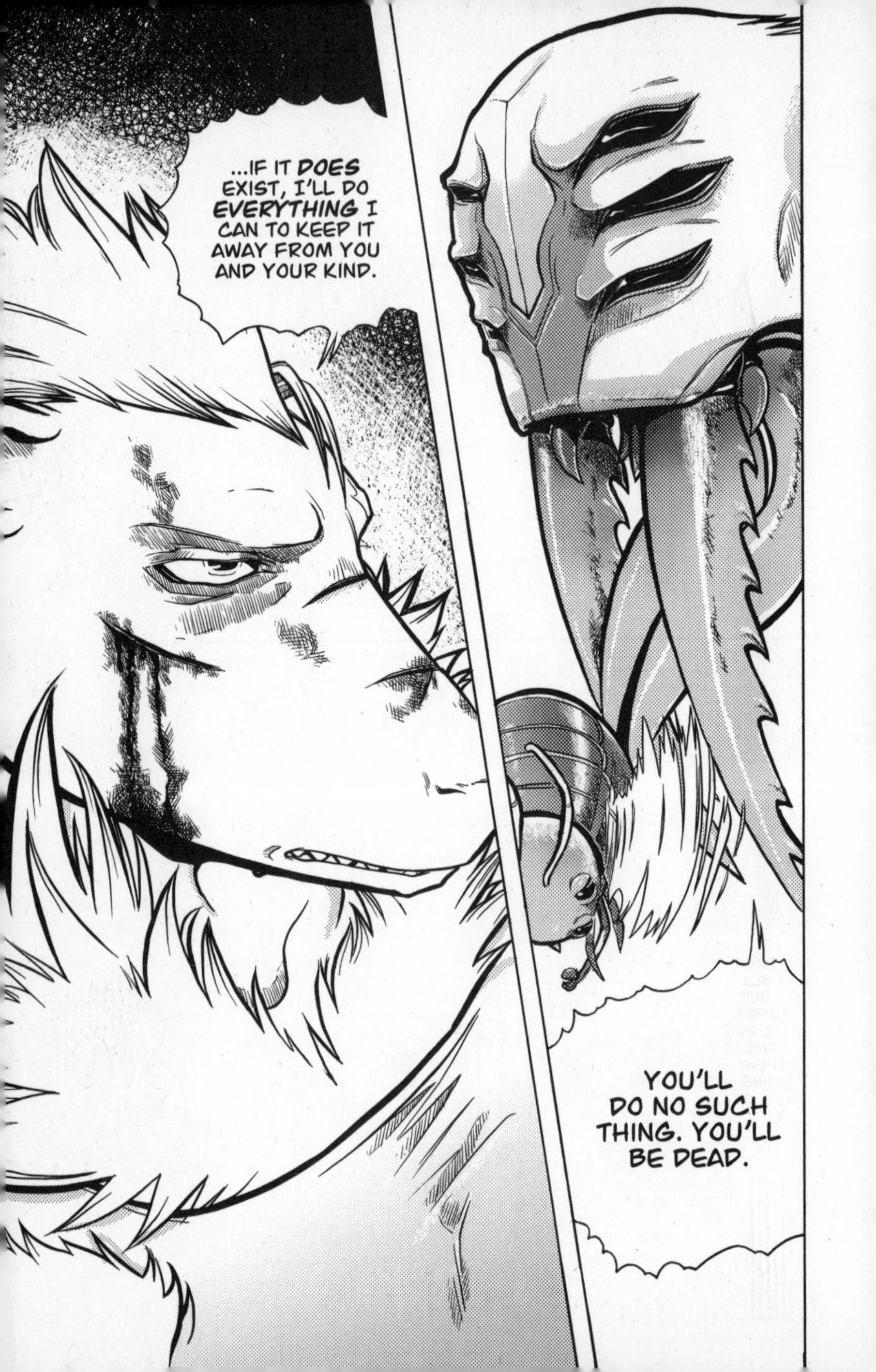
...IF IT DOES EXIST, I'LL DO EVERYTHING I CAN TO KEEP IT AWAY FROM YOU AND YOUR KIND.
YOU'LL DO NO SUCH THING. YOU'LL BE DEAD.

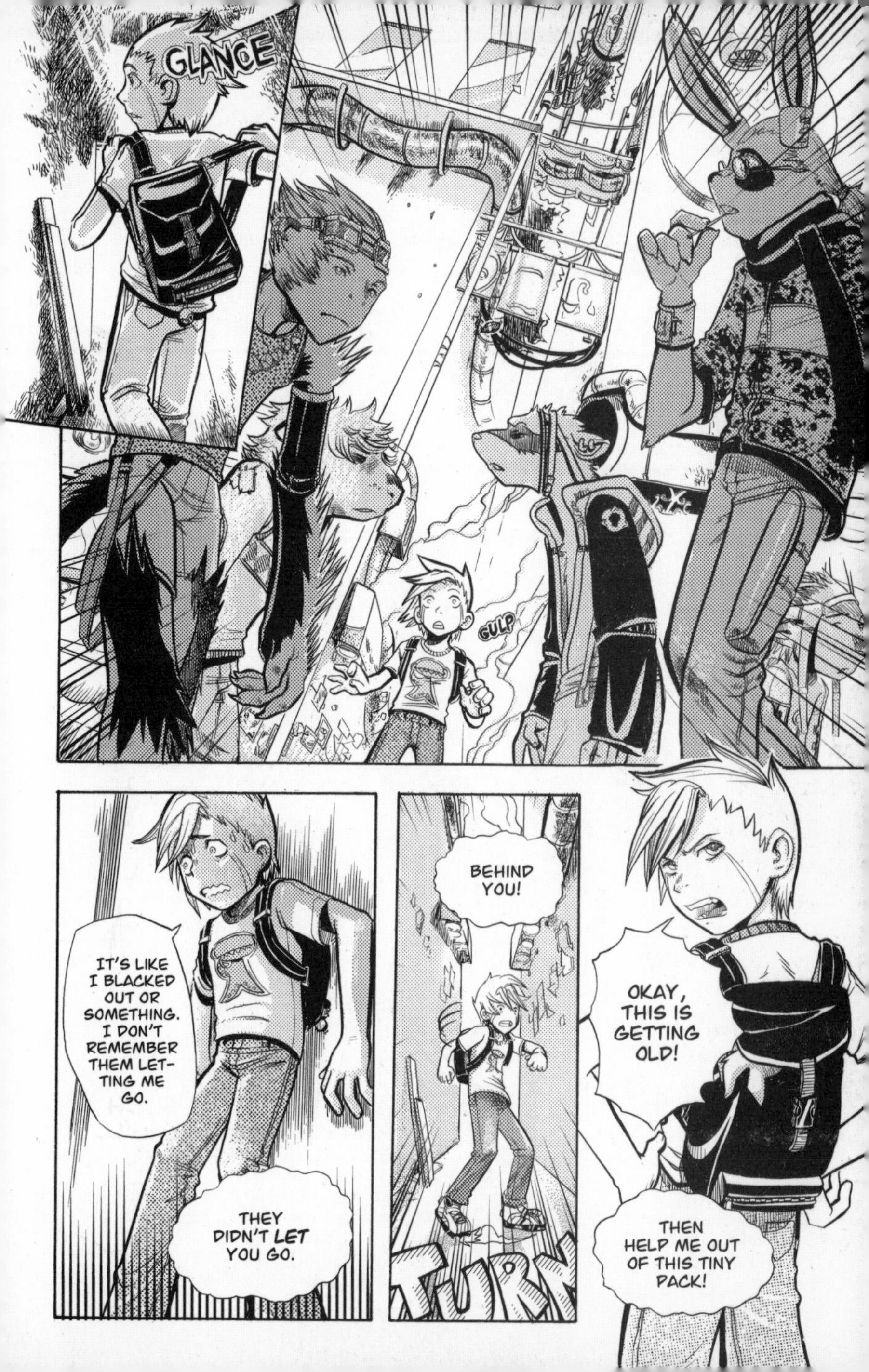
GLANCE
GULP
IT'S LIKE I BLACKED OUT OR SOMETHING. I DON'T REMEMBER THEM LETTING ME GO.
THEY DIDN'T LET YOU GO.
BEHIND YOU!
TURN
OKAY, THIS IS GETTING OLD!
THEN HELP ME OUT OF THIS TINY PACK!

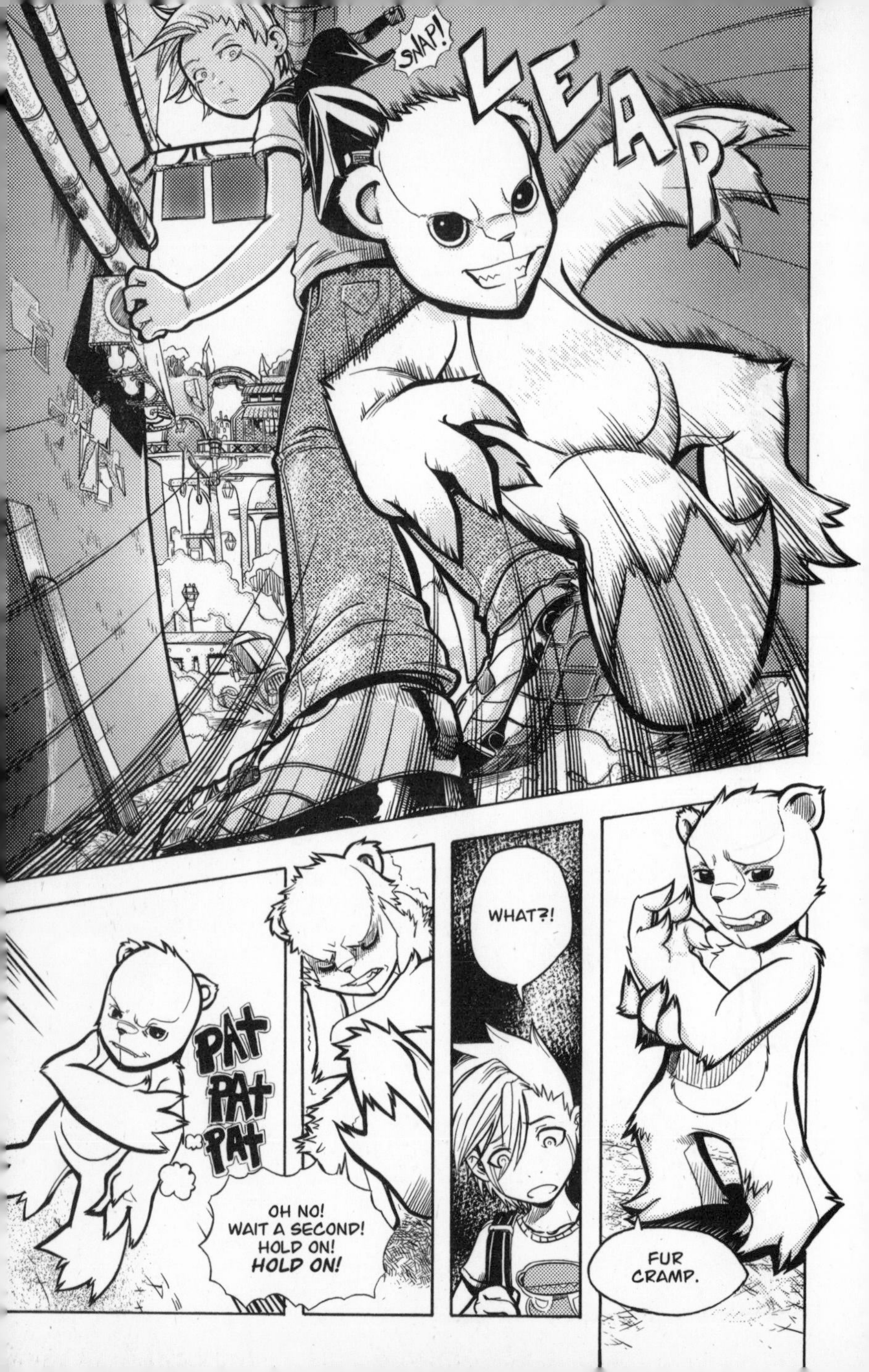
SNAP!
LEAP
PAT PAT PAT
OH NO! WAIT A SECOND! HOLD ON! **HOLD ON!**
WHAT?!
FUR CRAMP.

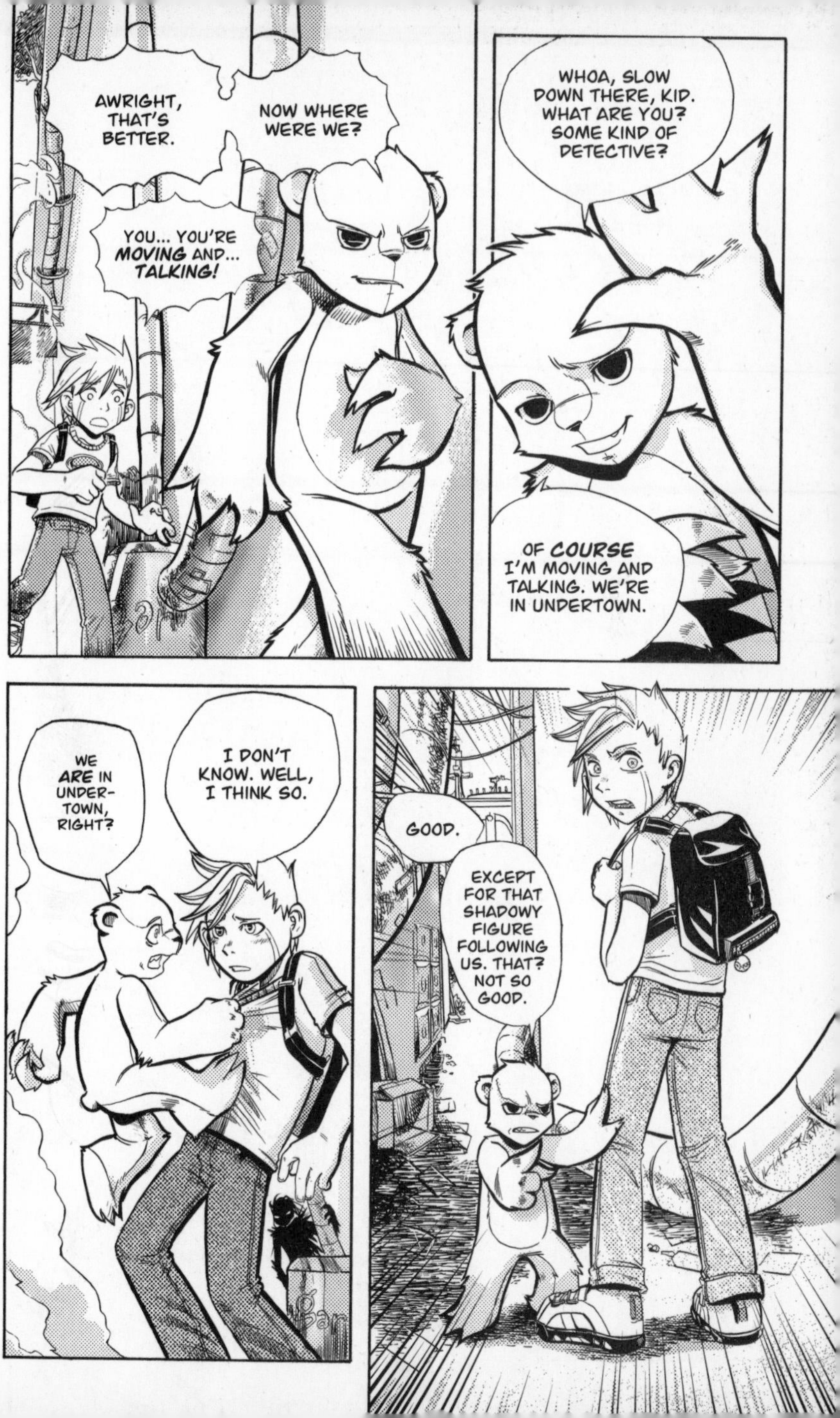
AWRIGHT, THAT'S BETTER.
NOW WHERE WERE WE?
YOU... YOU'RE *MOVING* AND... *TALKING!*
WHOA, SLOW DOWN THERE, KID. WHAT ARE YOU? SOME KIND OF DETECTIVE?
OF *COURSE* I'M MOVING AND TALKING. WE'RE IN UNDERTOWN.
WE *ARE* IN UNDER-TOWN, RIGHT?
I DON'T KNOW. WELL, I THINK SO.
GOOD.
EXCEPT FOR THAT SHADOWY FIGURE FOLLOWING US. THAT? NOT SO GOOD.

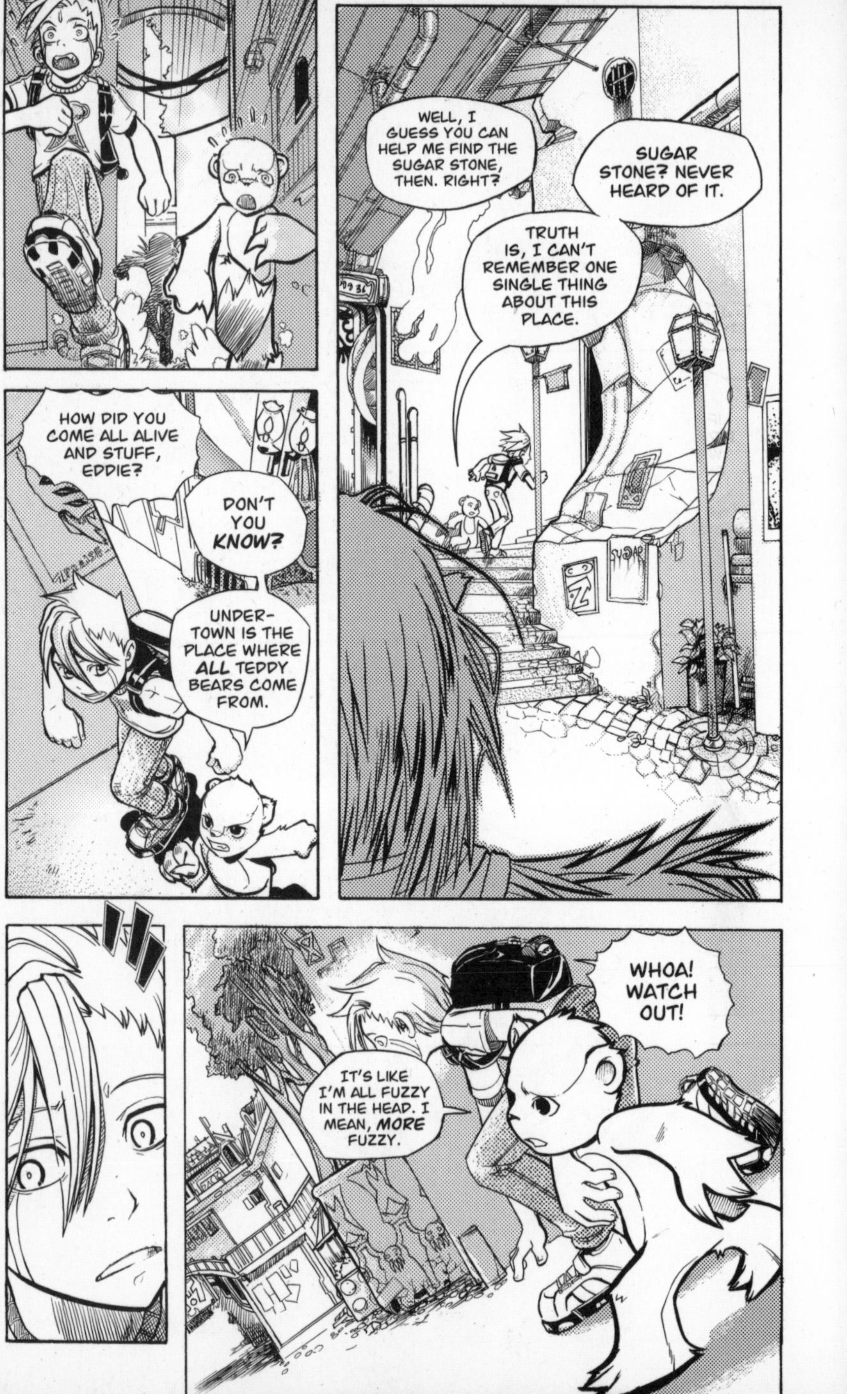
WELL, I GUESS YOU CAN HELP ME FIND THE SUGAR STONE, THEN. RIGHT?
SUGAR STONE? NEVER HEARD OF IT.
TRUTH IS, I CAN'T REMEMBER ONE SINGLE THING ABOUT THIS PLACE.
HOW DID YOU COME ALL ALIVE AND STUFF, EDDIE?
DON'T YOU KNOW?
UNDER-TOWN IS THE PLACE WHERE ALL TEDDY BEARS COME FROM.
SUGAR
IT'S LIKE I'M ALL FUZZY IN THE HEAD. I MEAN, MORE FUZZY.
WHOA! WATCH OUT!

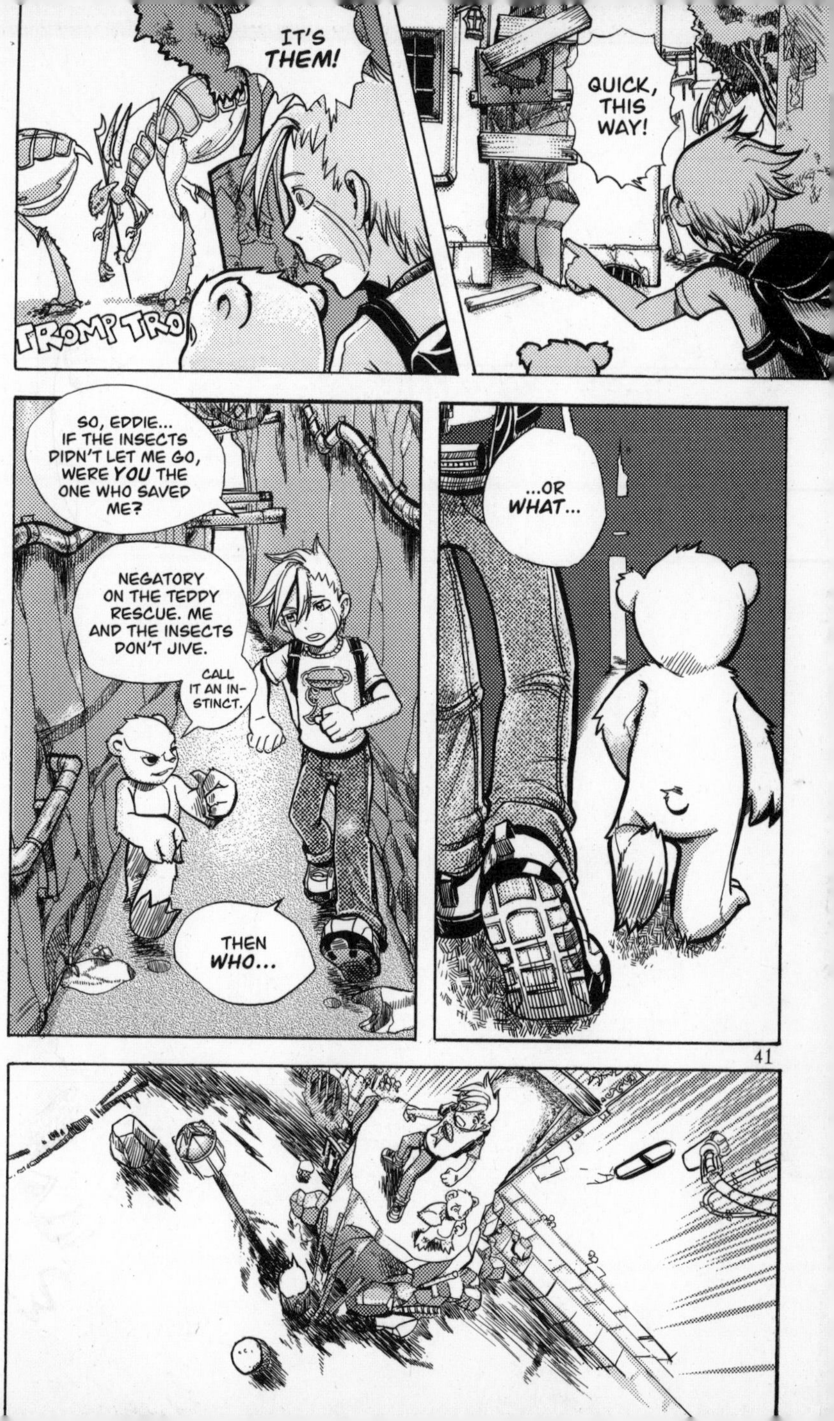
IT'S THEM!
TROMP TRO
QUICK, THIS WAY!
SO, EDDIE... IF THE INSECTS DIDN'T LET ME GO, WERE YOU THE ONE WHO SAVED ME?
NEGATORY ON THE TEDDY RESCUE. ME AND THE INSECTS DON'T JIVE.
CALL IT AN IN-STINCT.
THEN WHO...
...OR WHAT...

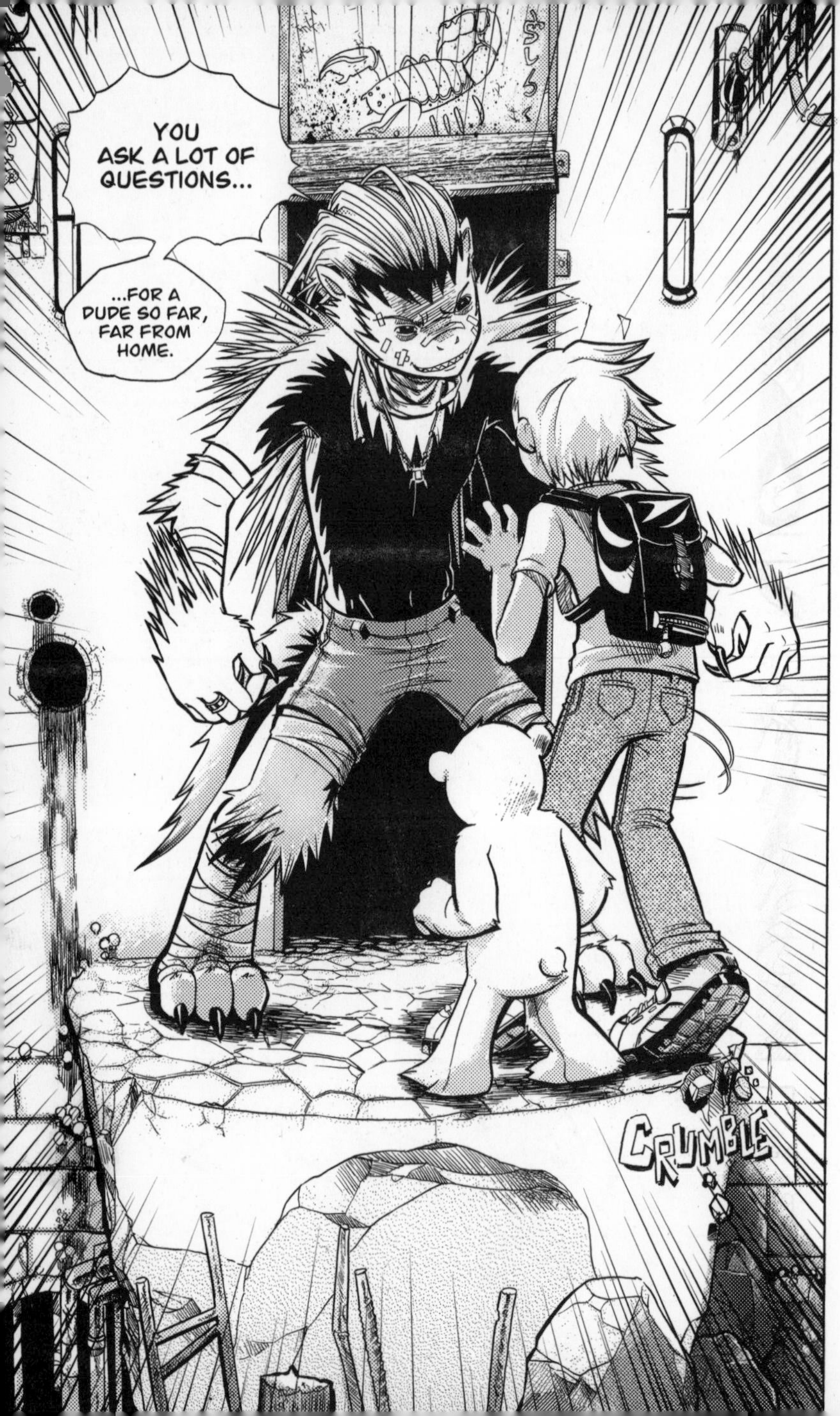
YOU ASK A LOT OF QUESTIONS...
...FOR A DUDE SO FAR, FAR FROM HOME.
CRUMBLE

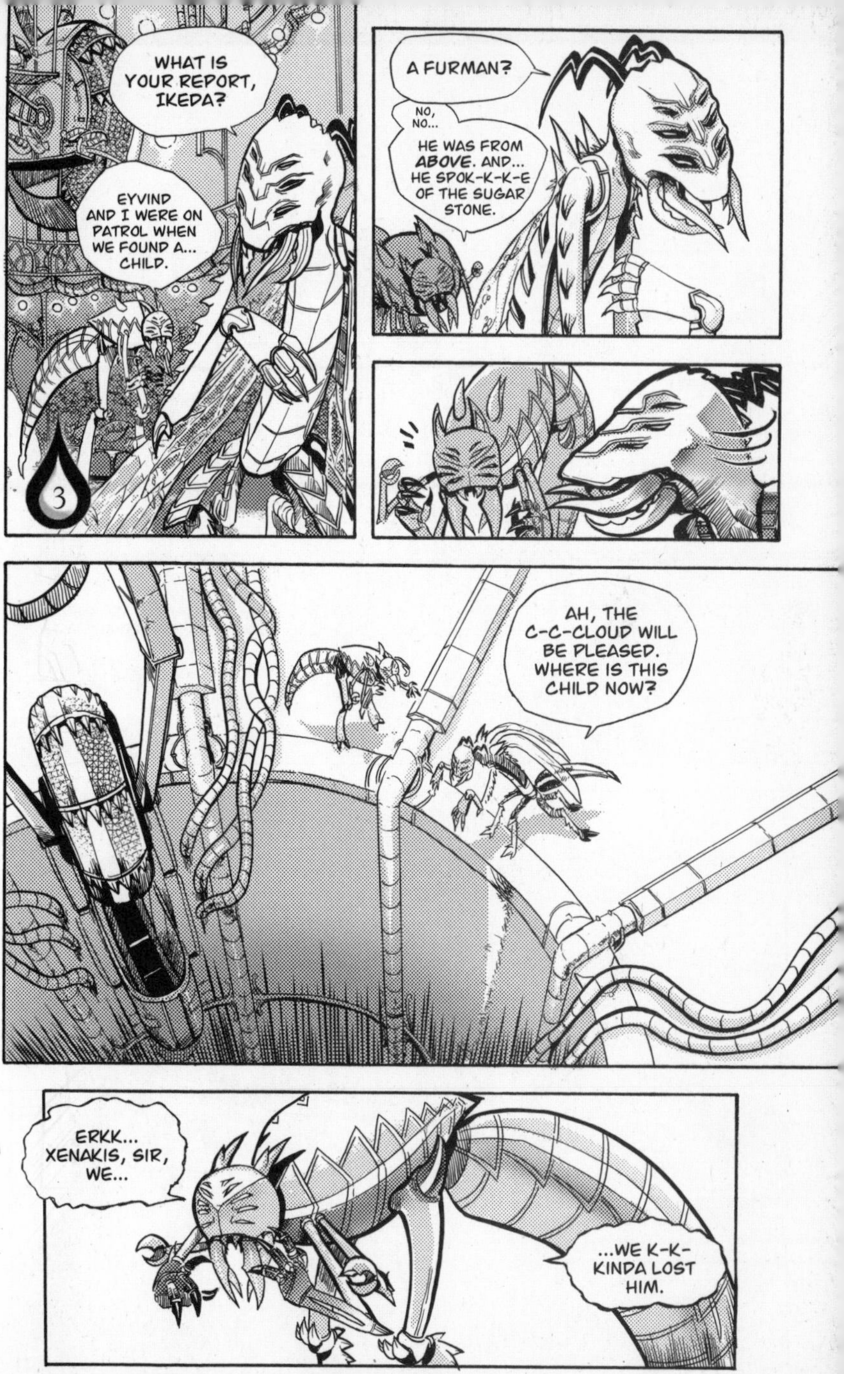
WHAT IS YOUR REPORT, IKEDA?
EYVIND AND I WERE ON PATROL WHEN WE FOUND A... CHILD.
3
A FURMAN?
NO, NO...
HE WAS FROM ABOVE. AND... HE SPOK-K-K-E OF THE SUGAR STONE.
AH, THE C-C-CLOUD WILL BE PLEASED. WHERE IS THIS CHILD NOW?
ERKK... XENAKIS, SIR, WE...
...WE K-K-KINDA LOST HIM.

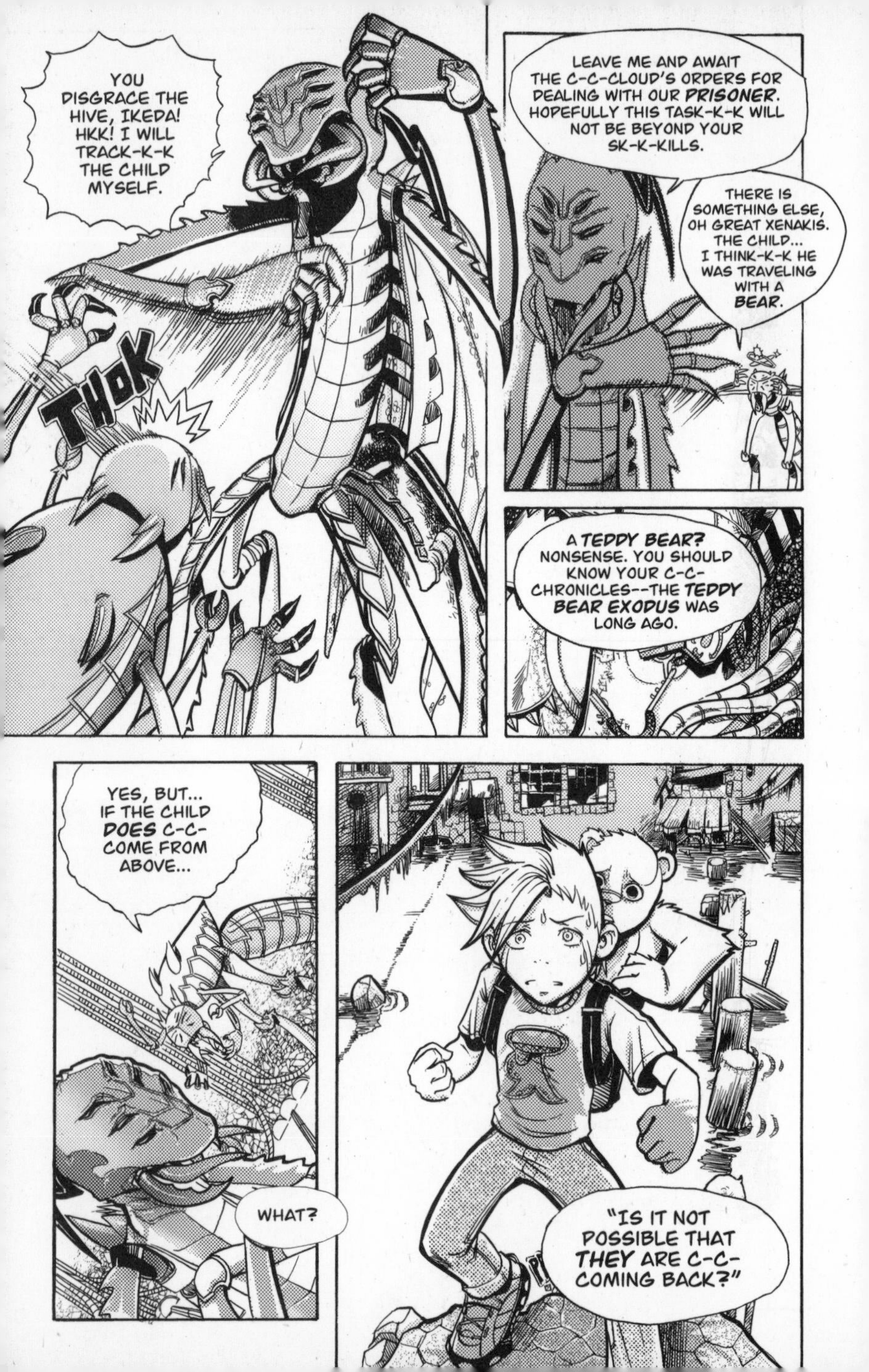
YOU DISGRACE THE HIVE, IKEDA! HKK! I WILL TRACK-K-K THE CHILD MYSELF.
THOK
LEAVE ME AND AWAIT THE C-C-CLOUD'S ORDERS FOR DEALING WITH OUR PRISONER. HOPEFULLY THIS TASK-K-K WILL NOT BE BEYOND YOUR SK-K-KILLS.
THERE IS SOMETHING ELSE, OH GREAT XENAKIS. THE CHILD... I THINK-K-K HE WAS TRAVELING WITH A BEAR.
A TEDDY BEAR? NONSENSE. YOU SHOULD KNOW YOUR C-C-CHRONICLES--THE TEDDY BEAR EXODUS WAS LONG AGO.
YES, BUT... IF THE CHILD DOES C-C-COME FROM ABOVE...
WHAT?
"IS IT NOT POSSIBLE THAT THEY ARE C-C-COMING BACK?"

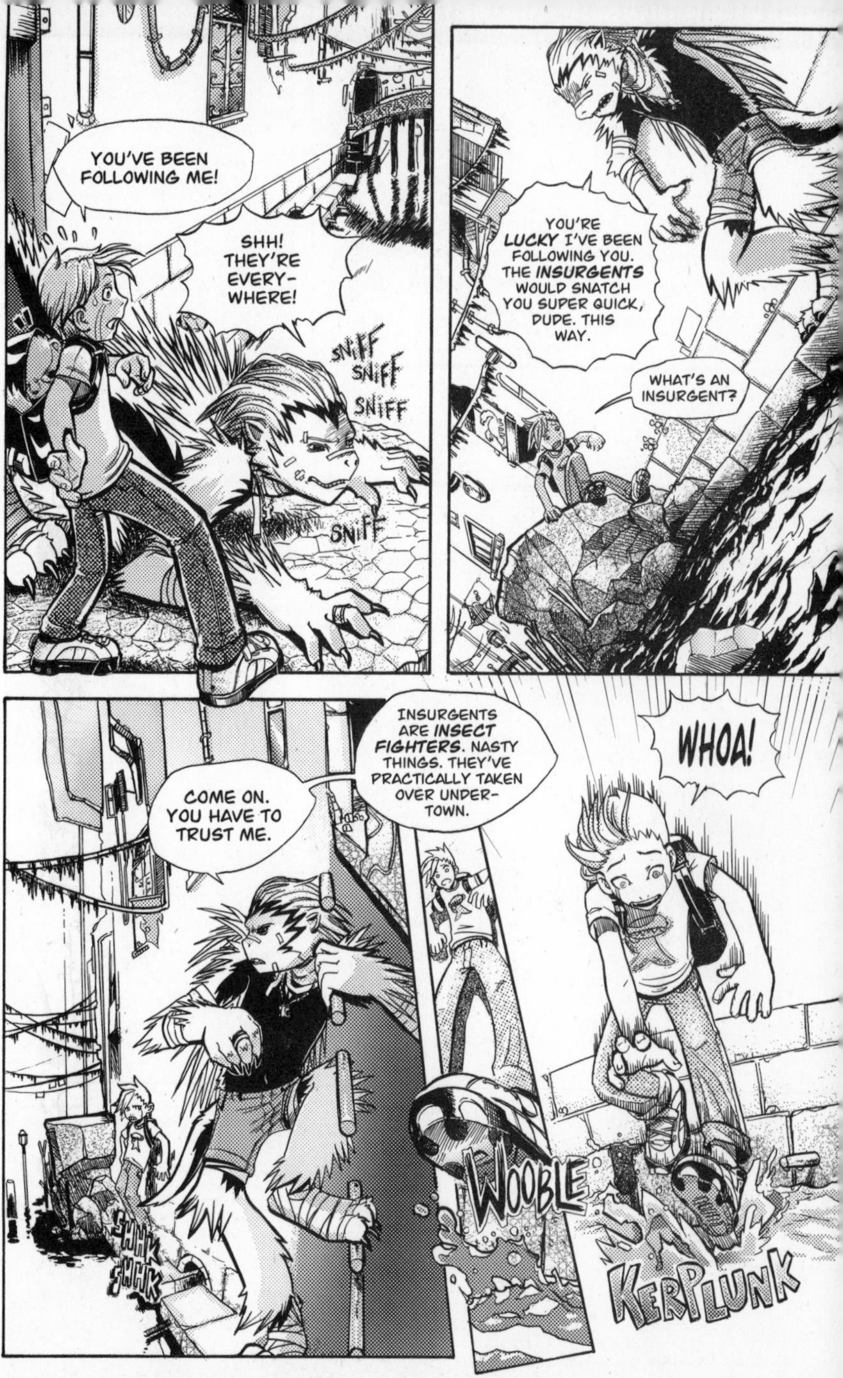
YOU'VE BEEN FOLLOWING ME!
SHH! THEY'RE EVERY-WHERE!
SNIFF SNIFF SNIFF
SNIFF
YOU'RE **LUCKY** I'VE BEEN FOLLOWING YOU. THE **INSURGENTS** WOULD SNATCH YOU SUPER QUICK, DUDE. THIS WAY.
WHAT'S AN INSURGENT?
COME ON. YOU HAVE TO TRUST ME.
INSURGENTS ARE **INSECT FIGHTERS**. NASTY THINGS. THEY'VE PRACTICALLY TAKEN OVER UNDER-TOWN.
SHHK SHHK
WOOBLE
WHOA!
KERPLUNK

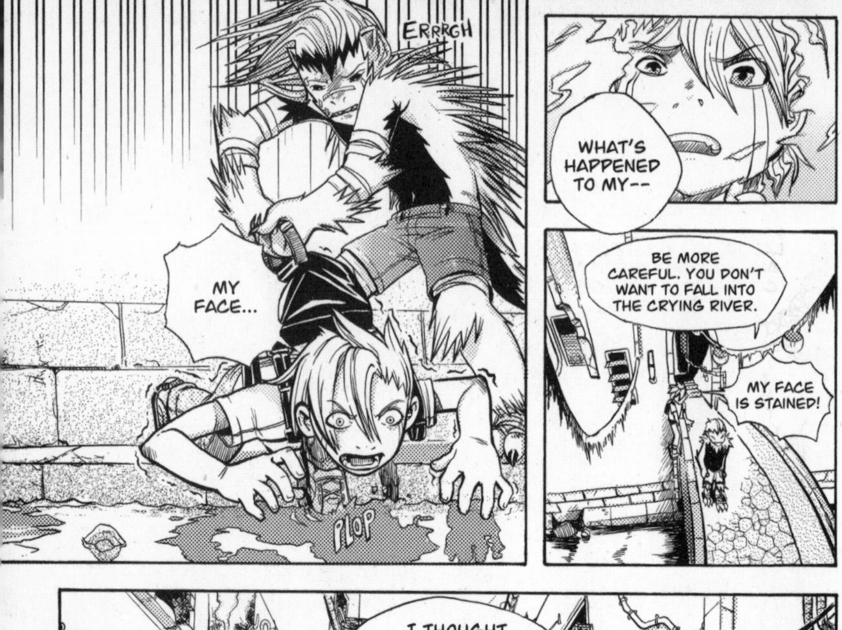
ERRRGH
MY FACE...
PLOP
WHAT'S HAPPENED TO MY--
BE MORE CAREFUL. YOU DON'T WANT TO FALL INTO THE CRYING RIVER.
MY FACE IS STAINED!
I THOUGHT THEY WERE WAR TATTOOS. DON'T WORRY, THEY LOOK COOL.

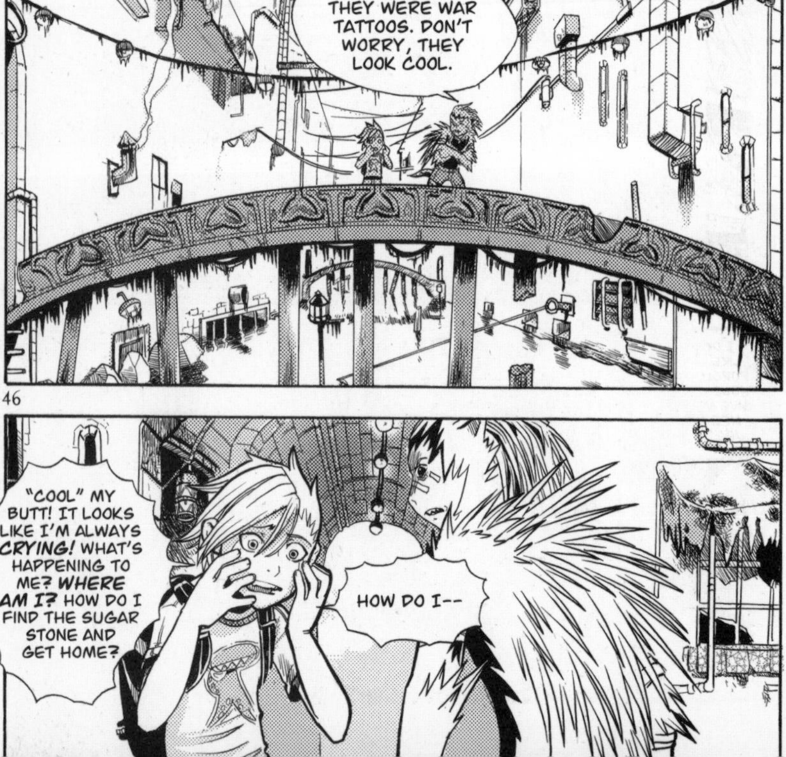
"COOL" MY BUTT! IT LOOKS LIKE I'M ALWAYS ***CRYING!*** WHAT'S HAPPENING TO ME? ***WHERE AM I?*** HOW DO I FIND THE SUGAR STONE AND GET HOME?
HOW DO I--

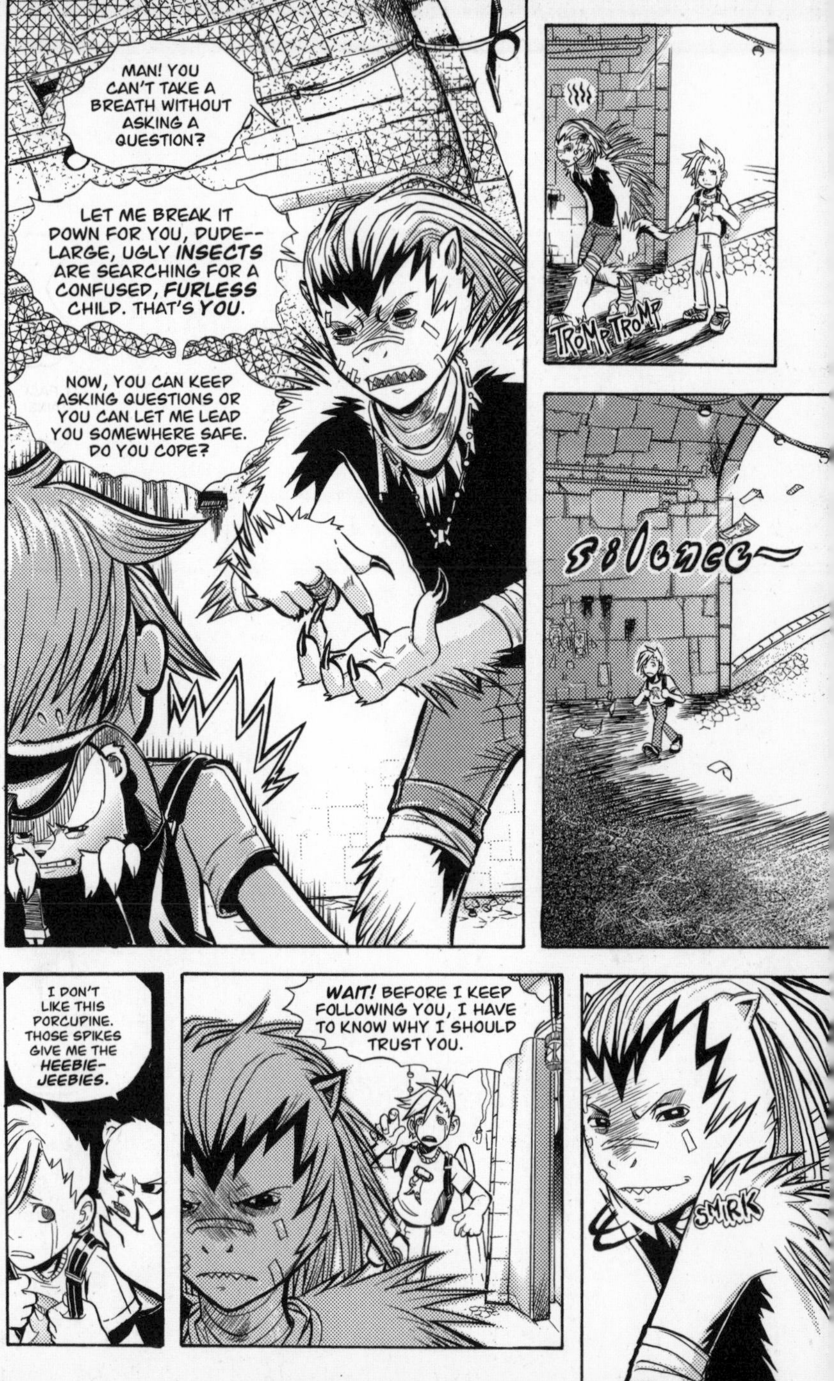
MAN! YOU CAN'T TAKE A BREATH WITHOUT ASKING A QUESTION?
LET ME BREAK IT DOWN FOR YOU, DUDE-- LARGE, UGLY INSECTS ARE SEARCHING FOR A CONFUSED, FURLESS CHILD. THAT'S YOU.
NOW, YOU CAN KEEP ASKING QUESTIONS OR YOU CAN LET ME LEAD YOU SOMEWHERE SAFE. DO YOU COPE?
TROMP TROMP
silence~
I DON'T LIKE THIS PORCUPINE. THOSE SPIKES GIVE ME THE HEEBIE-JEEBIES.
WAIT! BEFORE I KEEP FOLLOWING YOU, I HAVE TO KNOW WHY I SHOULD TRUST YOU.
SMIRK

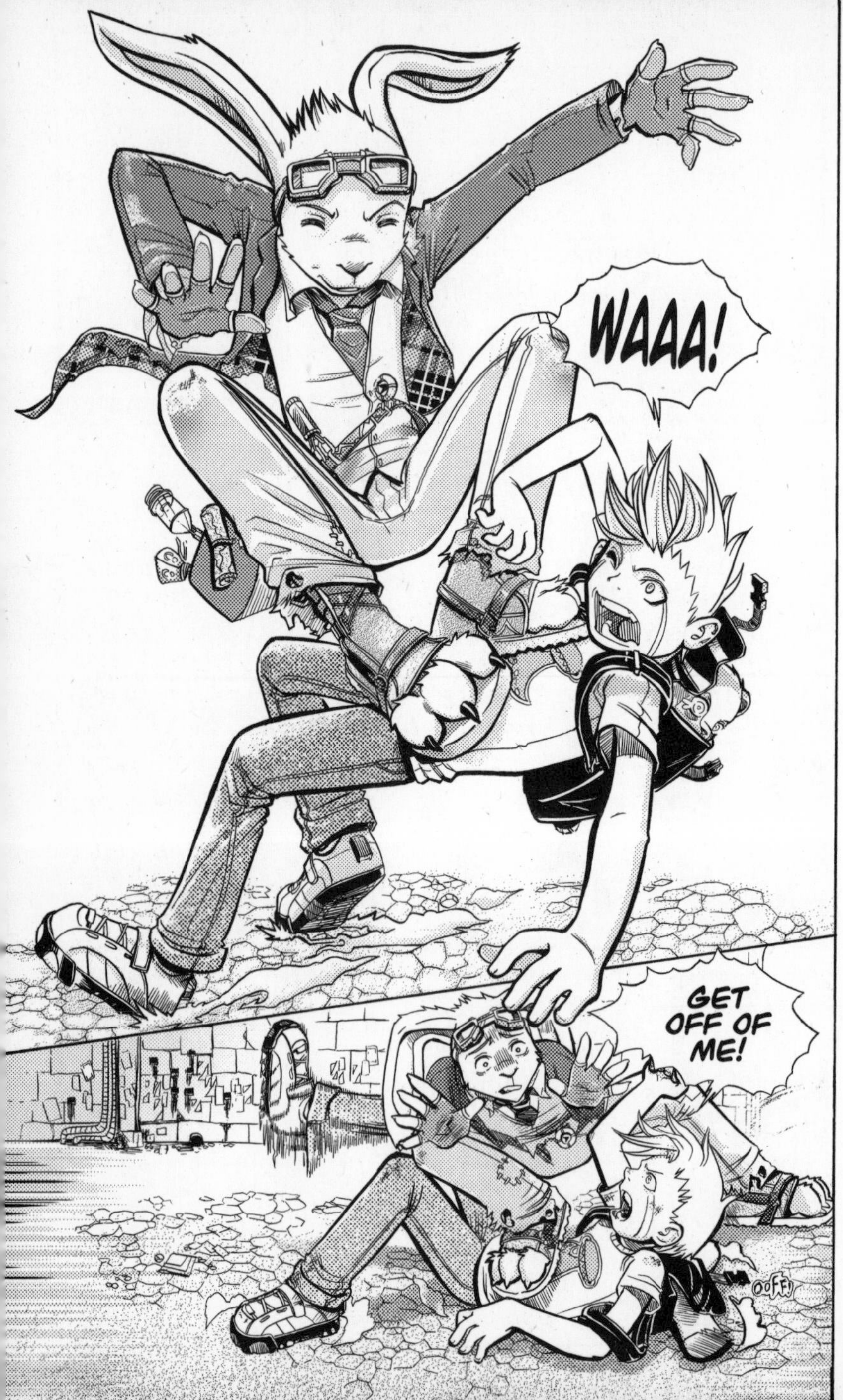
WAAA!
GET OFF OF ME!
OOFF!

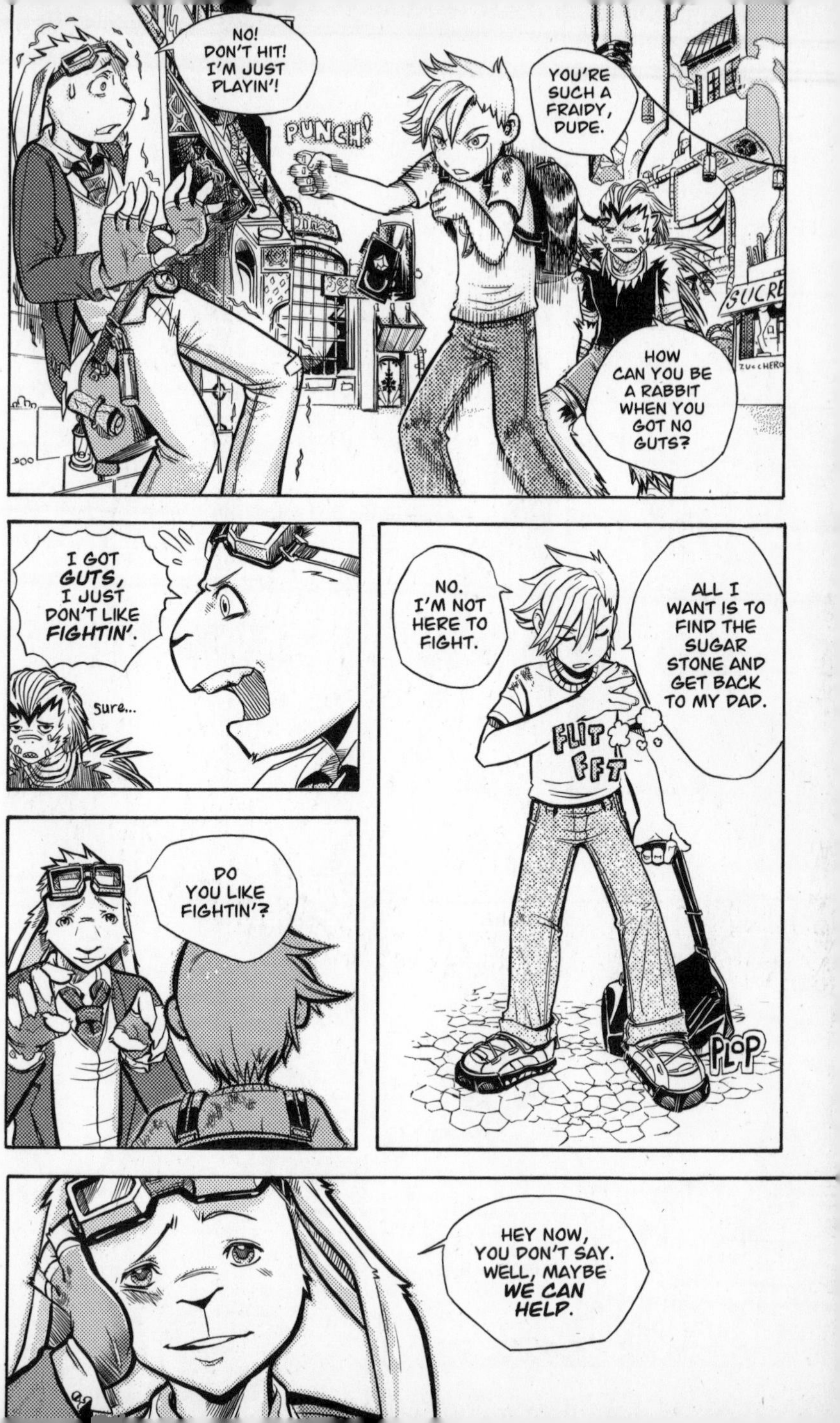
NO! DON'T HIT! I'M JUST PLAYIN'!
PUNCH!
YOU'RE SUCH A FRAIDY, DUDE.
SUCRE
HOW CAN YOU BE A RABBIT WHEN YOU GOT NO GUTS?
I GOT GUTS, I JUST DON'T LIKE FIGHTIN'.
sure...
DO YOU LIKE FIGHTIN'?
NO. I'M NOT HERE TO FIGHT.
ALL I WANT IS TO FIND THE SUGAR STONE AND GET BACK TO MY DAD.
FLIT FFT
PLOP
HEY NOW, YOU DON'T SAY. WELL, MAYBE WE CAN HELP.

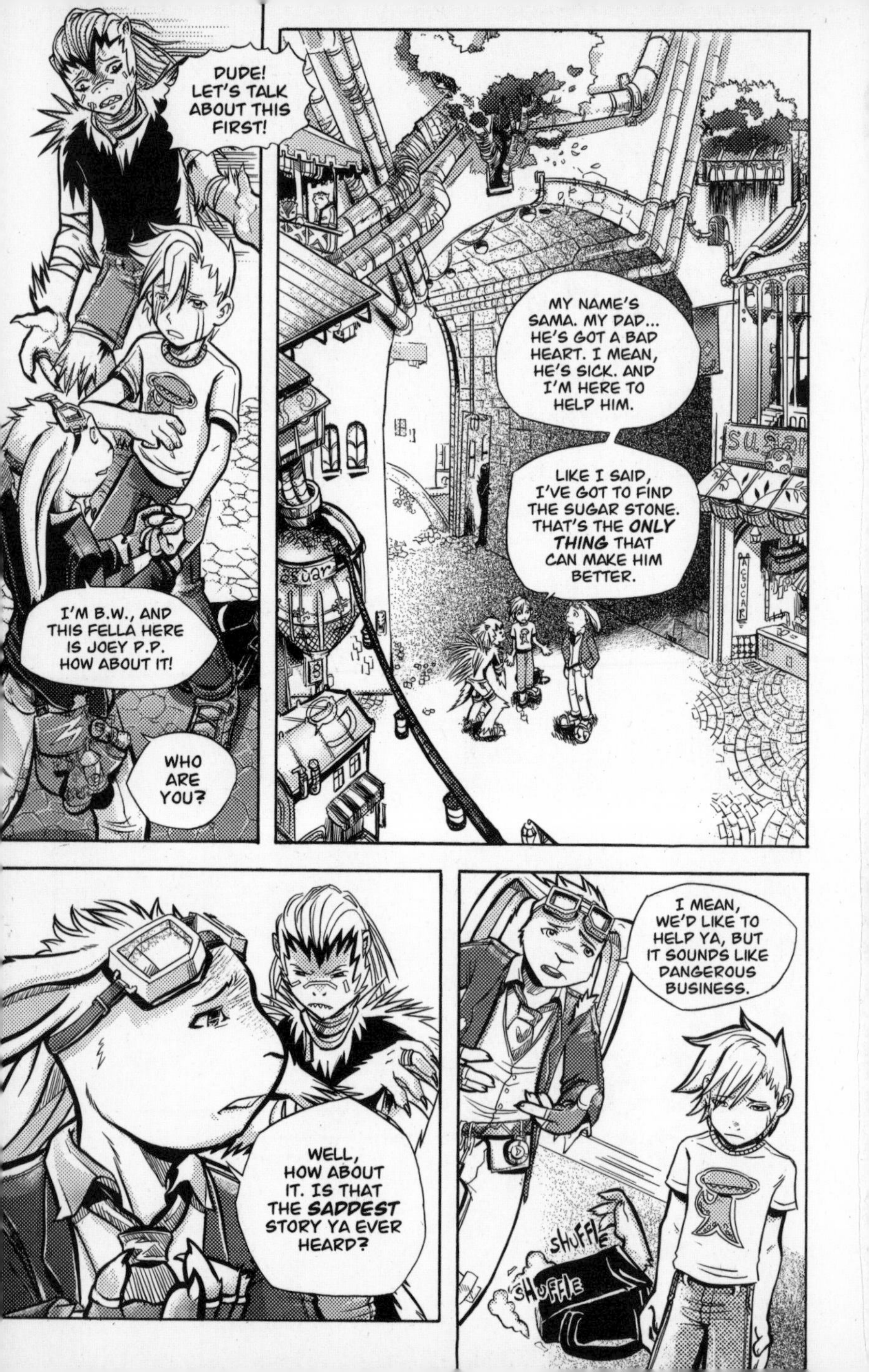
DUDE! LET'S TALK ABOUT THIS FIRST!
I'M B.W., AND THIS FELLA HERE IS JOEY P.P. HOW ABOUT IT!
WHO ARE YOU?
MY NAME'S SAMA. MY DAD... HE'S GOT A BAD HEART. I MEAN, HE'S SICK. AND I'M HERE TO HELP HIM.
LIKE I SAID, I'VE GOT TO FIND THE SUGAR STONE. THAT'S THE ONLY THING THAT CAN MAKE HIM BETTER.
WELL, HOW ABOUT IT. IS THAT THE SADDEST STORY YA EVER HEARD?
I MEAN, WE'D LIKE TO HELP YA, BUT IT SOUNDS LIKE DANGEROUS BUSINESS.
SHUFFLE
SHUFFLE

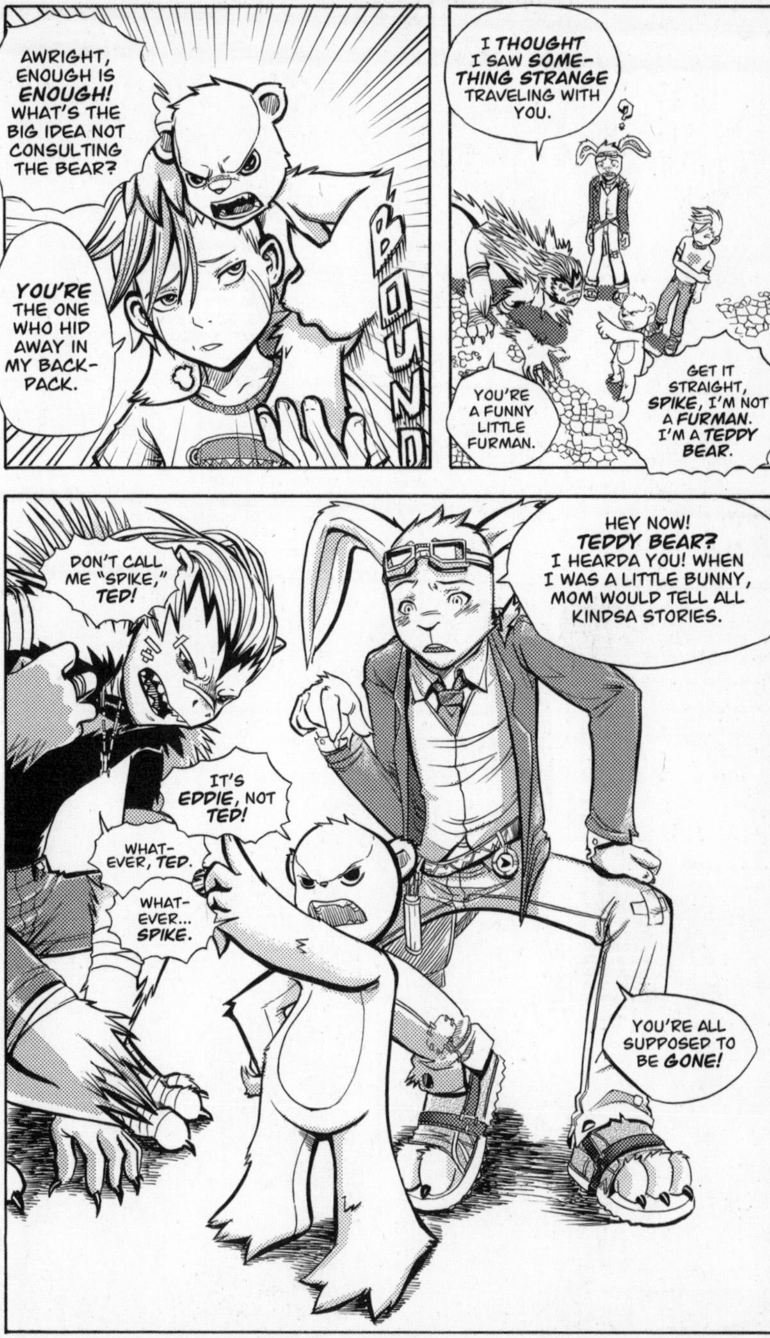
AWRIGHT, ENOUGH IS ENOUGH! WHAT'S THE BIG IDEA NOT CONSULTING THE BEAR?
YOU'RE THE ONE WHO HID AWAY IN MY BACK-PACK.
BOUND
I THOUGHT I SAW SOME-THING STRANGE TRAVELING WITH YOU.
?
YOU'RE A FUNNY LITTLE FURMAN.
GET IT STRAIGHT, SPIKE, I'M NOT A FURMAN. I'M A TEDDY BEAR.
DON'T CALL ME "SPIKE," TED!
HEY NOW! TEDDY BEAR? I HEARDA YOU! WHEN I WAS A LITTLE BUNNY, MOM WOULD TELL ALL KINDSA STORIES.
IT'S EDDIE, NOT TED!
WHAT-EVER, TED.
WHAT-EVER... SPIKE.
YOU'RE ALL SUPPOSED TO BE GONE!

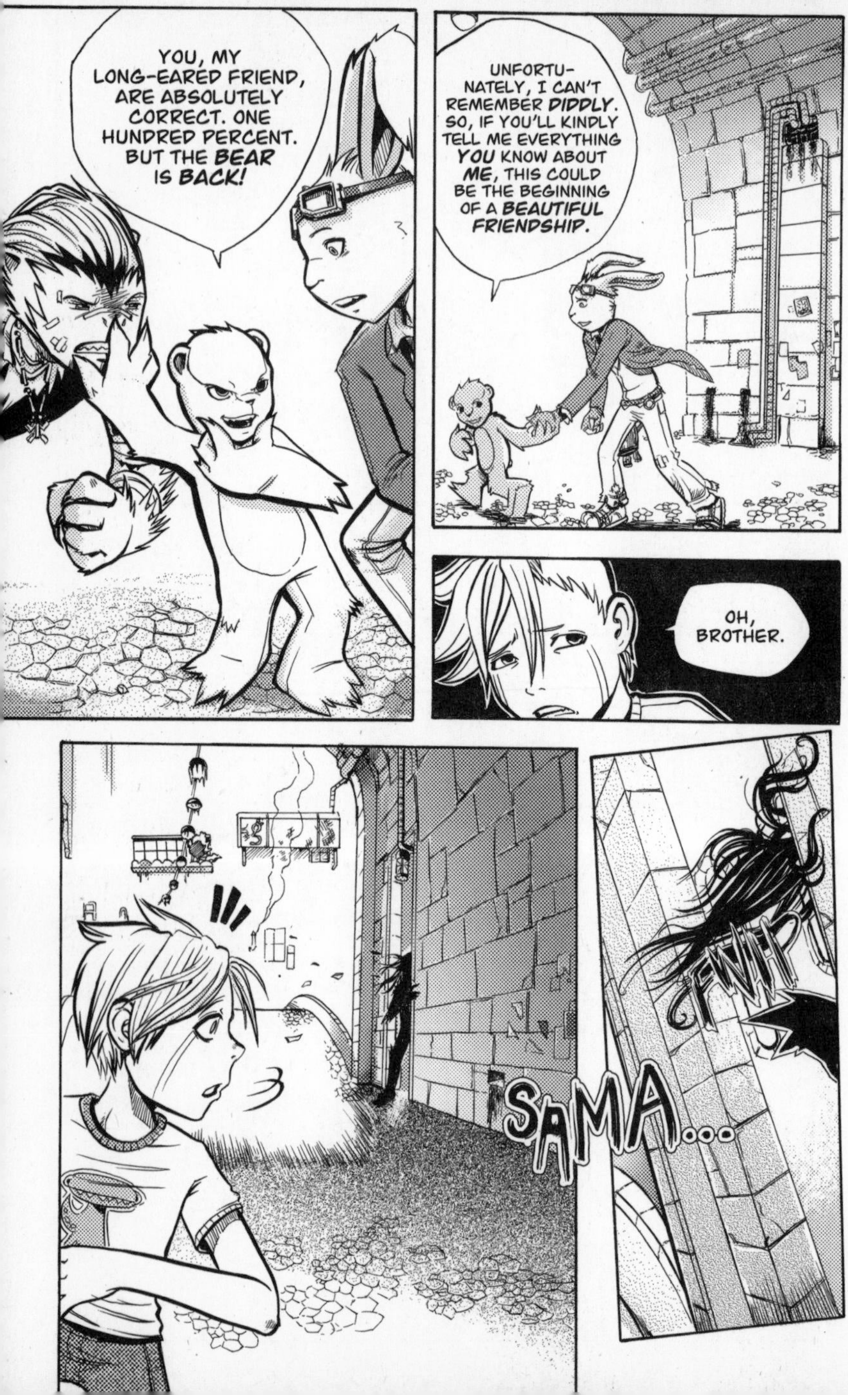
YOU, MY LONG-EARED FRIEND, ARE ABSOLUTELY CORRECT. ONE HUNDRED PERCENT. BUT THE BEAR IS BACK!
UNFORTU-NATELY, I CAN'T REMEMBER DIDDLY. SO, IF YOU'LL KINDLY TELL ME EVERYTHING YOU KNOW ABOUT ME, THIS COULD BE THE BEGINNING OF A BEAUTIFUL FRIENDSHIP.
OH, BROTHER.
SAMA...
FWIP

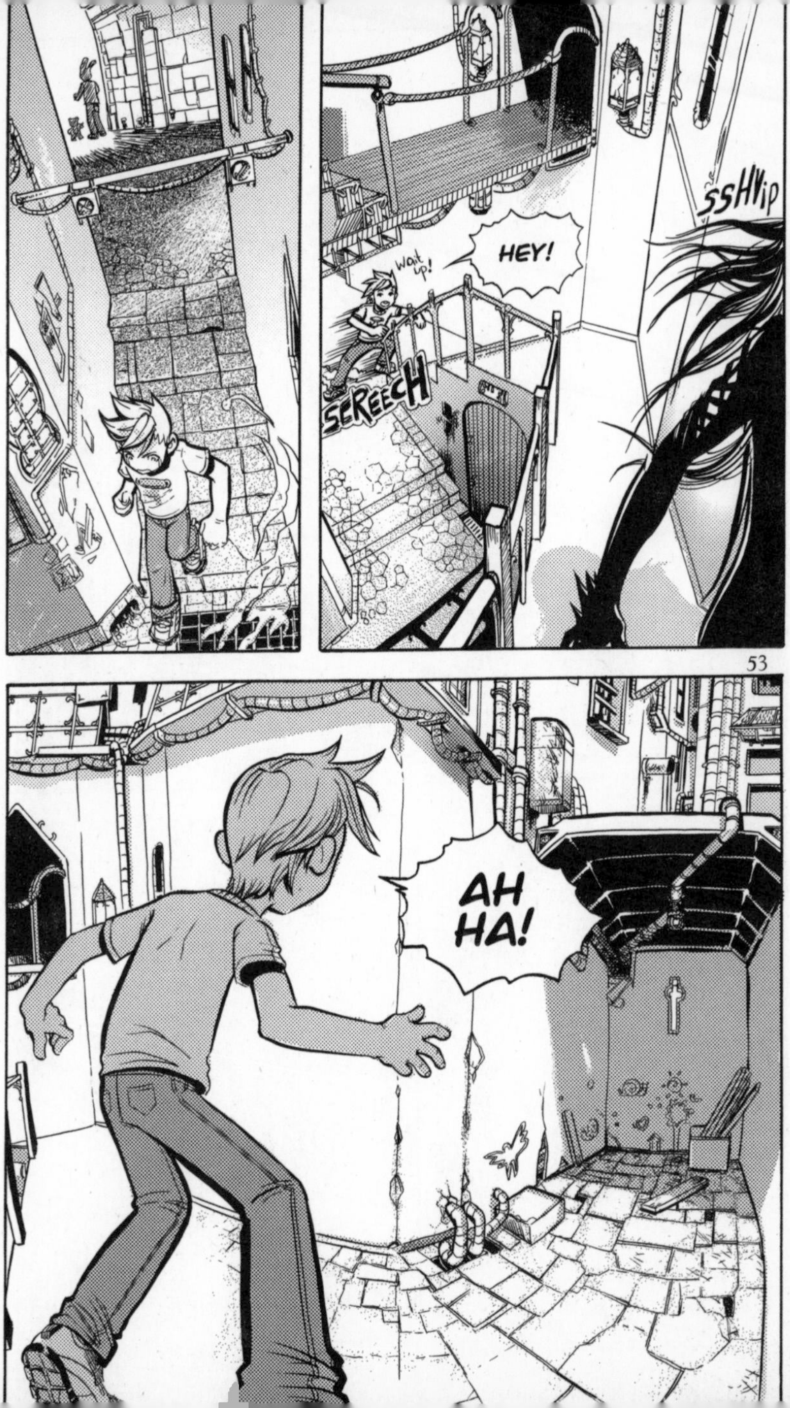
Wait up!
HEY!
SCREECH
SSHVip
AH HA!

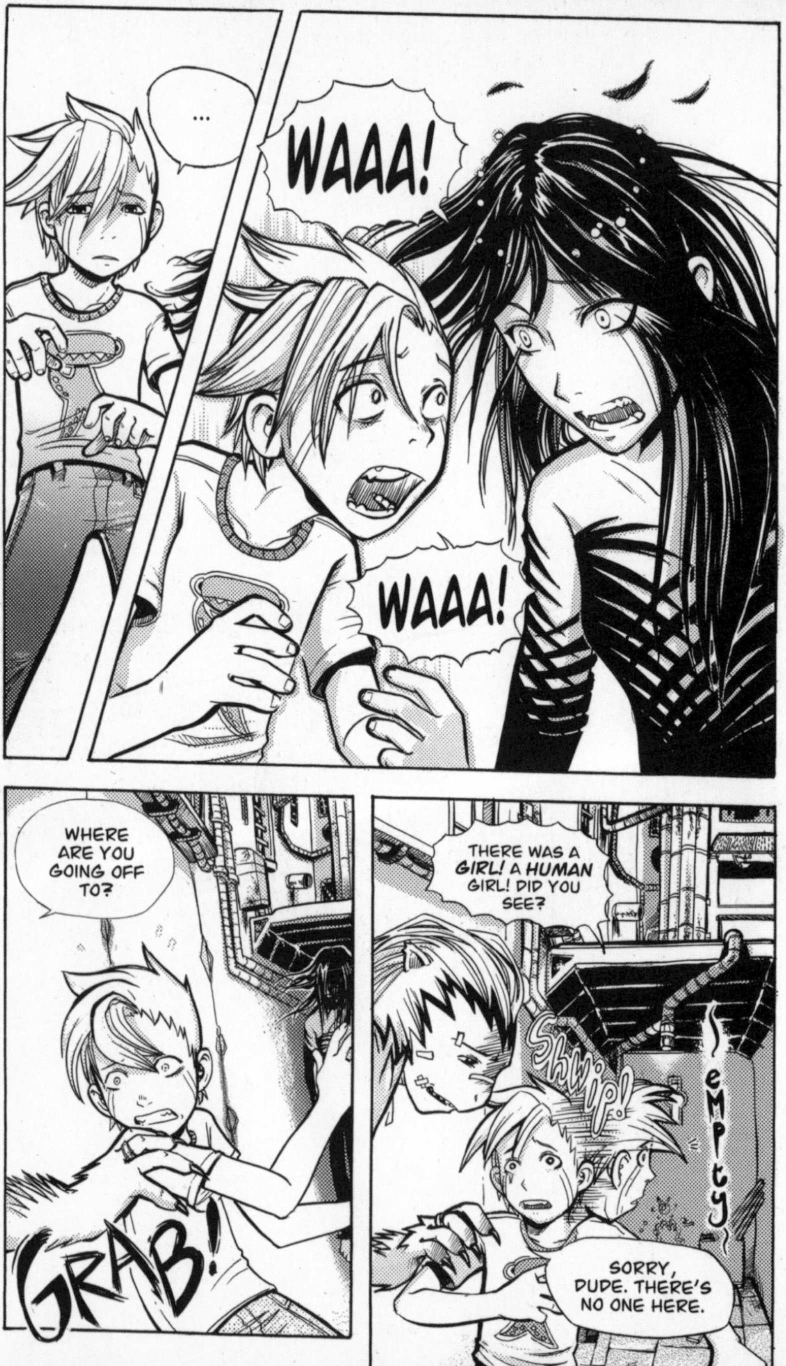
...
WAAA!
WAAA!
WHERE ARE YOU GOING OFF TO?
GRAB!
THERE WAS A **GIRL!** A **HUMAN** GIRL! DID YOU SEE?
Shwip!
empty
SORRY, DUDE. THERE'S NO ONE HERE.

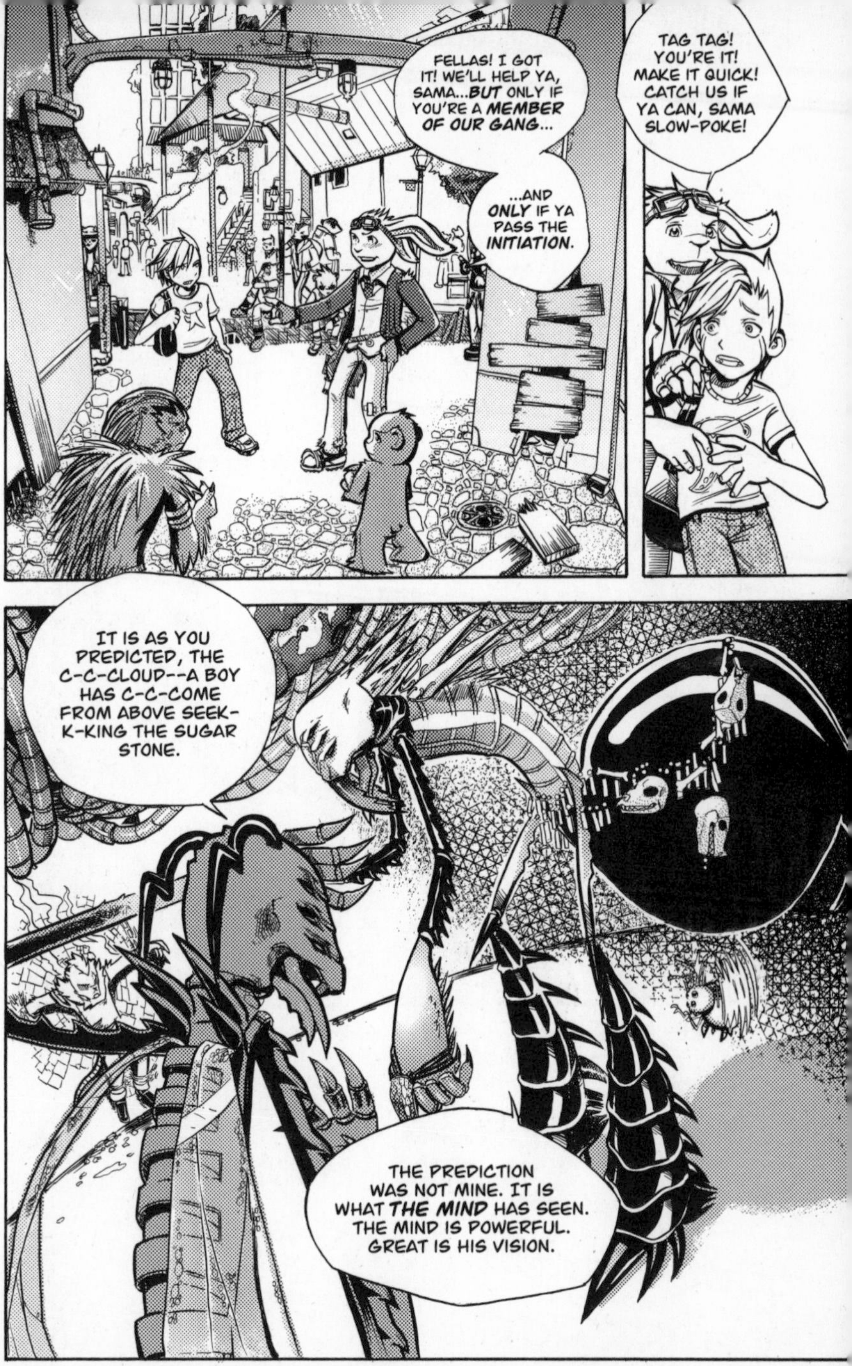
FELLAS! I GOT IT! WE'LL HELP YA, SAMA...BUT ONLY IF YOU'RE A MEMBER OF OUR GANG...
...AND ONLY IF YA PASS THE INITIATION.
TAG TAG! YOU'RE IT! MAKE IT QUICK! CATCH US IF YA CAN, SAMA SLOW-POKE!
IT IS AS YOU PREDICTED, THE C-C-CLOUD--A BOY HAS C-C-COME FROM ABOVE SEEK-K-KING THE SUGAR STONE.
THE PREDICTION WAS NOT MINE. IT IS WHAT THE MIND HAS SEEN. THE MIND IS POWERFUL. GREAT IS HIS VISION.

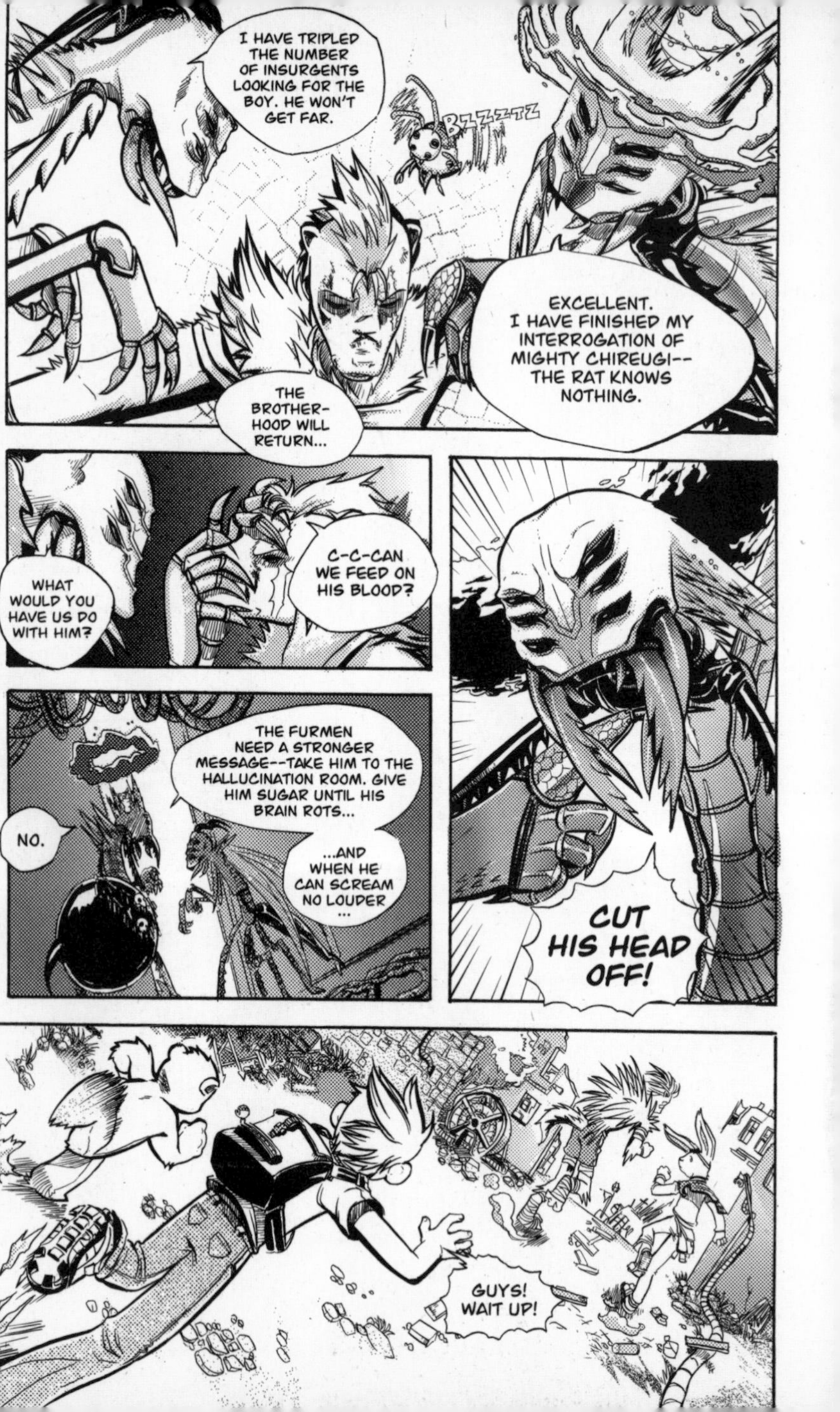
I HAVE TRIPLED THE NUMBER OF INSURGENTS LOOKING FOR THE BOY. HE WON'T GET FAR.
BZZZZTZ
EXCELLENT. I HAVE FINISHED MY INTERROGATION OF MIGHTY CHIREUGI-- THE RAT KNOWS NOTHING.
THE BROTHER-HOOD WILL RETURN...
WHAT WOULD YOU HAVE US DO WITH HIM?
C-C-CAN WE FEED ON HIS BLOOD?
THE FURMEN NEED A STRONGER MESSAGE--TAKE HIM TO THE HALLUCINATION ROOM. GIVE HIM SUGAR UNTIL HIS BRAIN ROTS...
NO.
...AND WHEN HE CAN SCREAM NO LOUDER ...
CUT HIS HEAD OFF!
GUYS! WAIT UP!

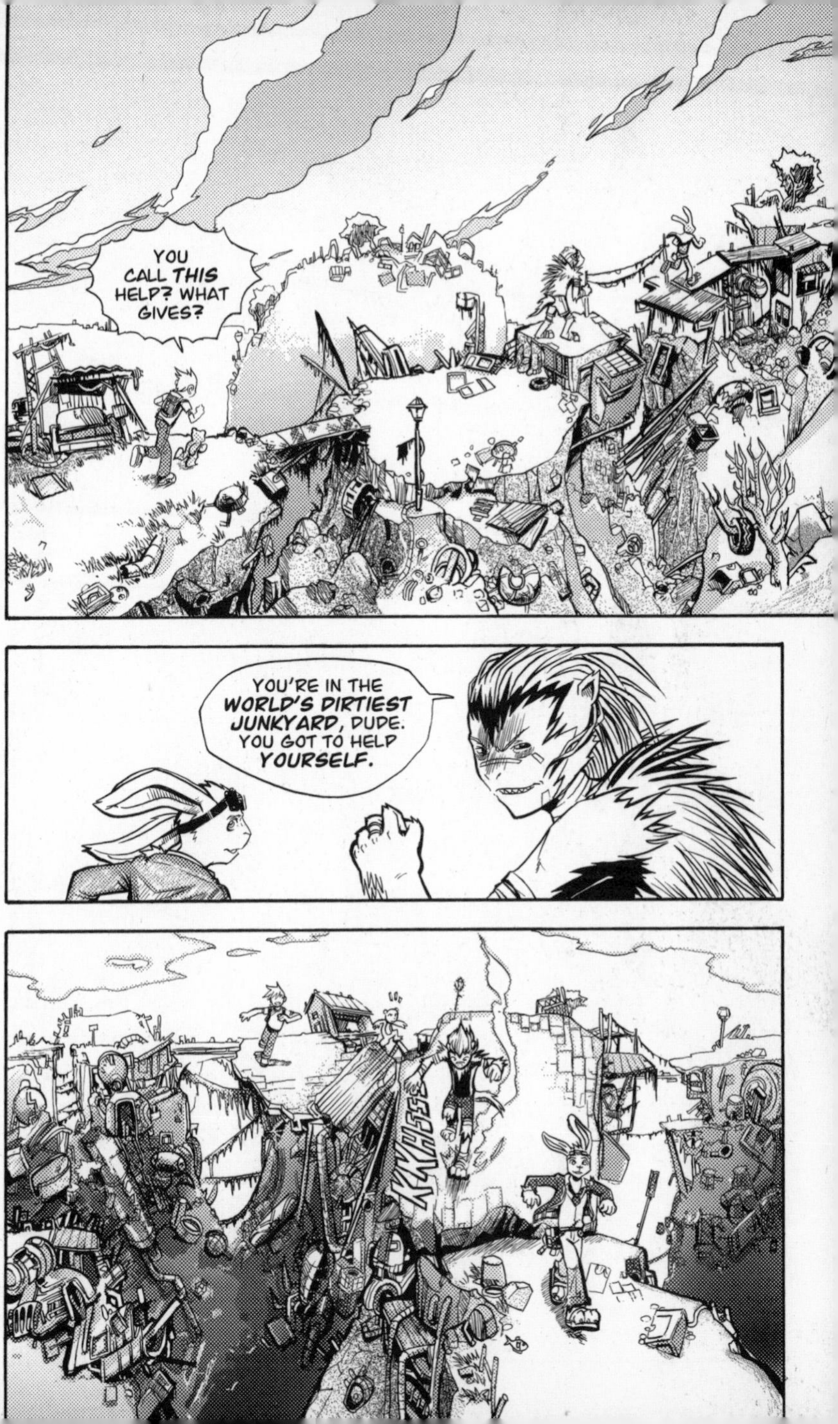
YOU CALL THIS HELP? WHAT GIVES?
YOU'RE IN THE WORLD'S DIRTIEST JUNKYARD, DUDE. YOU GOT TO HELP YOURSELF.
KKHSSS

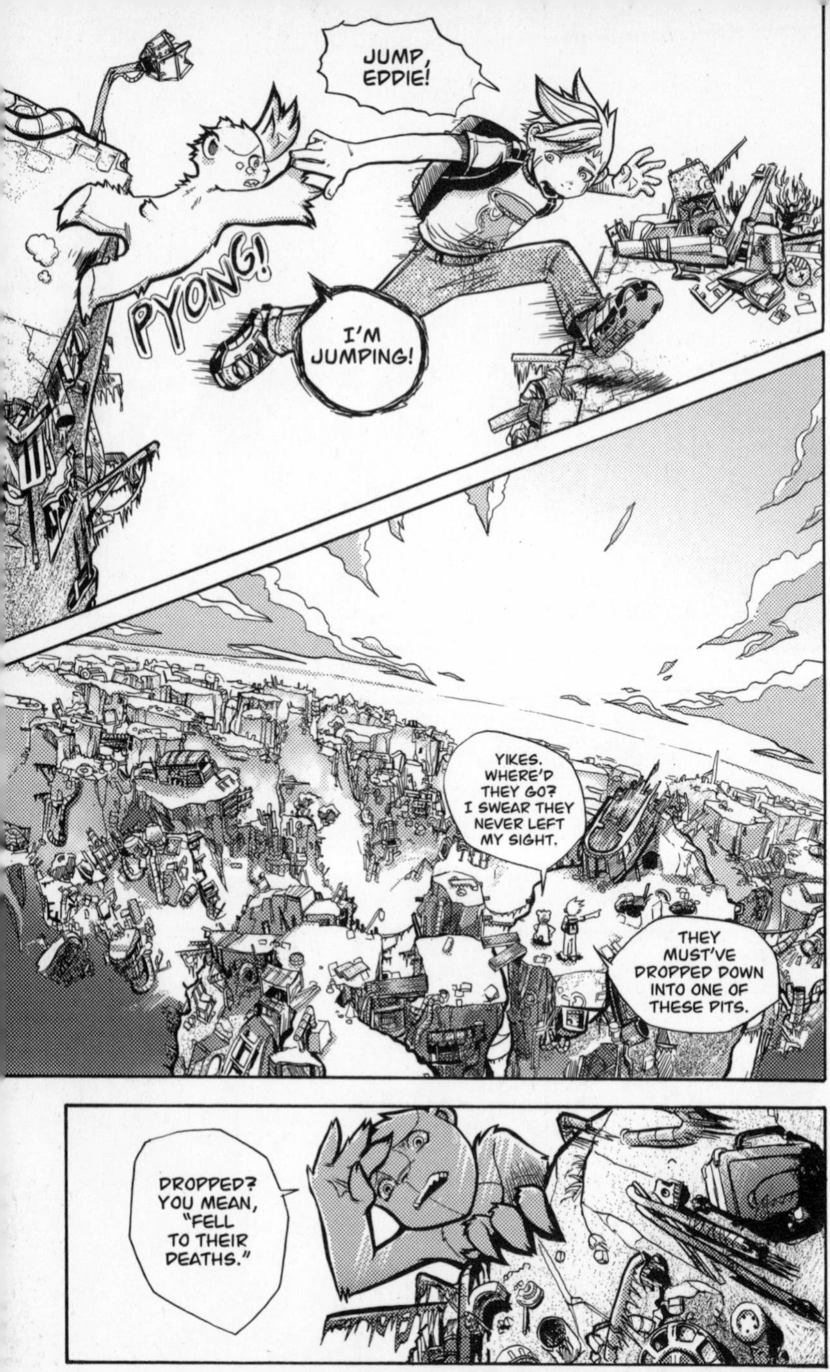
JUMP, EDDIE!
PYONG!
I'M JUMPING!
YIKES. WHERE'D THEY GO? I SWEAR THEY NEVER LEFT MY SIGHT.
THEY MUST'VE DROPPED DOWN INTO ONE OF THESE PITS.
DROPPED? YOU MEAN, "FELL TO THEIR DEATHS."

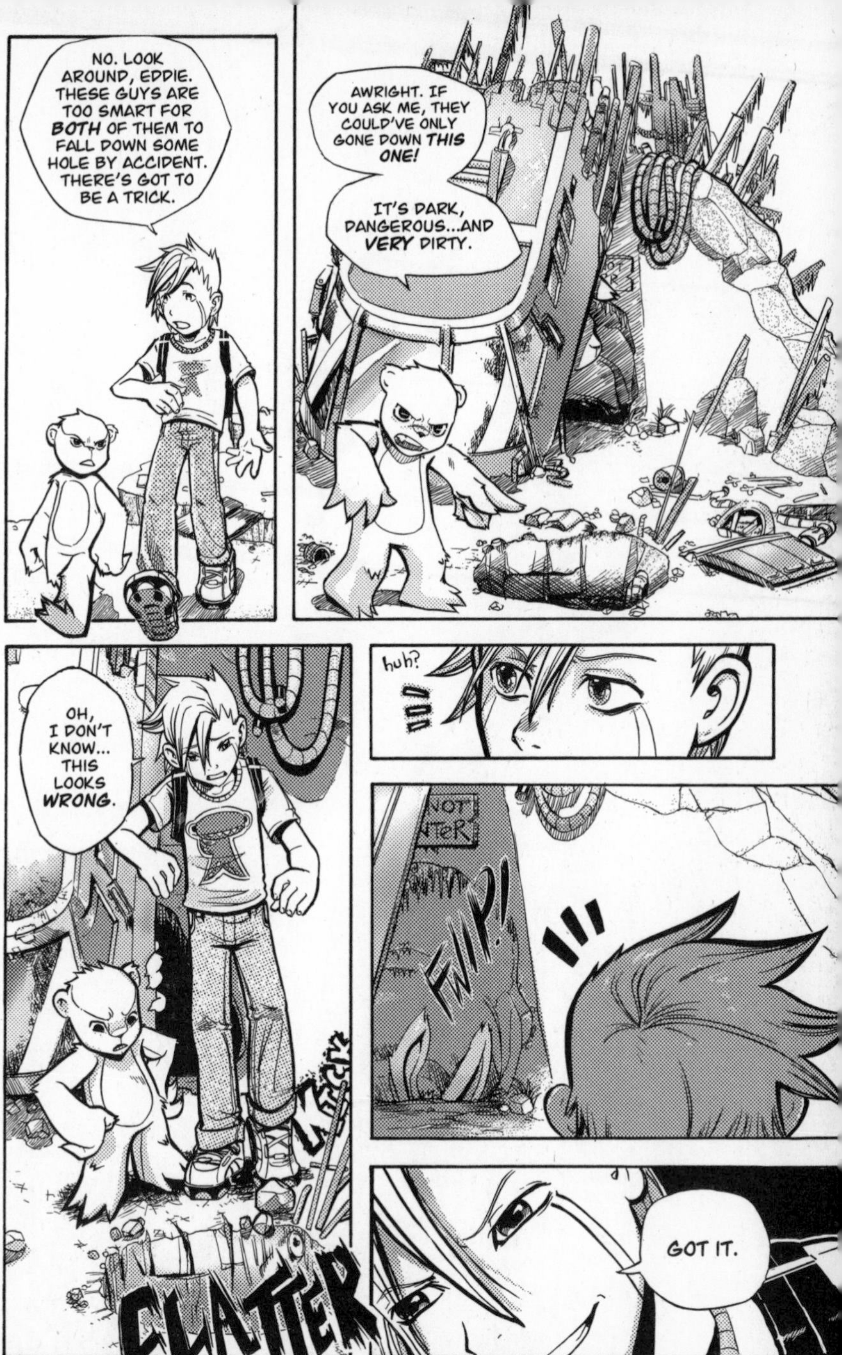
NO. LOOK AROUND, EDDIE. THESE GUYS ARE TOO SMART FOR BOTH OF THEM TO FALL DOWN SOME HOLE BY ACCIDENT. THERE'S GOT TO BE A TRICK.
AWRIGHT. IF YOU ASK ME, THEY COULD'VE ONLY GONE DOWN THIS ONE!
IT'S DARK, DANGEROUS...AND VERY DIRTY.
OH, I DON'T KNOW... THIS LOOKS WRONG.
CLATTER
huh?
NOT
NTER
FWIP!
GOT IT.

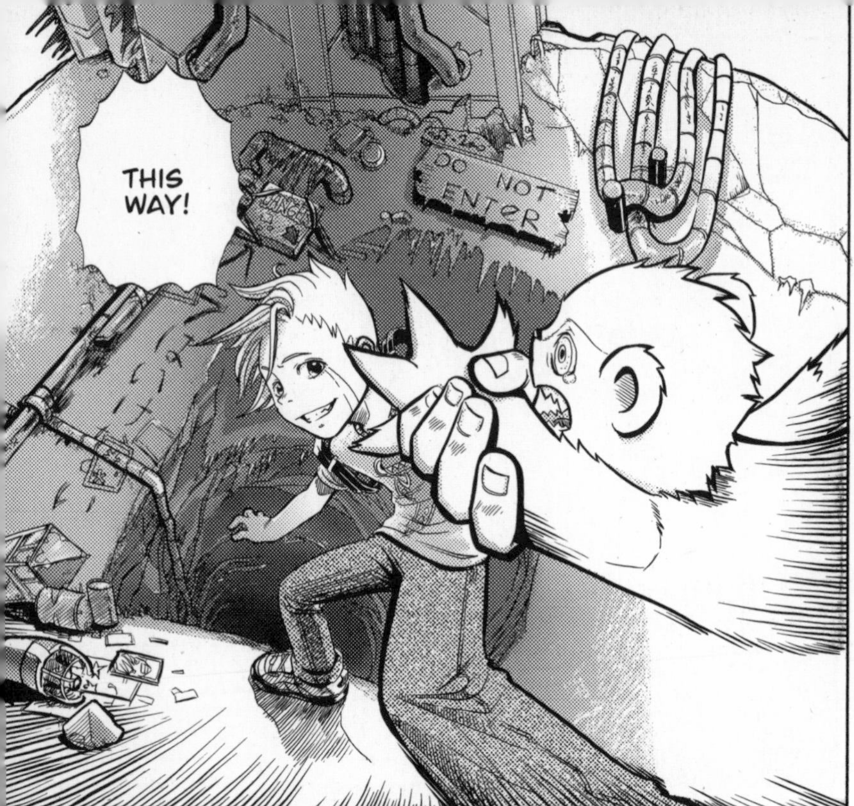
THIS WAY!
DO NOT ENTER

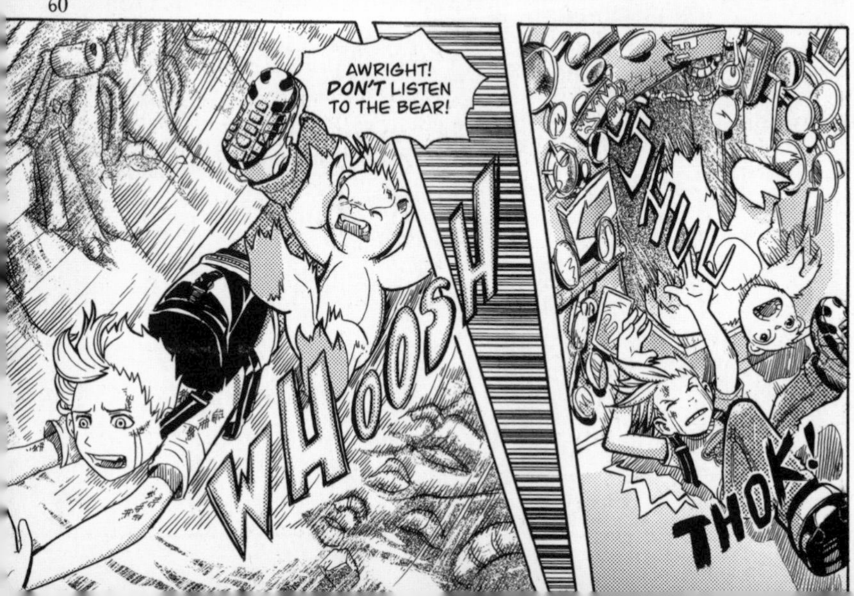
AWRIGHT! *DON'T* LISTEN TO THE BEAR!
WHOOSH
THOK!

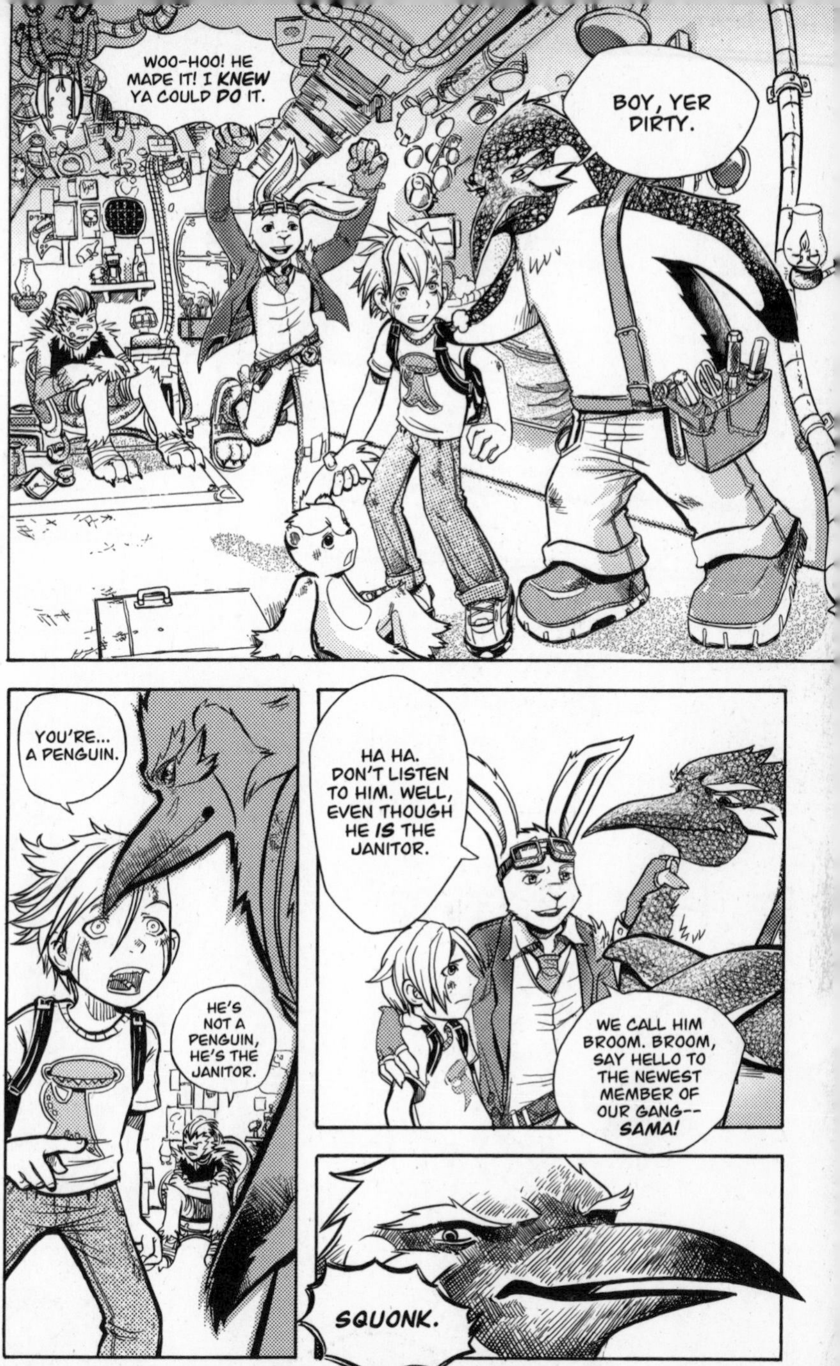
WOO-HOO! HE MADE IT! I KNEW YA COULD DO IT.
BOY, YER DIRTY.
YOU'RE... A PENGUIN.
HE'S NOT A PENGUIN, HE'S THE JANITOR.
HA HA. DON'T LISTEN TO HIM. WELL, EVEN THOUGH HE IS THE JANITOR.
WE CALL HIM BROOM. BROOM, SAY HELLO TO THE NEWEST MEMBER OF OUR GANG-- SAMA!
SQUONK.

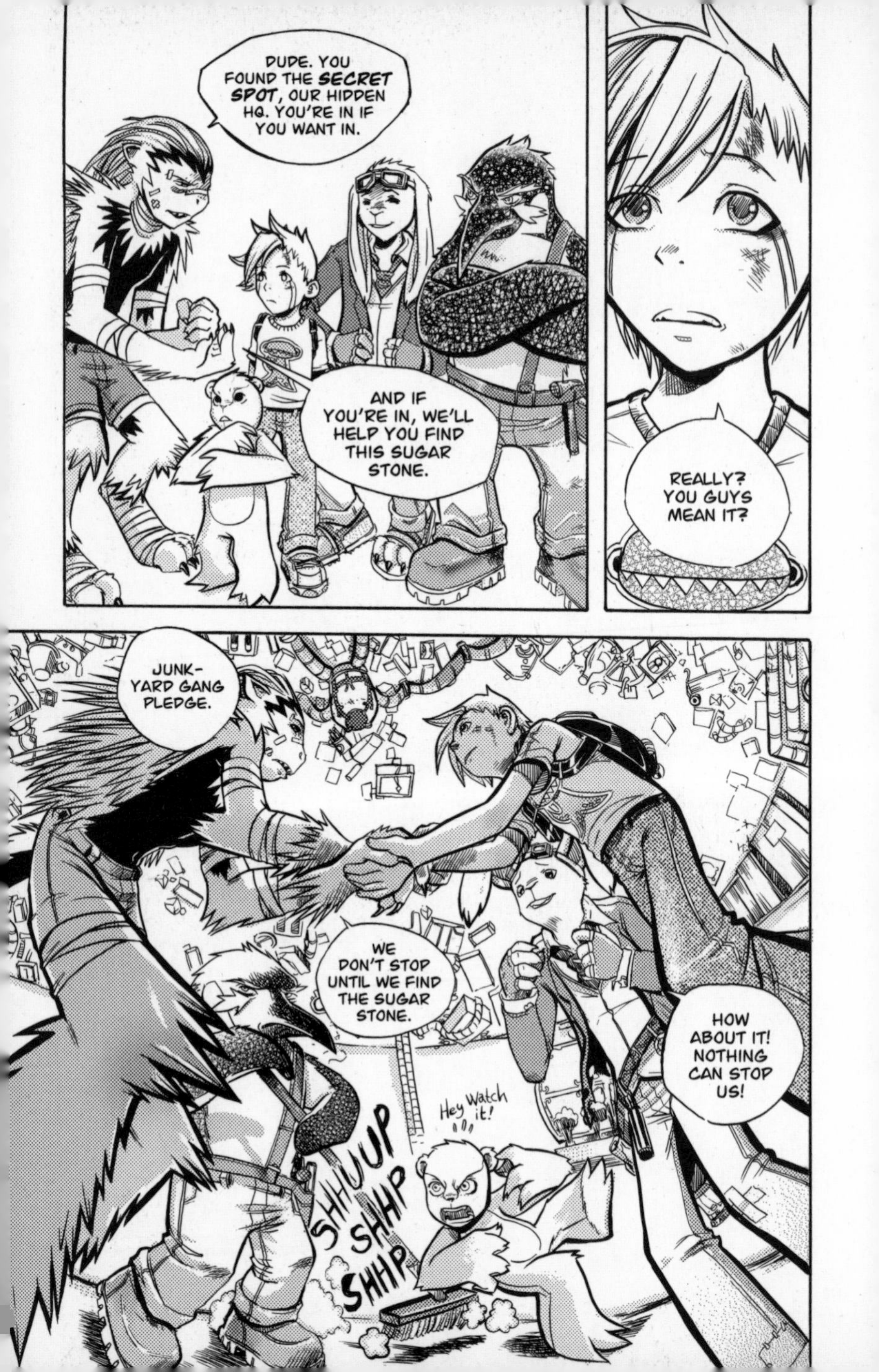
DUDE. YOU FOUND THE **SECRET SPOT**, OUR HIDDEN HQ. YOU'RE IN IF YOU WANT IN.
AND IF YOU'RE IN, WE'LL HELP YOU FIND THIS SUGAR STONE.
REALLY? YOU GUYS MEAN IT?
JUNK-YARD GANG PLEDGE.
WE DON'T STOP UNTIL WE FIND THE SUGAR STONE.
HOW ABOUT IT! NOTHING CAN STOP US!
Hey Watch it!
SHUUP SHHP SHHP

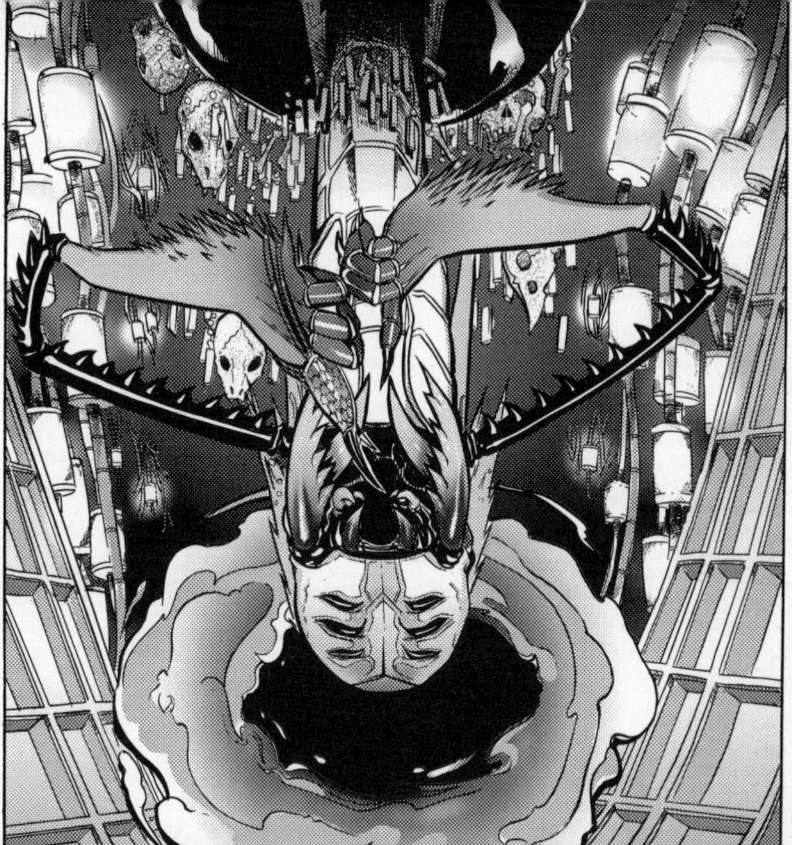
THE MIND, YOU ARE GREAT, POWERFUL, AND WISE.
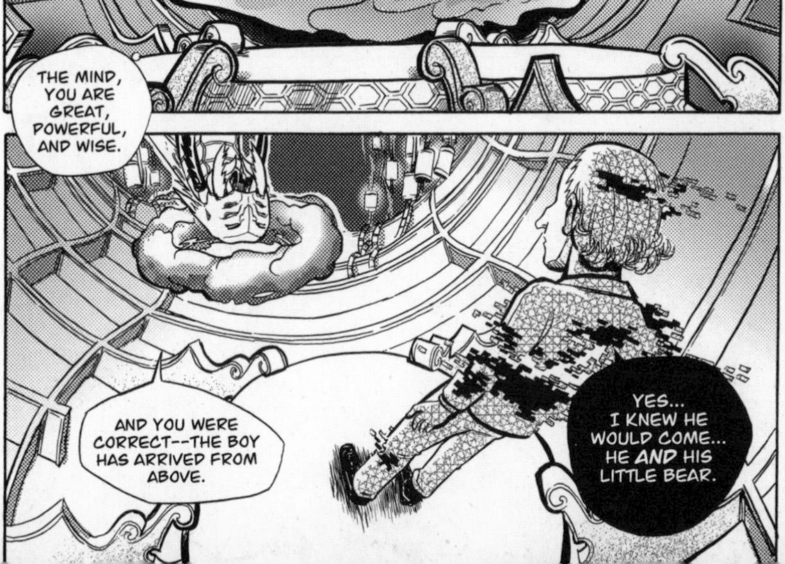
AND YOU WERE CORRECT--THE BOY HAS ARRIVED FROM ABOVE.
YES... I KNEW HE WOULD COME... HE AND HIS LITTLE BEAR.

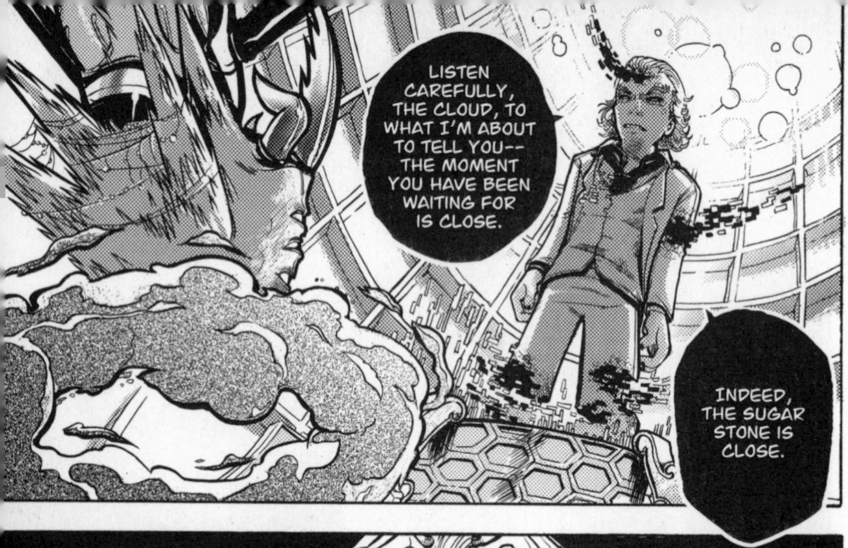
LISTEN CAREFULLY, THE CLOUD, TO WHAT I'M ABOUT TO TELL YOU-- THE MOMENT YOU HAVE BEEN WAITING FOR IS CLOSE.
INDEED, THE SUGAR STONE IS CLOSE.
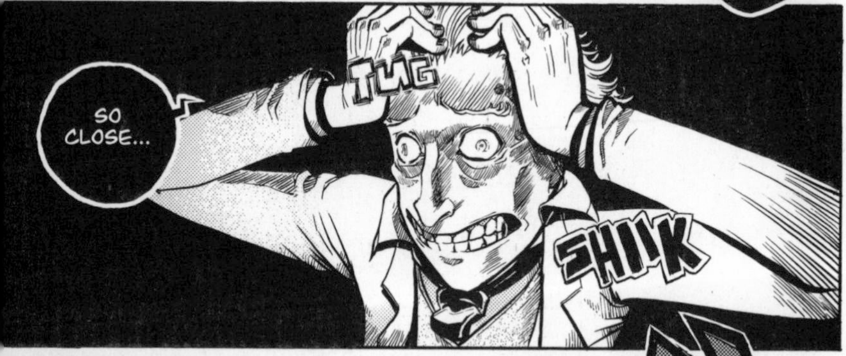
SO CLOSE...
TUG
SHIIK
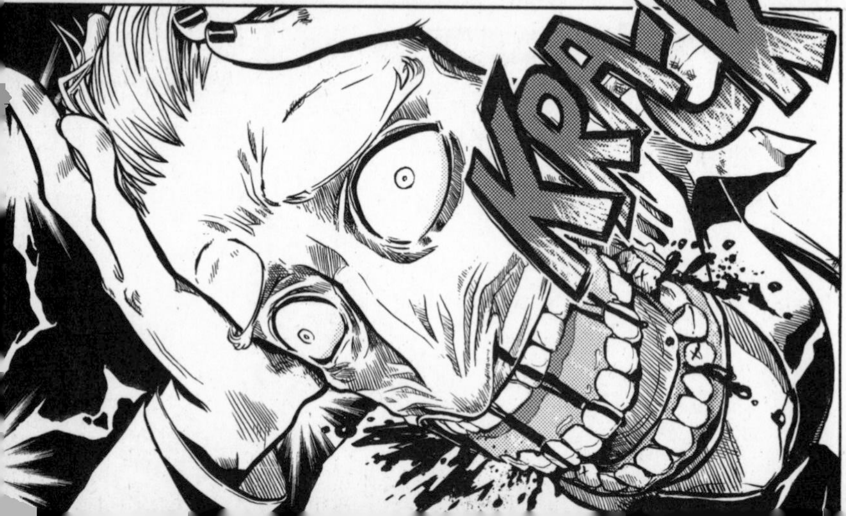
KRACK

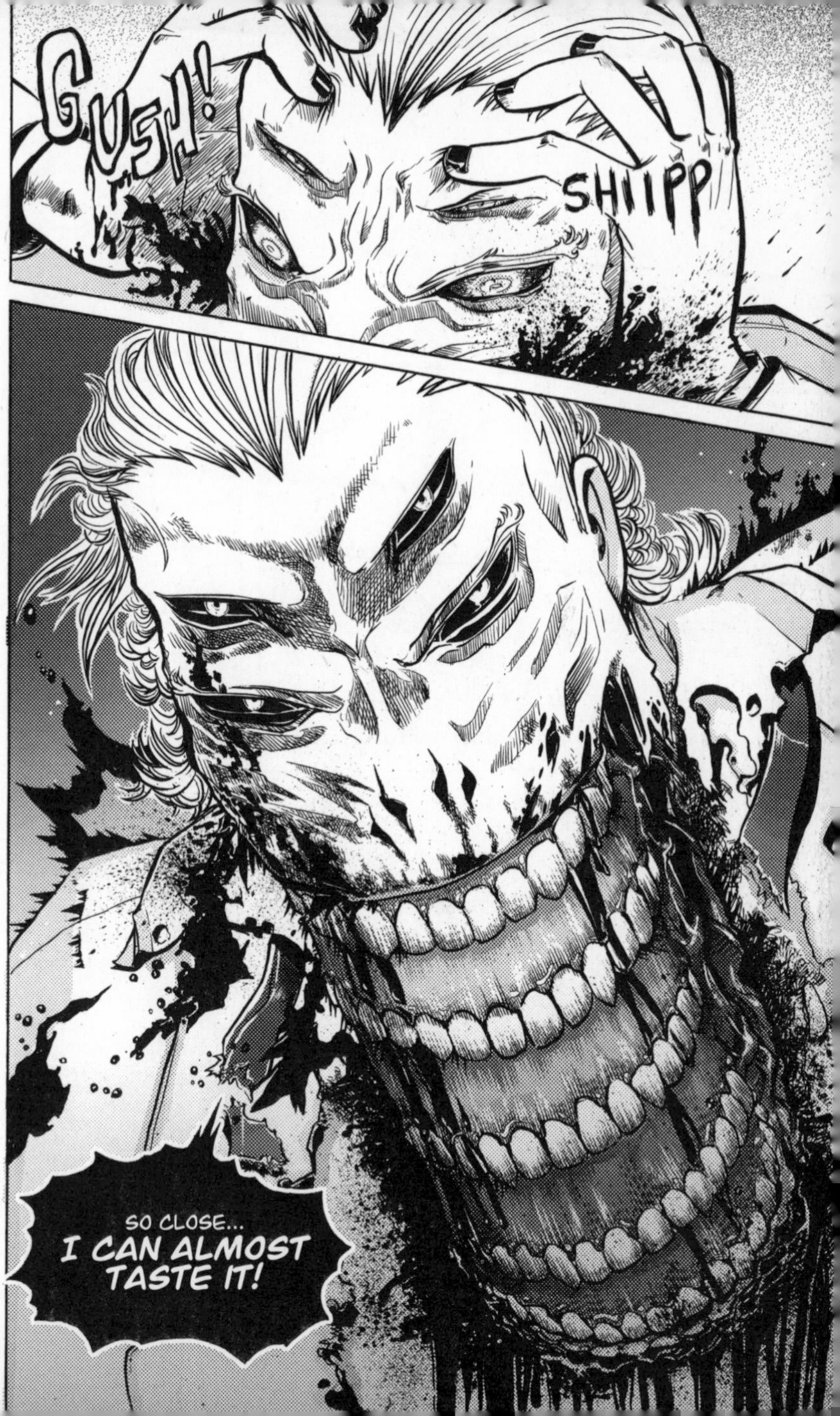
GUSH!
SHIIPP
SO CLOSE...
I CAN ALMOST TASTE IT!

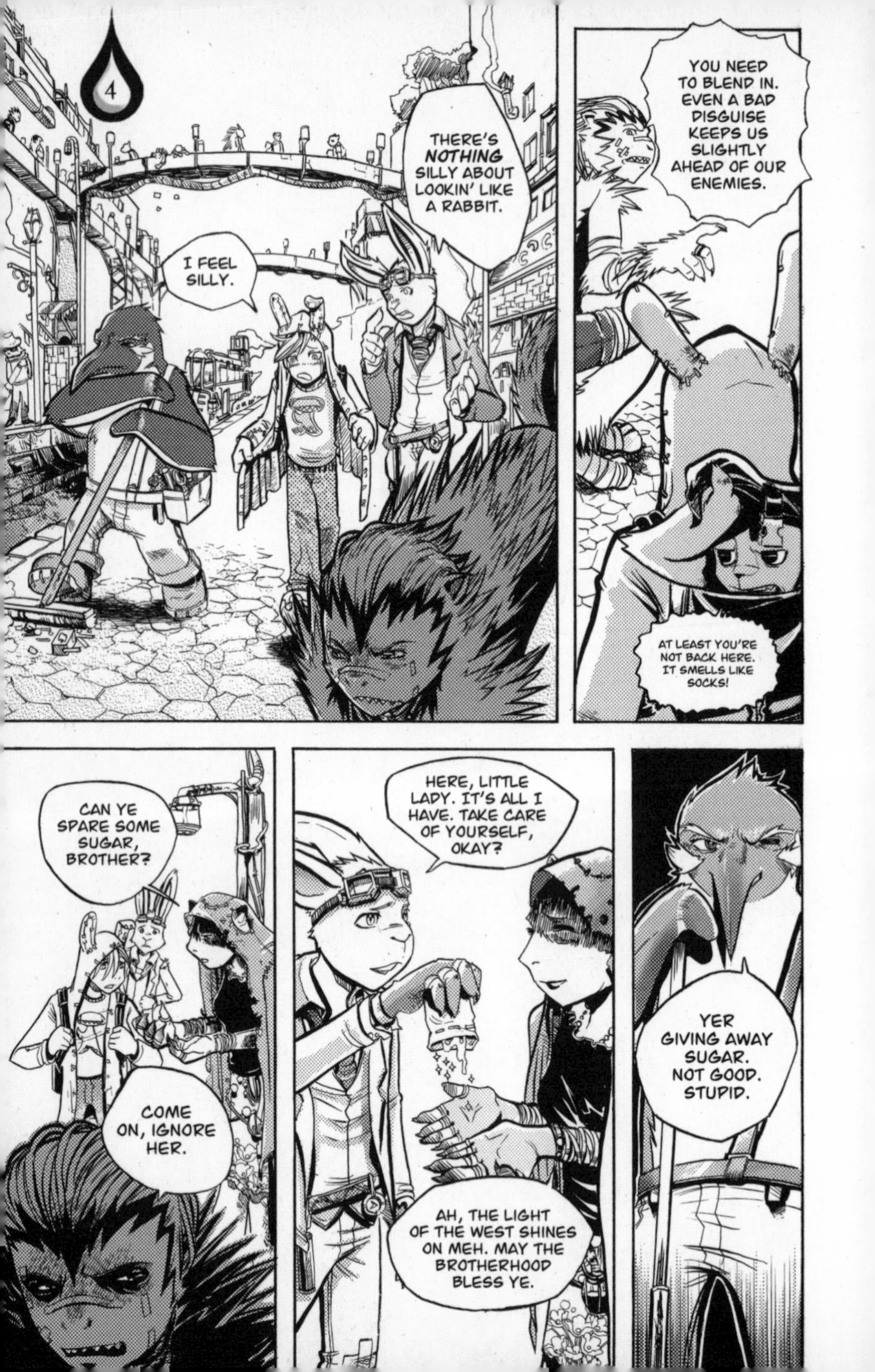
4
I FEEL SILLY.
THERE'S NOTHING SILLY ABOUT LOOKIN' LIKE A RABBIT.
YOU NEED TO BLEND IN. EVEN A BAD DISGUISE KEEPS US SLIGHTLY AHEAD OF OUR ENEMIES.
AT LEAST YOU'RE NOT BACK HERE. IT SMELLS LIKE SOCKS!
CAN YE SPARE SOME SUGAR, BROTHER?
COME ON, IGNORE HER.
HERE, LITTLE LADY. IT'S ALL I HAVE. TAKE CARE OF YOURSELF, OKAY?
AH, THE LIGHT OF THE WEST SHINES ON MEH. MAY THE BROTHERHOOD BLESS YE.
YER GIVING AWAY SUGAR. NOT GOOD. STUPID.

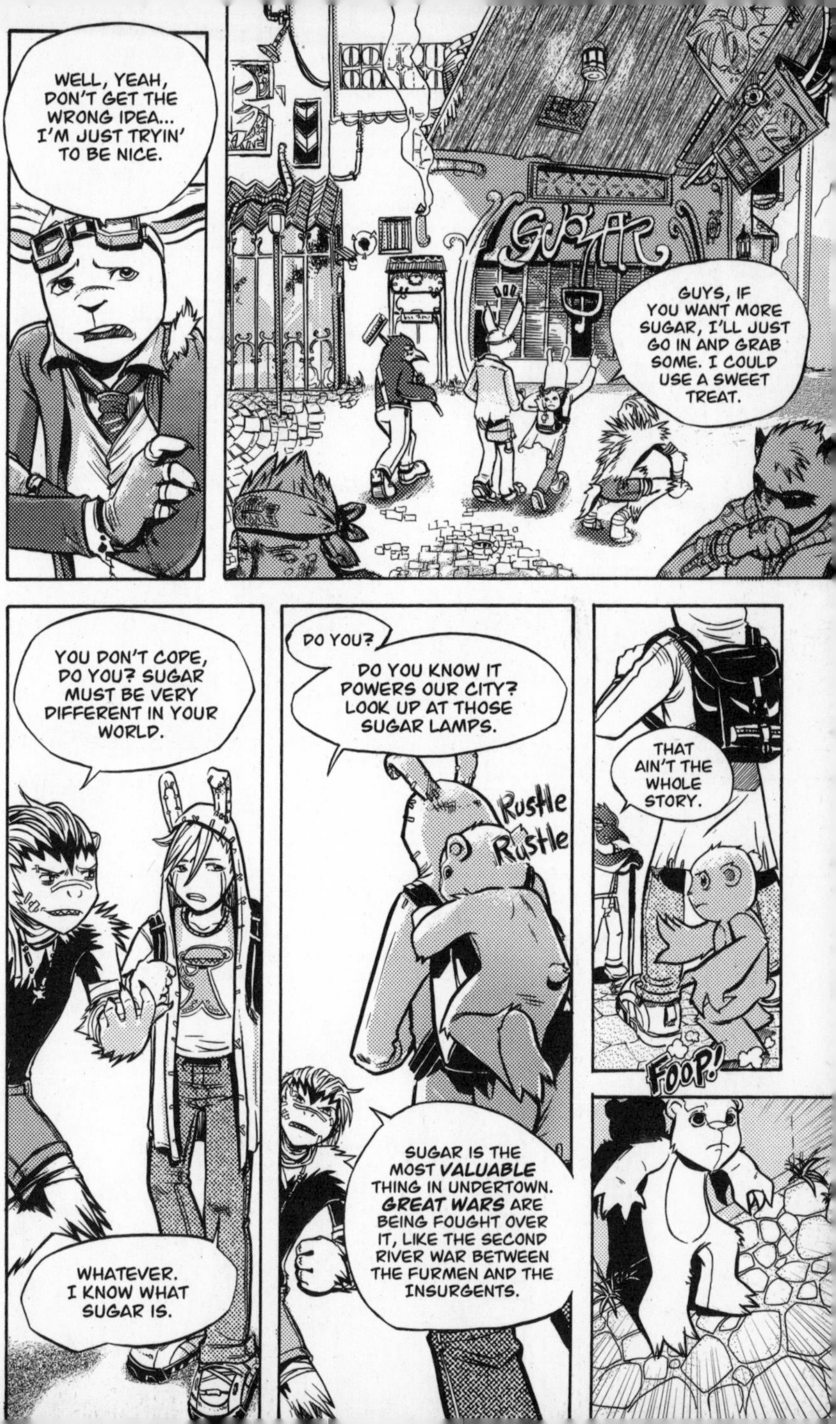
WELL, YEAH, DON'T GET THE WRONG IDEA... I'M JUST TRYIN' TO BE NICE.
SUGAR
GUYS, IF YOU WANT MORE SUGAR, I'LL JUST GO IN AND GRAB SOME. I COULD USE A SWEET TREAT.
YOU DON'T COPE, DO YOU? SUGAR MUST BE VERY DIFFERENT IN YOUR WORLD.
WHATEVER. I KNOW WHAT SUGAR IS.
DO YOU?
DO YOU KNOW IT POWERS OUR CITY? LOOK UP AT THOSE SUGAR LAMPS.
Rustle Rustle
SUGAR IS THE MOST ***VALUABLE*** THING IN UNDERTOWN. ***GREAT WARS*** ARE BEING FOUGHT OVER IT, LIKE THE SECOND RIVER WAR BETWEEN THE FURMEN AND THE INSURGENTS.
THAT AIN'T THE WHOLE STORY.
FOOP!

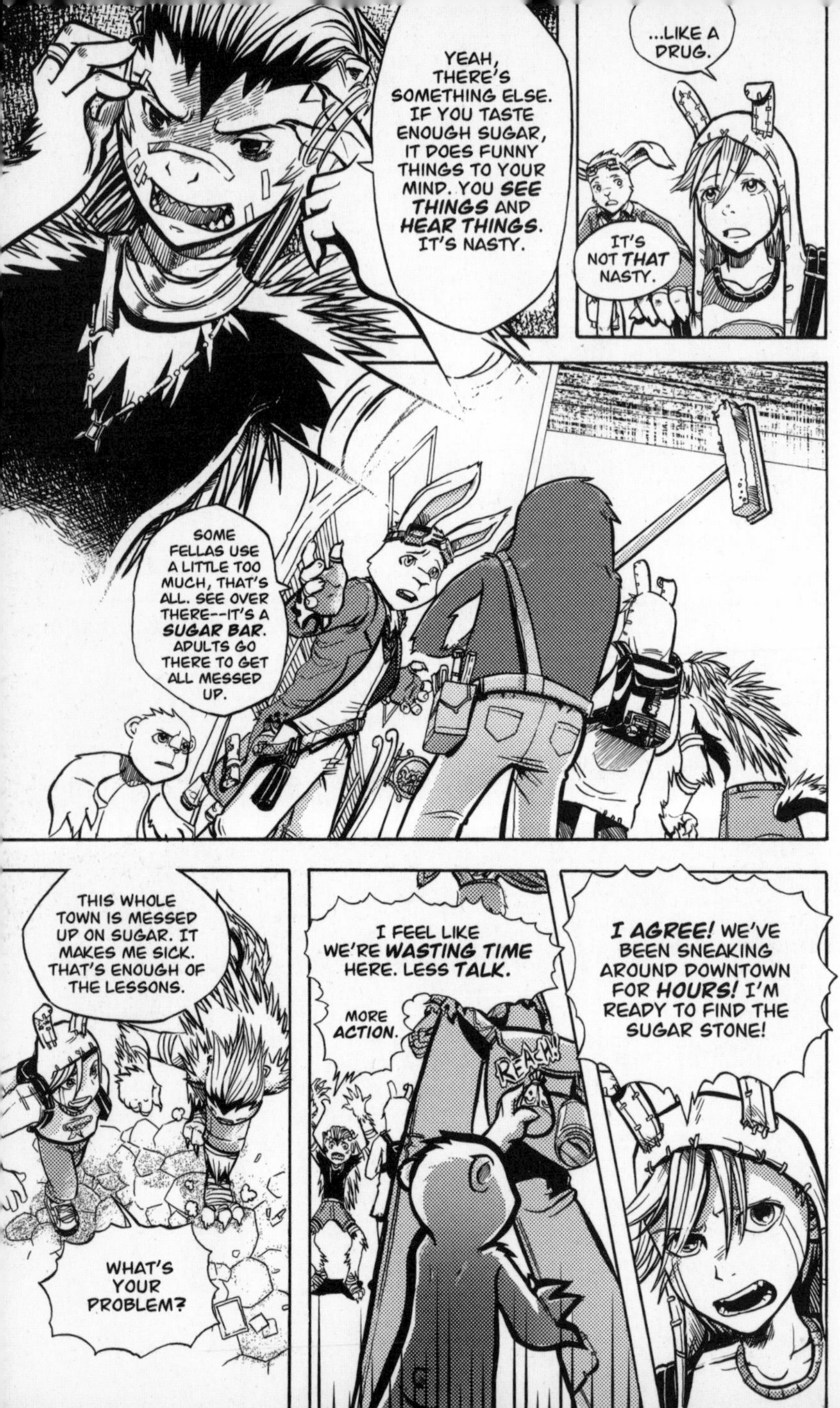
YEAH, THERE'S SOMETHING ELSE. IF YOU TASTE ENOUGH SUGAR, IT DOES FUNNY THINGS TO YOUR MIND. YOU **SEE THINGS** AND **HEAR THINGS**. IT'S NASTY.
...LIKE A DRUG.
IT'S NOT **THAT** NASTY.
SOME FELLAS USE A LITTLE TOO MUCH, THAT'S ALL. SEE OVER THERE--IT'S A **SUGAR BAR**. ADULTS GO THERE TO GET ALL MESSED UP.
THIS WHOLE TOWN IS MESSED UP ON SUGAR. IT MAKES ME SICK. THAT'S ENOUGH OF THE LESSONS.
WHAT'S YOUR PROBLEM?
I FEEL LIKE WE'RE **WASTING TIME** HERE. LESS **TALK**.
MORE **ACTION**.
REACH
I AGREE! WE'VE BEEN SNEAKING AROUND DOWNTOWN FOR **HOURS!** I'M READY TO FIND THE SUGAR STONE!

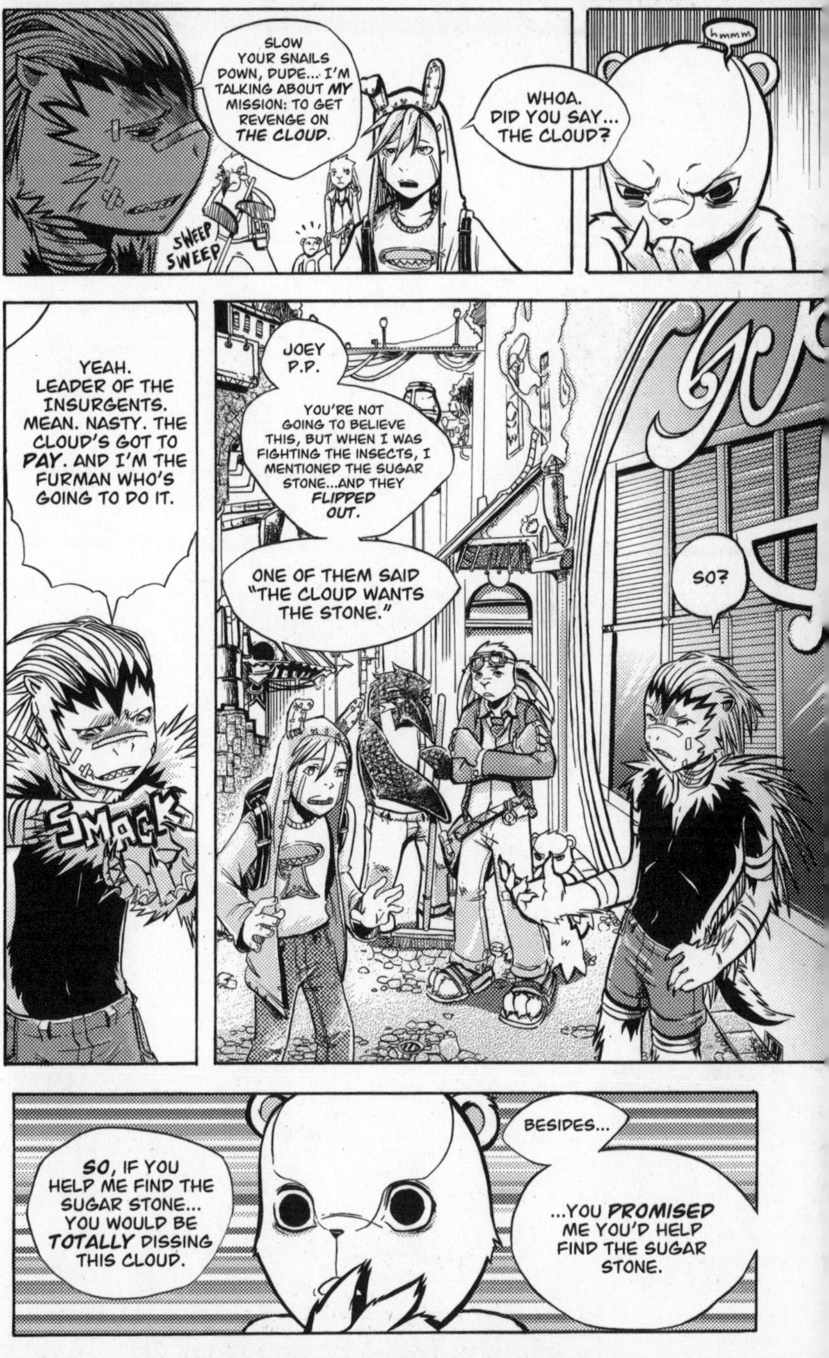
SLOW YOUR SNAILS DOWN, DUDE... I'M TALKING ABOUT *MY* MISSION: TO GET REVENGE ON *THE CLOUD*.
SWEEP SWEEP
hmmm
WHOA. DID YOU SAY... THE CLOUD?
YEAH. LEADER OF THE INSURGENTS. MEAN. NASTY. THE CLOUD'S GOT TO *PAY*. AND I'M THE FURMAN WHO'S GOING TO DO IT.
SMACK
JOEY P.P.
YOU'RE NOT GOING TO BELIEVE THIS, BUT WHEN I WAS FIGHTING THE INSECTS, I MENTIONED THE SUGAR STONE...AND THEY *FLIPPED OUT*.
ONE OF THEM SAID "THE CLOUD WANTS THE STONE."
SO?
SO, IF YOU HELP ME FIND THE SUGAR STONE... YOU WOULD BE *TOTALLY* DISSING THIS CLOUD.
BESIDES...
...YOU *PROMISED* ME YOU'D HELP FIND THE SUGAR STONE.

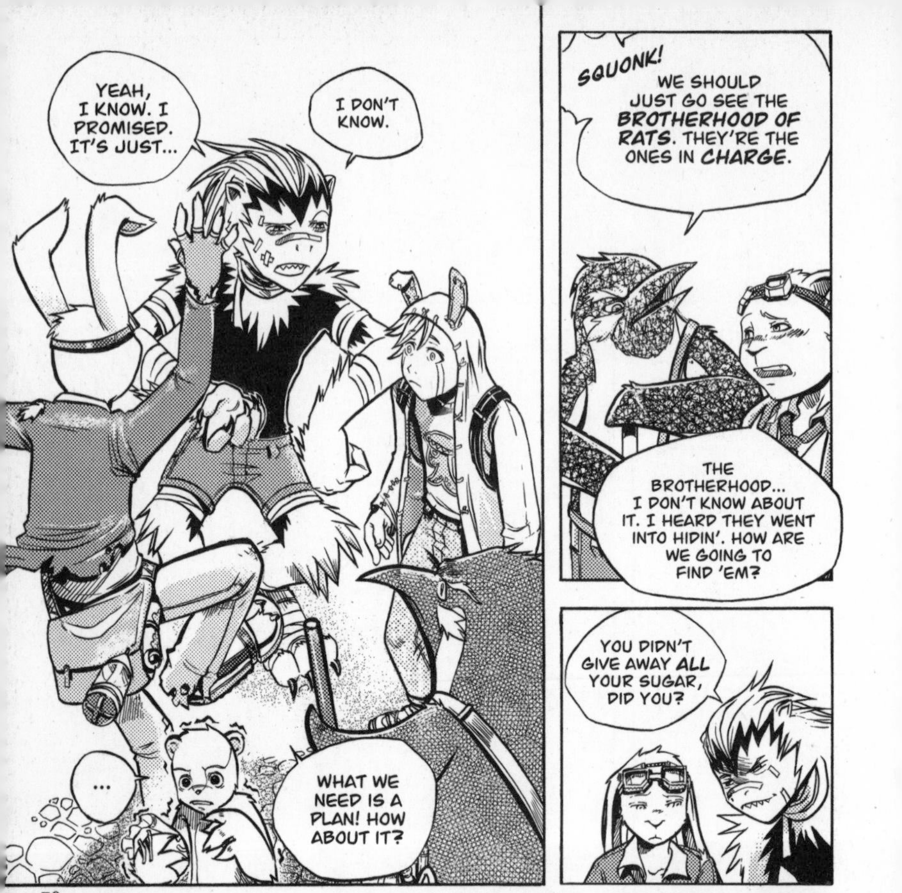
YEAH, I KNOW. I PROMISED. IT'S JUST...
I DON'T KNOW.
...
WHAT WE NEED IS A PLAN! HOW ABOUT IT?
SQUONK!
WE SHOULD JUST GO SEE THE BROTHERHOOD OF RATS. THEY'RE THE ONES IN CHARGE.
THE BROTHERHOOD... I DON'T KNOW ABOUT IT. I HEARD THEY WENT INTO HIDIN'. HOW ARE WE GOING TO FIND 'EM?
YOU DIDN'T GIVE AWAY ALL YOUR SUGAR, DID YOU?

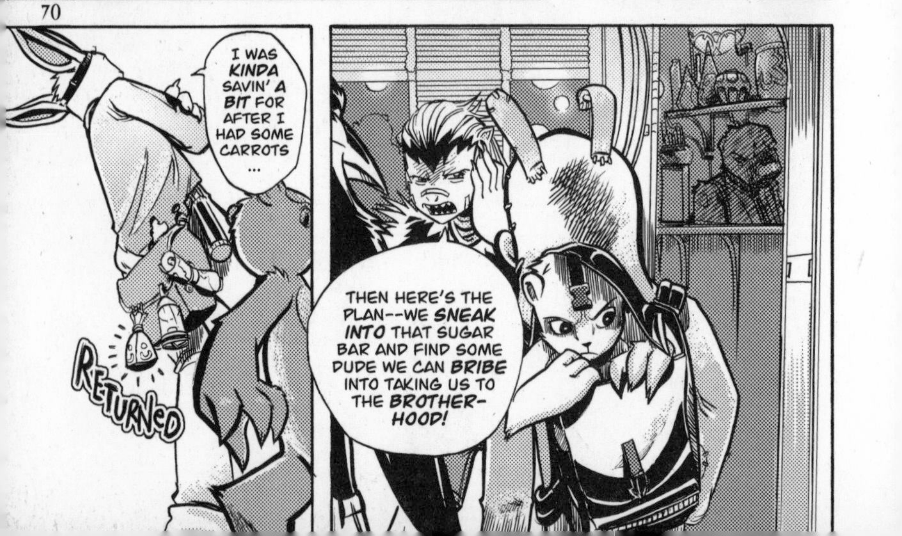
I WAS KINDA SAVIN' A BIT FOR AFTER I HAD SOME CARROTS ...
RETURNED
THEN HERE'S THE PLAN--WE SNEAK INTO THAT SUGAR BAR AND FIND SOME DUDE WE CAN BRIBE INTO TAKING US TO THE BROTHER-HOOD!

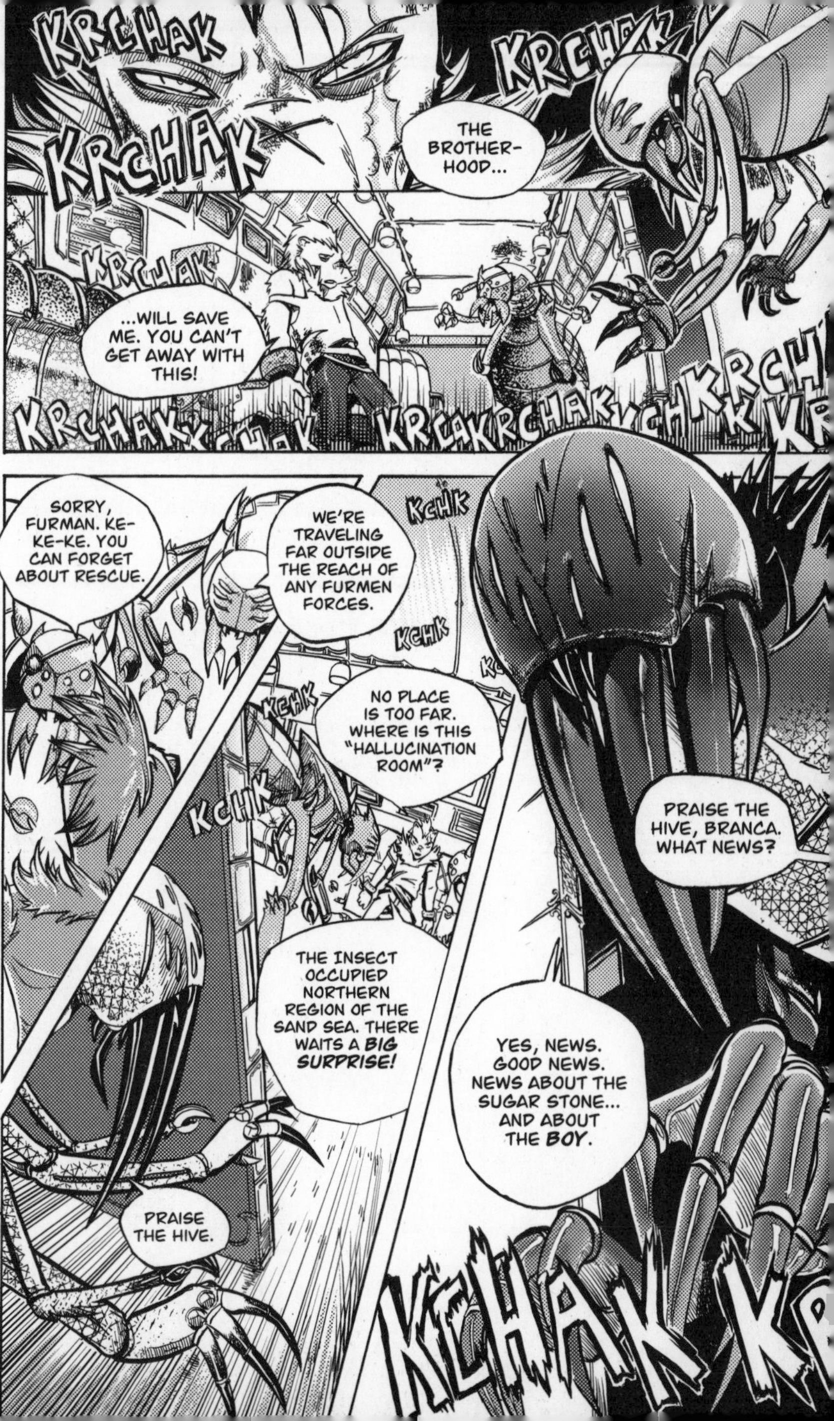
KRCHAK
KRCHAK
KRCHAK
THE BROTHER-HOOD...
KRCHAK
...WILL SAVE ME. YOU CAN'T GET AWAY WITH THIS!
KRCHAK
SORRY, FURMAN. KE-KE-KE. YOU CAN FORGET ABOUT RESCUE.
WE'RE TRAVELING FAR OUTSIDE THE REACH OF ANY FURMEN FORCES.
KCHK
KCHK
KCHK
NO PLACE IS TOO FAR. WHERE IS THIS "HALLUCINATION ROOM"?
KCHK
THE INSECT OCCUPIED NORTHERN REGION OF THE SAND SEA. THERE WAITS A **BIG SURPRISE!**
PRAISE THE HIVE.
PRAISE THE HIVE, BRANCA. WHAT NEWS?
YES, NEWS. GOOD NEWS. NEWS ABOUT THE SUGAR STONE... AND ABOUT THE **BOY**.
KCHAK

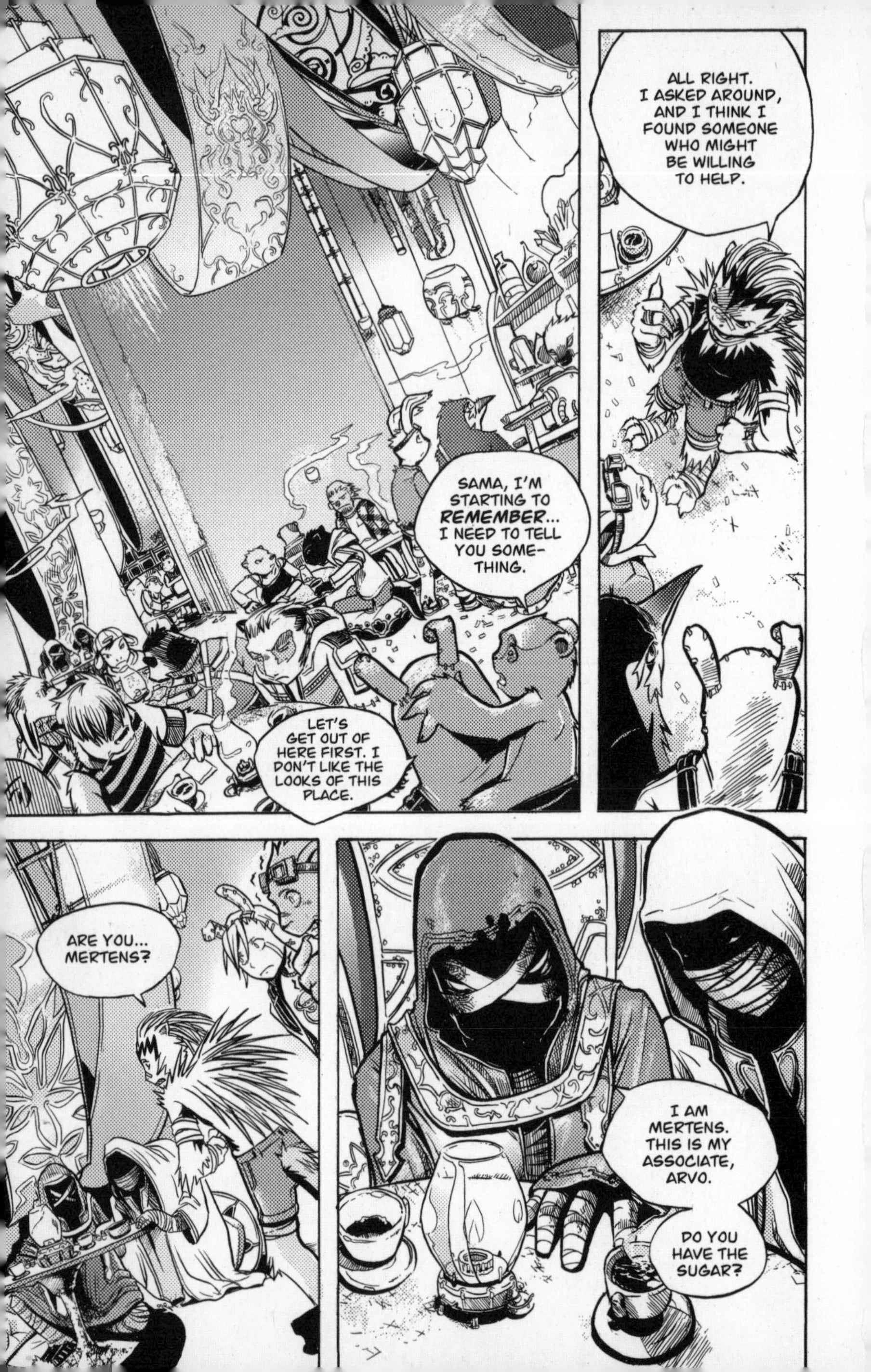
SAMA, I'M STARTING TO REMEMBER... I NEED TO TELL YOU SOME-THING.
LET'S GET OUT OF HERE FIRST. I DON'T LIKE THE LOOKS OF THIS PLACE.
ALL RIGHT. I ASKED AROUND, AND I THINK I FOUND SOMEONE WHO MIGHT BE WILLING TO HELP.
ARE YOU... MERTENS?
I AM MERTENS. THIS IS MY ASSOCIATE, ARVO.
DO YOU HAVE THE SUGAR?

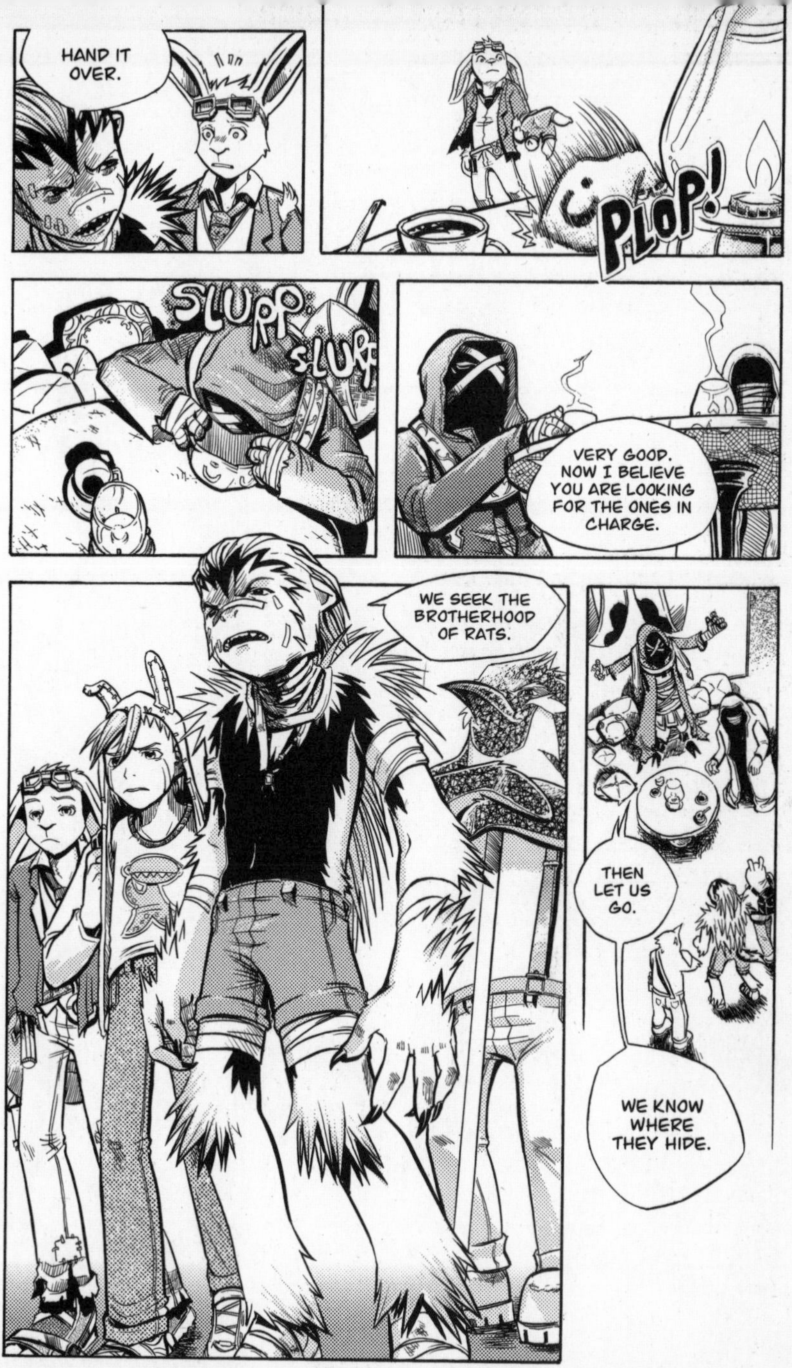
HAND IT OVER.
PLOP!
SLUPP
SLURP
VERY GOOD. NOW I BELIEVE YOU ARE LOOKING FOR THE ONES IN CHARGE.
WE SEEK THE BROTHERHOOD OF RATS.
THEN LET US GO.
WE KNOW WHERE THEY HIDE.

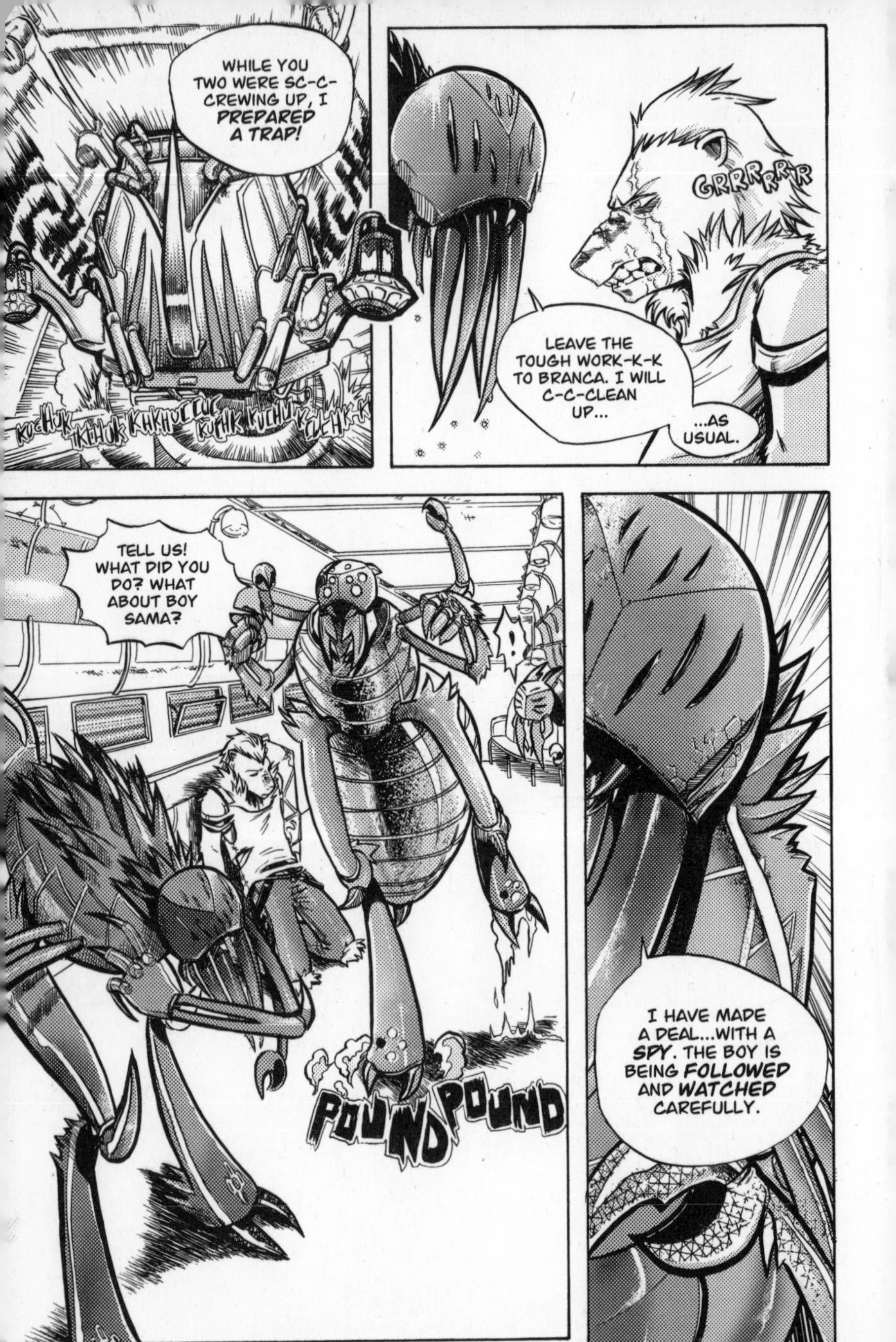
WHILE YOU TWO WERE SC-C-CREWING UP, I *PREPARED A TRAP!*
KUCHUK TKCHUK KHKHUCCUC KUCHK KUCHUK KCHK-K
GRRRRRR
LEAVE THE TOUGH WORK-K-K TO BRANCA. I WILL C-C-CLEAN UP...
...AS USUAL.
TELL US! WHAT DID YOU DO? WHAT ABOUT BOY SAMA?
!
POUND POUND
I HAVE MADE A DEAL...WITH A *SPY*. THE BOY IS BEING *FOLLOWED* AND *WATCHED* CAREFULLY.

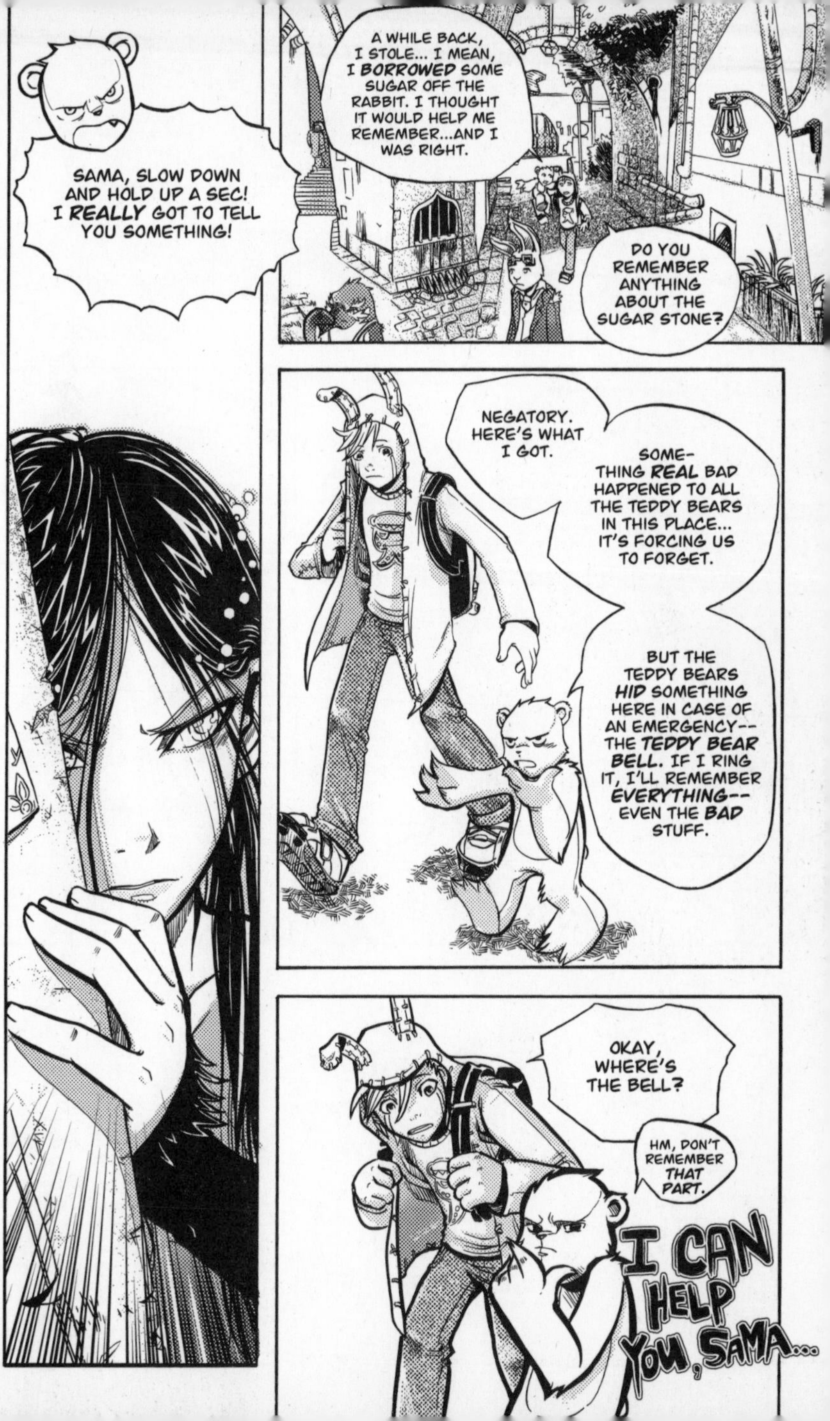
SAMA, SLOW DOWN AND HOLD UP A SEC! I REALLY GOT TO TELL YOU SOMETHING!
A WHILE BACK, I STOLE... I MEAN, I BORROWED SOME SUGAR OFF THE RABBIT. I THOUGHT IT WOULD HELP ME REMEMBER...AND I WAS RIGHT.
DO YOU REMEMBER ANYTHING ABOUT THE SUGAR STONE?
NEGATORY. HERE'S WHAT I GOT.
SOME-THING REAL BAD HAPPENED TO ALL THE TEDDY BEARS IN THIS PLACE... IT'S FORCING US TO FORGET.
BUT THE TEDDY BEARS HID SOMETHING HERE IN CASE OF AN EMERGENCY--THE TEDDY BEAR BELL. IF I RING IT, I'LL REMEMBER EVERYTHING--EVEN THE BAD STUFF.
OKAY, WHERE'S THE BELL?
HM, DON'T REMEMBER THAT PART.
I CAN HELP YOU, SAMA...

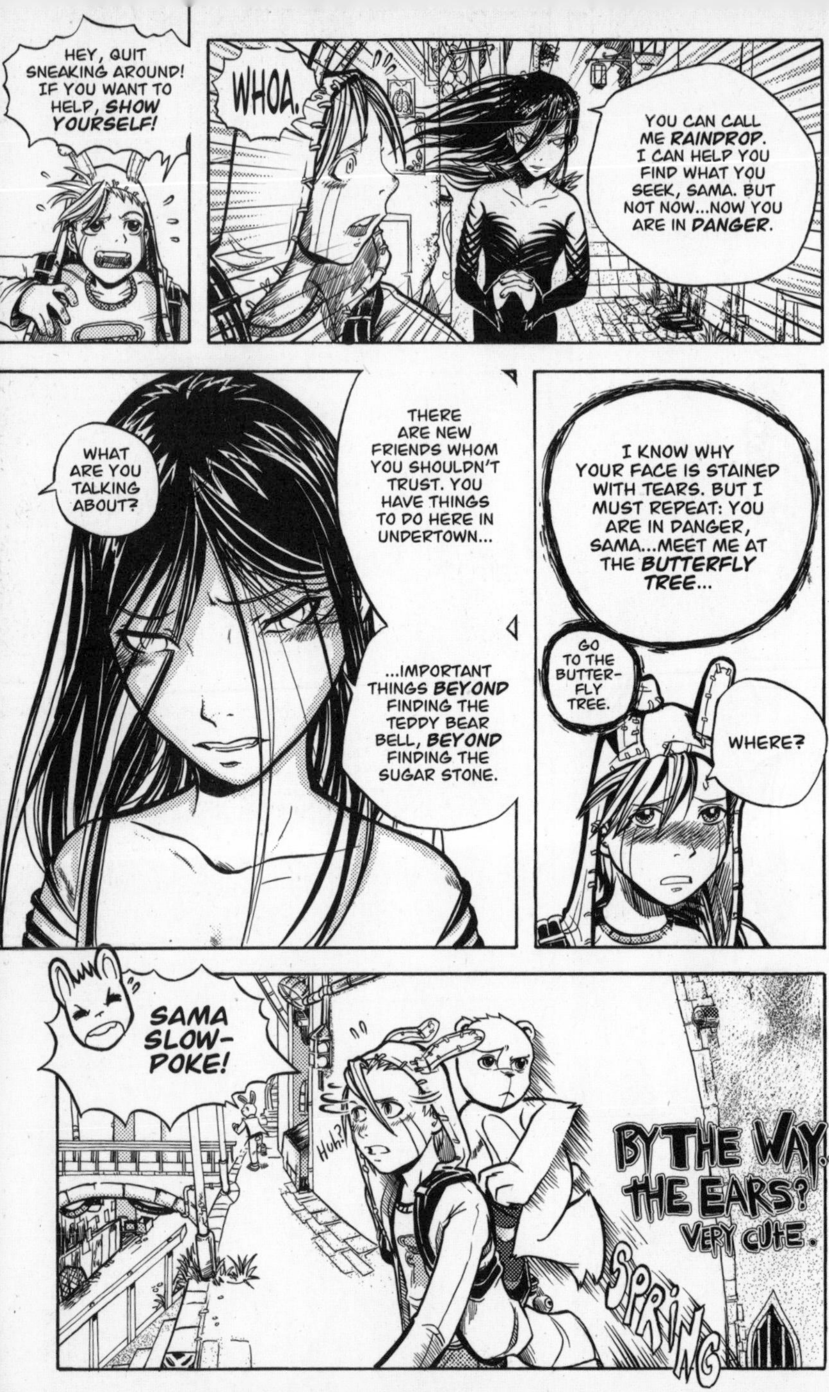
HEY, QUIT SNEAKING AROUND! IF YOU WANT TO HELP, SHOW YOURSELF!
WHOA.
YOU CAN CALL ME RAINDROP. I CAN HELP YOU FIND WHAT YOU SEEK, SAMA. BUT NOT NOW...NOW YOU ARE IN DANGER.
WHAT ARE YOU TALKING ABOUT?
THERE ARE NEW FRIENDS WHOM YOU SHOULDN'T TRUST. YOU HAVE THINGS TO DO HERE IN UNDERTOWN...
...IMPORTANT THINGS BEYOND FINDING THE TEDDY BEAR BELL, BEYOND FINDING THE SUGAR STONE.
I KNOW WHY YOUR FACE IS STAINED WITH TEARS. BUT I MUST REPEAT: YOU ARE IN DANGER, SAMA...MEET ME AT THE BUTTERFLY TREE...
GO TO THE BUTTER-FLY TREE.
WHERE?
SAMA SLOW-POKE!
Huh?
BY THE WAY... THE EARS? VERY CUTE.
SPRING

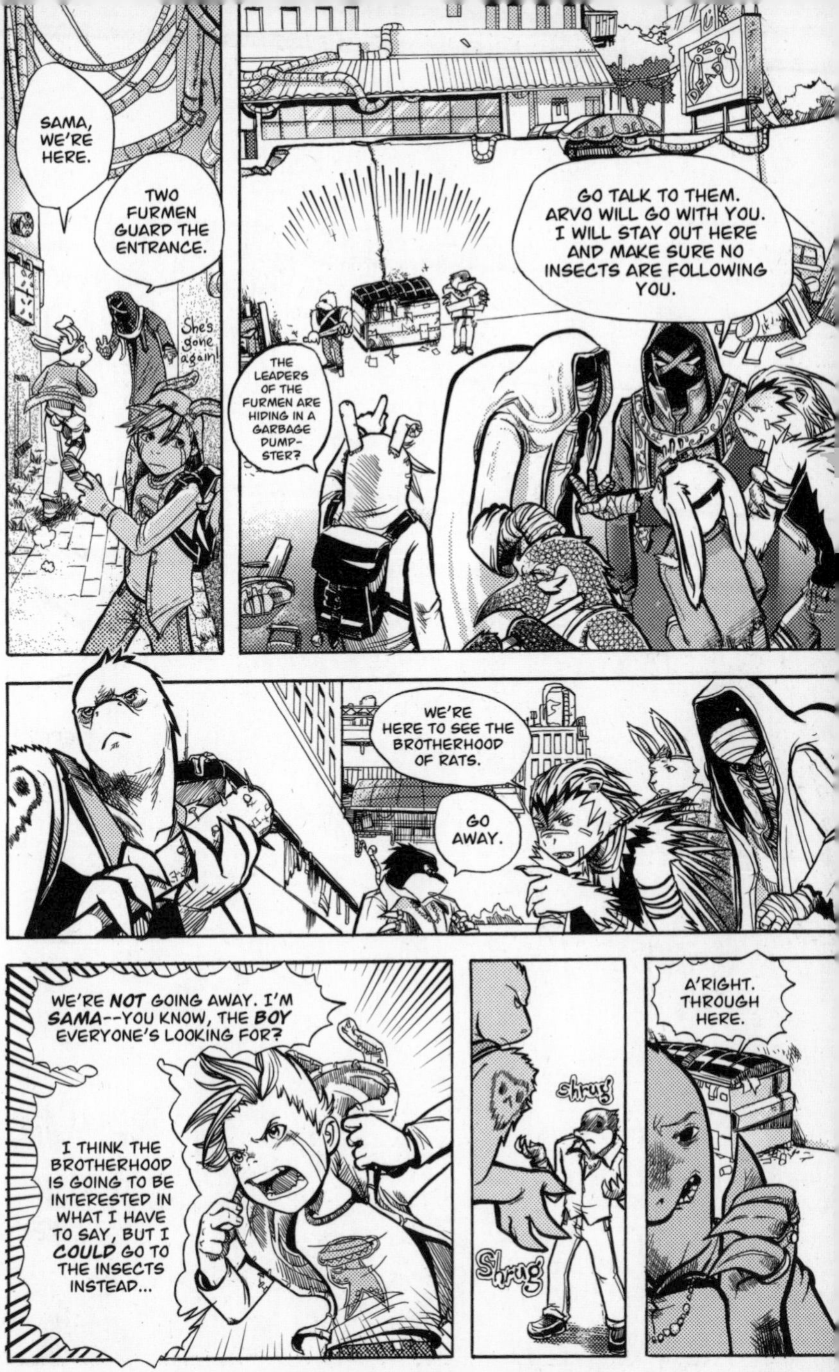
SAMA, WE'RE HERE.
TWO FURMEN GUARD THE ENTRANCE.
She's gone again!
GO TALK TO THEM. ARVO WILL GO WITH YOU. I WILL STAY OUT HERE AND MAKE SURE NO INSECTS ARE FOLLOWING YOU.
THE LEADERS OF THE FURMEN ARE HIDING IN A GARBAGE DUMP-STER?
WE'RE HERE TO SEE THE BROTHERHOOD OF RATS.
GO AWAY.
WE'RE NOT GOING AWAY. I'M SAMA--YOU KNOW, THE BOY EVERYONE'S LOOKING FOR?
I THINK THE BROTHERHOOD IS GOING TO BE INTERESTED IN WHAT I HAVE TO SAY, BUT I COULD GO TO THE INSECTS INSTEAD...
shrug
Shrug
A'RIGHT. THROUGH HERE.

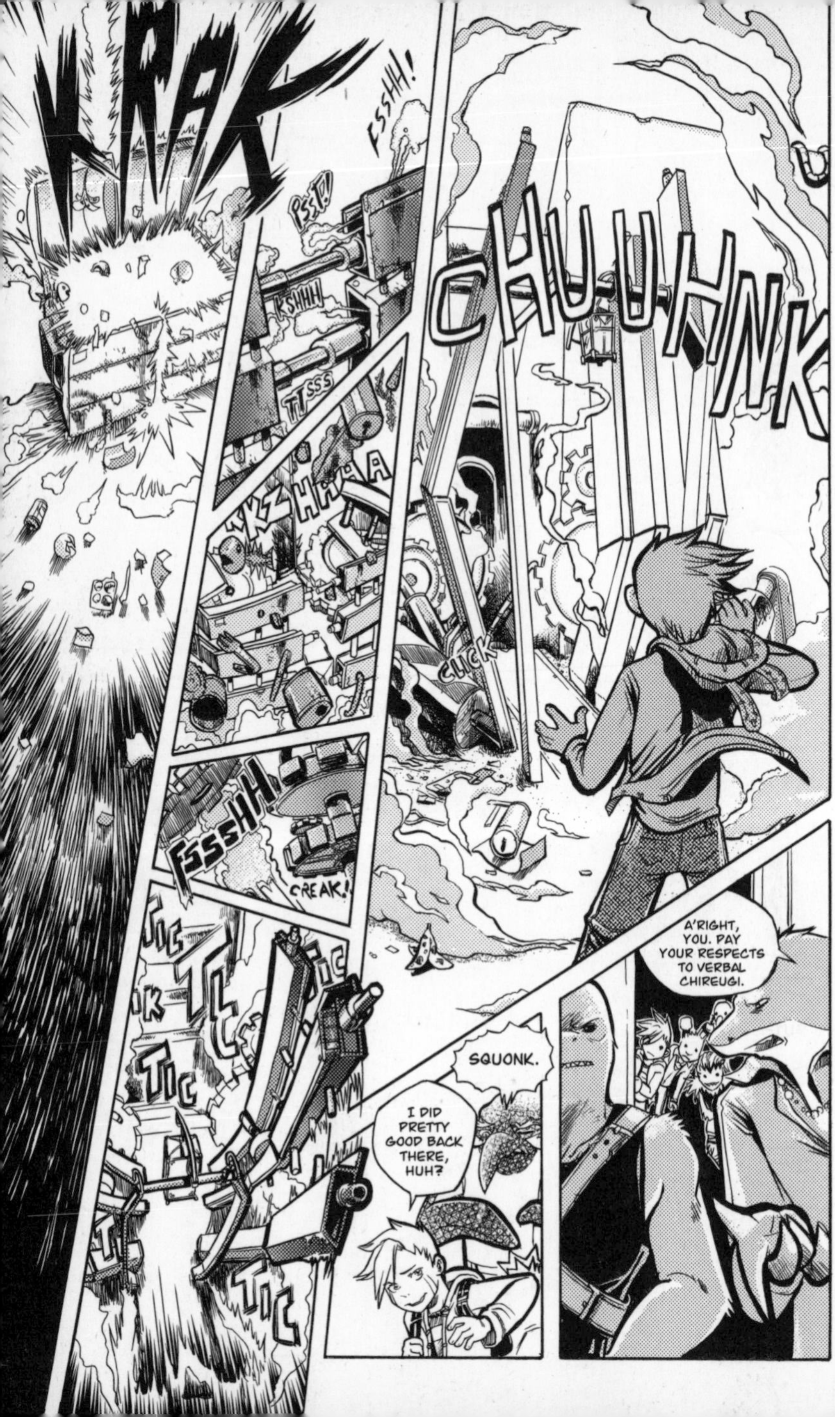
KRAK
FSSHH!
PSST!
KSHHH
TTSSS
CHUUUHNK
CLICK
FSSSHH
CREAK!
TIC
TIC
TIC
SQUONK.
I DID PRETTY GOOD BACK THERE, HUH?
A'RIGHT, YOU. PAY YOUR RESPECTS TO VERBAL CHIREUGI.

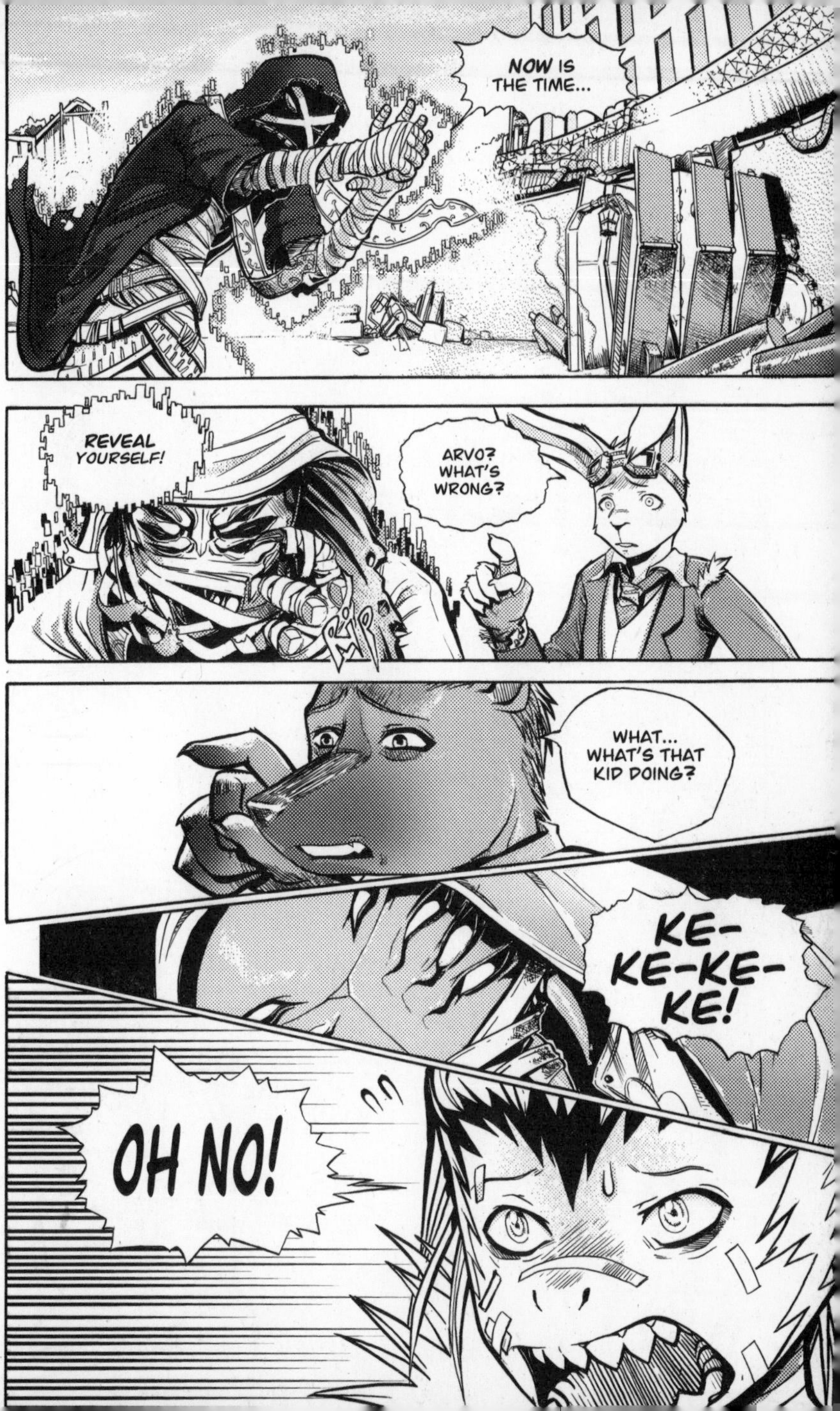
NOW IS THE TIME...
REVEAL YOURSELF!
ARVO? WHAT'S WRONG?
RIP
WHAT... WHAT'S THAT KID DOING?
KE-KE-KE-KE-KE!
OH NO!

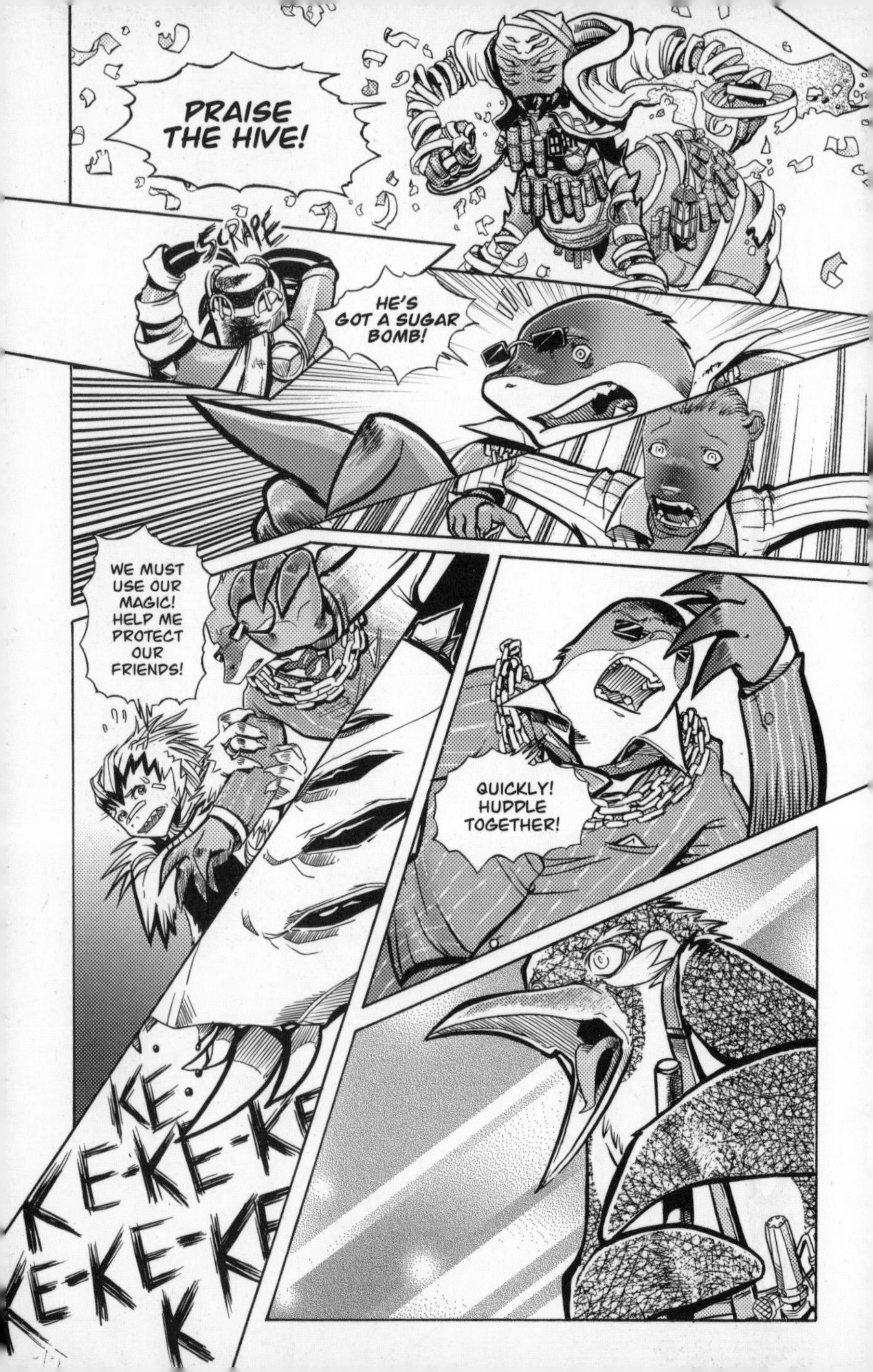
PRAISE THE HIVE!
SCRAPE
HE'S GOT A SUGAR BOMB!
WE MUST USE OUR MAGIC! HELP ME PROTECT OUR FRIENDS!
QUICKLY! HUDDLE TOGETHER!
KE KE-KE-KE KE-KE-KE-KE K

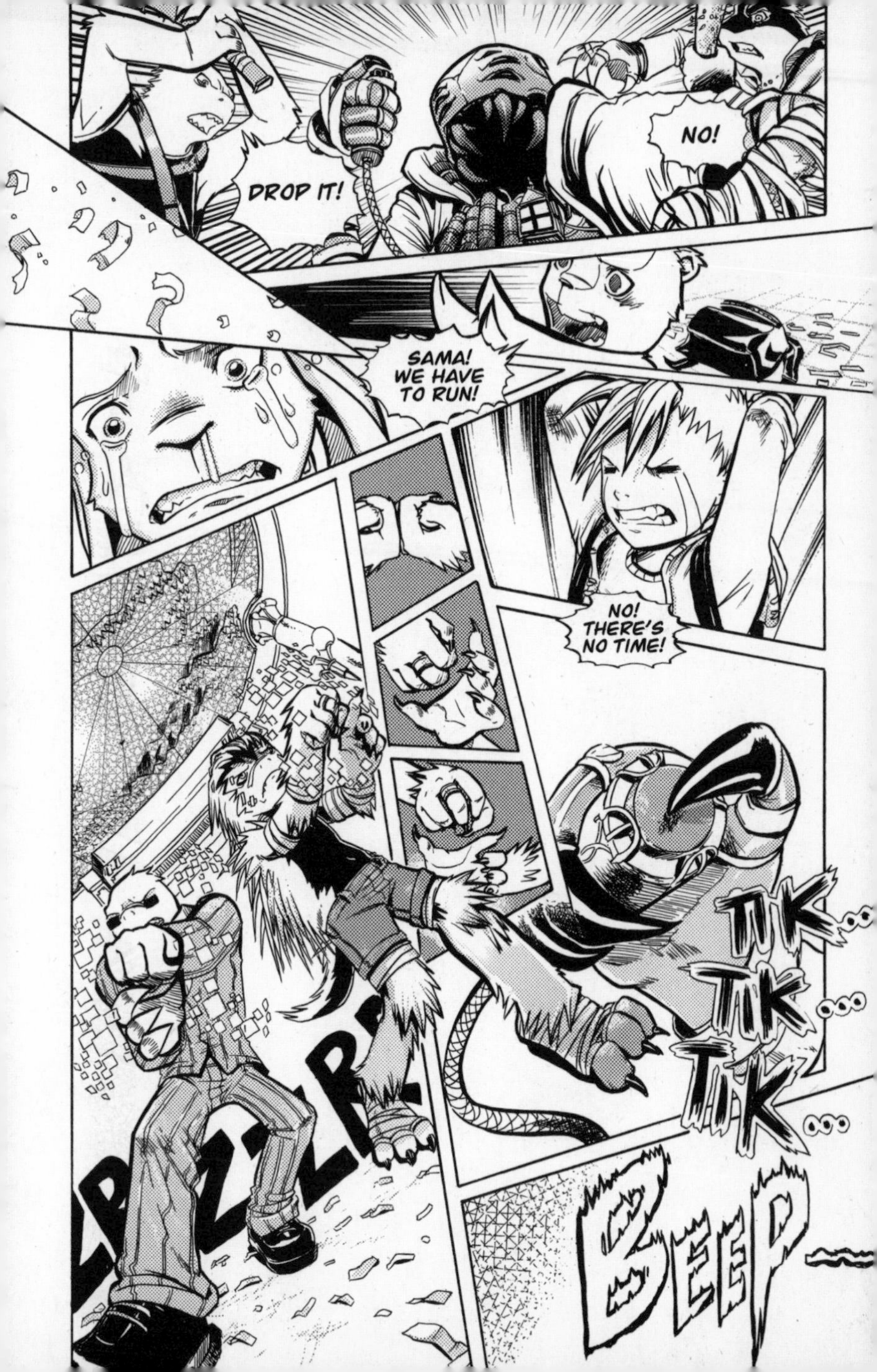
DROP IT!
NO!
SAMA! WE HAVE TO RUN!
NO! THERE'S NO TIME!
BZZRR
TIK...
TIK...
TIK...
BEEP~

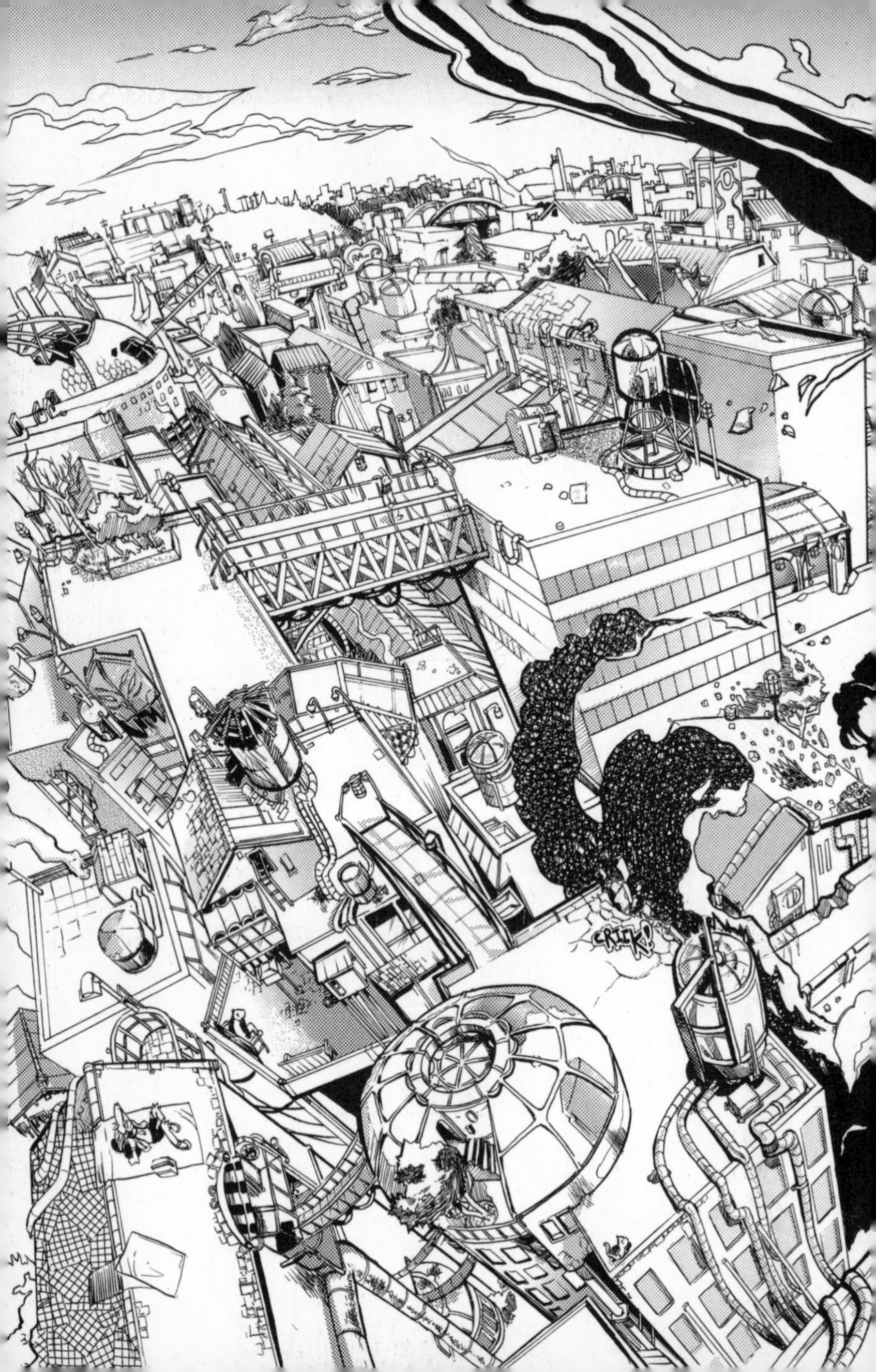
CRICK!

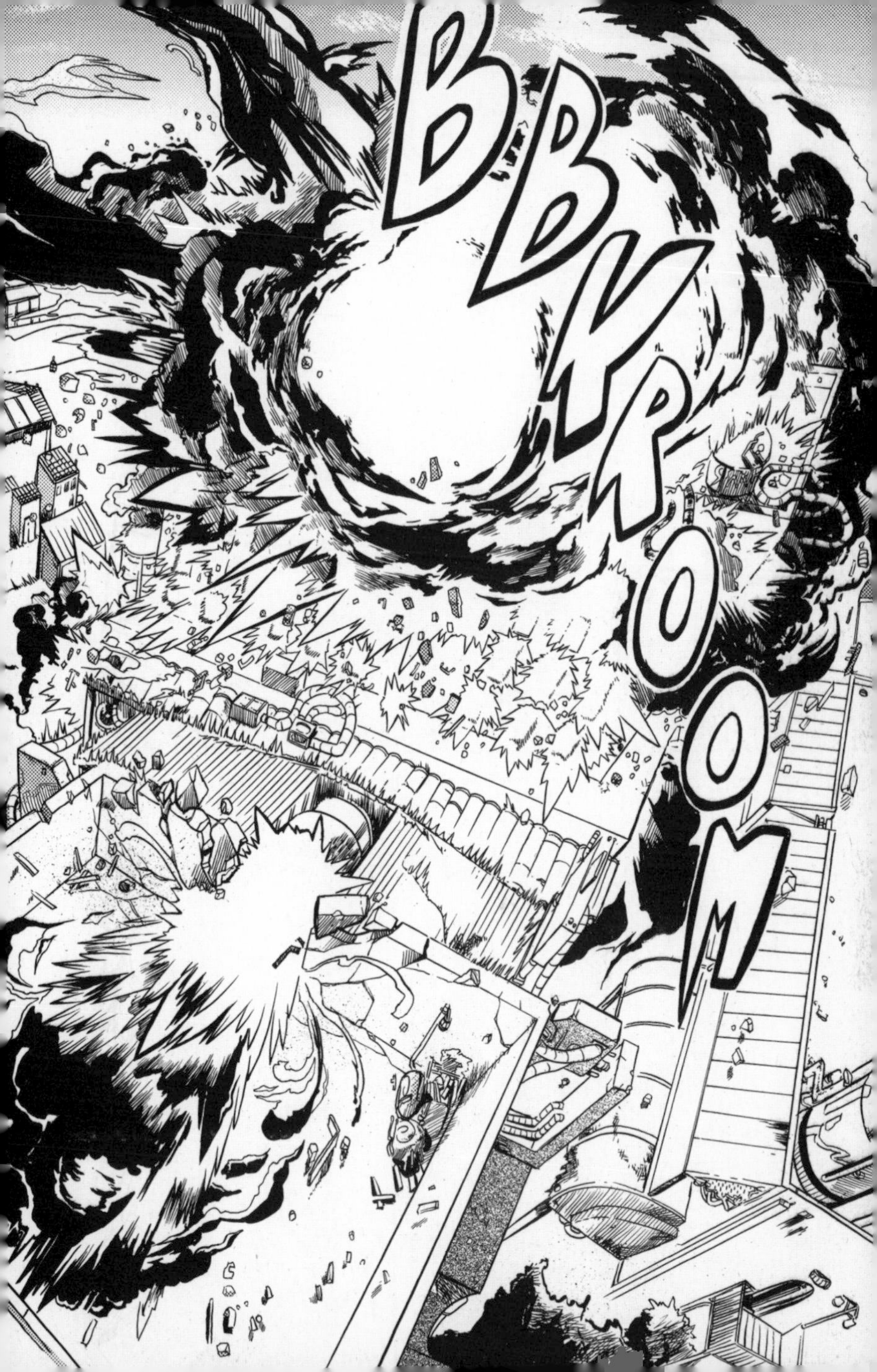
BBUROOOM

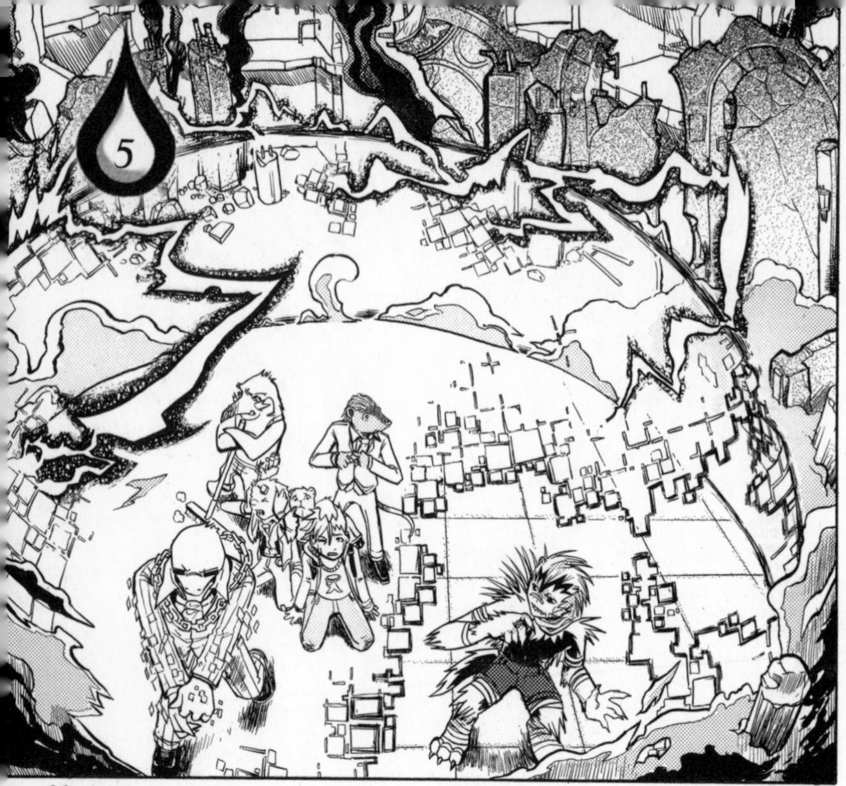
5

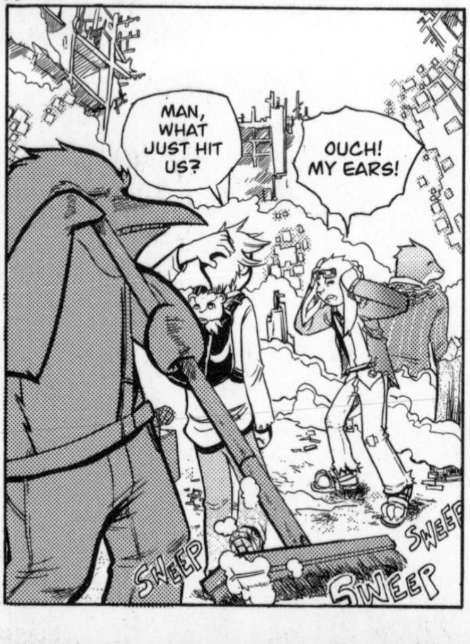
MAN, WHAT JUST HIT US?
OUCH! MY EARS!
SWEEP
SWEEP
SWEEP

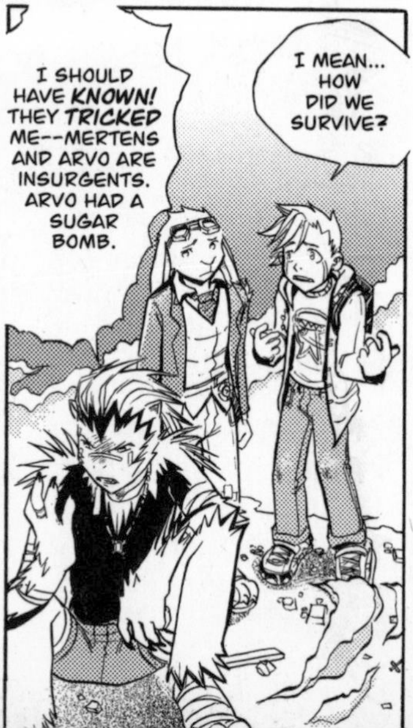
I SHOULD HAVE KNOWN! THEY TRICKED ME--MERTENS AND ARVO ARE INSURGENTS. ARVO HAD A SUGAR BOMB.
I MEAN... HOW DID WE SURVIVE?

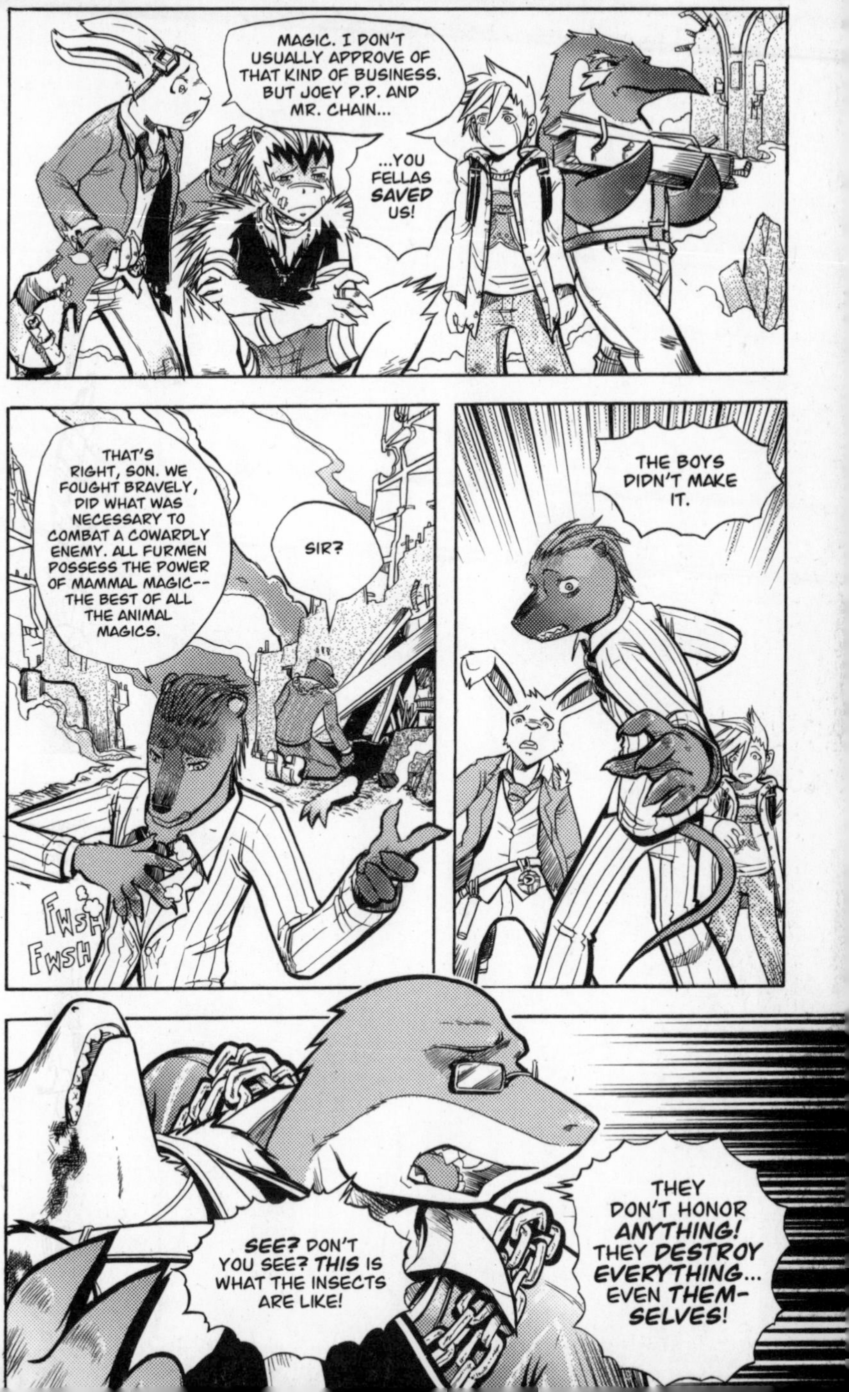
MAGIC. I DON'T USUALLY APPROVE OF THAT KIND OF BUSINESS. BUT JOEY P.P. AND MR. CHAIN...
...YOU FELLAS SAVED US!
THAT'S RIGHT, SON. WE FOUGHT BRAVELY, DID WHAT WAS NECESSARY TO COMBAT A COWARDLY ENEMY. ALL FURMEN POSSESS THE POWER OF MAMMAL MAGIC-- THE BEST OF ALL THE ANIMAL MAGICS.
SIR?
FWSH
FWSH
THE BOYS DIDN'T MAKE IT.
SEE? DON'T YOU SEE? THIS IS WHAT THE INSECTS ARE LIKE!
THEY DON'T HONOR ANYTHING! THEY DESTROY EVERYTHING... EVEN THEM-SELVES!

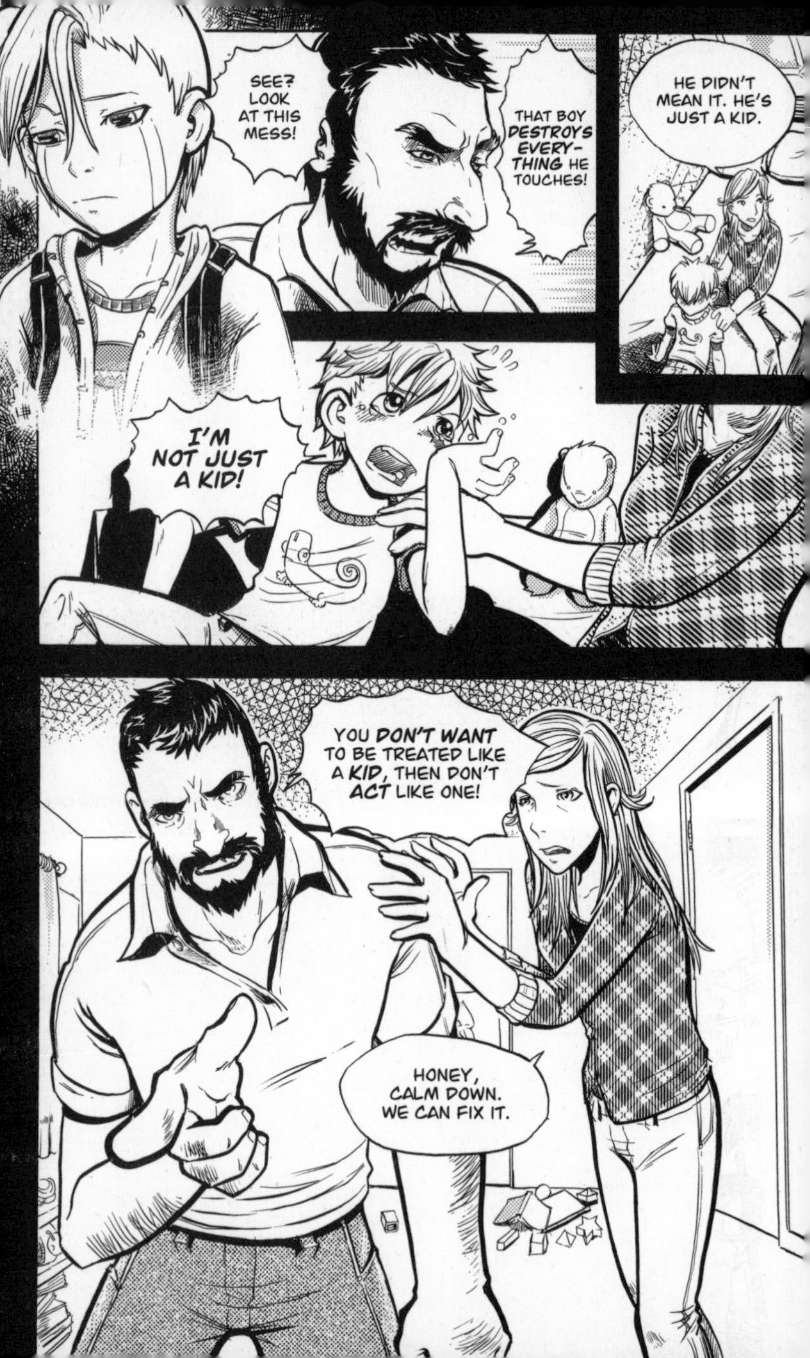
SEE? LOOK AT THIS MESS!
THAT BOY DESTROYS EVERY-THING HE TOUCHES!
HE DIDN'T MEAN IT. HE'S JUST A KID.
I'M NOT JUST A KID!
YOU DON'T WANT TO BE TREATED LIKE A KID, THEN DON'T ACT LIKE ONE!
HONEY, CALM DOWN. WE CAN FIX IT.

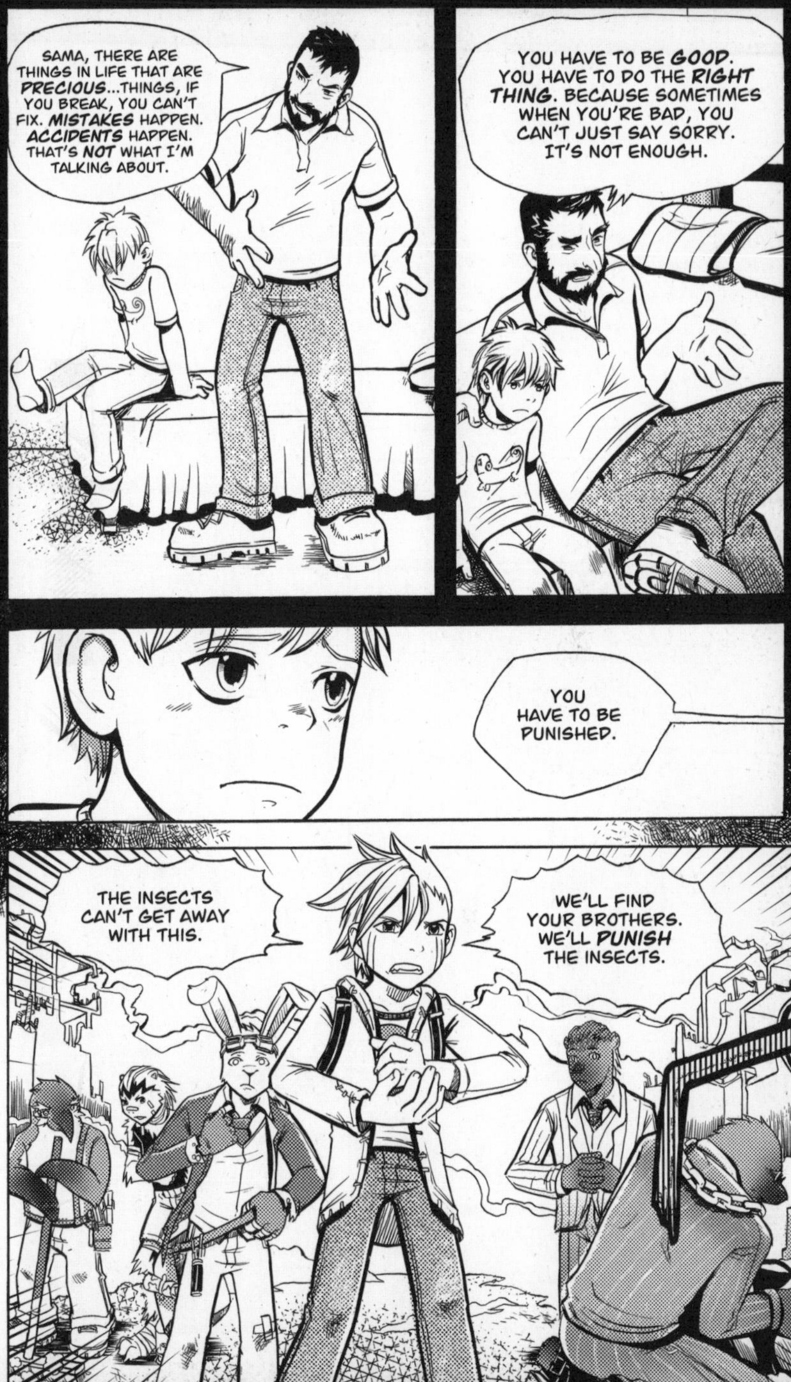
SAMA, THERE ARE THINGS IN LIFE THAT ARE PRECIOUS...THINGS, IF YOU BREAK, YOU CAN'T FIX. MISTAKES HAPPEN. ACCIDENTS HAPPEN. THAT'S NOT WHAT I'M TALKING ABOUT.
YOU HAVE TO BE GOOD. YOU HAVE TO DO THE RIGHT THING. BECAUSE SOMETIMES WHEN YOU'RE BAD, YOU CAN'T JUST SAY SORRY. IT'S NOT ENOUGH.
YOU HAVE TO BE PUNISHED.
THE INSECTS CAN'T GET AWAY WITH THIS.
WE'LL FIND YOUR BROTHERS. WE'LL PUNISH THE INSECTS.

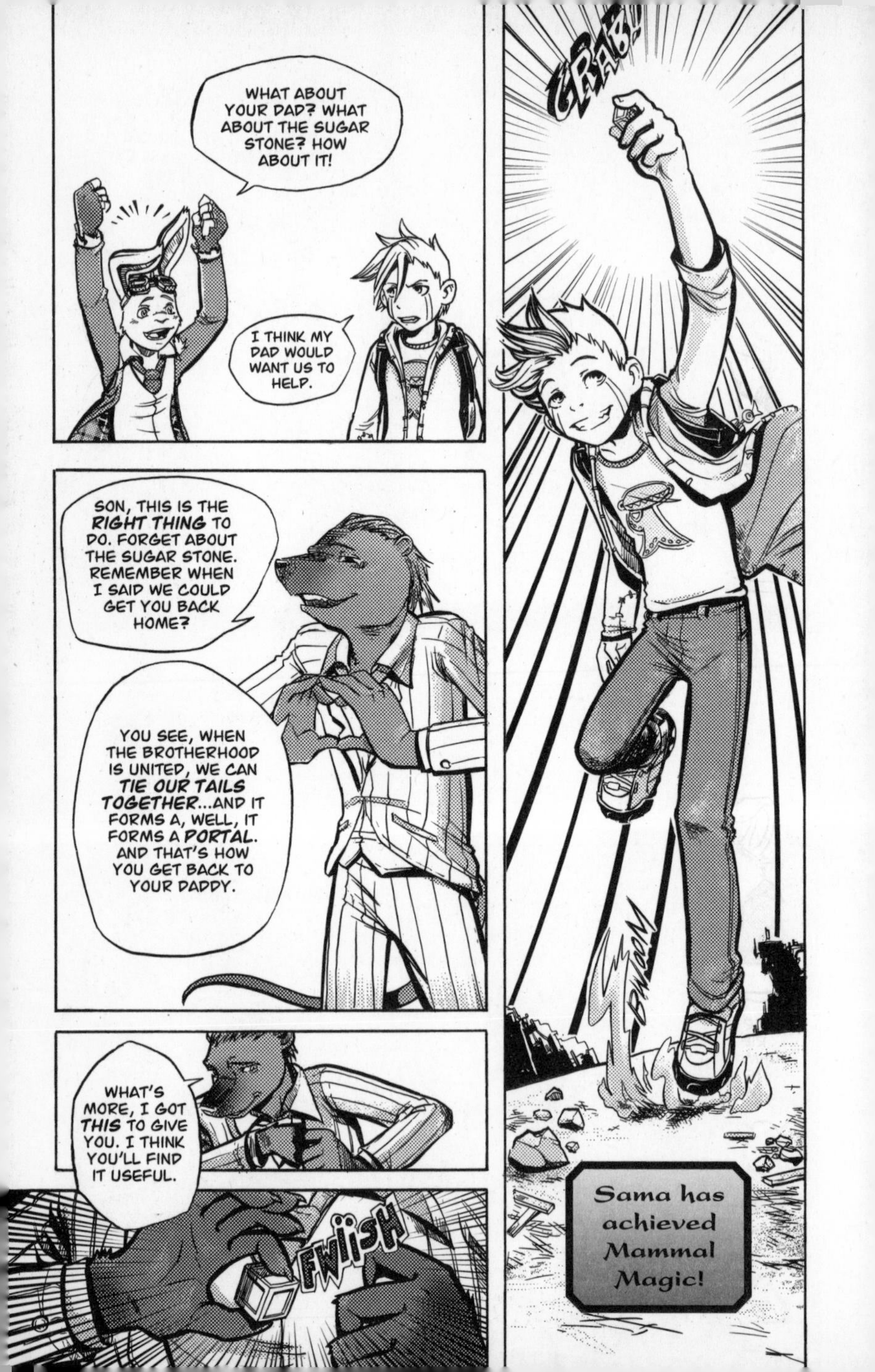
WHAT ABOUT YOUR DAD? WHAT ABOUT THE SUGAR STONE? HOW ABOUT IT!
I THINK MY DAD WOULD WANT US TO HELP.
SON, THIS IS THE ***RIGHT THING*** TO DO. FORGET ABOUT THE SUGAR STONE. REMEMBER WHEN I SAID WE COULD GET YOU BACK HOME?
YOU SEE, WHEN THE BROTHERHOOD IS UNITED, WE CAN ***TIE OUR TAILS TOGETHER***...AND IT FORMS A, WELL, IT FORMS A ***PORTAL***. AND THAT'S HOW YOU GET BACK TO YOUR DADDY.
WHAT'S MORE, I GOT **THIS** TO GIVE YOU. I THINK YOU'LL FIND IT USEFUL.
FWÏSH
GRAB!!
BWOOM
Sama has achieved Mammal Magic!

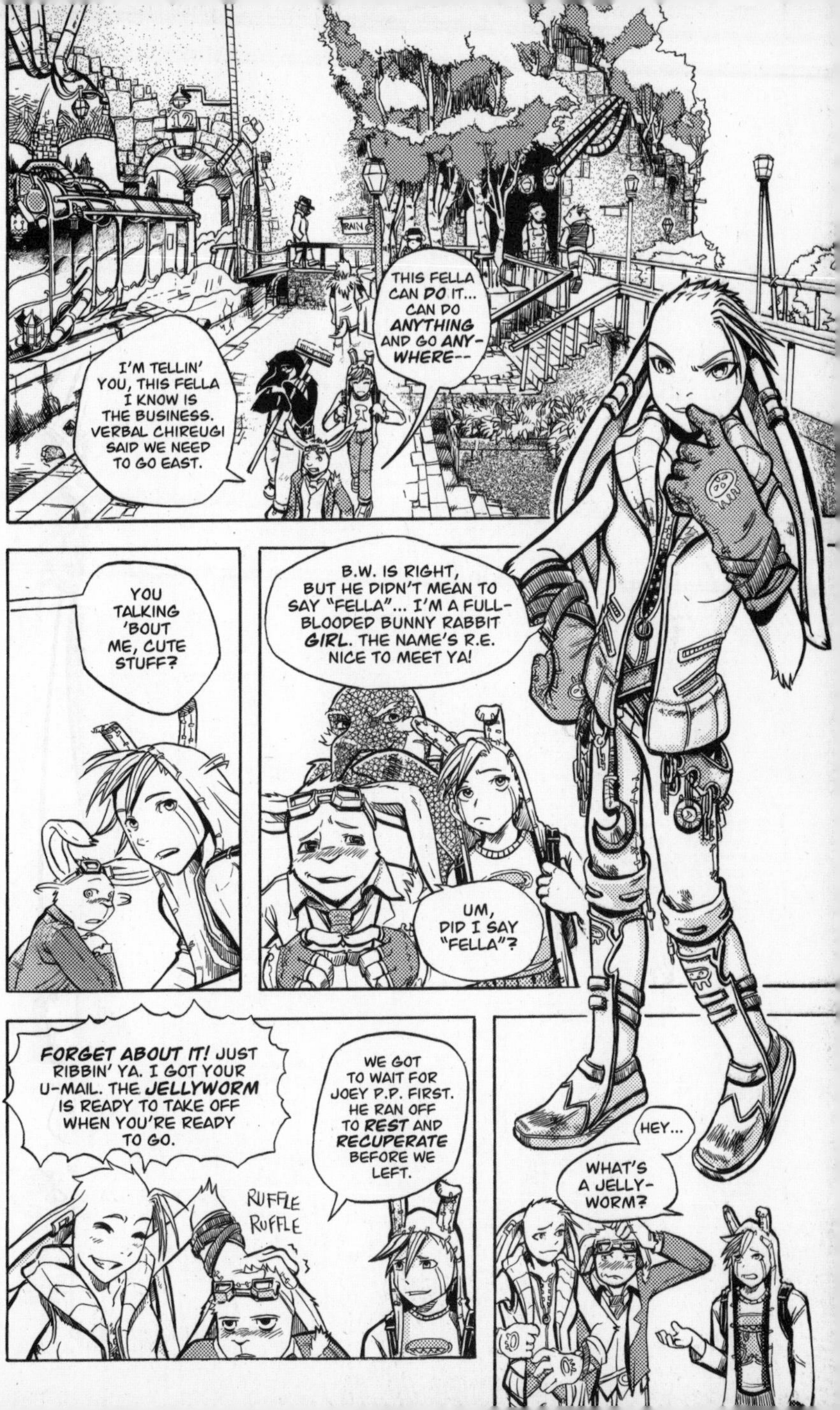
12
RAIN
I'M TELLIN' YOU, THIS FELLA I KNOW IS THE BUSINESS. VERBAL CHIREUGI SAID WE NEED TO GO EAST.
THIS FELLA CAN **DO** IT... CAN DO **ANYTHING** AND GO **ANY-WHERE**--
YOU TALKING 'BOUT ME, CUTE STUFF?
B.W. IS RIGHT, BUT HE DIDN'T MEAN TO SAY "FELLA"... I'M A FULL-BLOODED BUNNY RABBIT **GIRL**. THE NAME'S R.E. NICE TO MEET YA!
UM, DID I SAY "FELLA"?
FORGET ABOUT IT! JUST RIBBIN' YA. I GOT YOUR U-MAIL. THE **JELLYWORM** IS READY TO TAKE OFF WHEN YOU'RE READY TO GO.
WE GOT TO WAIT FOR JOEY P.P. FIRST. HE RAN OFF TO **REST** AND **RECUPERATE** BEFORE WE LEFT.
RUFFLE RUFFLE
HEY...
WHAT'S A JELLY-WORM?

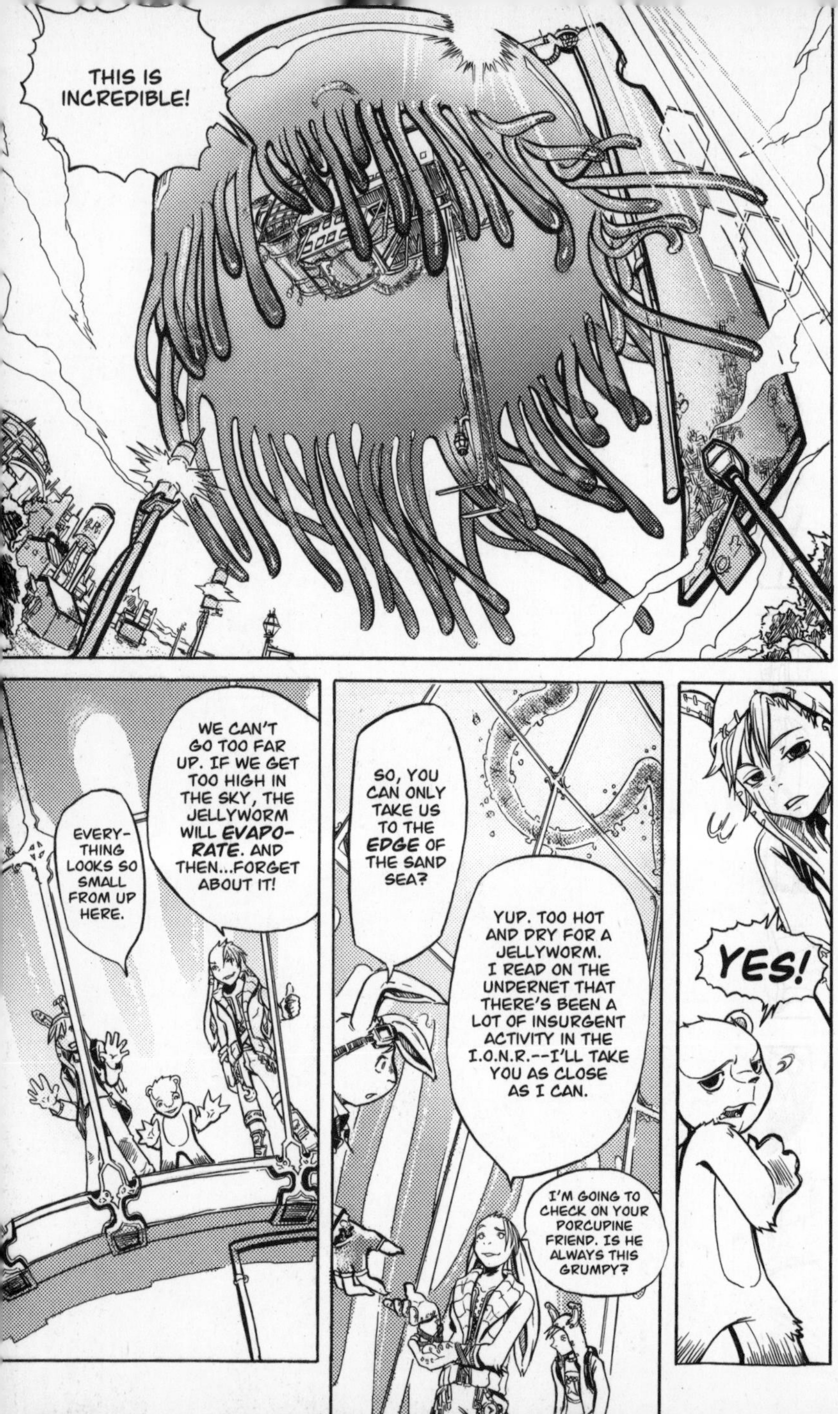
THIS IS INCREDIBLE!
EVERY-THING LOOKS SO SMALL FROM UP HERE.
WE CAN'T GO TOO FAR UP. IF WE GET TOO HIGH IN THE SKY, THE JELLYWORM WILL EVAPO-RATE. AND THEN...FORGET ABOUT IT!
SO, YOU CAN ONLY TAKE US TO THE EDGE OF THE SAND SEA?
YUP. TOO HOT AND DRY FOR A JELLYWORM. I READ ON THE UNDERNET THAT THERE'S BEEN A LOT OF INSURGENT ACTIVITY IN THE I.O.N.R.--I'LL TAKE YOU AS CLOSE AS I CAN.
I'M GOING TO CHECK ON YOUR PORCUPINE FRIEND. IS HE ALWAYS THIS GRUMPY?
YES!

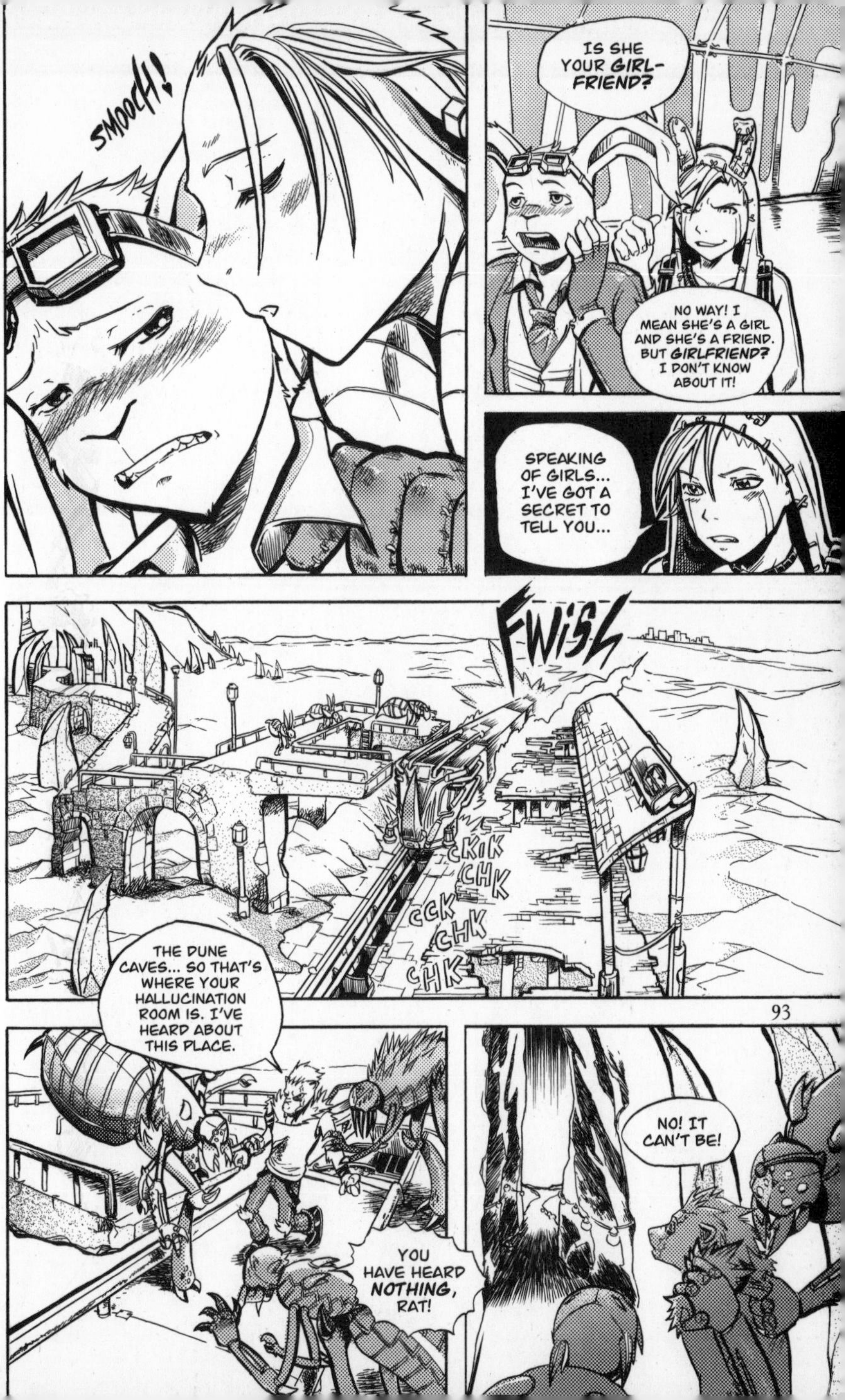
SMOOCH!
IS SHE YOUR GIRL-FRIEND?
NO WAY! I MEAN SHE'S A GIRL AND SHE'S A FRIEND. BUT GIRLFRIEND? I DON'T KNOW ABOUT IT!
SPEAKING OF GIRLS... I'VE GOT A SECRET TO TELL YOU...
FWISH
CKIK CHK CCK CHK CHK
THE DUNE CAVES... SO THAT'S WHERE YOUR HALLUCINATION ROOM IS. I'VE HEARD ABOUT THIS PLACE.
YOU HAVE HEARD NOTHING, RAT!
NO! IT CAN'T BE!

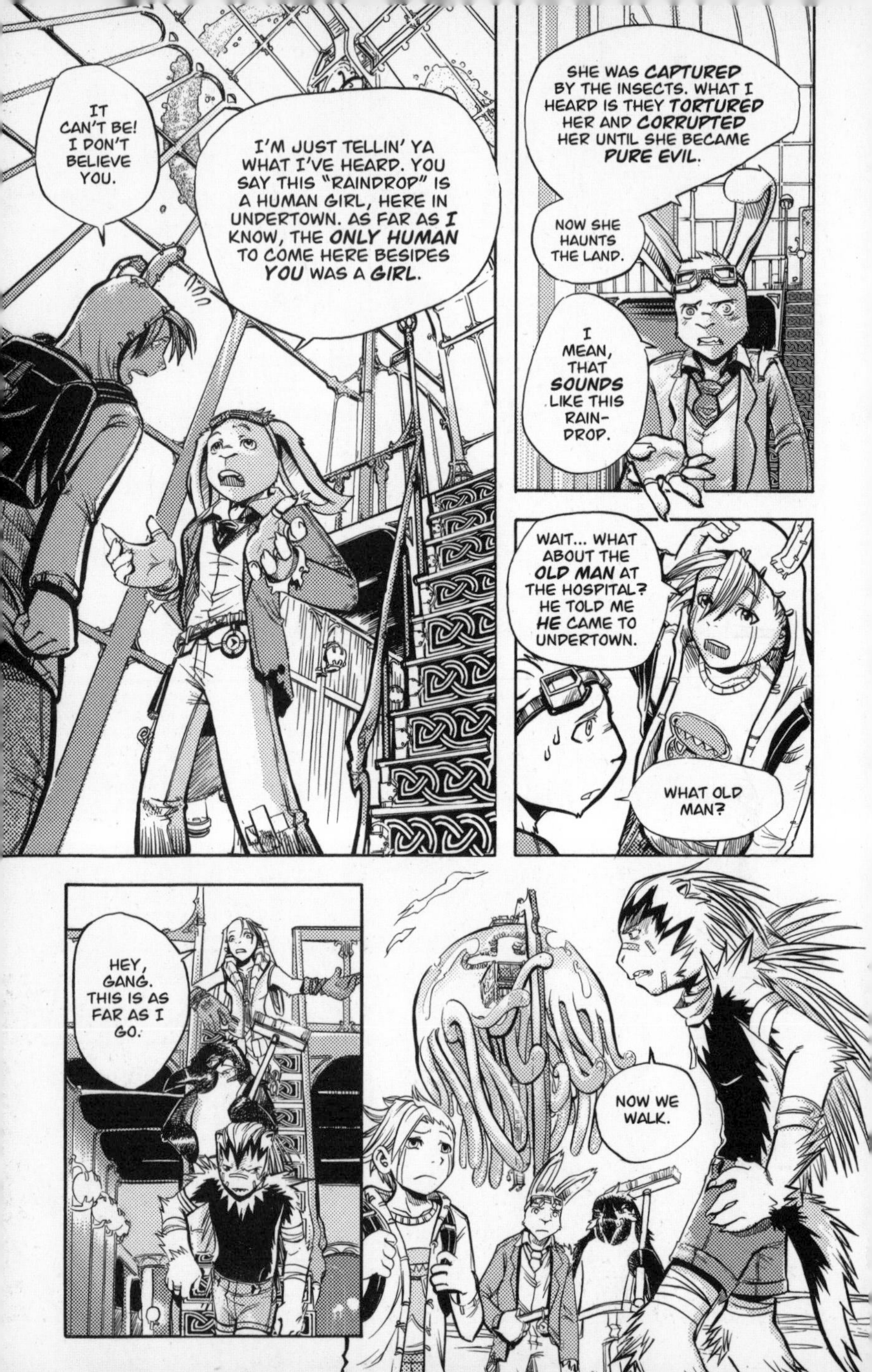
IT CAN'T BE! I DON'T BELIEVE YOU.
I'M JUST TELLIN' YA WHAT I'VE HEARD. YOU SAY THIS "RAINDROP" IS A HUMAN GIRL, HERE IN UNDERTOWN. AS FAR AS I KNOW, THE ONLY HUMAN TO COME HERE BESIDES YOU WAS A GIRL.
SHE WAS CAPTURED BY THE INSECTS. WHAT I HEARD IS THEY TORTURED HER AND CORRUPTED HER UNTIL SHE BECAME PURE EVIL.
NOW SHE HAUNTS THE LAND.
I MEAN, THAT SOUNDS LIKE THIS RAIN-DROP.
WAIT... WHAT ABOUT THE OLD MAN AT THE HOSPITAL? HE TOLD ME HE CAME TO UNDERTOWN.
WHAT OLD MAN?
HEY, GANG. THIS IS AS FAR AS I GO.
NOW WE WALK.

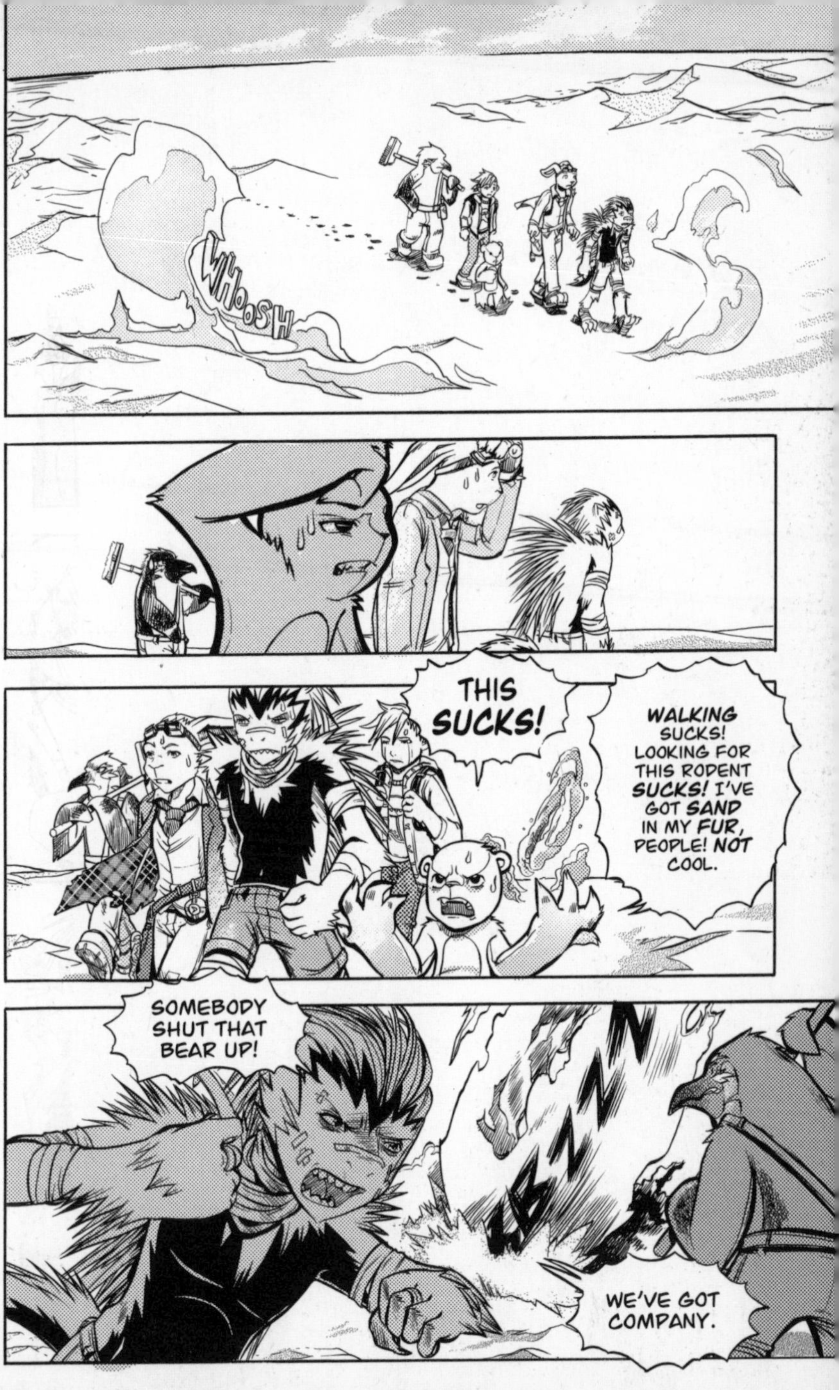
WHOOSH
THIS SUCKS!
WALKING SUCKS! LOOKING FOR THIS RODENT SUCKS! I'VE GOT SAND IN MY FUR, PEOPLE! NOT COOL.
SOMEBODY SHUT THAT BEAR UP!
WE'VE GOT COMPANY.

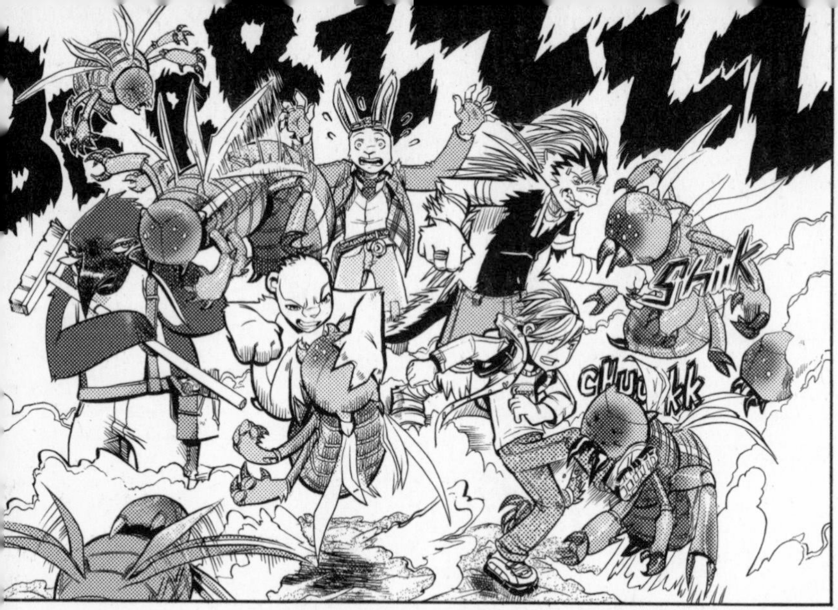
SHIK

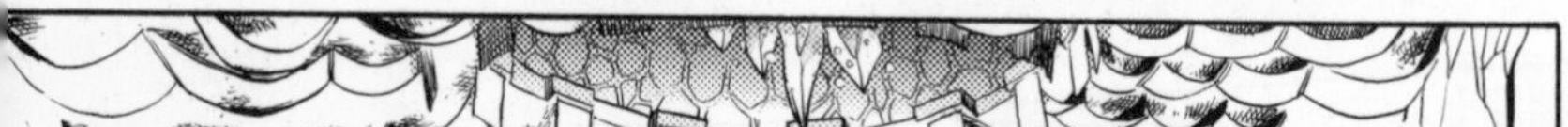
HAK-HAK-HAK! WELC-C-COME TO OUR SECRET STOCK-K-KPILE OF SUGAR!
WHY?
WHY TAKE CONTROL OF THE FACTORY? SO MANY INNOCENT FURMEN DIED...BUT YOU HAVE SO MUCH SUGAR. YOU DON'T NEED IT!

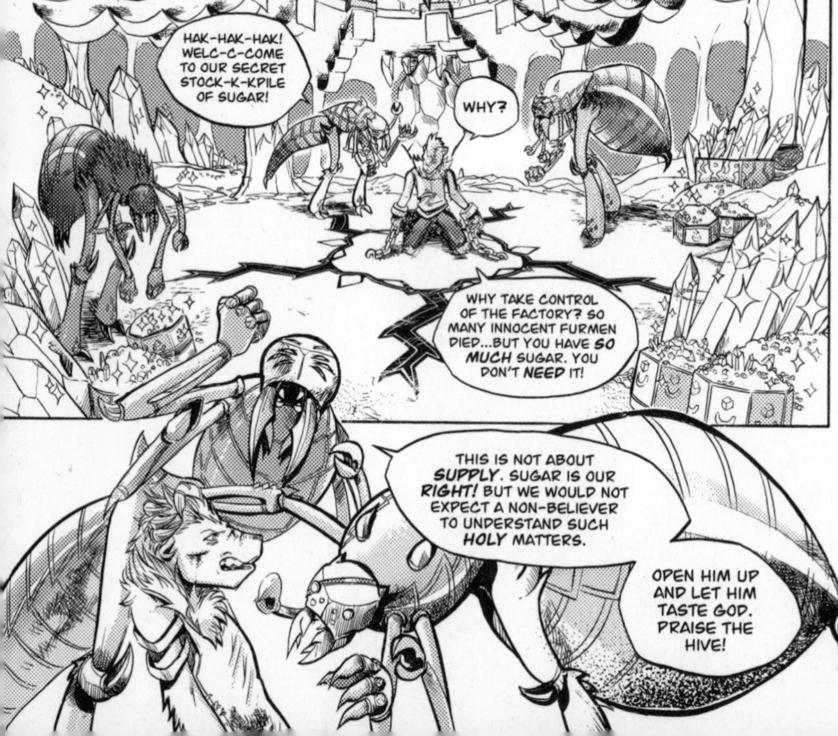
THIS IS NOT ABOUT SUPPLY. SUGAR IS OUR RIGHT! BUT WE WOULD NOT EXPECT A NON-BELIEVER TO UNDERSTAND SUCH HOLY MATTERS.
OPEN HIM UP AND LET HIM TASTE GOD. PRAISE THE HIVE!

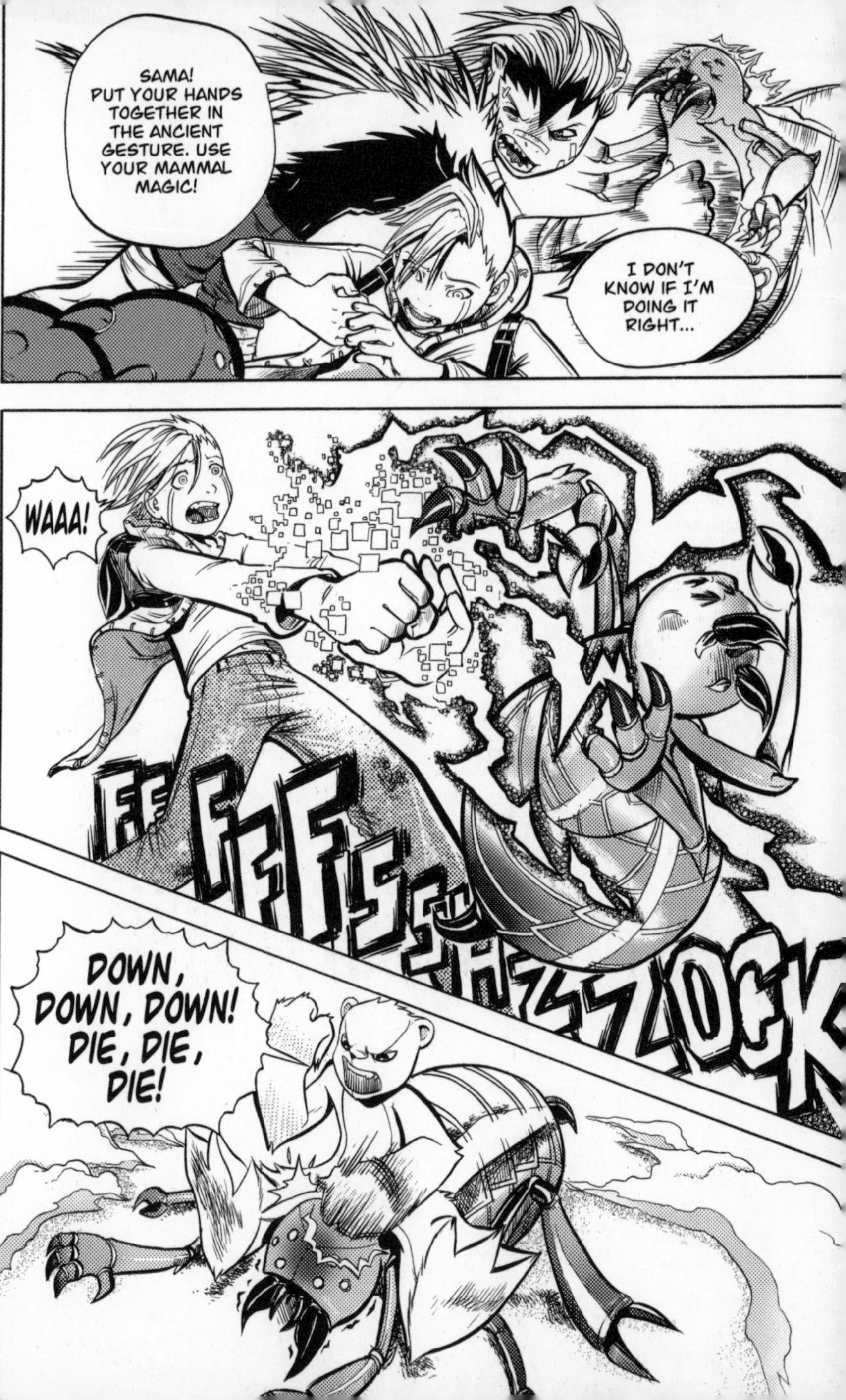
SAMA! PUT YOUR HANDS TOGETHER IN THE ANCIENT GESTURE. USE YOUR MAMMAL MAGIC!
I DON'T KNOW IF I'M DOING IT RIGHT...
WAAA!
DOWN, DOWN, DOWN! DIE, DIE, DIE!

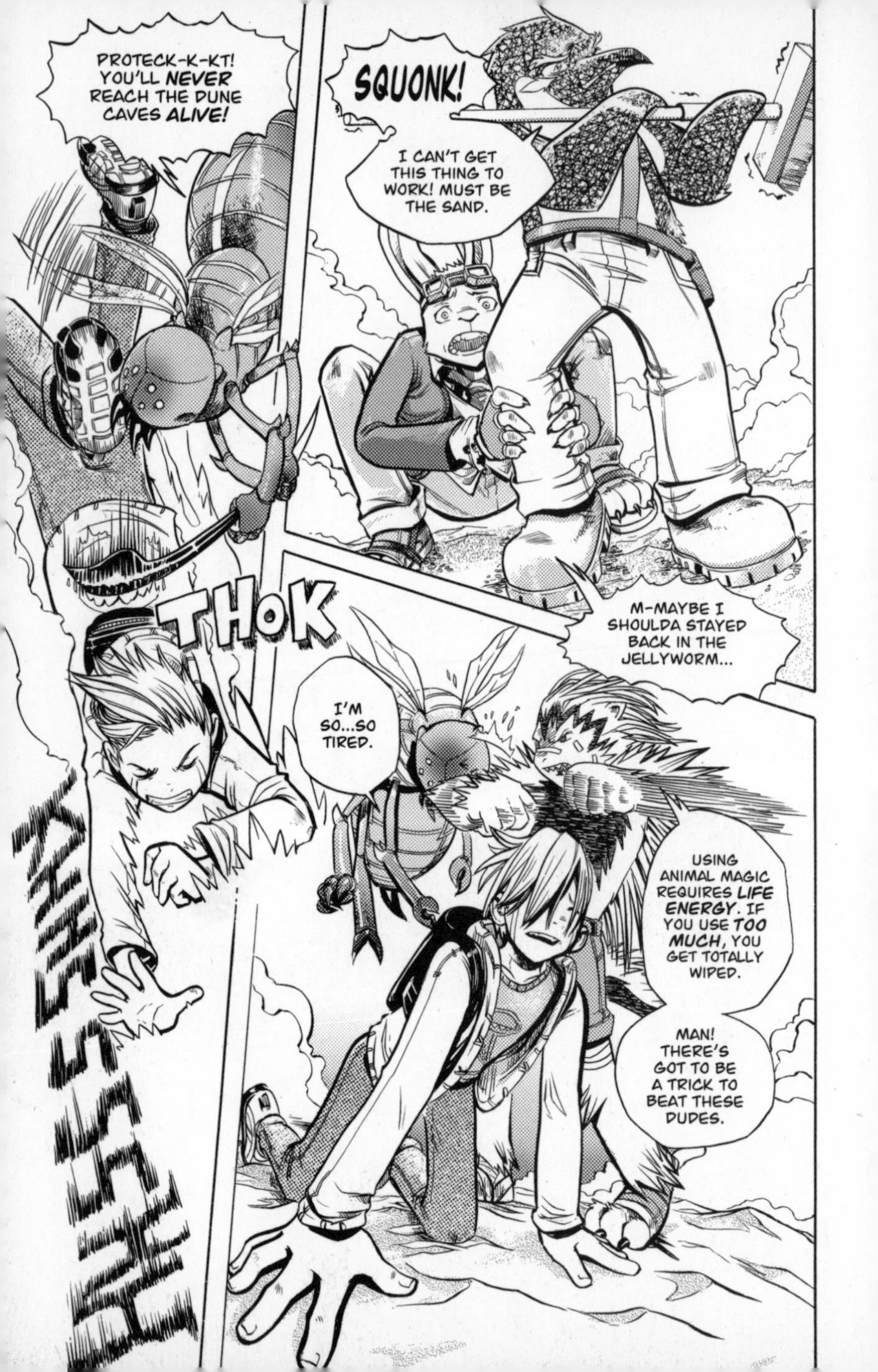
PROTECK-K-KT! YOU'LL NEVER REACH THE DUNE CAVES ALIVE!
SQUONK!
I CAN'T GET THIS THING TO WORK! MUST BE THE SAND.
THOK
KHSSSHH
M-MAYBE I SHOULDA STAYED BACK IN THE JELLYWORM...
I'M SO...SO TIRED.
USING ANIMAL MAGIC REQUIRES LIFE ENERGY. IF YOU USE TOO MUCH, YOU GET TOTALLY WIPED.
MAN! THERE'S GOT TO BE A TRICK TO BEAT THESE DUDES.

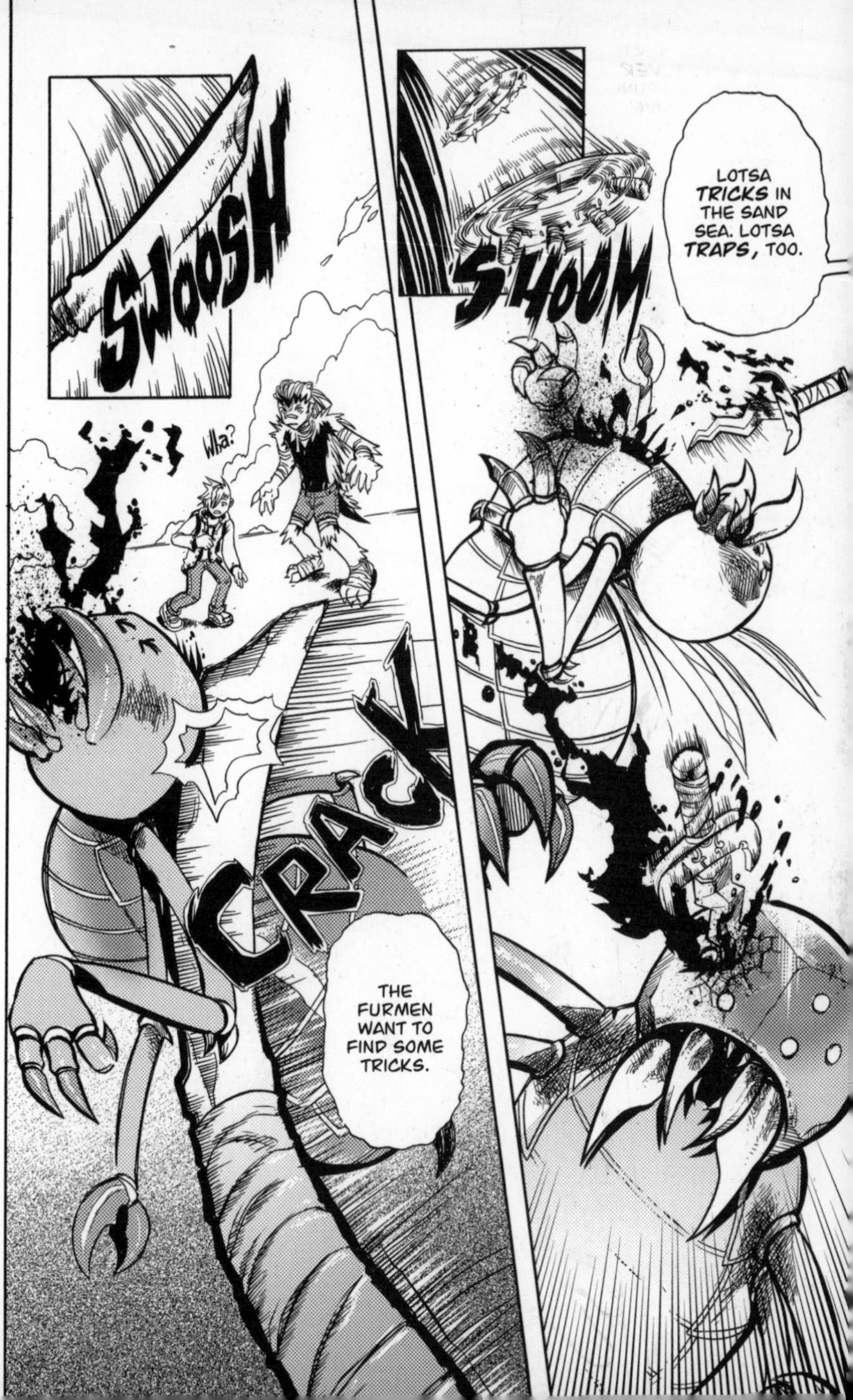
SWOOSH
Wha?
CRACK
THE FURMEN WANT TO FIND SOME TRICKS.
SHOOM
LOTSA TRICKS IN THE SAND SEA. LOTSA TRAPS, TOO.

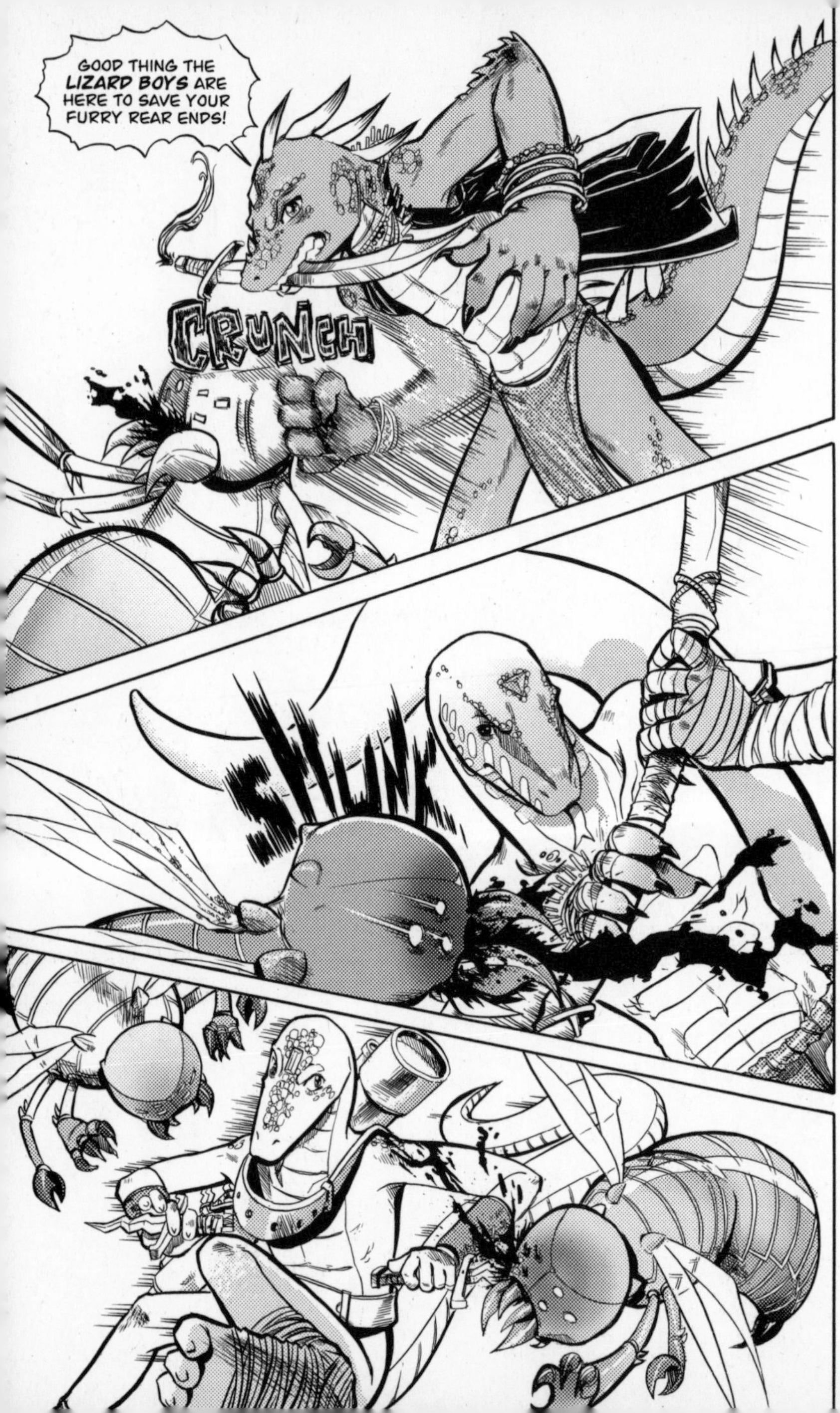
GOOD THING THE LIZARD BOYS ARE HERE TO SAVE YOUR FURRY REAR ENDS!
CRUNCH
SHUNK

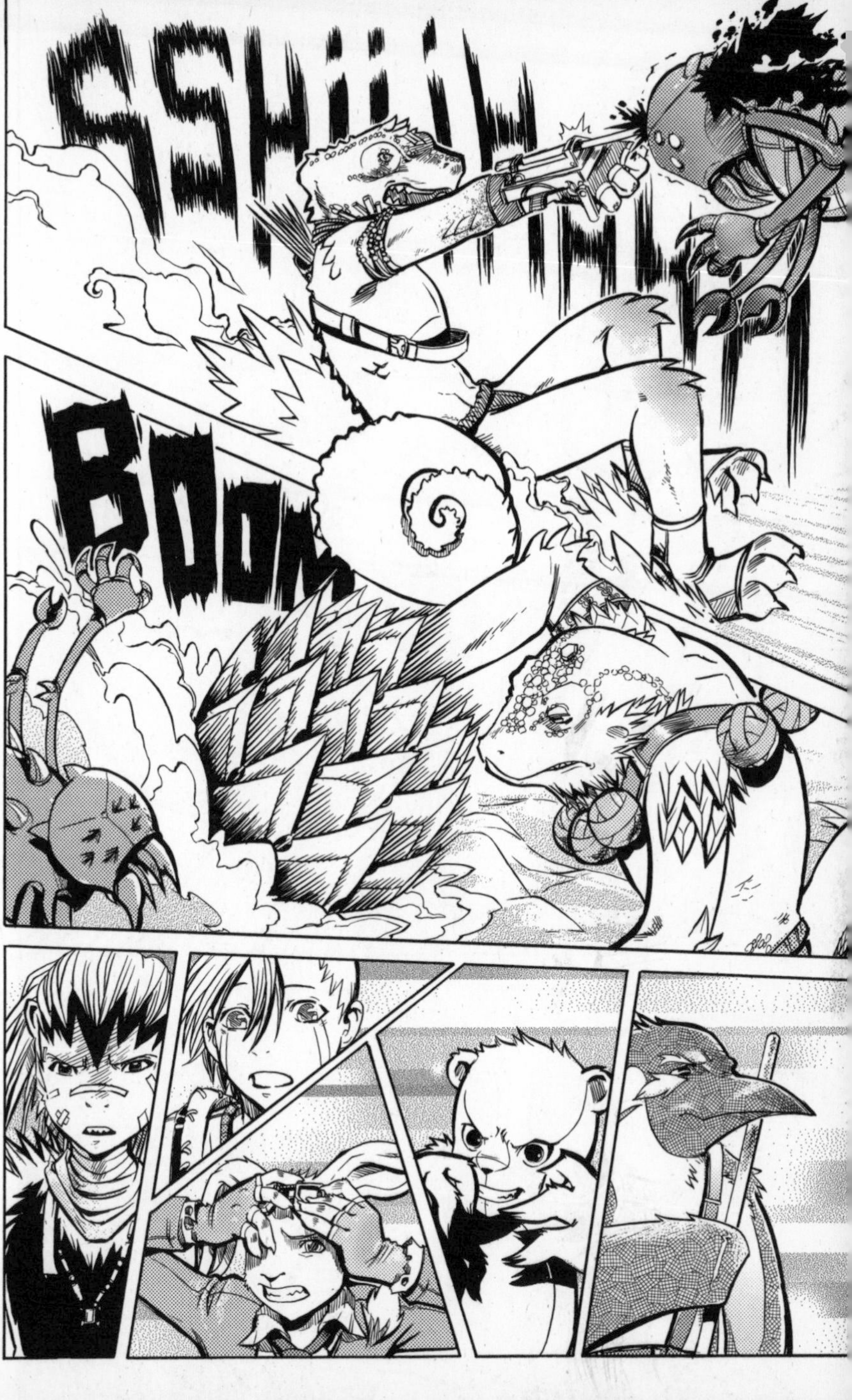
SSHiiiH
BOOM

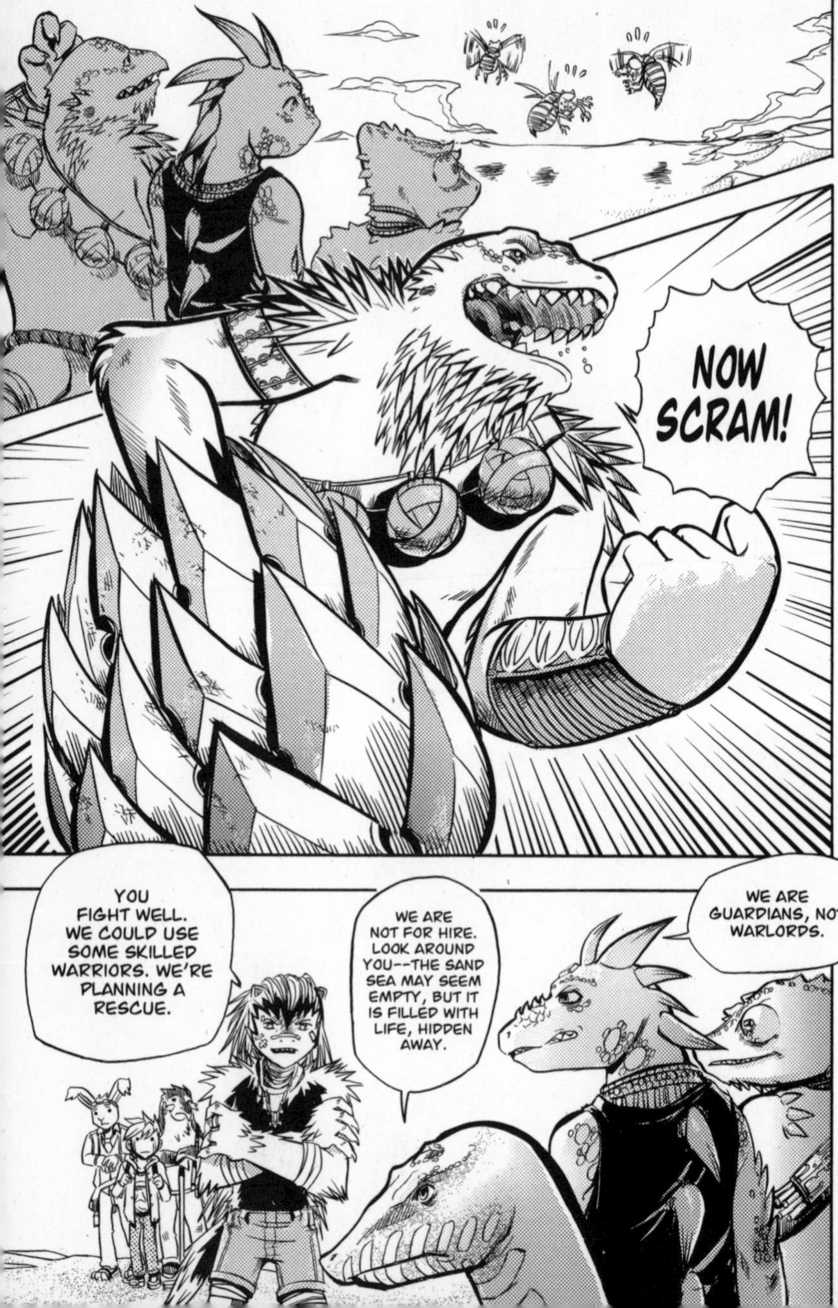
NOW SCRAM!
YOU FIGHT WELL. WE COULD USE SOME SKILLED WARRIORS. WE'RE PLANNING A RESCUE.
WE ARE NOT FOR HIRE. LOOK AROUND YOU--THE SAND SEA MAY SEEM EMPTY, BUT IT IS FILLED WITH LIFE, HIDDEN AWAY.
WE ARE GUARDIANS, NOT WARLORDS.

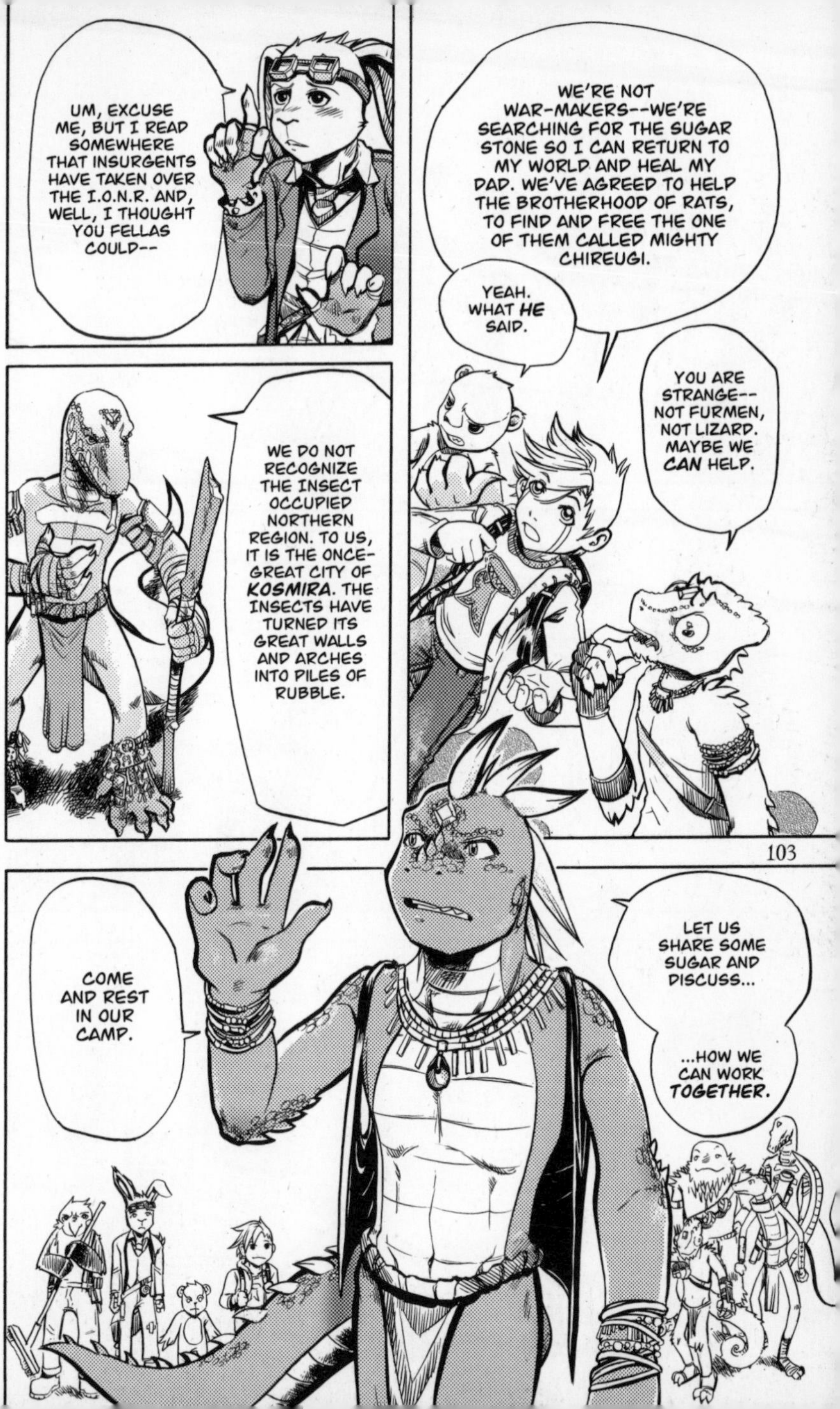
UM, EXCUSE ME, BUT I READ SOMEWHERE THAT INSURGENTS HAVE TAKEN OVER THE I.O.N.R. AND, WELL, I THOUGHT YOU FELLAS COULD--
WE DO NOT RECOGNIZE THE INSECT OCCUPIED NORTHERN REGION. TO US, IT IS THE ONCE-GREAT CITY OF **KOSMIRA**. THE INSECTS HAVE TURNED ITS GREAT WALLS AND ARCHES INTO PILES OF RUBBLE.
WE'RE NOT WAR-MAKERS--WE'RE SEARCHING FOR THE SUGAR STONE SO I CAN RETURN TO MY WORLD AND HEAL MY DAD. WE'VE AGREED TO HELP THE BROTHERHOOD OF RATS, TO FIND AND FREE THE ONE OF THEM CALLED MIGHTY CHIREUGI.
YEAH. WHAT **HE** SAID.
YOU ARE STRANGE--NOT FURMEN, NOT LIZARD. MAYBE WE **CAN** HELP.
COME AND REST IN OUR CAMP.
LET US SHARE SOME SUGAR AND DISCUSS...
...HOW WE CAN WORK **TOGETHER**.

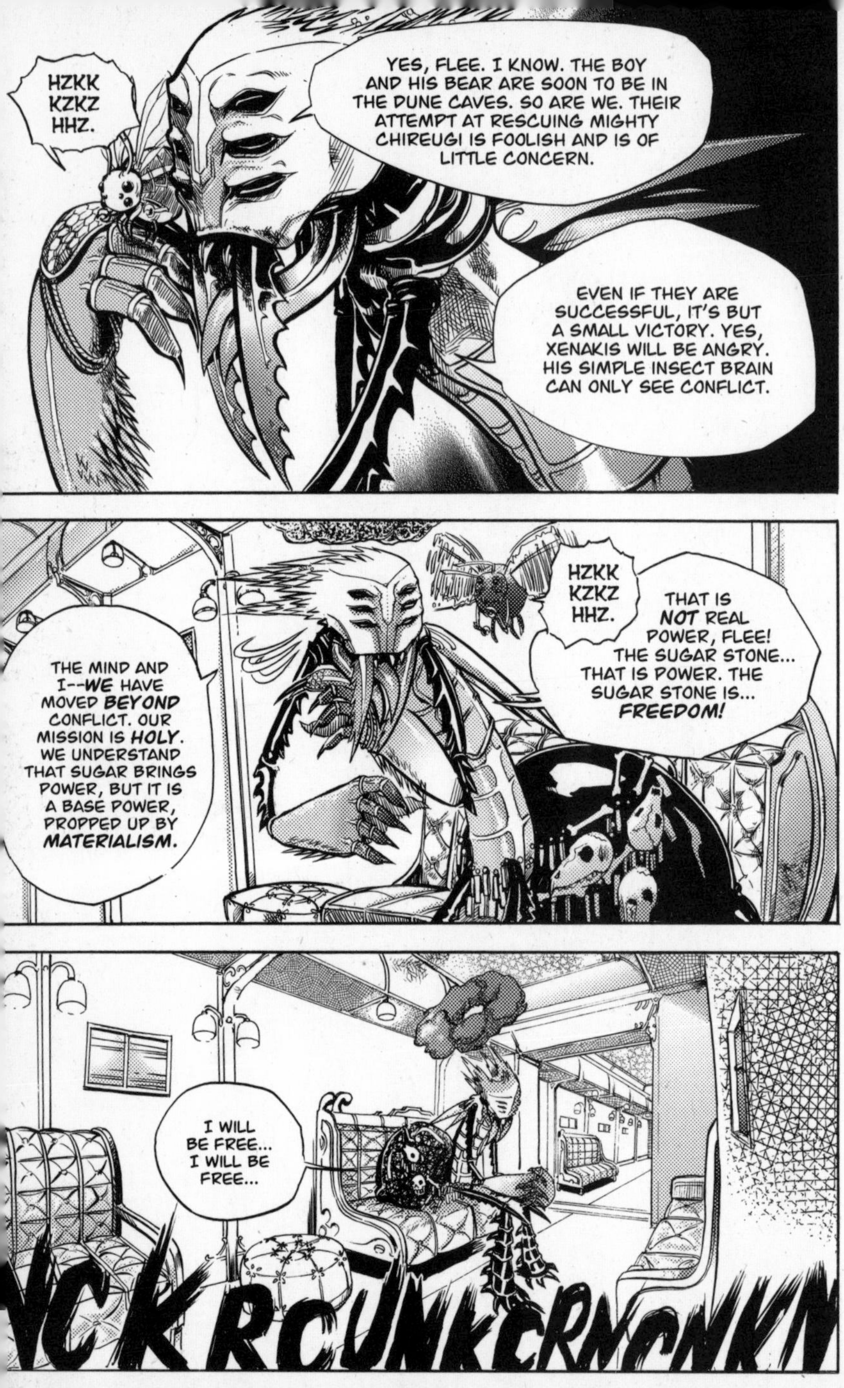
HZKK KZKZ HHZ.
YES, FLEE. I KNOW. THE BOY AND HIS BEAR ARE SOON TO BE IN THE DUNE CAVES. SO ARE WE. THEIR ATTEMPT AT RESCUING MIGHTY CHIREUGI IS FOOLISH AND IS OF LITTLE CONCERN.
EVEN IF THEY ARE SUCCESSFUL, IT'S BUT A SMALL VICTORY. YES, XENAKIS WILL BE ANGRY. HIS SIMPLE INSECT BRAIN CAN ONLY SEE CONFLICT.
THE MIND AND I--**WE** HAVE MOVED **BEYOND** CONFLICT. OUR MISSION IS **HOLY**. WE UNDERSTAND THAT SUGAR BRINGS POWER, BUT IT IS A BASE POWER, PROPPED UP BY ***MATERIALISM***.
HZKK KZKZ HHZ.
THAT IS ***NOT*** REAL POWER, FLEE! THE SUGAR STONE... THAT IS POWER. THE SUGAR STONE IS... ***FREEDOM!***
I WILL BE FREE... I WILL BE FREE...
NCK RCUNKCRNCNKN

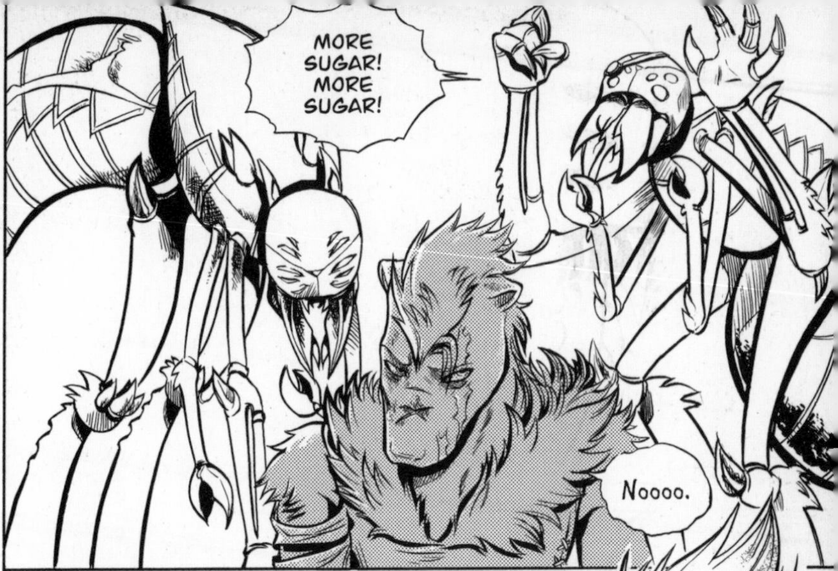
MORE SUGAR! MORE SUGAR!
Noooo.
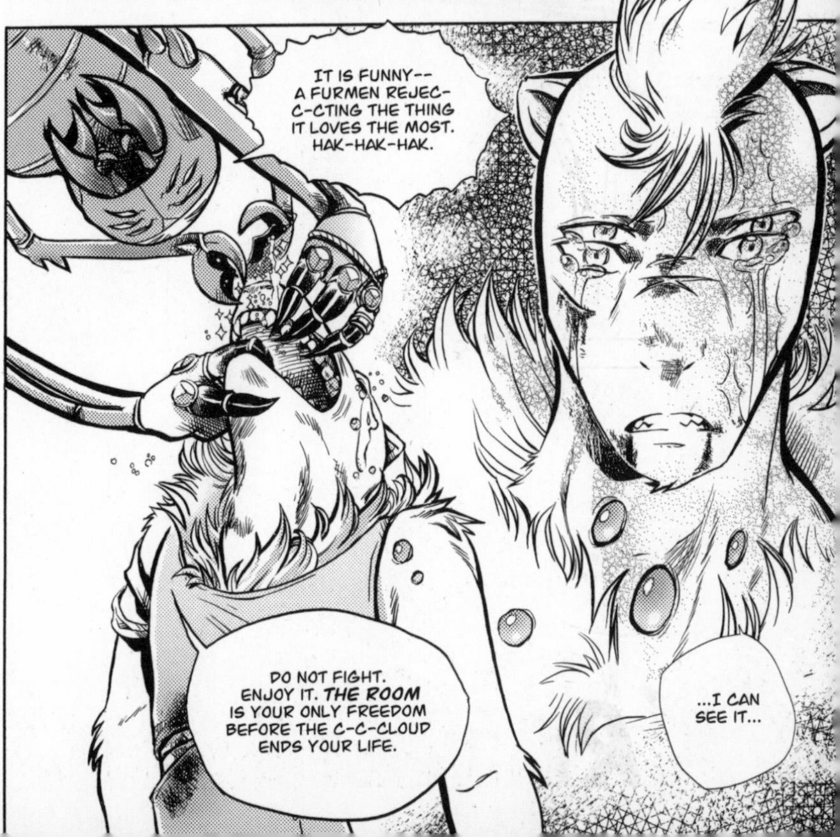
IT IS FUNNY-- A FURMEN REJEC-C-CTING THE THING IT LOVES THE MOST. HAK-HAK-HAK.
DO NOT FIGHT. ENJOY IT. ***THE ROOM*** IS YOUR ONLY FREEDOM BEFORE THE C-C-CLOUD ENDS YOUR LIFE.
...I CAN SEE IT...

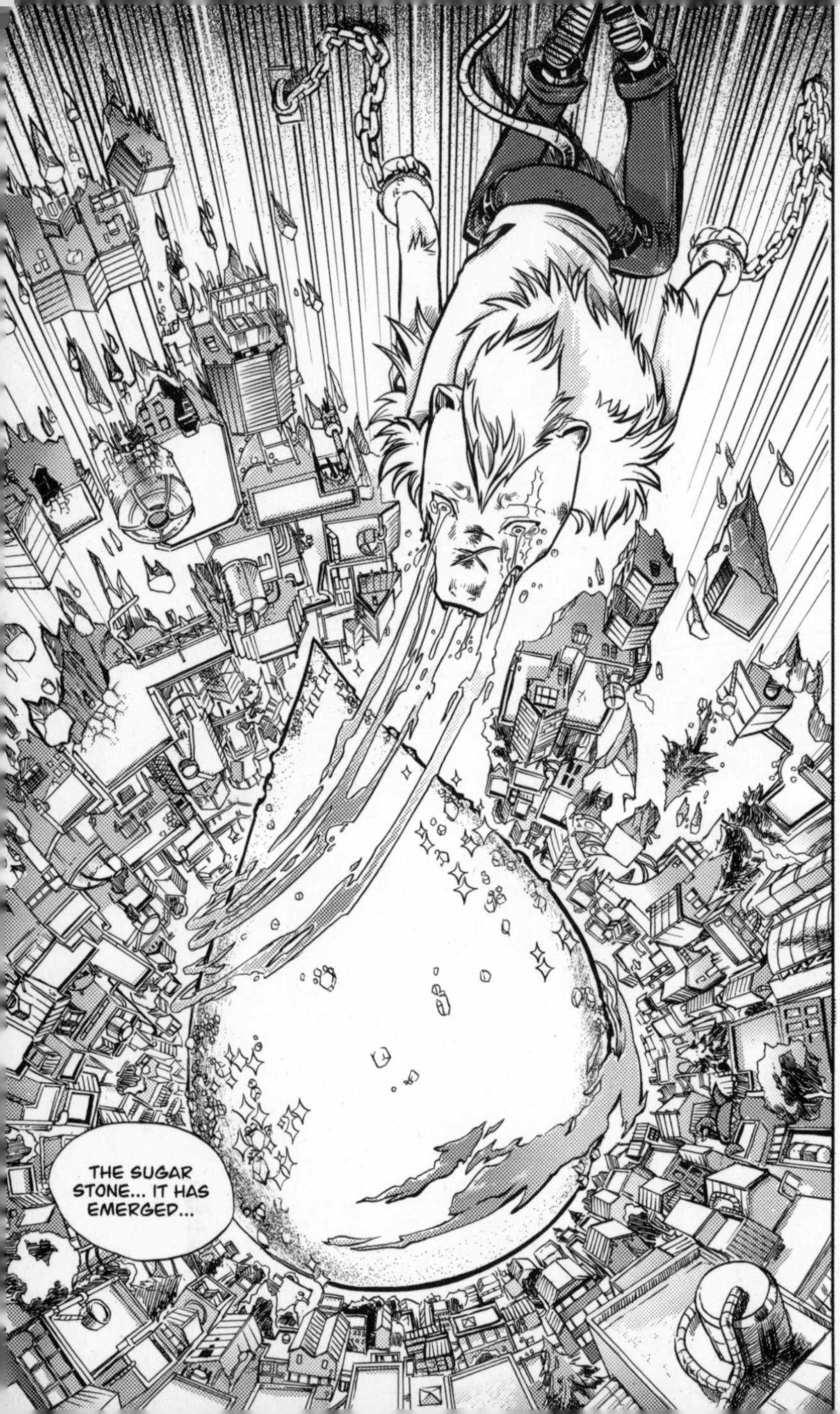
THE SUGAR STONE... IT HAS EMERGED...

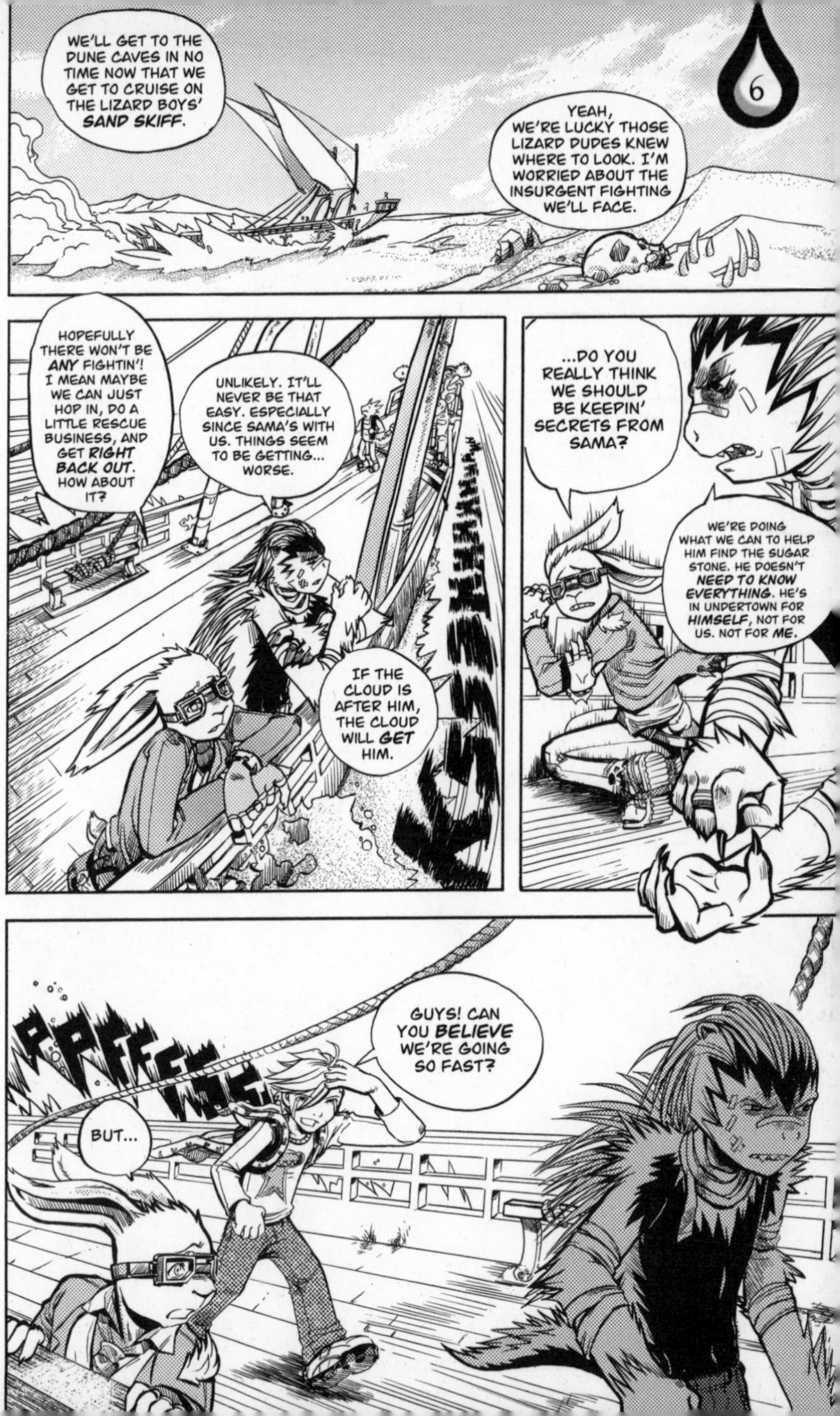
6
WE'LL GET TO THE DUNE CAVES IN NO TIME NOW THAT WE GET TO CRUISE ON THE LIZARD BOYS' SAND SKIFF.
YEAH, WE'RE LUCKY THOSE LIZARD DUDES KNEW WHERE TO LOOK. I'M WORRIED ABOUT THE INSURGENT FIGHTING WE'LL FACE.
HOPEFULLY THERE WON'T BE ANY FIGHTIN'! I MEAN MAYBE WE CAN JUST HOP IN, DO A LITTLE RESCUE BUSINESS, AND GET RIGHT BACK OUT. HOW ABOUT IT?
UNLIKELY. IT'LL NEVER BE THAT EASY. ESPECIALLY SINCE SAMA'S WITH US. THINGS SEEM TO BE GETTING... WORSE.
IF THE CLOUD IS AFTER HIM, THE CLOUD WILL GET HIM.
KSSHHHHHHHHH
...DO YOU REALLY THINK WE SHOULD BE KEEPIN' SECRETS FROM SAMA?
WE'RE DOING WHAT WE CAN TO HELP HIM FIND THE SUGAR STONE. HE DOESN'T NEED TO KNOW EVERYTHING. HE'S IN UNDERTOWN FOR HIMSELF, NOT FOR US. NOT FOR ME.
PPFFFSSS
BUT...
GUYS! CAN YOU BELIEVE WE'RE GOING SO FAST?

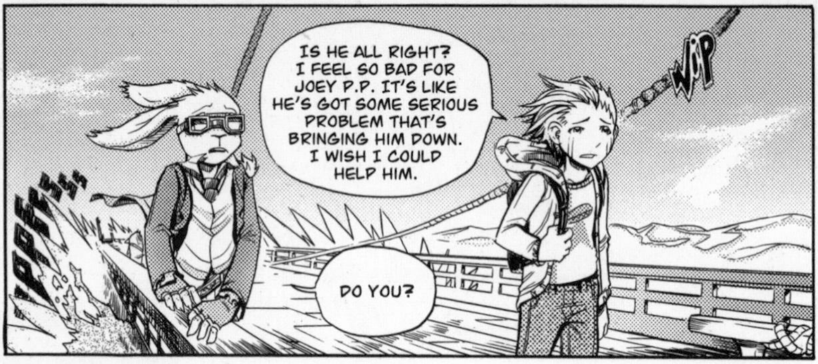
WHIP
IS HE ALL RIGHT? I FEEL SO BAD FOR JOEY P.P. IT'S LIKE HE'S GOT SOME SERIOUS PROBLEM THAT'S BRINGING HIM DOWN. I WISH I COULD HELP HIM.
DO YOU?

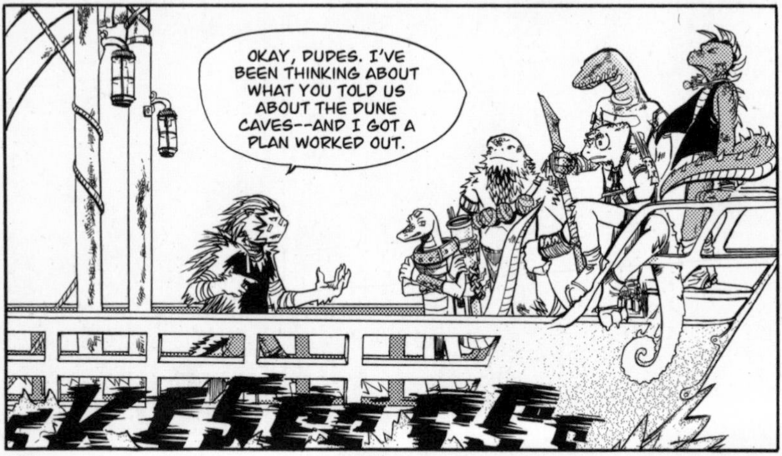
OKAY, DUDES. I'VE BEEN THINKING ABOUT WHAT YOU TOLD US ABOUT THE DUNE CAVES--AND I GOT A PLAN WORKED OUT.

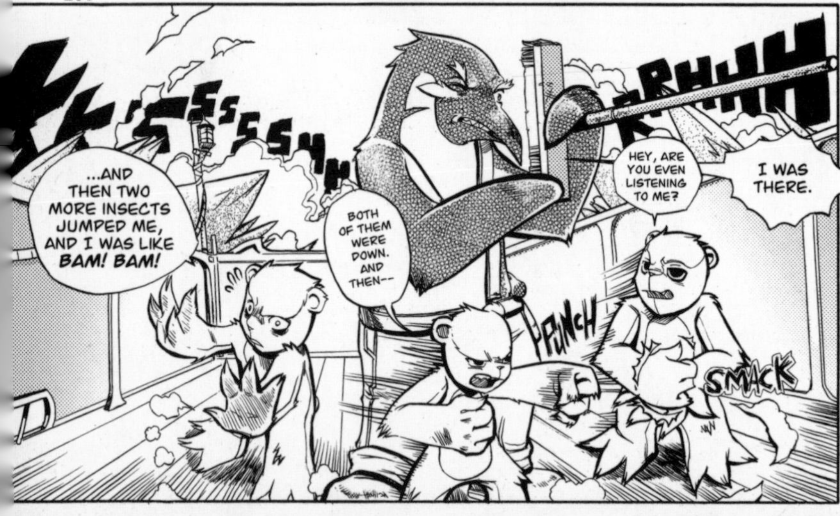
...AND THEN TWO MORE INSECTS JUMPED ME, AND I WAS LIKE **BAM! BAM!**
BOTH OF THEM WERE DOWN. AND THEN--
HEY, ARE YOU EVEN LISTENING TO ME?
I WAS THERE.
PUNCH
SMACK

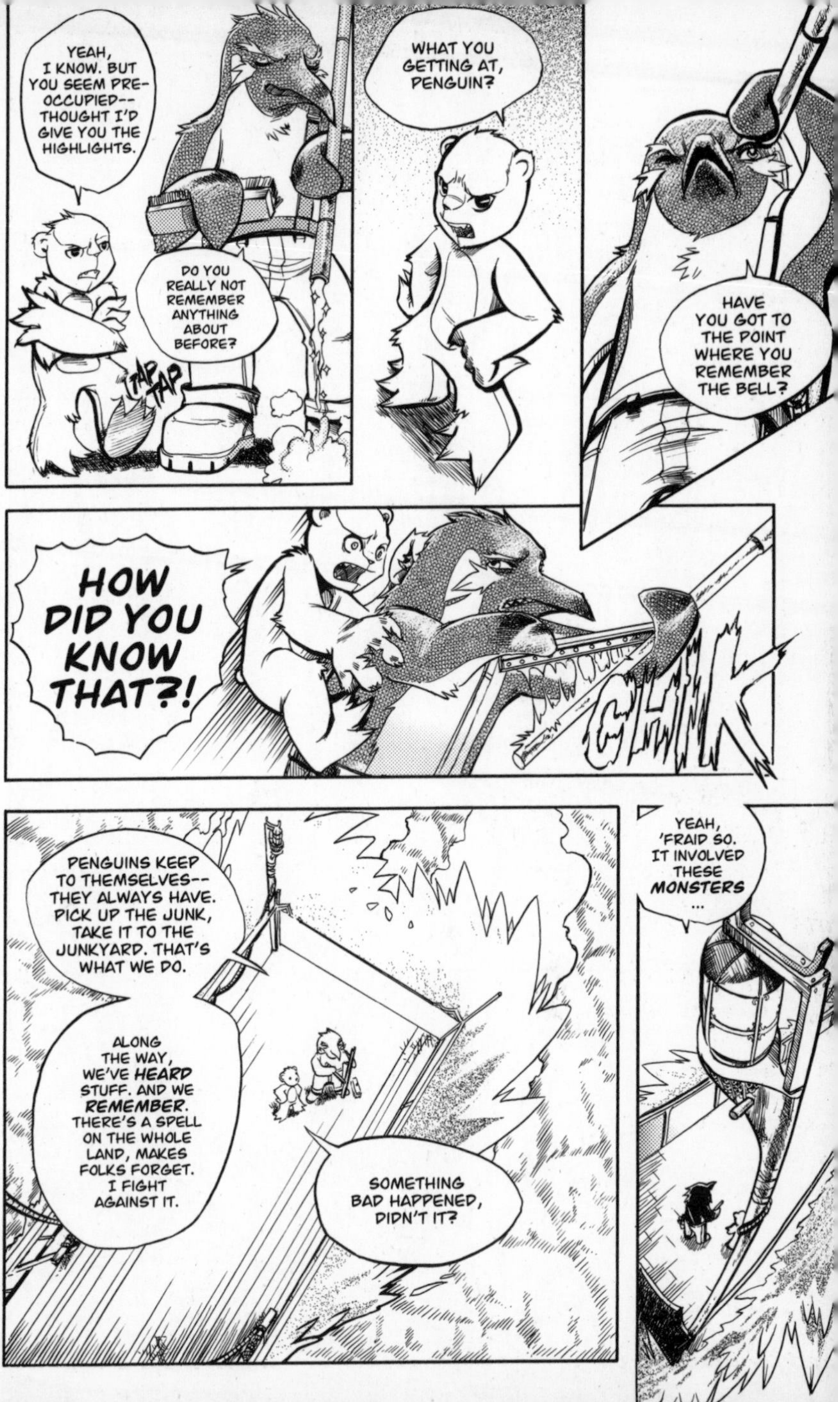
YEAH, I KNOW. BUT YOU SEEM PRE-OCCUPIED--THOUGHT I'D GIVE YOU THE HIGHLIGHTS.
DO YOU REALLY NOT REMEMBER ANYTHING ABOUT BEFORE?
TAP TAP
WHAT YOU GETTING AT, PENGUIN?
HAVE YOU GOT TO THE POINT WHERE YOU REMEMBER THE BELL?
HOW DID YOU KNOW THAT?!
CHIK
PENGUINS KEEP TO THEMSELVES--THEY ALWAYS HAVE. PICK UP THE JUNK, TAKE IT TO THE JUNKYARD. THAT'S WHAT WE DO.
ALONG THE WAY, WE'VE HEARD STUFF. AND WE REMEMBER. THERE'S A SPELL ON THE WHOLE LAND, MAKES FOLKS FORGET. I FIGHT AGAINST IT.
SOMETHING BAD HAPPENED, DIDN'T IT?
YEAH, 'FRAID SO. IT INVOLVED THESE MONSTERS...

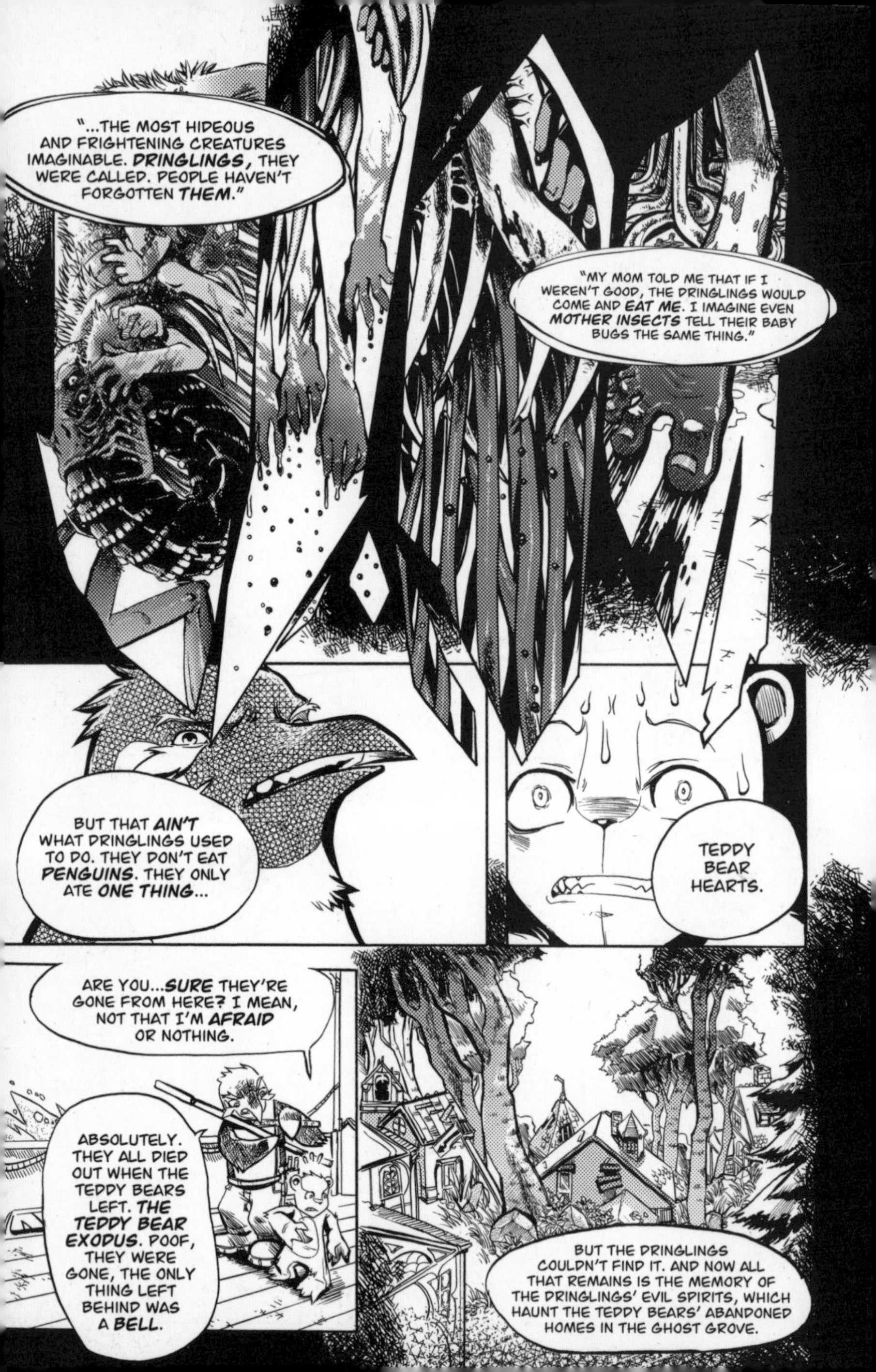
"...THE MOST HIDEOUS AND FRIGHTENING CREATURES IMAGINABLE. DRINGLINGS, THEY WERE CALLED. PEOPLE HAVEN'T FORGOTTEN THEM."
"MY MOM TOLD ME THAT IF I WEREN'T GOOD, THE DRINGLINGS WOULD COME AND EAT ME. I IMAGINE EVEN MOTHER INSECTS TELL THEIR BABY BUGS THE SAME THING."
BUT THAT AIN'T WHAT DRINGLINGS USED TO DO. THEY DON'T EAT PENGUINS. THEY ONLY ATE ONE THING...
TEDDY BEAR HEARTS.
ARE YOU...SURE THEY'RE GONE FROM HERE? I MEAN, NOT THAT I'M AFRAID OR NOTHING.
ABSOLUTELY. THEY ALL DIED OUT WHEN THE TEDDY BEARS LEFT. THE TEDDY BEAR EXODUS. POOF, THEY WERE GONE, THE ONLY THING LEFT BEHIND WAS A BELL.
BUT THE DRINGLINGS COULDN'T FIND IT. AND NOW ALL THAT REMAINS IS THE MEMORY OF THE DRINGLINGS' EVIL SPIRITS, WHICH HAUNT THE TEDDY BEARS' ABANDONED HOMES IN THE GHOST GROVE.

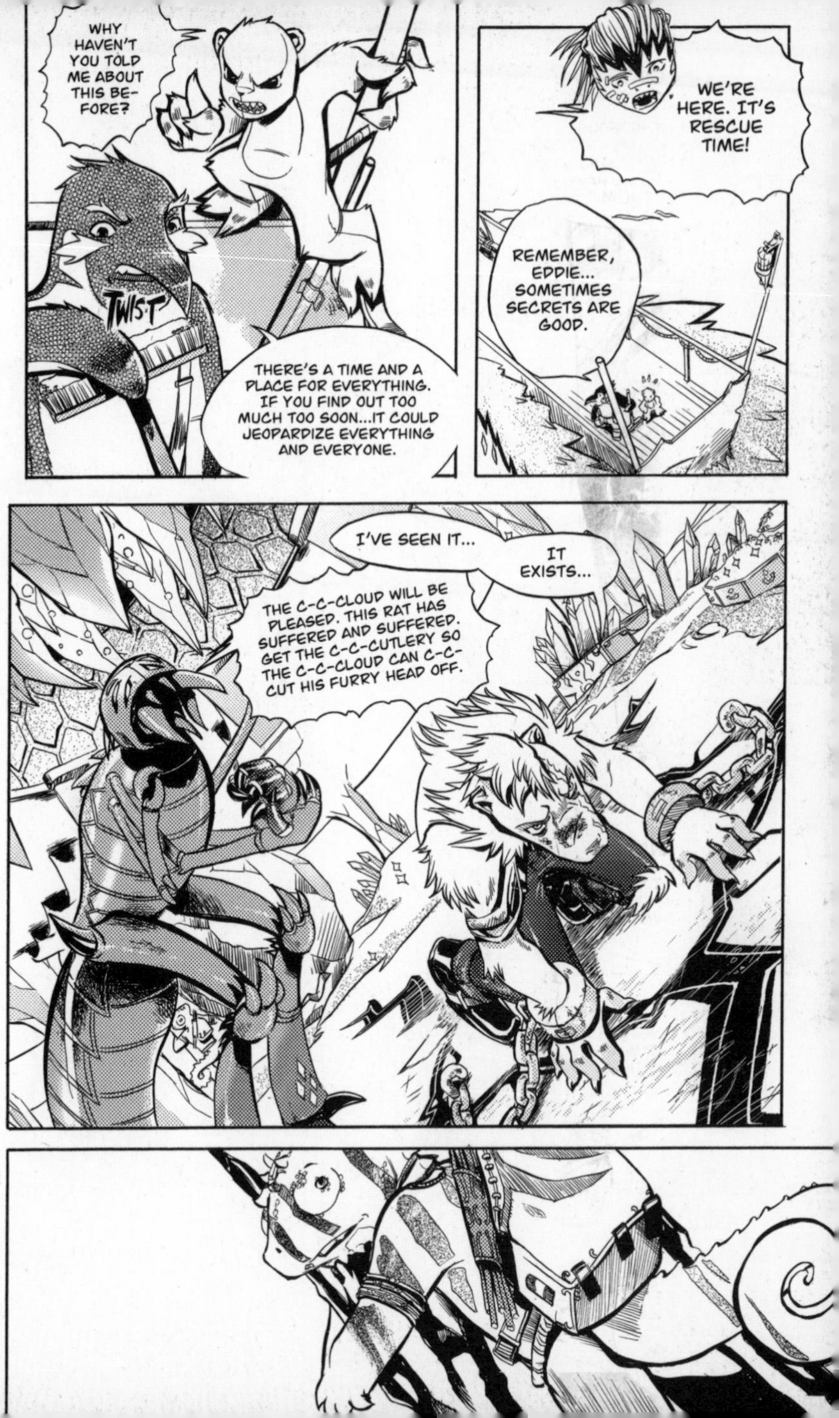
WHY HAVEN'T YOU TOLD ME ABOUT THIS BE-FORE?
TWIST
THERE'S A TIME AND A PLACE FOR EVERYTHING. IF YOU FIND OUT TOO MUCH TOO SOON...IT COULD JEOPARDIZE EVERYTHING AND EVERYONE.
WE'RE HERE. IT'S RESCUE TIME!
REMEMBER, EDDIE... SOMETIMES SECRETS ARE GOOD.
I'VE SEEN IT...
IT EXISTS...
THE C-C-CLOUD WILL BE PLEASED. THIS RAT HAS SUFFERED AND SUFFERED. GET THE C-C-CUTLERY SO THE C-C-CLOUD CAN C-C-CUT HIS FURRY HEAD OFF.

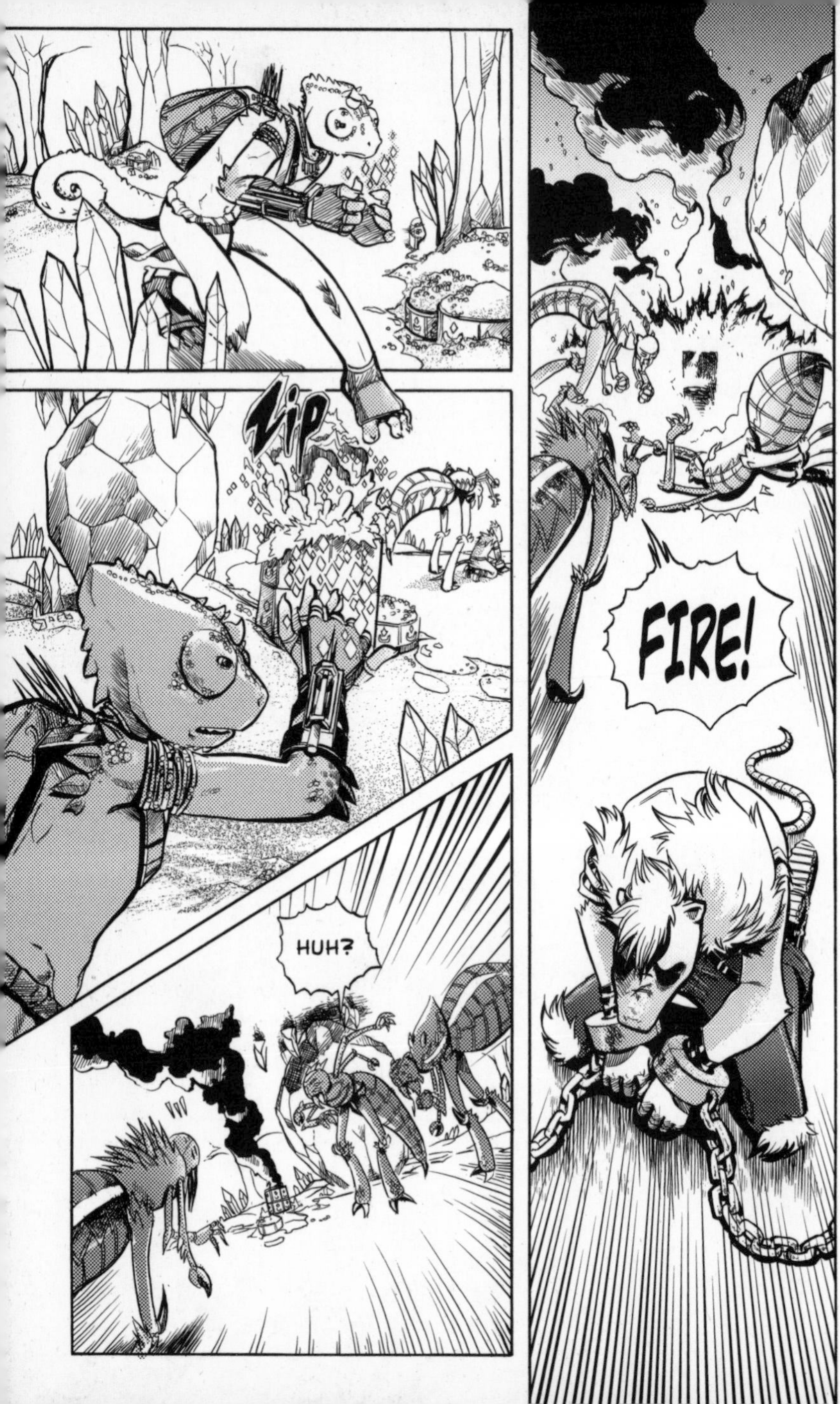
ZIP
HUH?
FIRE!

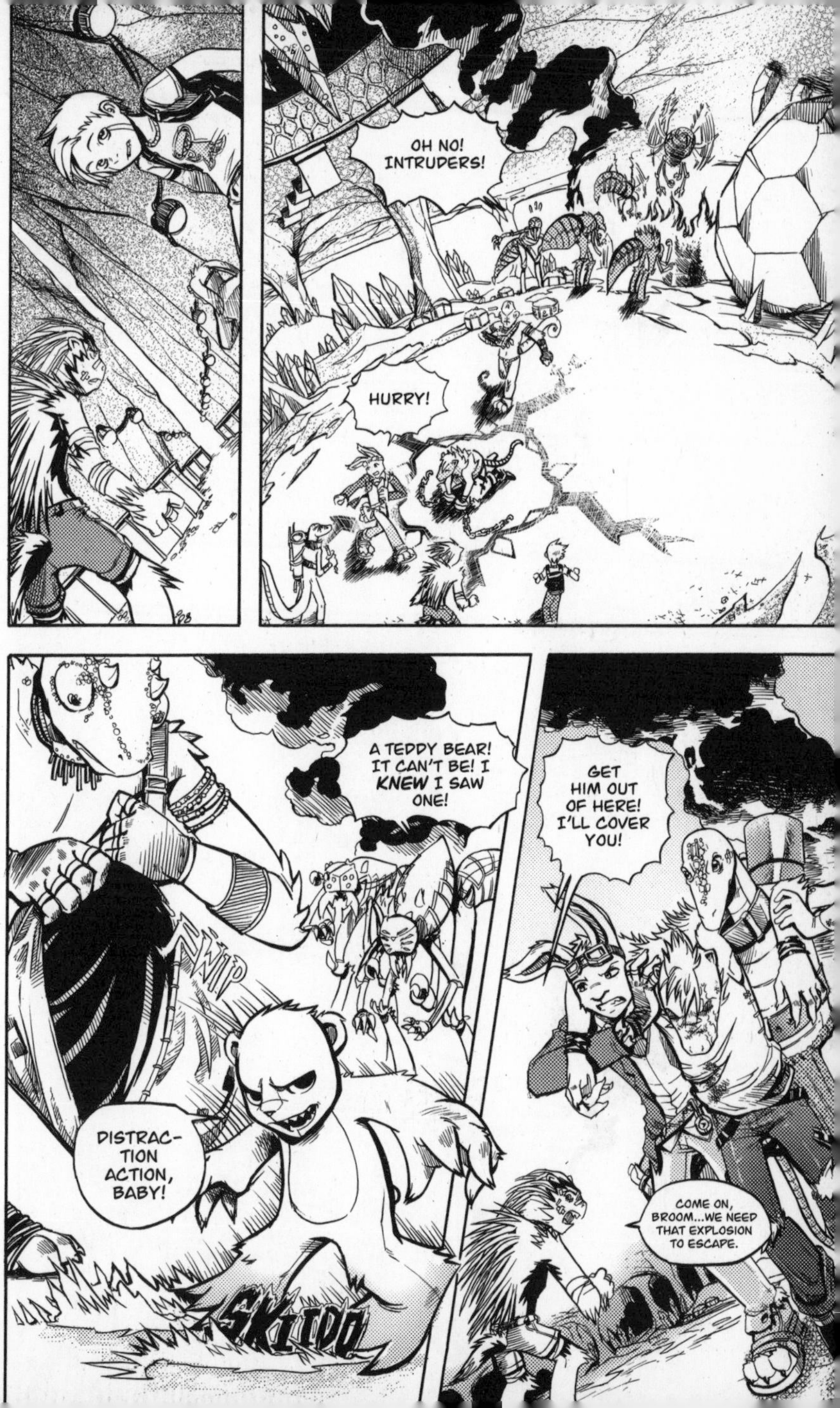
OH NO! INTRUDERS!
HURRY!
A TEDDY BEAR! IT CAN'T BE! I **KNEW** I SAW ONE!
SWIP
DISTRACTION ACTION, BABY!
SKIDDO
GET HIM OUT OF HERE! I'LL COVER YOU!
COME ON, BROOM...WE NEED THAT EXPLOSION TO ESCAPE.

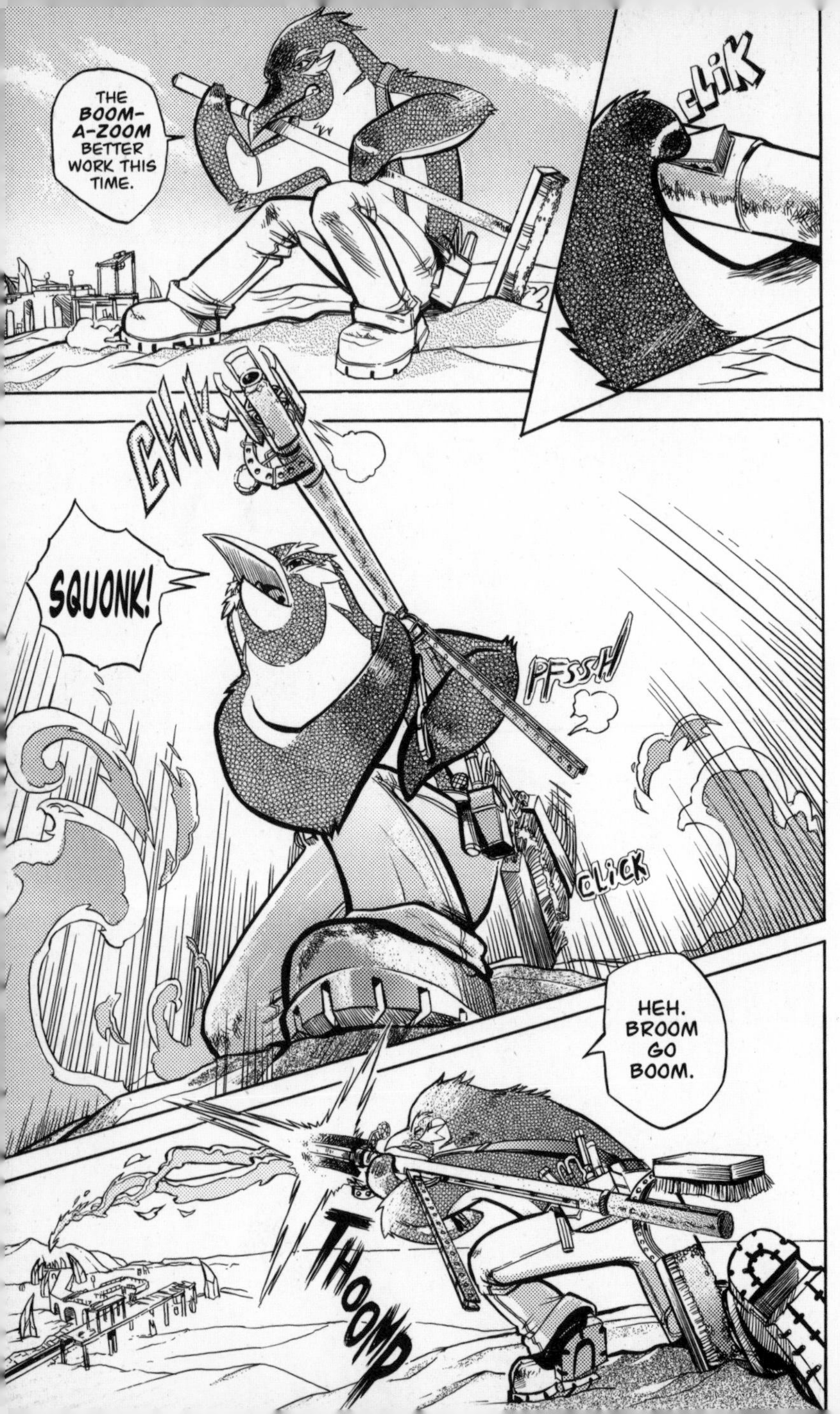
THE BOOM-A-ZOOM BETTER WORK THIS TIME.
CLIK
CHIK
SQUONK!
PFSSH
CLICK
HEH. BROOM GO BOOM.
THOOMP

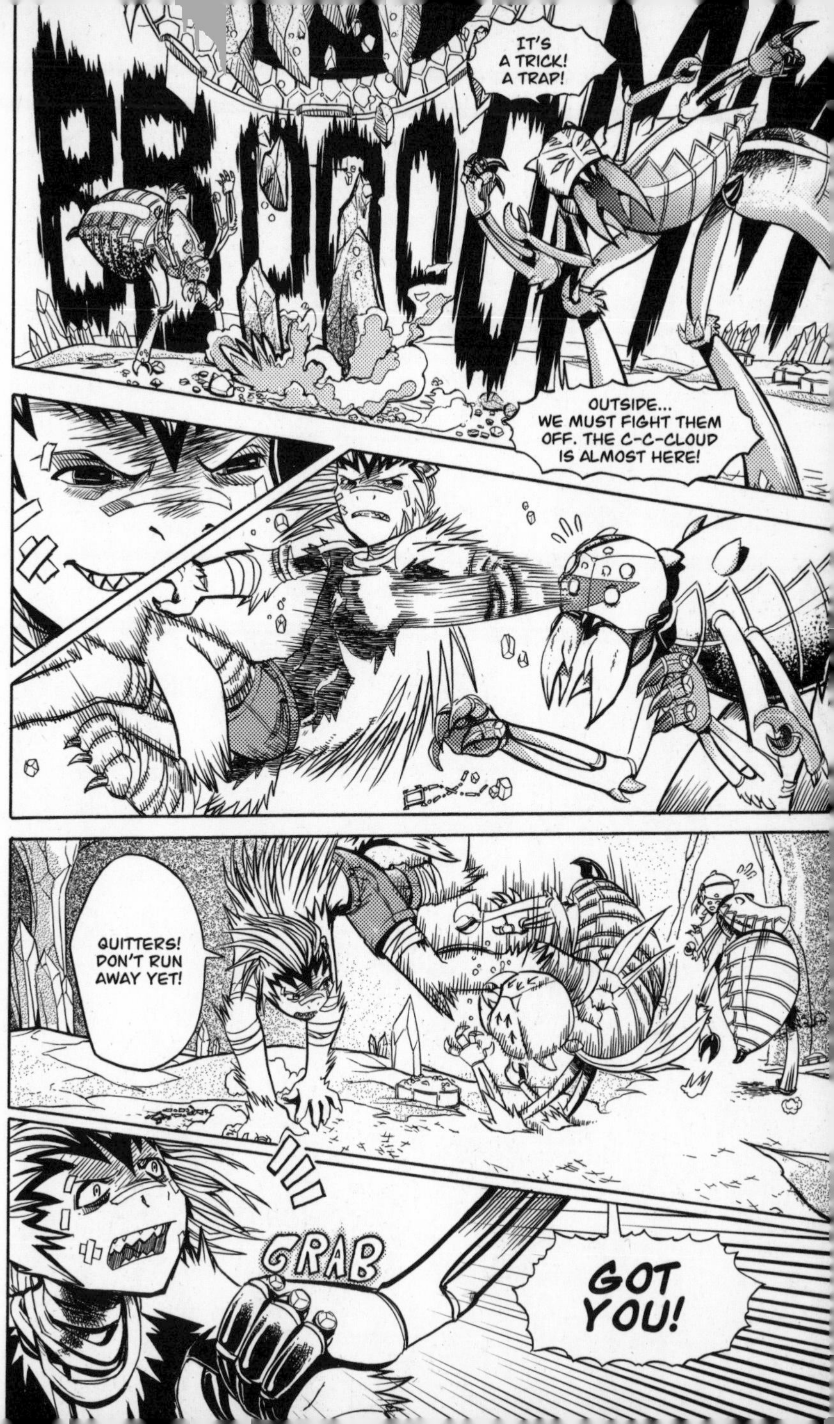
BROOOM
IT'S A TRICK! A TRAP!
OUTSIDE... WE MUST FIGHT THEM OFF. THE C-C-CLOUD IS ALMOST HERE!
QUITTERS! DON'T RUN AWAY YET!
GRAB
GOT YOU!

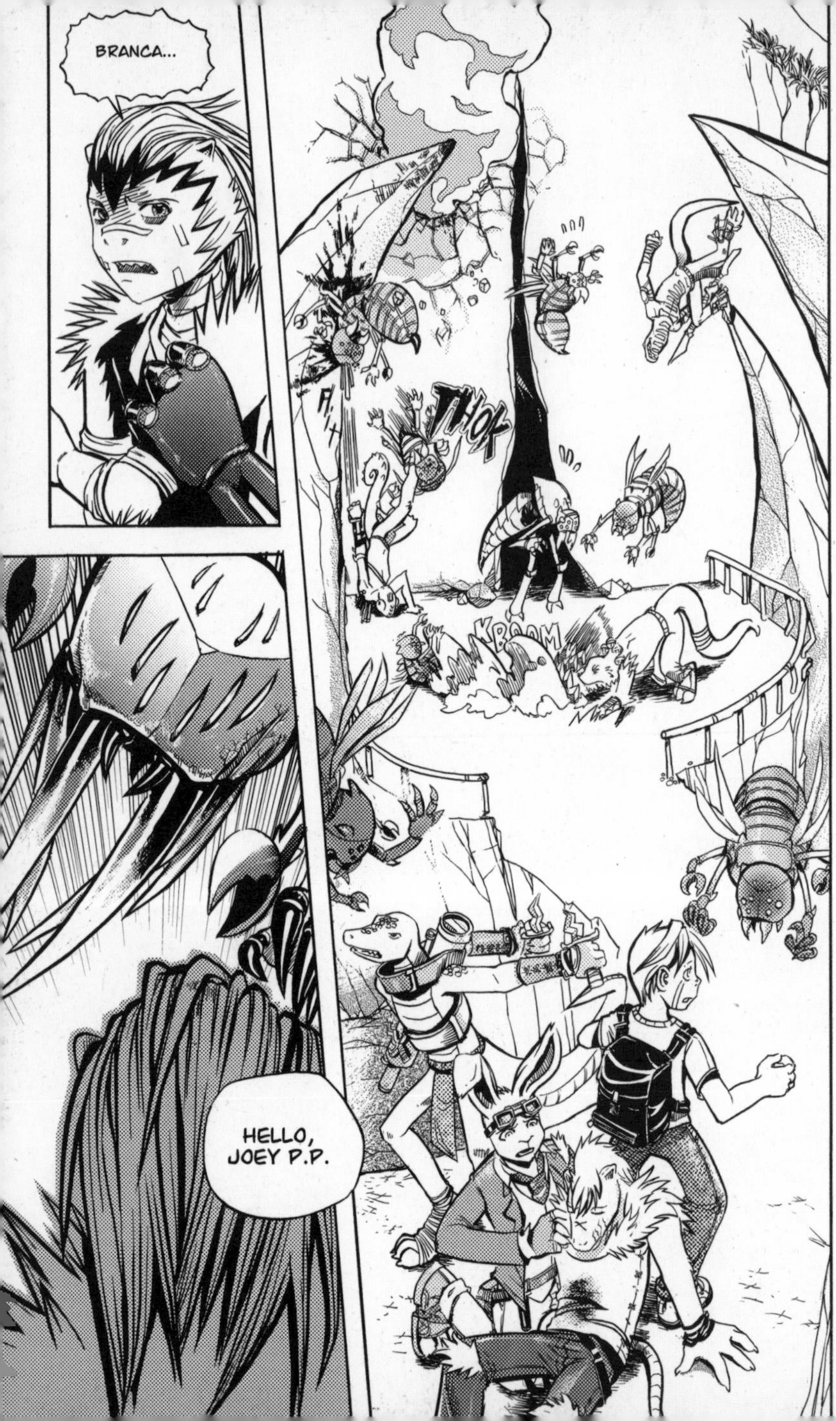
BRANCA...
HELLO, JOEY P.P.
THOK
KBOOM

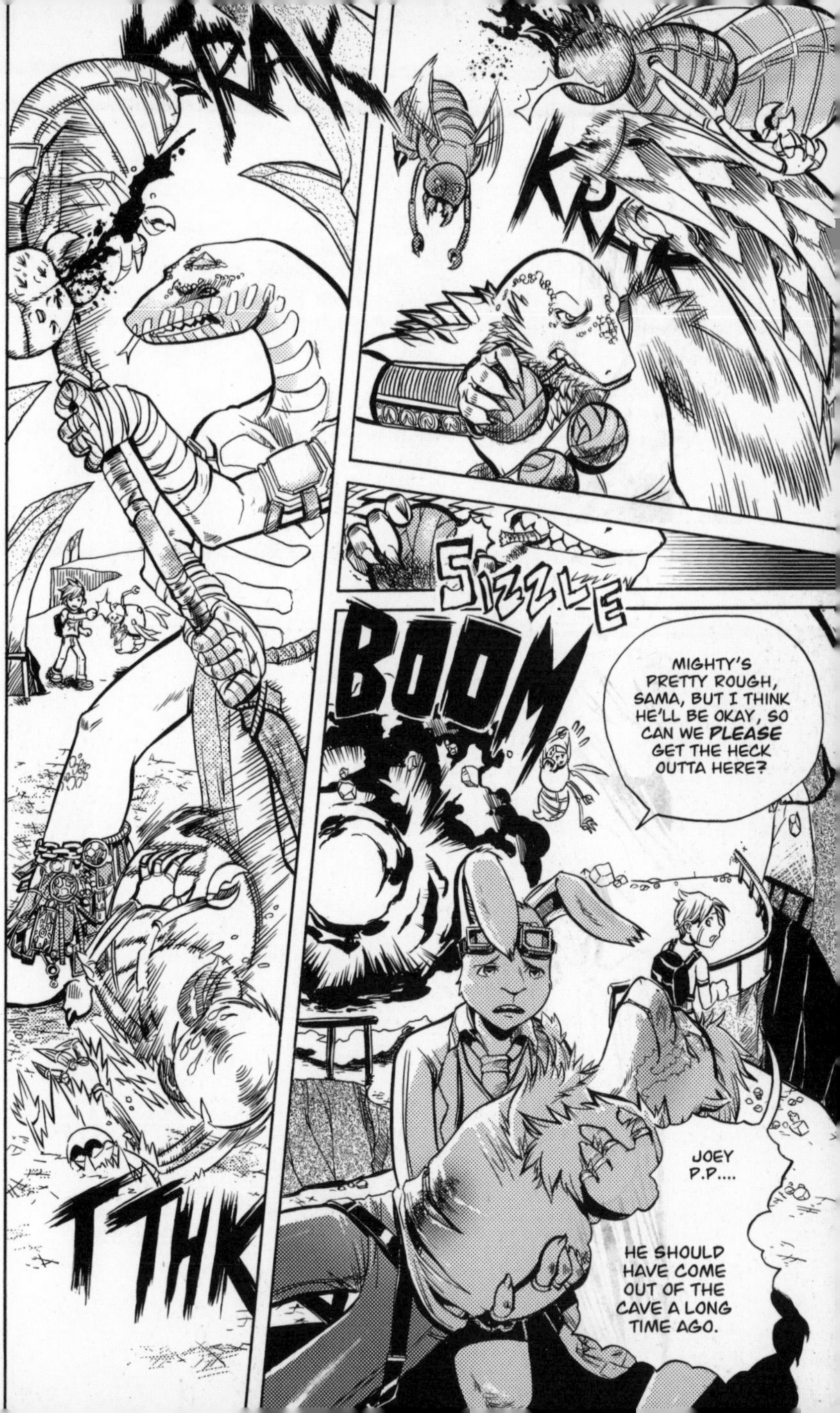
KRAK
TTHK
KRAK
SIZZLE
BOOM
MIGHTY'S PRETTY ROUGH, SAMA, BUT I THINK HE'LL BE OKAY, SO CAN WE *PLEASE* GET THE HECK OUTTA HERE?
JOEY P.P....
HE SHOULD HAVE COME OUT OF THE CAVE A LONG TIME AGO.

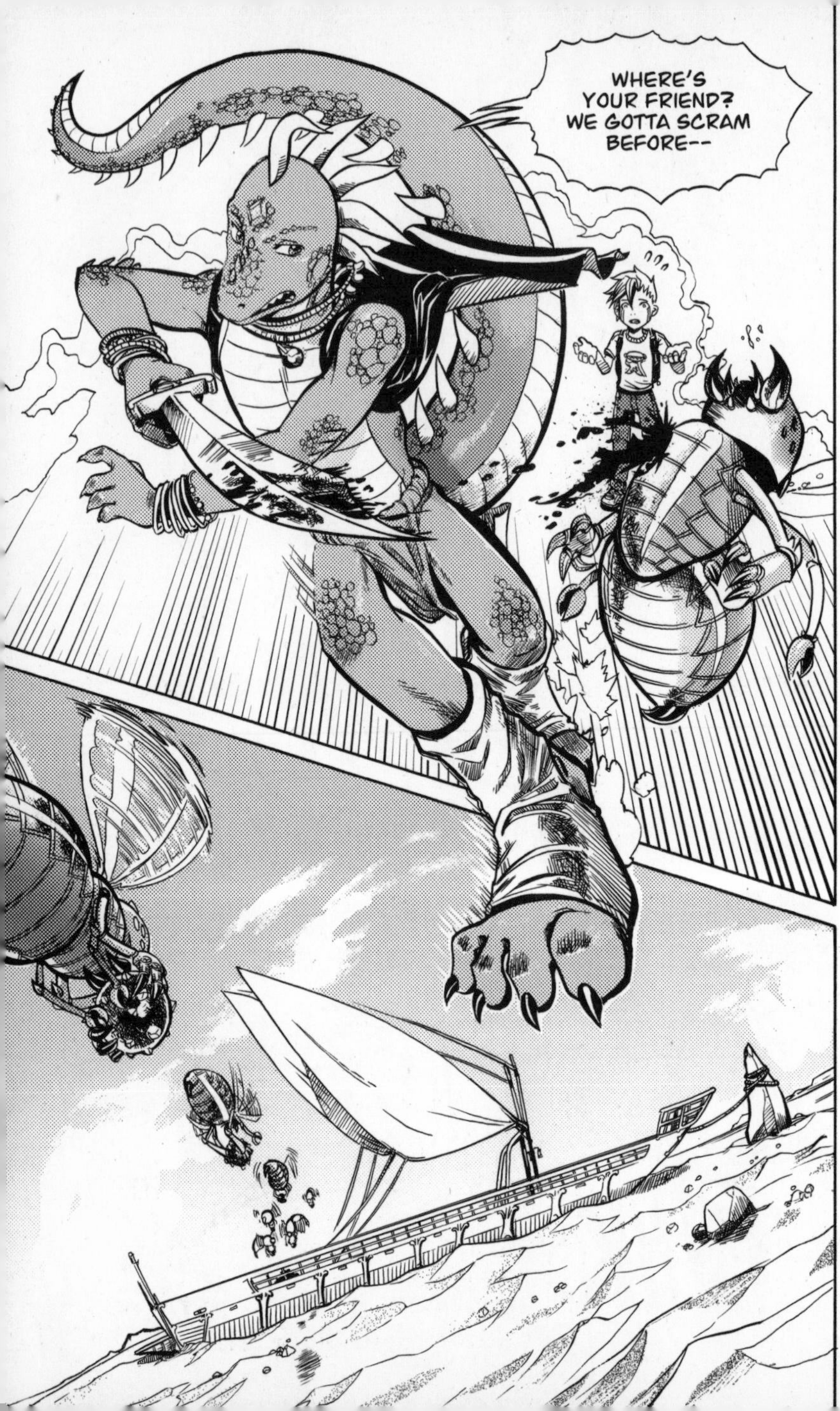
WHERE'S YOUR FRIEND? WE GOTTA SCRAM BEFORE--

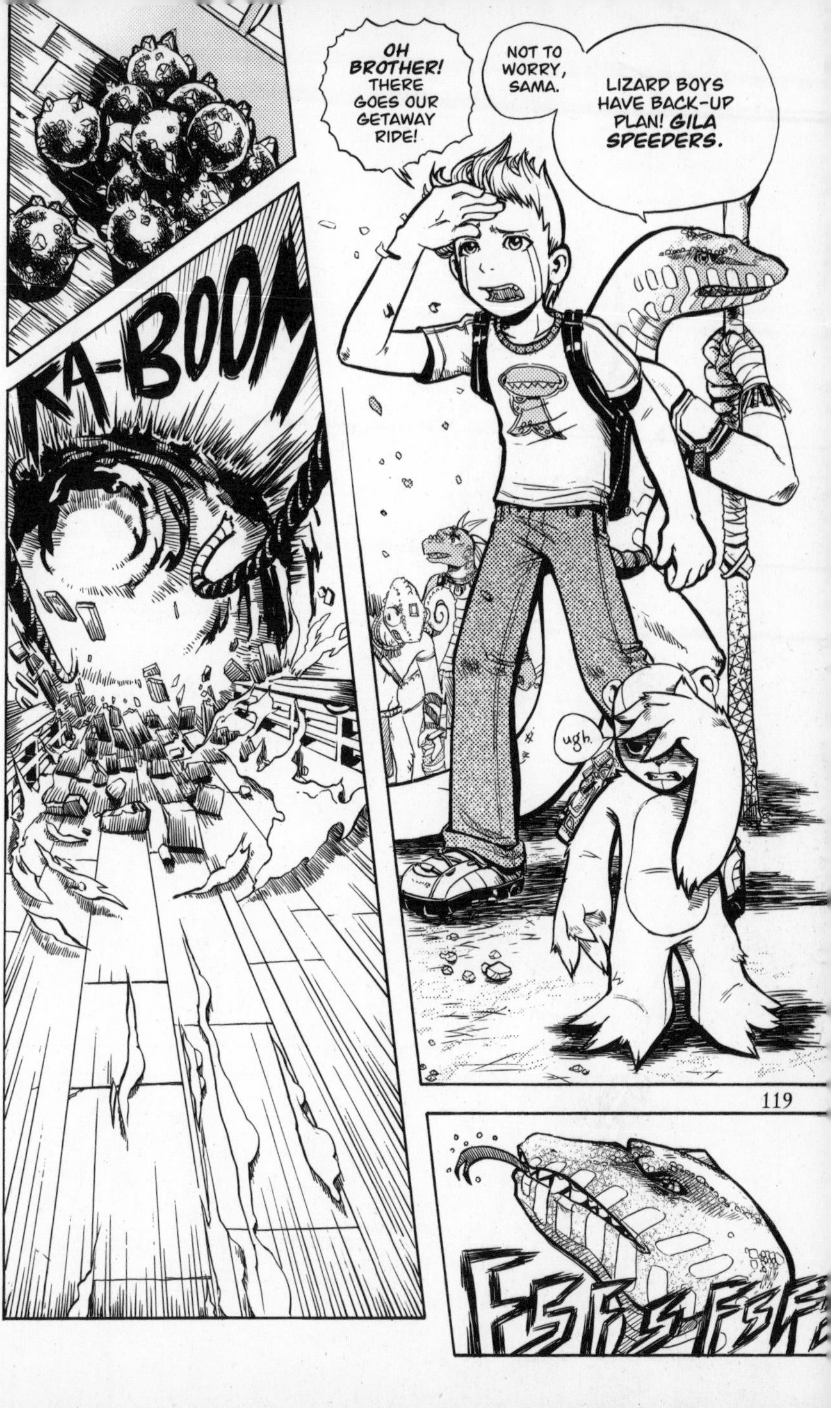
KA-BOOM
OH BROTHER! THERE GOES OUR GETAWAY RIDE!
NOT TO WORRY, SAMA.
LIZARD BOYS HAVE BACK-UP PLAN! GILA SPEEDERS.
ugh.

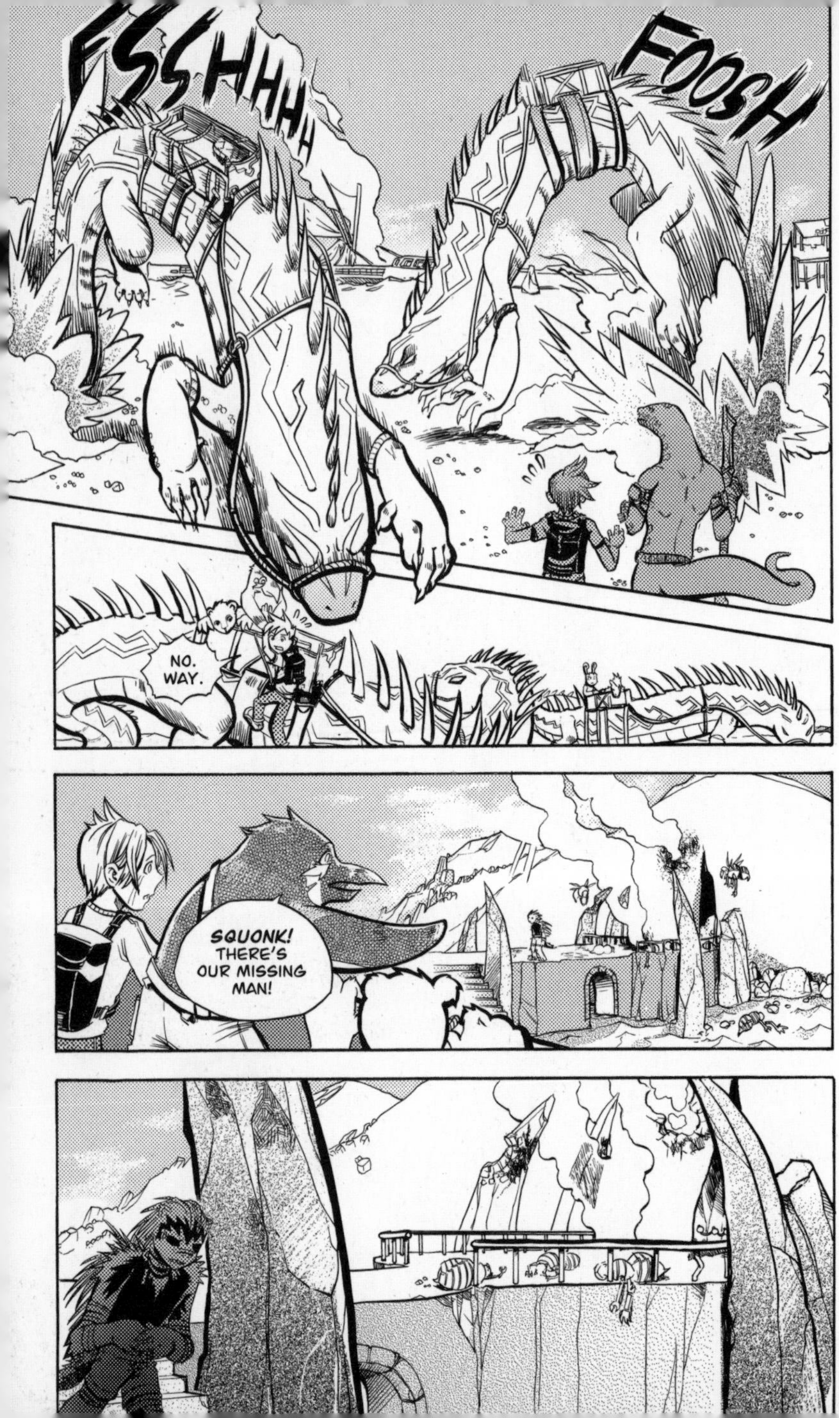
FSSHHHH
FOOSH
NO. WAY.
SQUONK! THERE'S OUR MISSING MAN!

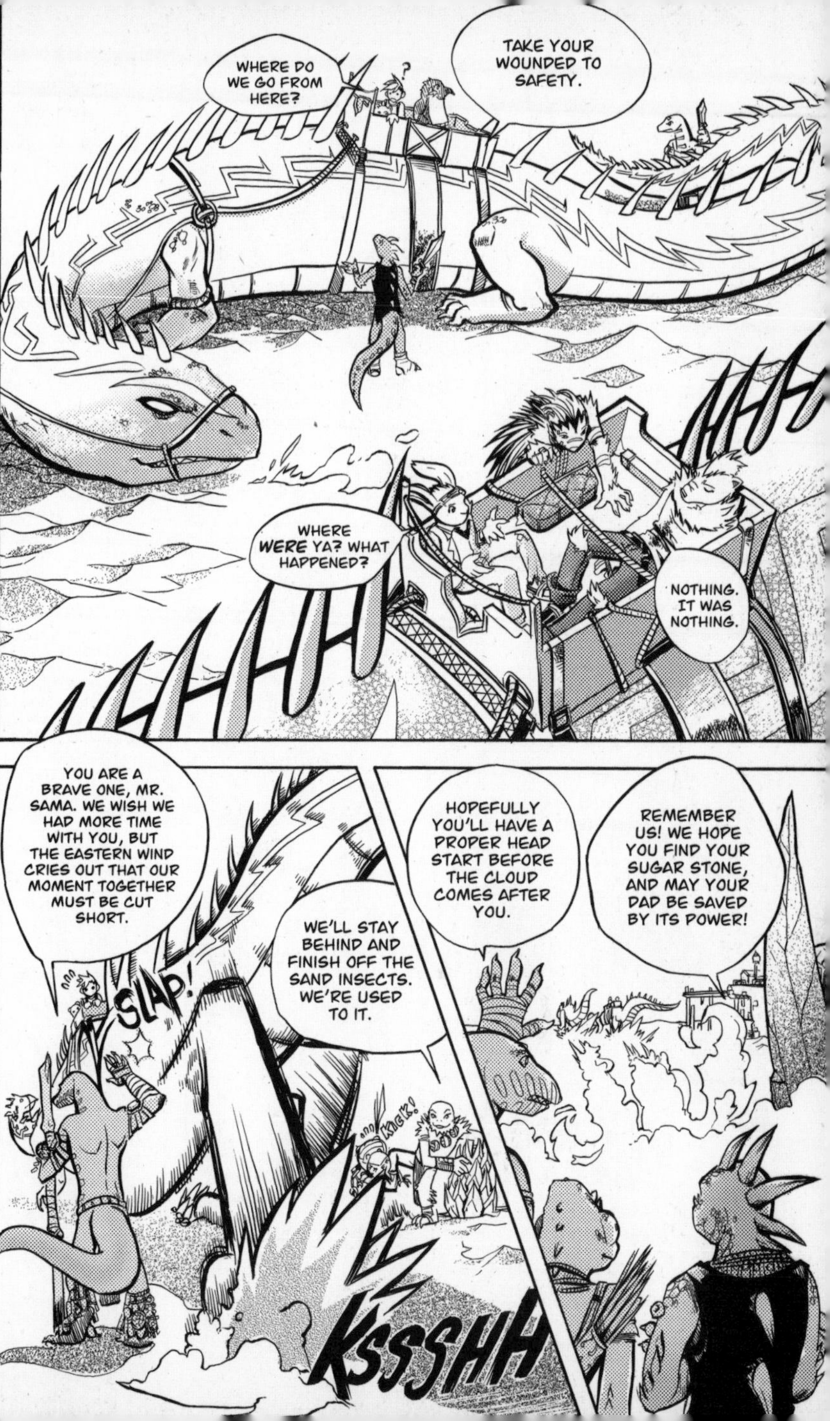
WHERE DO WE GO FROM HERE?
?
TAKE YOUR WOUNDED TO SAFETY.
WHERE WERE YA? WHAT HAPPENED?
NOTHING. IT WAS NOTHING.
YOU ARE A BRAVE ONE, MR. SAMA. WE WISH WE HAD MORE TIME WITH YOU, BUT THE EASTERN WIND CRIES OUT THAT OUR MOMENT TOGETHER MUST BE CUT SHORT.
SLAP!
WE'LL STAY BEHIND AND FINISH OFF THE SAND INSECTS. WE'RE USED TO IT.
KSSSHH
HOPEFULLY YOU'LL HAVE A PROPER HEAD START BEFORE THE CLOUD COMES AFTER YOU.
REMEMBER US! WE HOPE YOU FIND YOUR SUGAR STONE, AND MAY YOUR DAD BE SAVED BY ITS POWER!

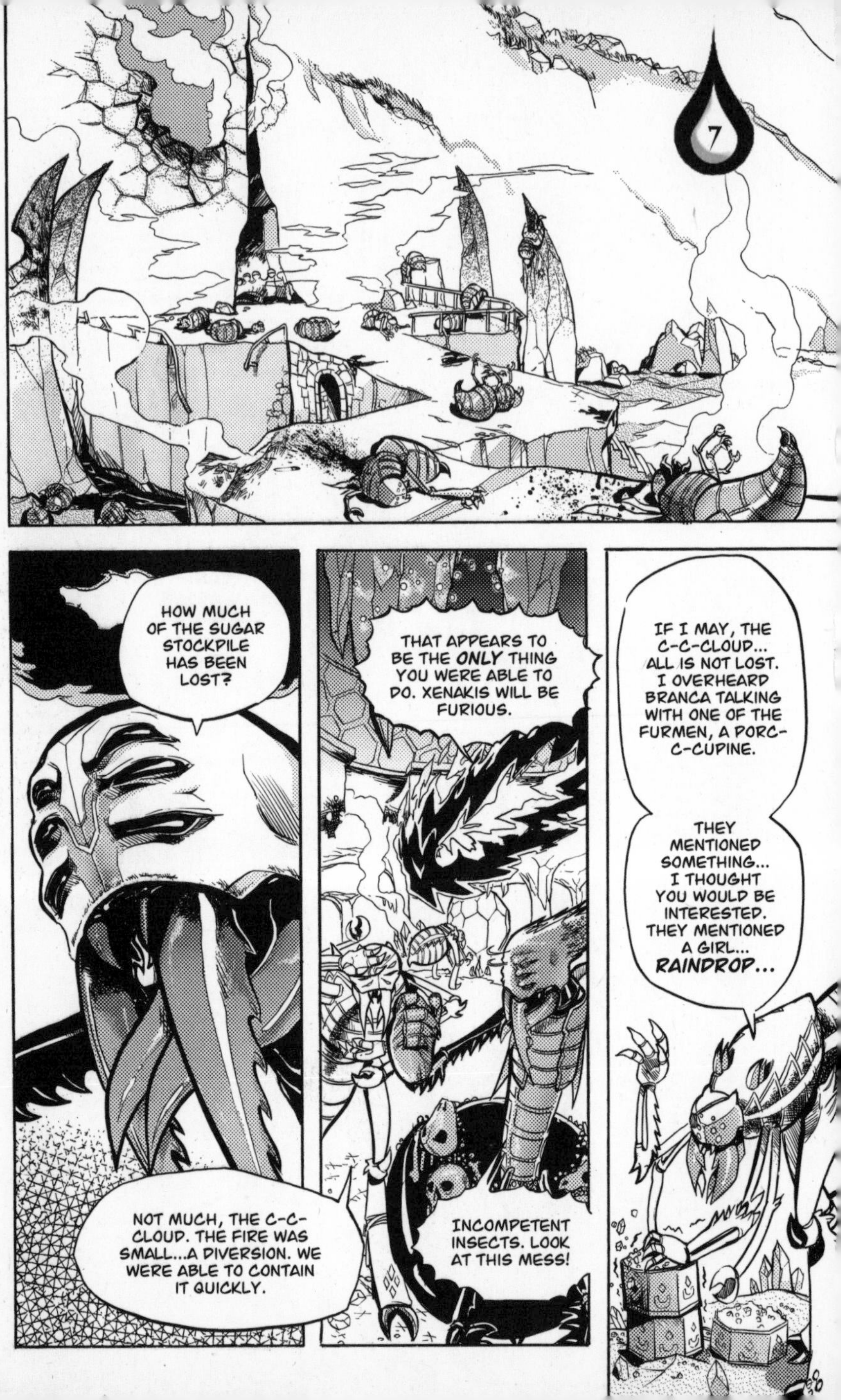
7
HOW MUCH OF THE SUGAR STOCKPILE HAS BEEN LOST?
NOT MUCH, THE C-C-CLOUD. THE FIRE WAS SMALL...A DIVERSION. WE WERE ABLE TO CONTAIN IT QUICKLY.
THAT APPEARS TO BE THE ONLY THING YOU WERE ABLE TO DO. XENAKIS WILL BE FURIOUS.
INCOMPETENT INSECTS. LOOK AT THIS MESS!
IF I MAY, THE C-C-CLOUD... ALL IS NOT LOST. I OVERHEARD BRANCA TALKING WITH ONE OF THE FURMEN, A PORC-C-CUPINE.
THEY MENTIONED SOMETHING... I THOUGHT YOU WOULD BE INTERESTED. THEY MENTIONED A GIRL... RAINDROP...

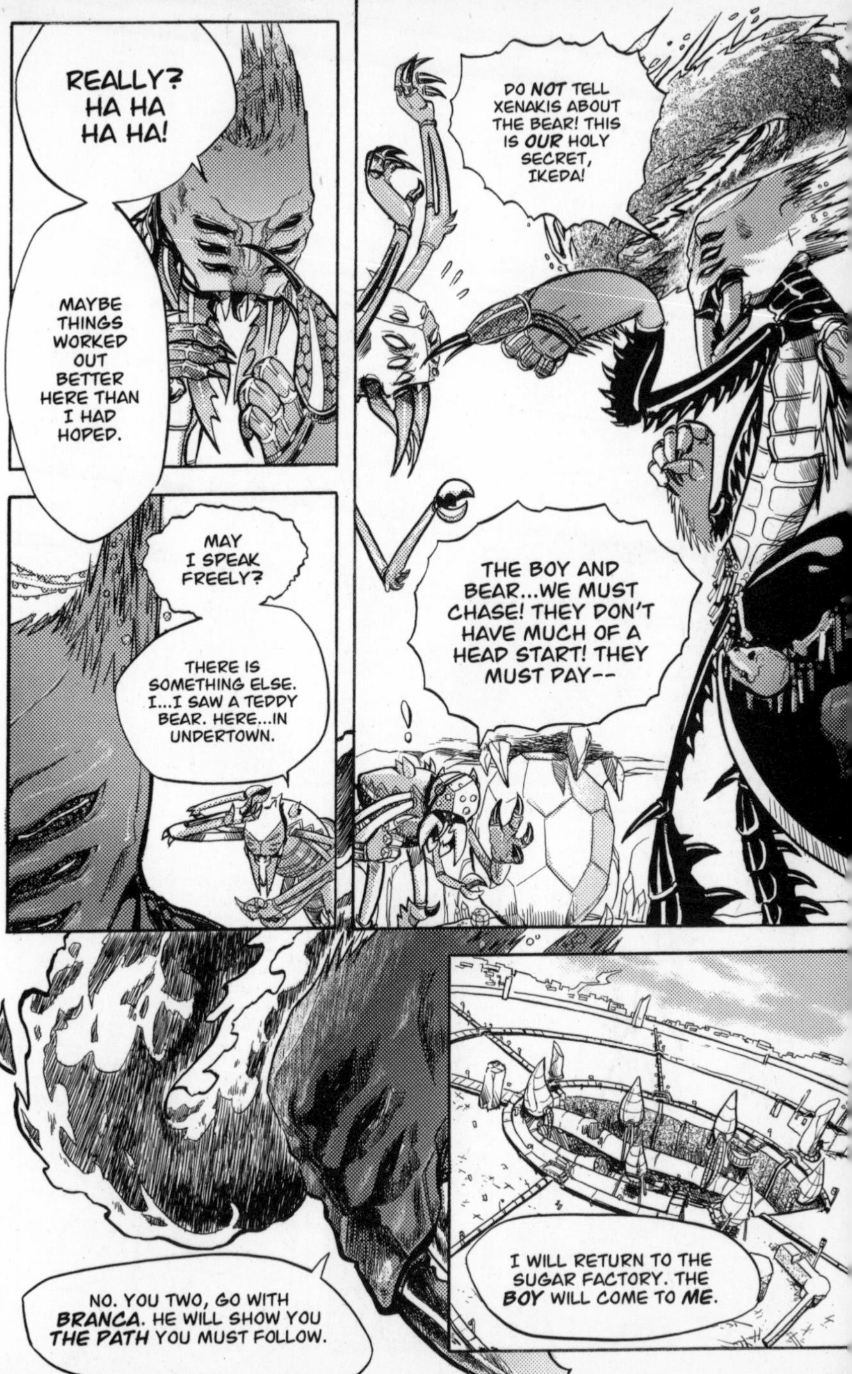
REALLY? HA HA HA HA!
MAYBE THINGS WORKED OUT BETTER HERE THAN I HAD HOPED.
MAY I SPEAK FREELY?
THERE IS SOMETHING ELSE. I...I SAW A TEDDY BEAR. HERE...IN UNDERTOWN.
DO NOT TELL XENAKIS ABOUT THE BEAR! THIS IS OUR HOLY SECRET, IKEDA!
THE BOY AND BEAR...WE MUST CHASE! THEY DON'T HAVE MUCH OF A HEAD START! THEY MUST PAY--
!
NO. YOU TWO, GO WITH BRANCA. HE WILL SHOW YOU THE PATH YOU MUST FOLLOW.
I WILL RETURN TO THE SUGAR FACTORY. THE BOY WILL COME TO ME.

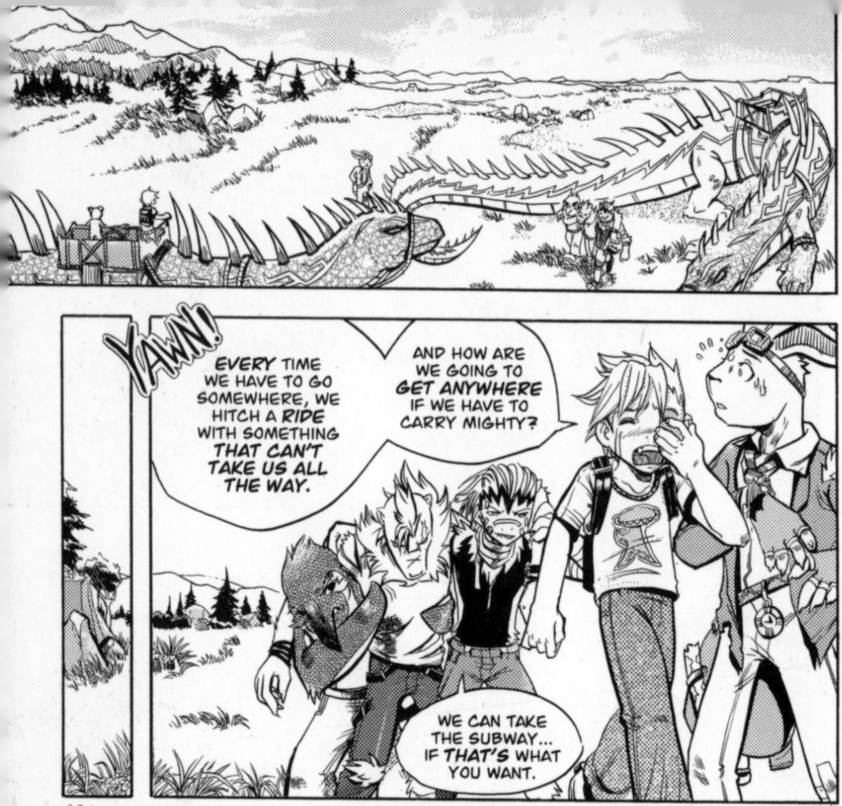
YAWN!
EVERY TIME WE HAVE TO GO SOMEWHERE, WE HITCH A RIDE WITH SOMETHING THAT CAN'T TAKE US ALL THE WAY.
AND HOW ARE WE GOING TO GET ANYWHERE IF WE HAVE TO CARRY MIGHTY?
WE CAN TAKE THE SUBWAY... IF THAT'S WHAT YOU WANT.

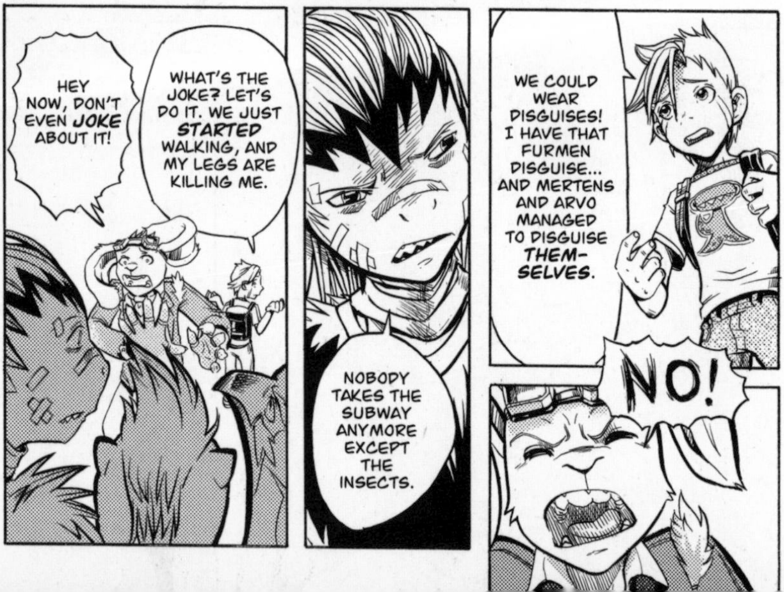
HEY NOW, DON'T EVEN JOKE ABOUT IT!
WHAT'S THE JOKE? LET'S DO IT. WE JUST STARTED WALKING, AND MY LEGS ARE KILLING ME.
NOBODY TAKES THE SUBWAY ANYMORE EXCEPT THE INSECTS.
WE COULD WEAR DISGUISES! I HAVE THAT FURMEN DISGUISE... AND MERTENS AND ARVO MANAGED TO DISGUISE THEM-SELVES.
NO!

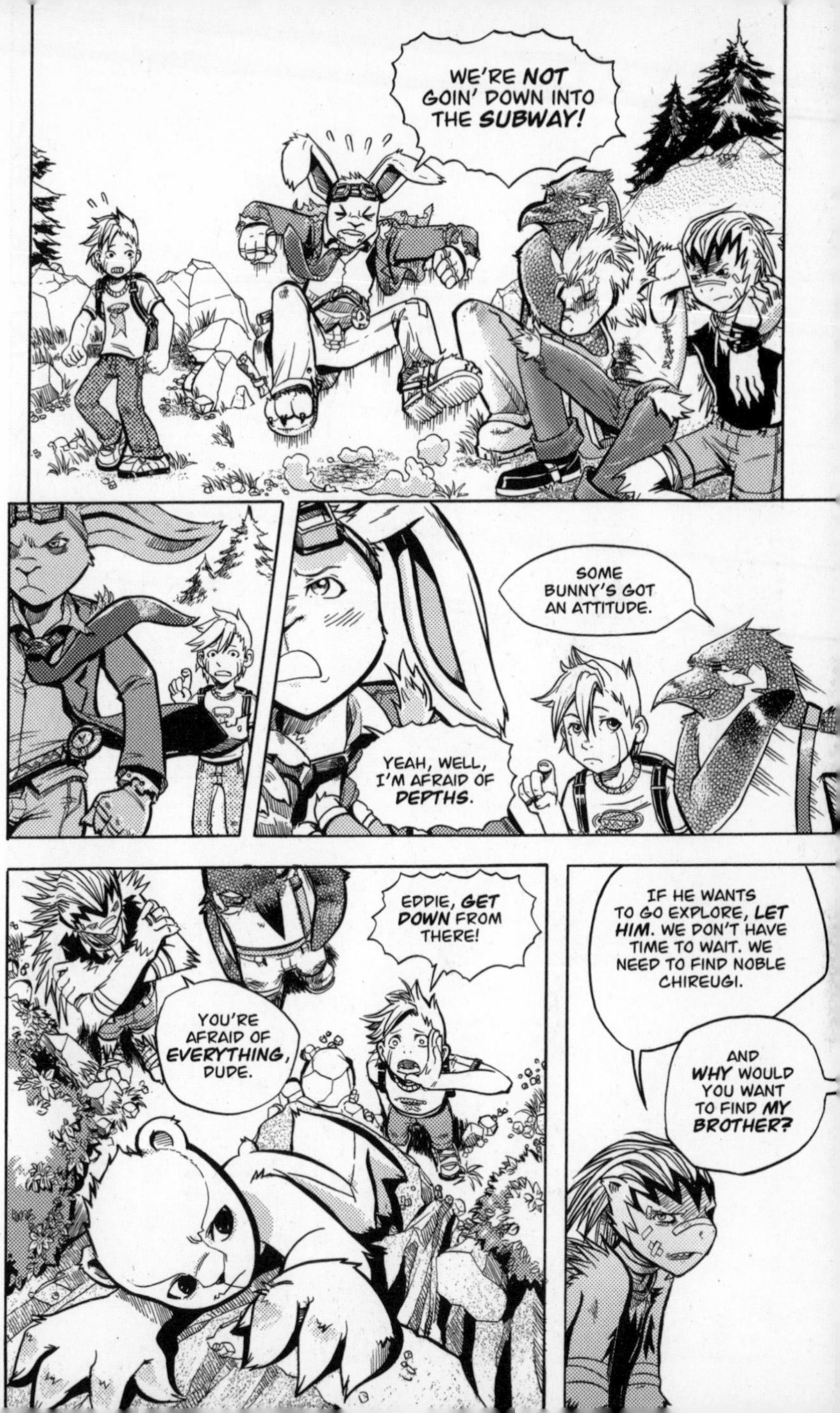
WE'RE NOT GOIN' DOWN INTO THE SUBWAY!
SOME BUNNY'S GOT AN ATTITUDE.
YEAH, WELL, I'M AFRAID OF DEPTHS.
EDDIE, GET DOWN FROM THERE!
YOU'RE AFRAID OF EVERYTHING, DUDE.
IF HE WANTS TO GO EXPLORE, LET HIM. WE DON'T HAVE TIME TO WAIT. WE NEED TO FIND NOBLE CHIREUGI.
AND WHY WOULD YOU WANT TO FIND MY BROTHER?

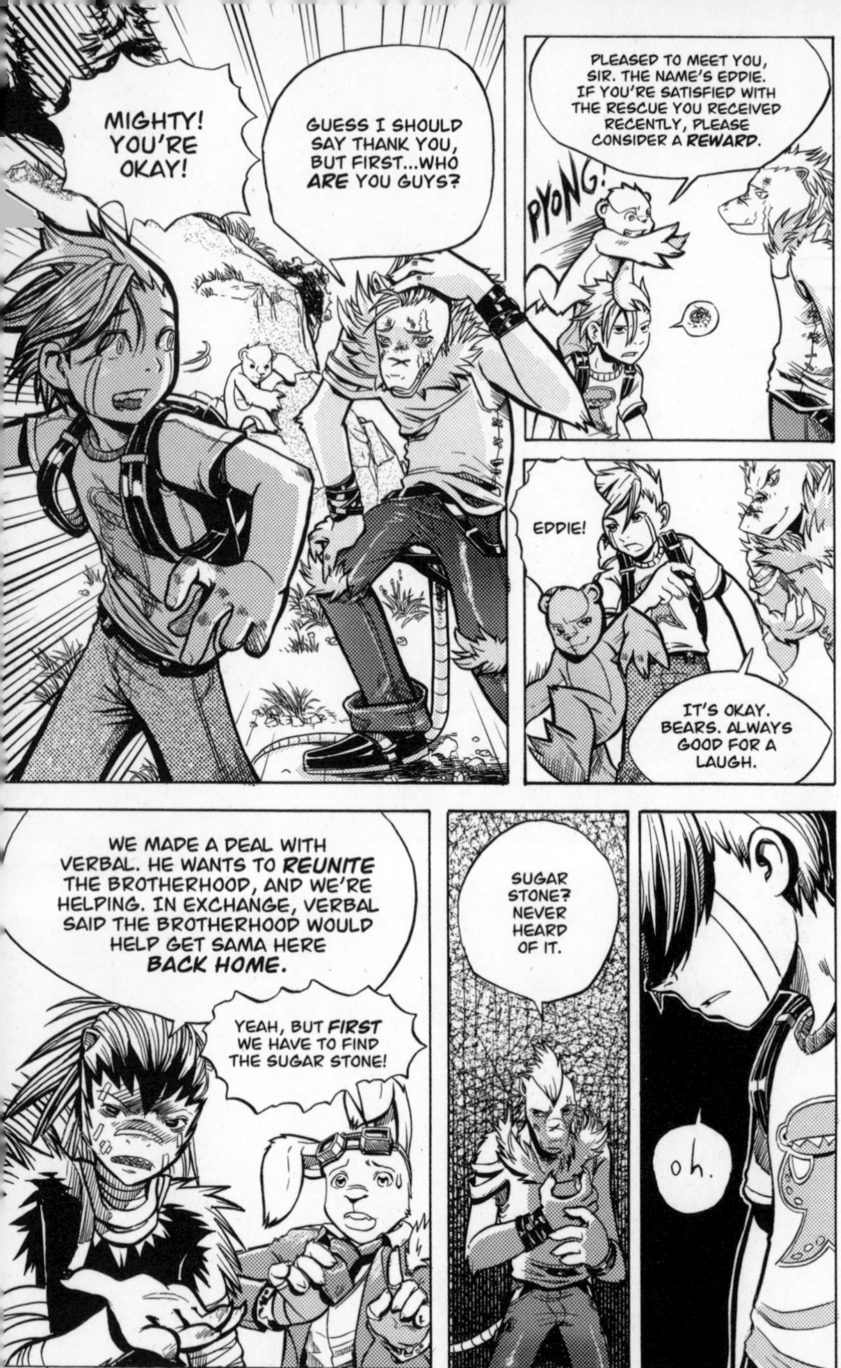
MIGHTY! YOU'RE OKAY!
GUESS I SHOULD SAY THANK YOU, BUT FIRST...WHO ARE YOU GUYS?
PLEASED TO MEET YOU, SIR. THE NAME'S EDDIE. IF YOU'RE SATISFIED WITH THE RESCUE YOU RECEIVED RECENTLY, PLEASE CONSIDER A REWARD.
PYONG!
EDDIE!
IT'S OKAY. BEARS. ALWAYS GOOD FOR A LAUGH.
WE MADE A DEAL WITH VERBAL. HE WANTS TO REUNITE THE BROTHERHOOD, AND WE'RE HELPING. IN EXCHANGE, VERBAL SAID THE BROTHERHOOD WOULD HELP GET SAMA HERE BACK HOME.
YEAH, BUT FIRST WE HAVE TO FIND THE SUGAR STONE!
SUGAR STONE? NEVER HEARD OF IT.
oh.

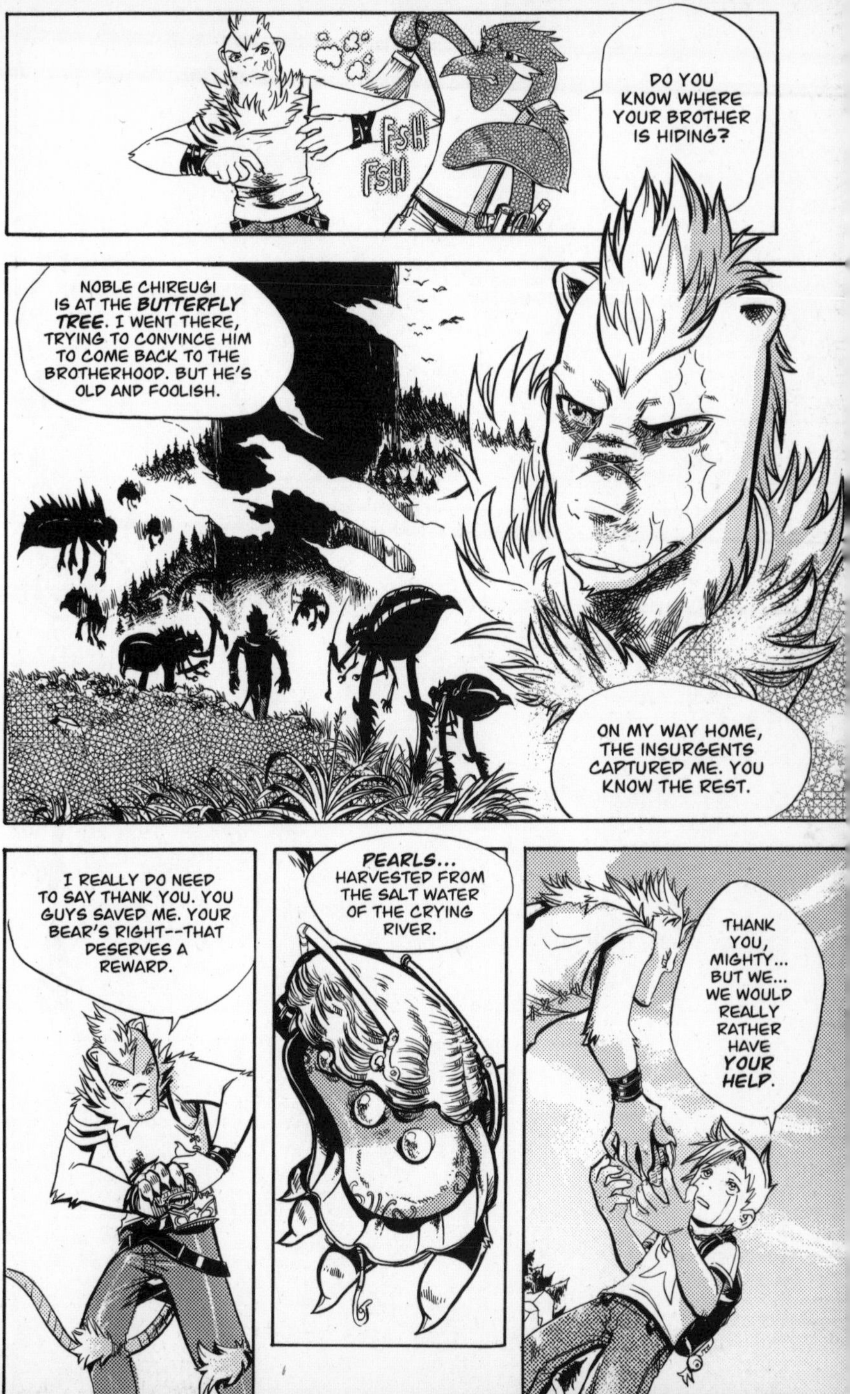
FSH FSH
DO YOU KNOW WHERE YOUR BROTHER IS HIDING?
NOBLE CHIREUGI IS AT THE **BUTTERFLY TREE**. I WENT THERE, TRYING TO CONVINCE HIM TO COME BACK TO THE BROTHERHOOD. BUT HE'S OLD AND FOOLISH.
ON MY WAY HOME, THE INSURGENTS CAPTURED ME. YOU KNOW THE REST.
I REALLY DO NEED TO SAY THANK YOU. YOU GUYS SAVED ME. YOUR BEAR'S RIGHT--THAT DESERVES A REWARD.
PEARLS... HARVESTED FROM THE SALT WATER OF THE CRYING RIVER.
THANK YOU, MIGHTY... BUT WE... WE WOULD REALLY RATHER HAVE ***YOUR HELP***.

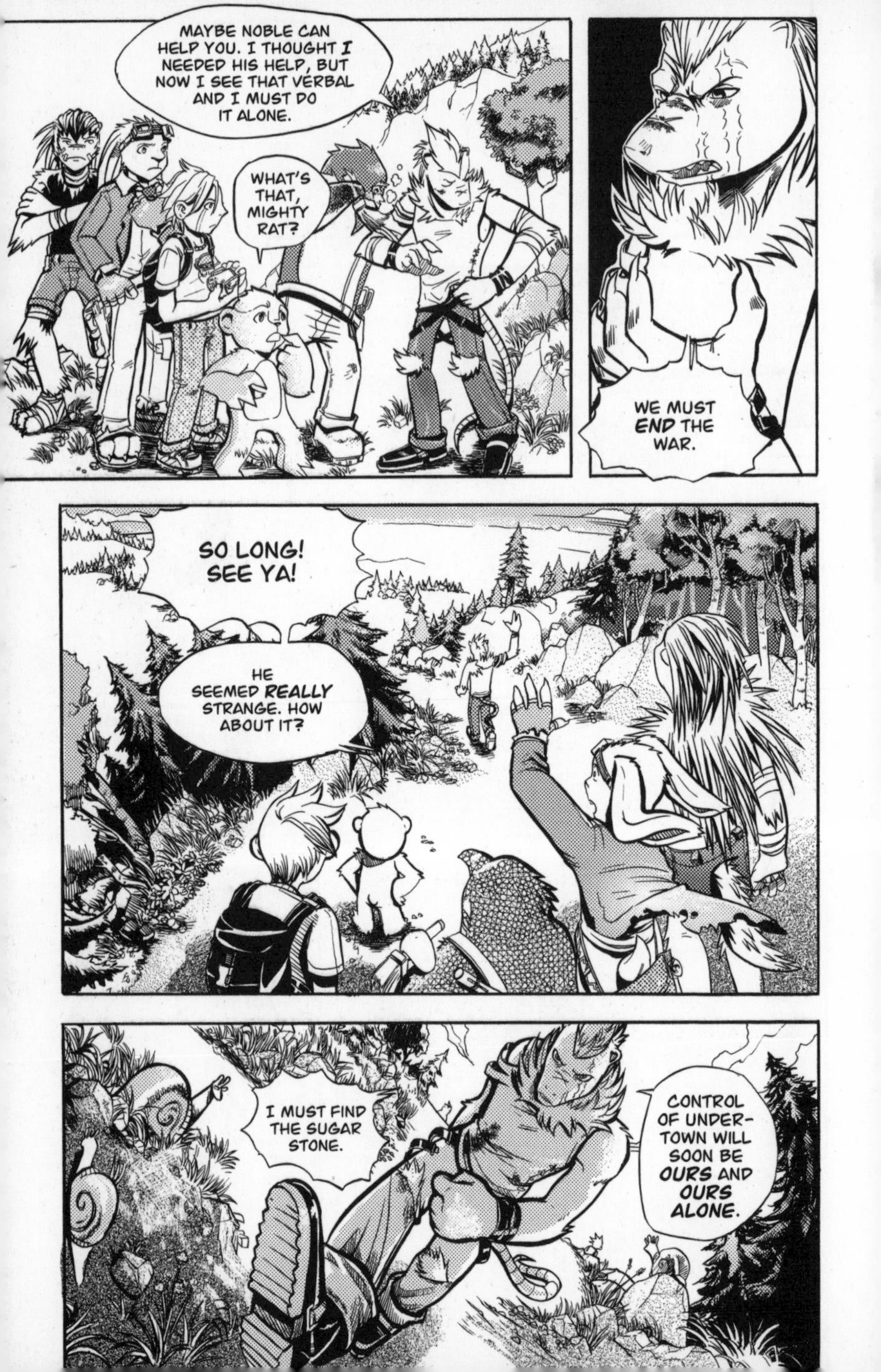
MAYBE NOBLE CAN HELP YOU. I THOUGHT I NEEDED HIS HELP, BUT NOW I SEE THAT VERBAL AND I MUST DO IT ALONE.
WHAT'S THAT, MIGHTY RAT?
WE MUST END THE WAR.
SO LONG! SEE YA!
HE SEEMED REALLY STRANGE. HOW ABOUT IT?
I MUST FIND THE SUGAR STONE.
CONTROL OF UNDER-TOWN WILL SOON BE OURS AND OURS ALONE.

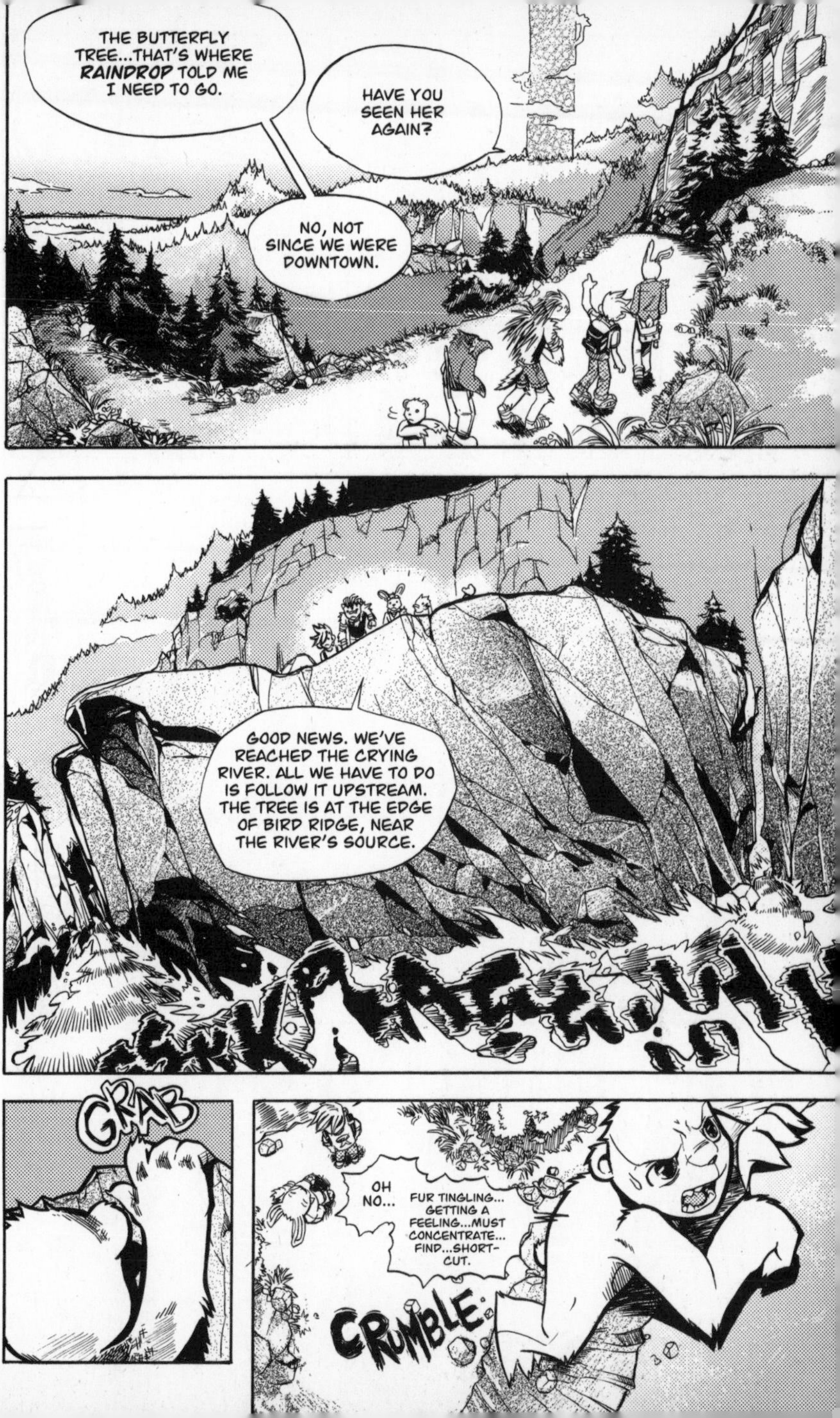
THE BUTTERFLY TREE...THAT'S WHERE RAINDROP TOLD ME I NEED TO GO.
HAVE YOU SEEN HER AGAIN?
NO, NOT SINCE WE WERE DOWNTOWN.
GOOD NEWS. WE'VE REACHED THE CRYING RIVER. ALL WE HAVE TO DO IS FOLLOW IT UPSTREAM. THE TREE IS AT THE EDGE OF BIRD RIDGE, NEAR THE RIVER'S SOURCE.
GRAB
OH NO...
FUR TINGLING... GETTING A FEELING...MUST CONCENTRATE... FIND...SHORT-CUT.
CRUMBLE

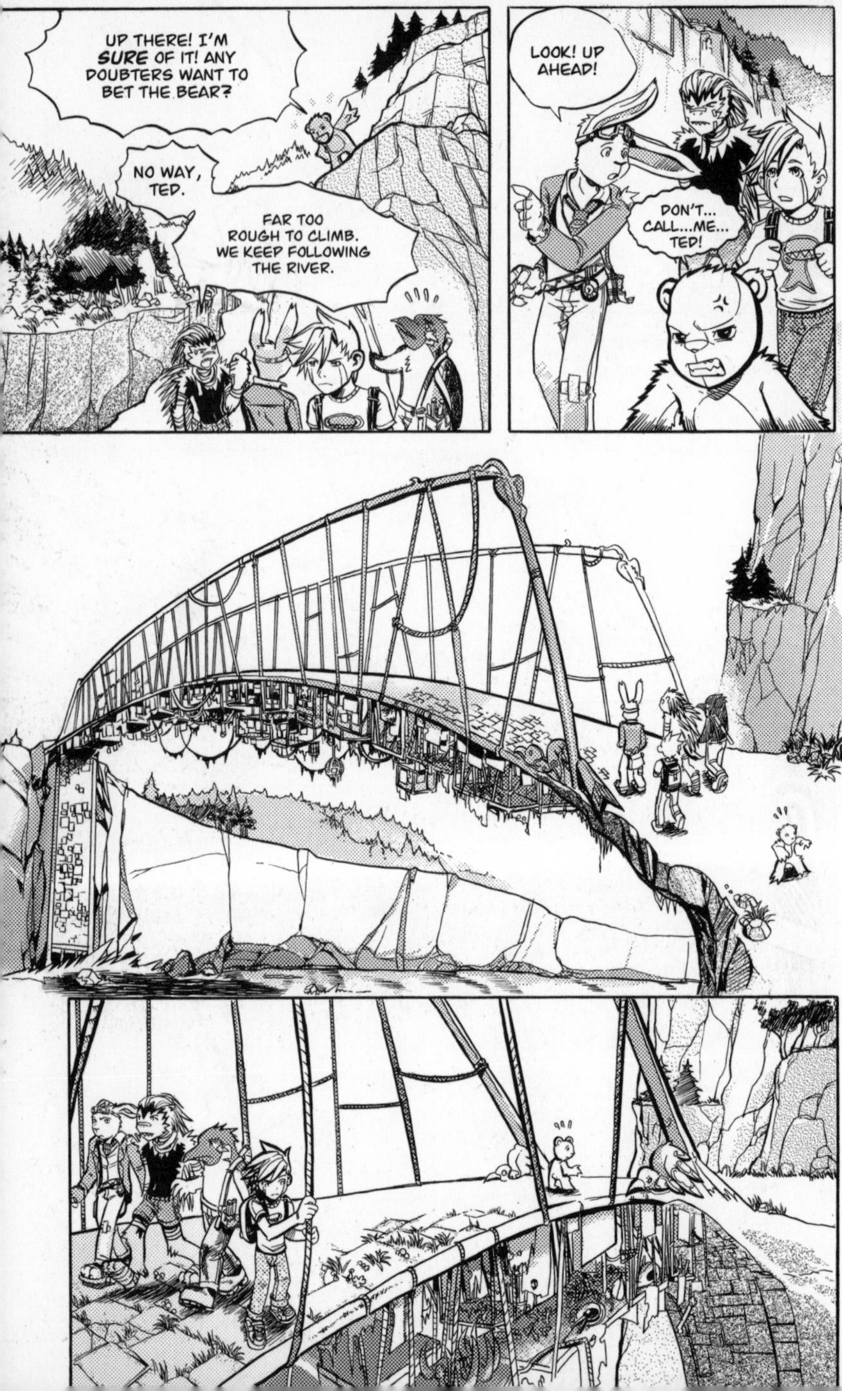
UP THERE! I'M SURE OF IT! ANY DOUBTERS WANT TO BET THE BEAR?
NO WAY, TED.
FAR TOO ROUGH TO CLIMB. WE KEEP FOLLOWING THE RIVER.
LOOK! UP AHEAD!
DON'T... CALL...ME... TED!

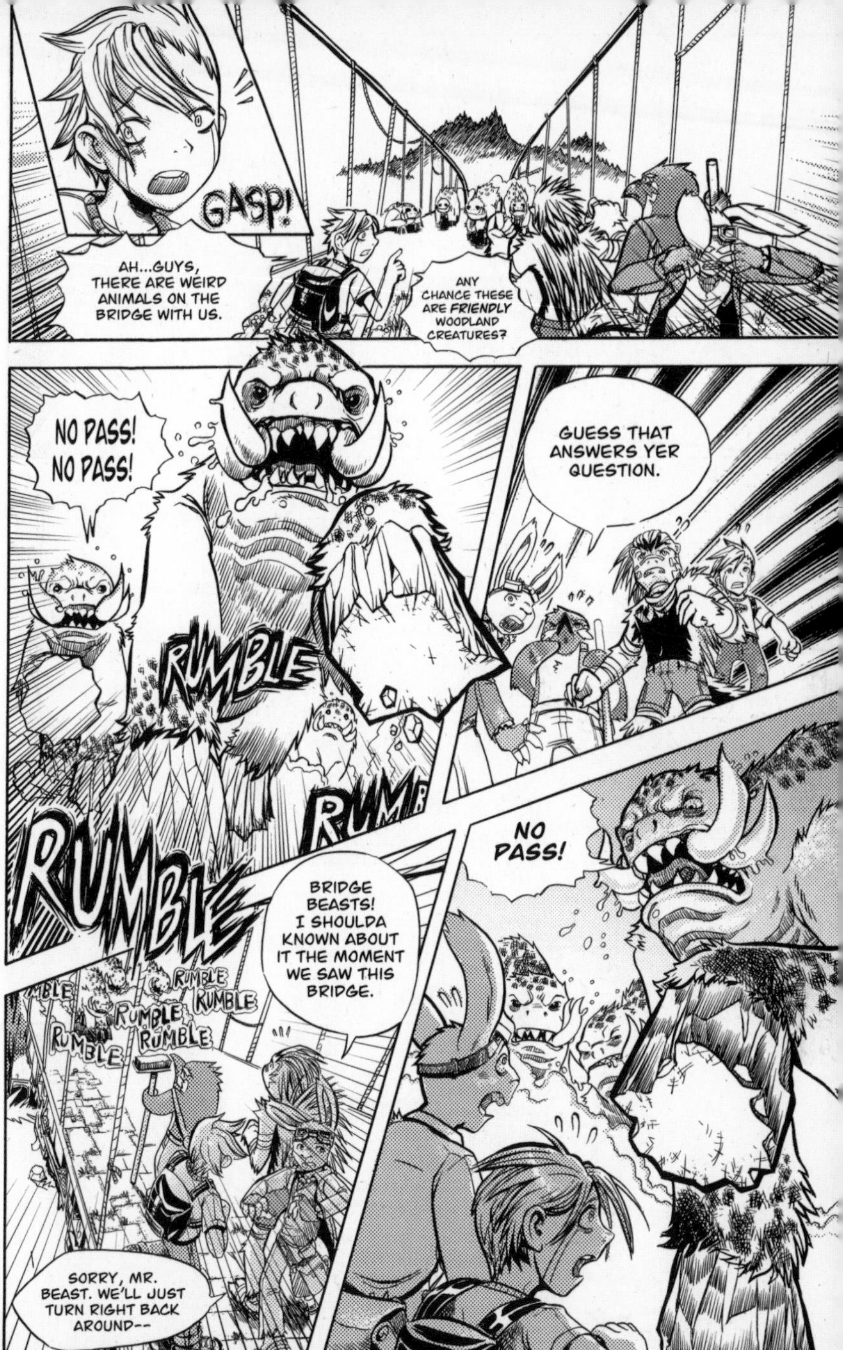
GASP!
AH...GUYS, THERE ARE WEIRD ANIMALS ON THE BRIDGE WITH US.
ANY CHANCE THESE ARE FRIENDLY WOODLAND CREATURES?
NO PASS! NO PASS!
RUMBLE
RUMBLE
RUMB
GUESS THAT ANSWERS YER QUESTION.
RUMBLE RUMBLE
RUMBLE RUMBLE
RUMBLE RUMBLE
BRIDGE BEASTS! I SHOULDA KNOWN ABOUT IT THE MOMENT WE SAW THIS BRIDGE.
SORRY, MR. BEAST. WE'LL JUST TURN RIGHT BACK AROUND--
NO PASS!

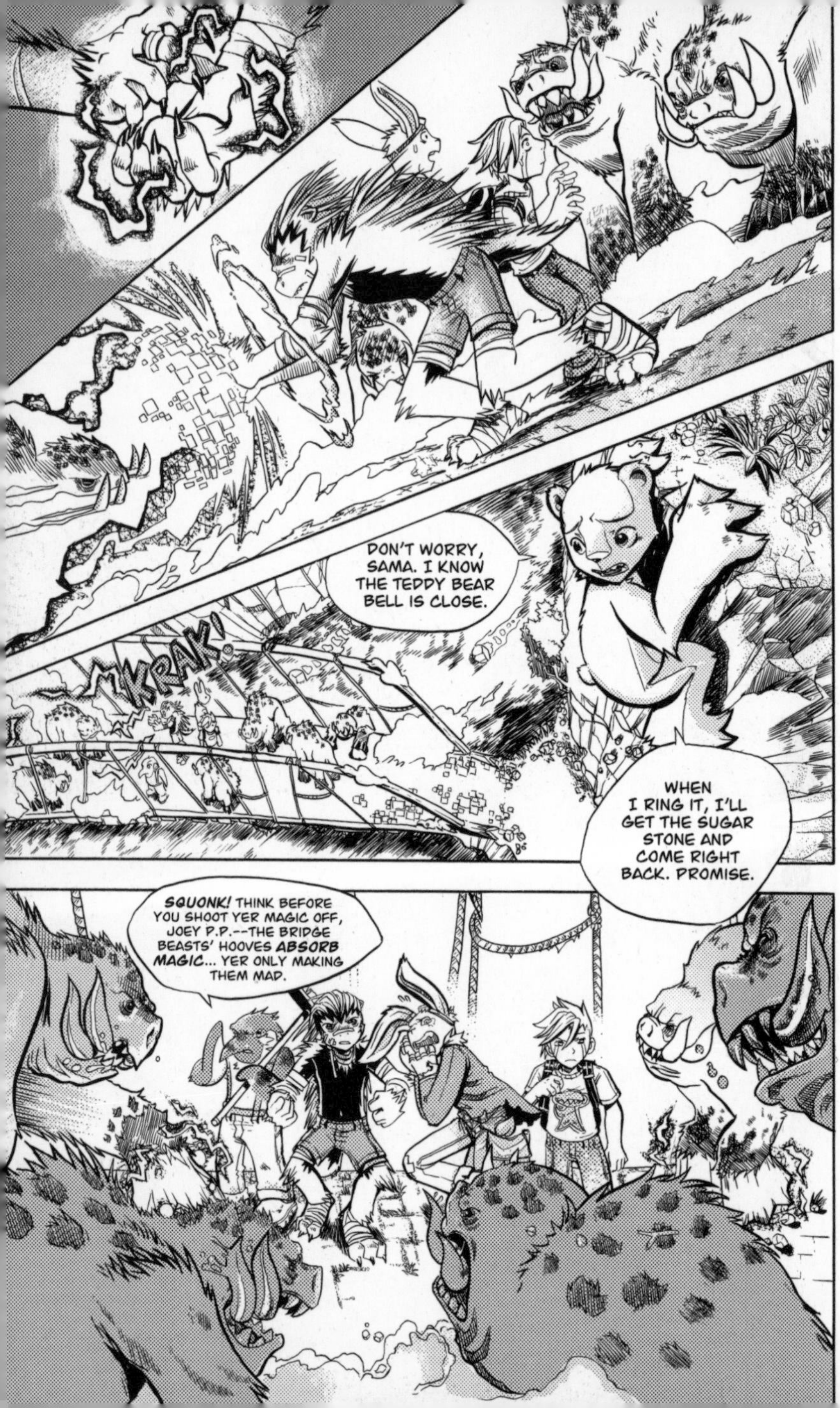
KRAK!
DON'T WORRY, SAMA. I KNOW THE TEDDY BEAR BELL IS CLOSE.
WHEN I RING IT, I'LL GET THE SUGAR STONE AND COME RIGHT BACK. PROMISE.
SQUONK! THINK BEFORE YOU SHOOT YER MAGIC OFF, JOEY P.P.--THE BRIDGE BEASTS' HOOVES ABSORB MAGIC... YER ONLY MAKING THEM MAD.

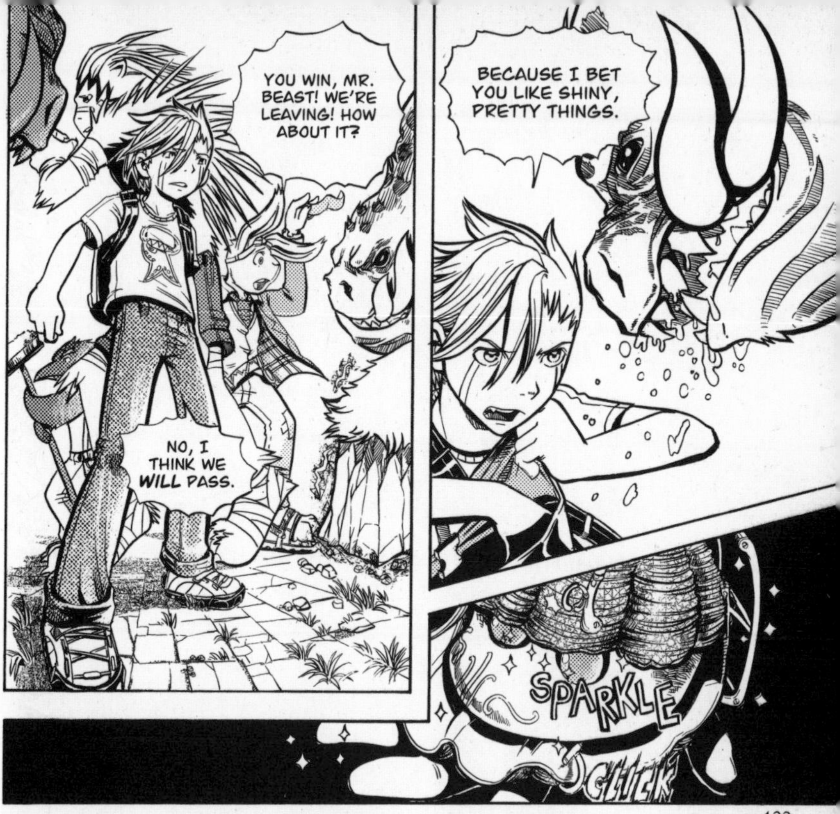
YOU WIN, MR. BEAST! WE'RE LEAVING! HOW ABOUT IT?
NO, I THINK WE **WILL** PASS.
BECAUSE I BET YOU LIKE SHINY, PRETTY THINGS.
SPARKLE
CLICK

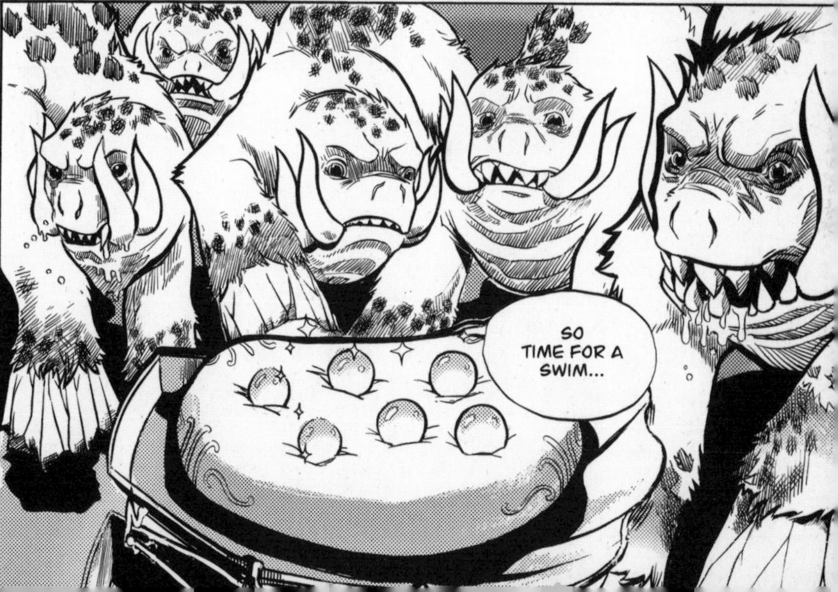
SO TIME FOR A SWIM...

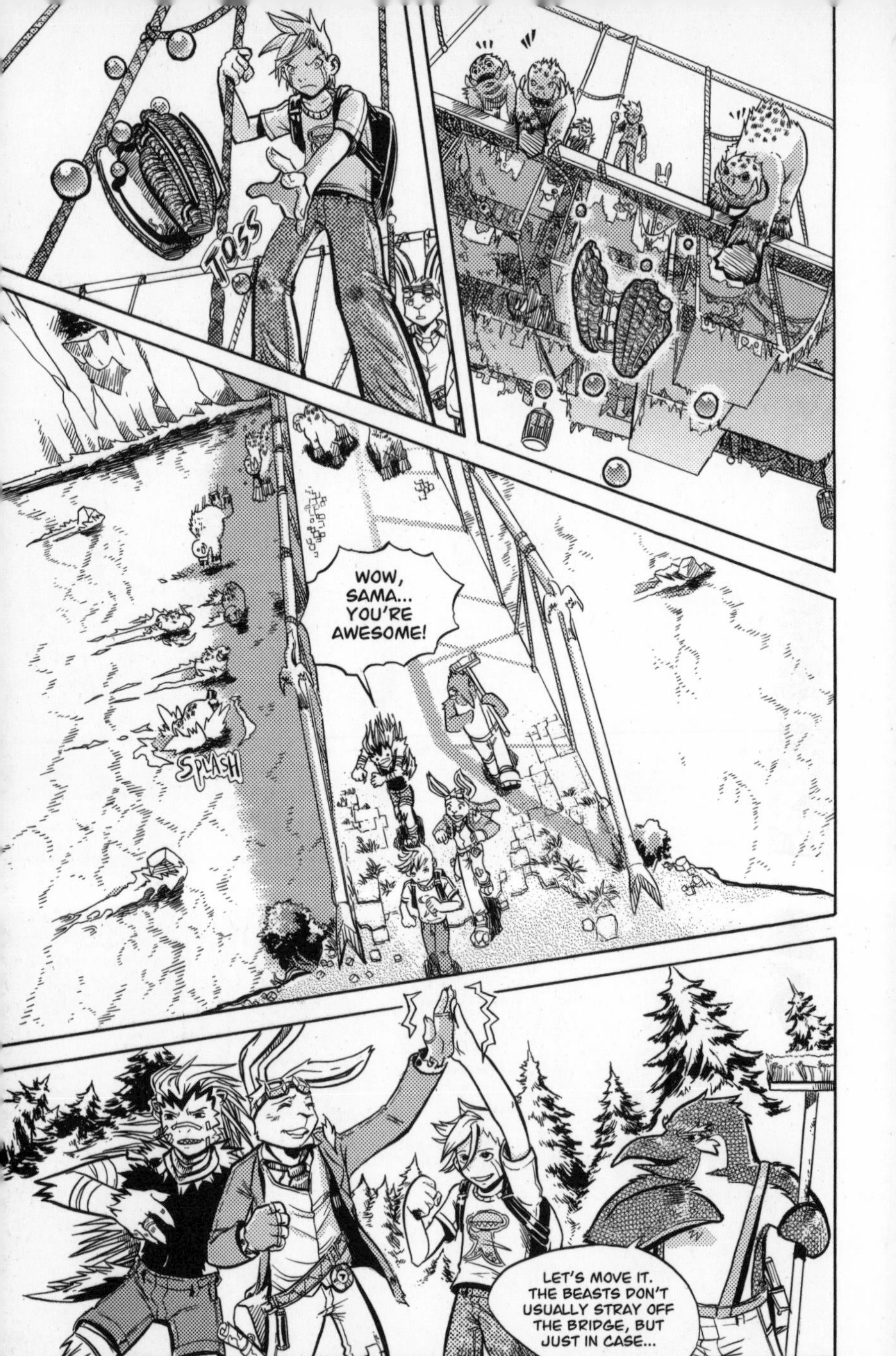
TOSS
SPLASH
WOW, SAMA... YOU'RE AWESOME!
LET'S MOVE IT. THE BEASTS DON'T USUALLY STRAY OFF THE BRIDGE, BUT JUST IN CASE...

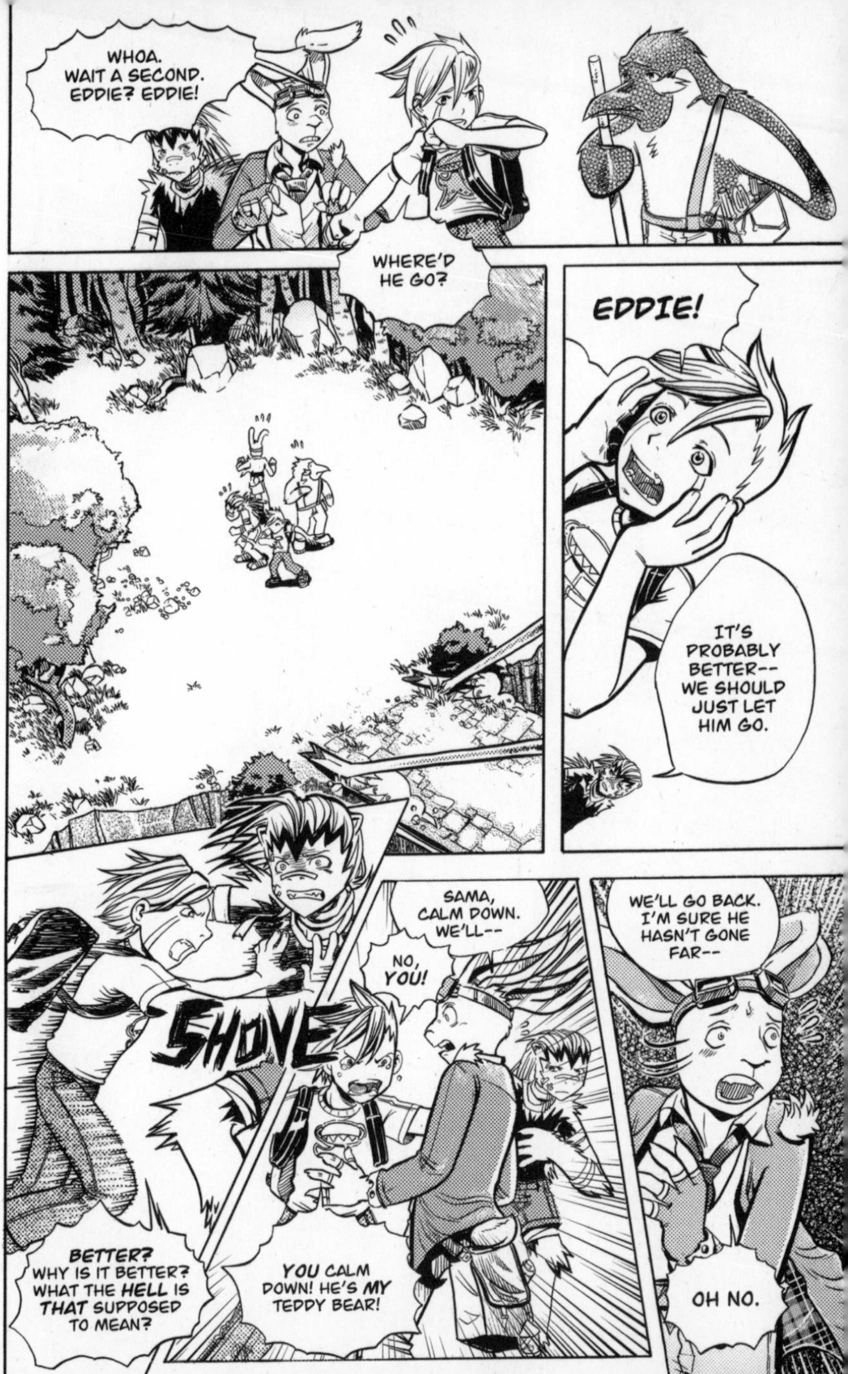
WHOA. WAIT A SECOND. EDDIE? EDDIE!
WHERE'D HE GO?
EDDIE!
IT'S PROBABLY BETTER-- WE SHOULD JUST LET HIM GO.
BETTER? WHY IS IT BETTER? WHAT THE HELL IS THAT SUPPOSED TO MEAN?
SHOVE
SAMA, CALM DOWN. WE'LL--
NO, YOU!
YOU CALM DOWN! HE'S MY TEDDY BEAR!
WE'LL GO BACK. I'M SURE HE HASN'T GONE FAR--
OH NO.

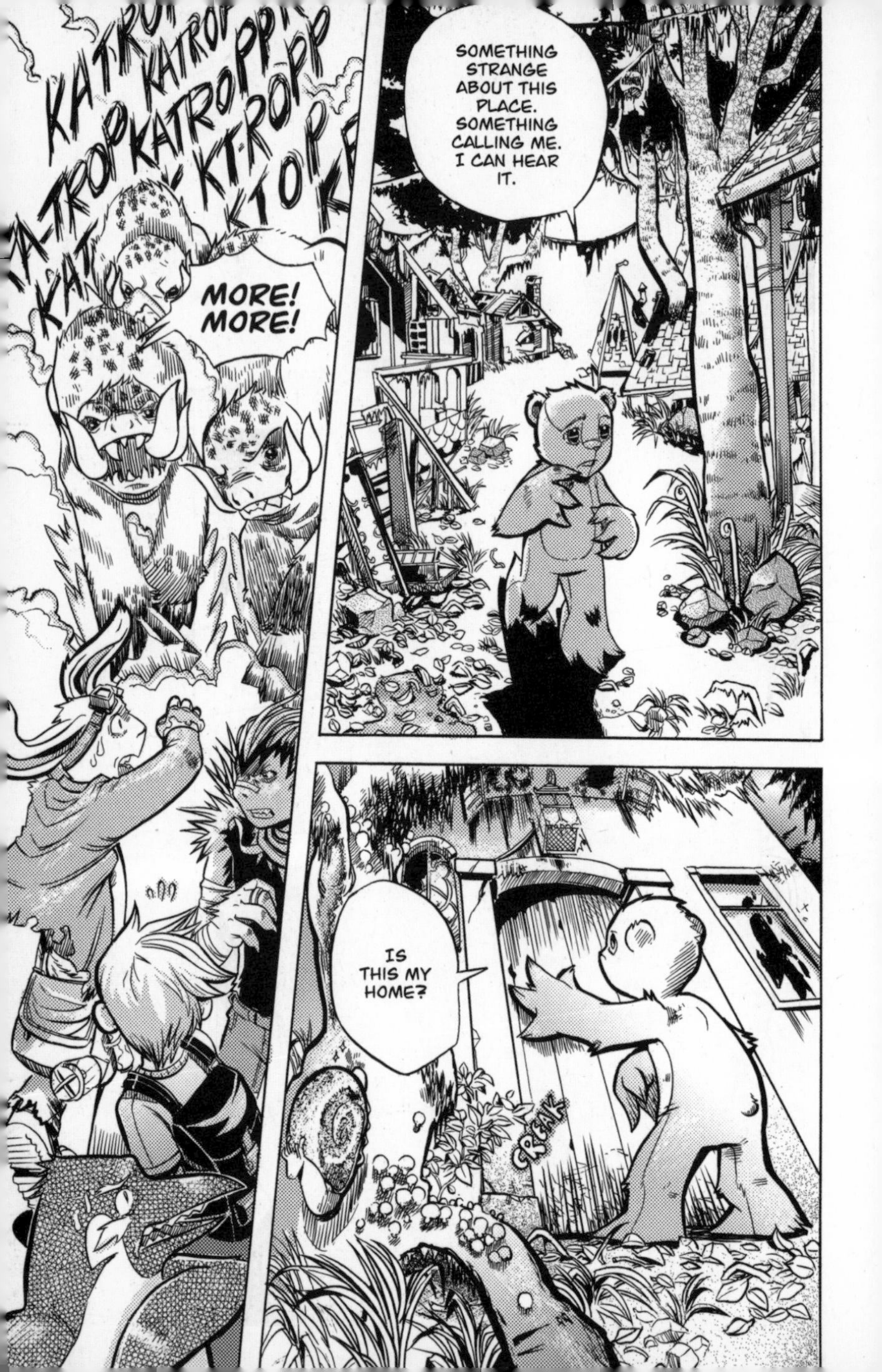
KATROPP
KATROPP
KT-ROPP
MORE! MORE!
SOMETHING STRANGE ABOUT THIS PLACE. SOMETHING CALLING ME. I CAN HEAR IT.
IS THIS MY HOME?
CREAK

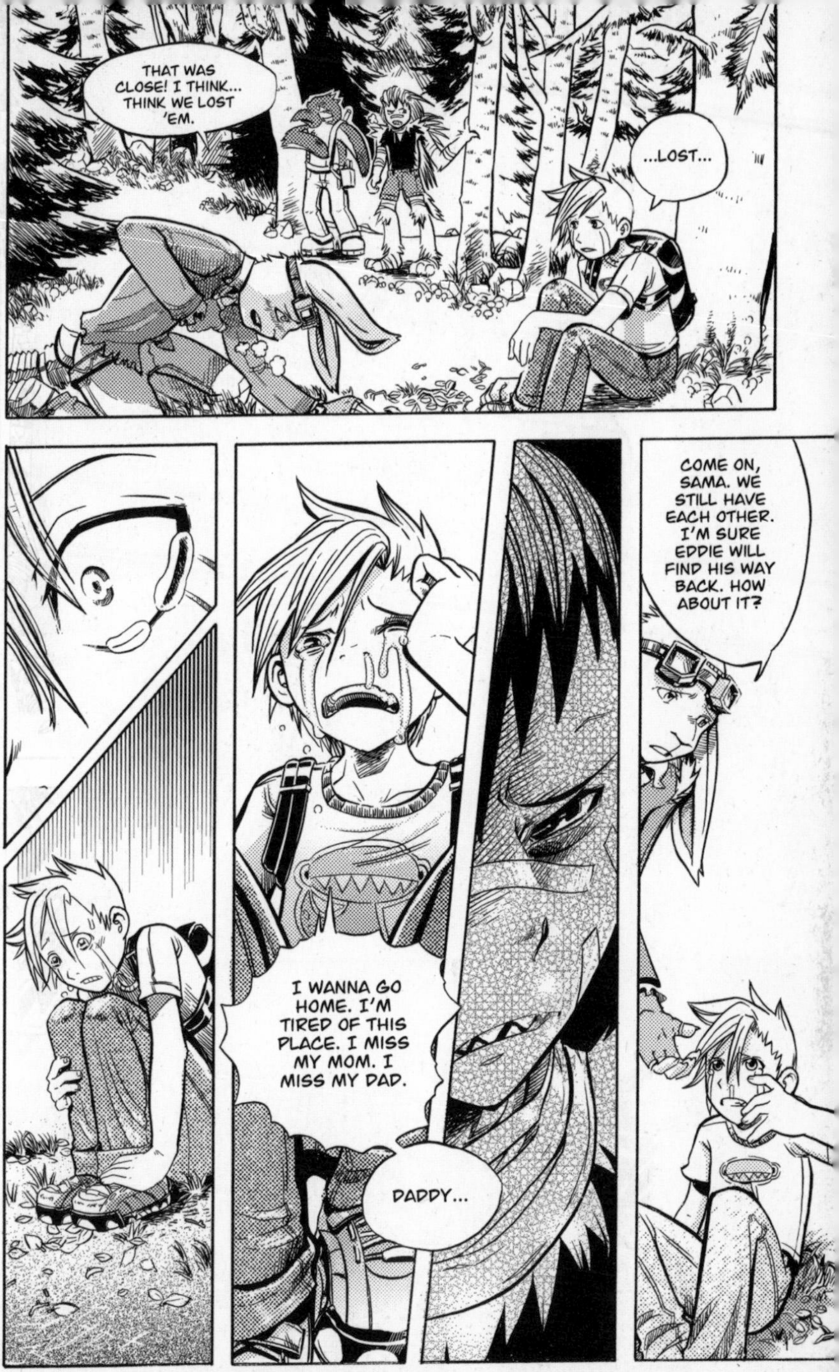
THAT WAS CLOSE! I THINK... THINK WE LOST 'EM.
...LOST...
I WANNA GO HOME. I'M TIRED OF THIS PLACE. I MISS MY MOM. I MISS MY DAD.
DADDY...
COME ON, SAMA. WE STILL HAVE EACH OTHER. I'M SURE EDDIE WILL FIND HIS WAY BACK. HOW ABOUT IT?

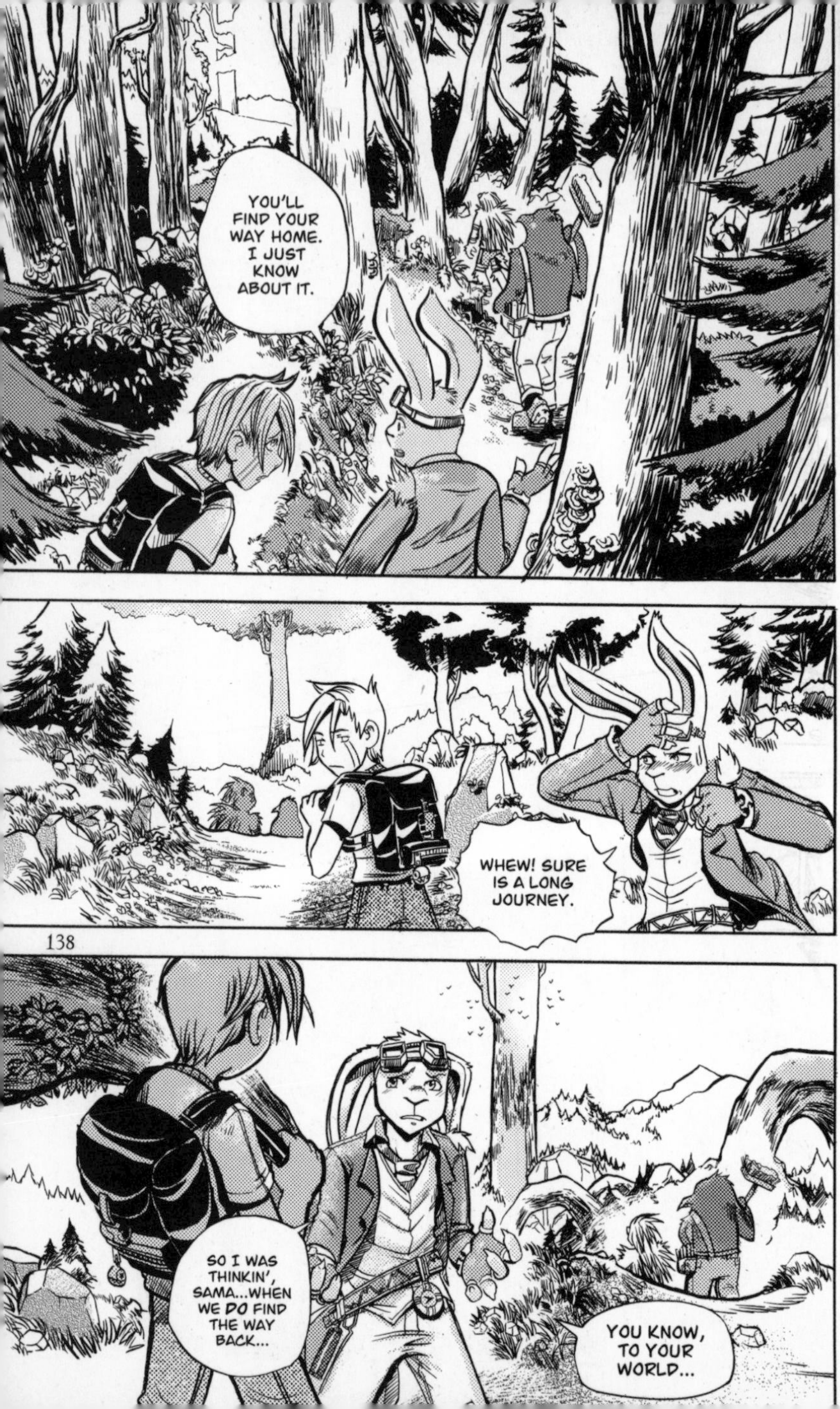
YOU'LL FIND YOUR WAY HOME. I JUST KNOW ABOUT IT.
WHEW! SURE IS A LONG JOURNEY.
SO I WAS THINKIN', SAMA...WHEN WE *DO* FIND THE WAY BACK...
YOU KNOW, TO YOUR WORLD...

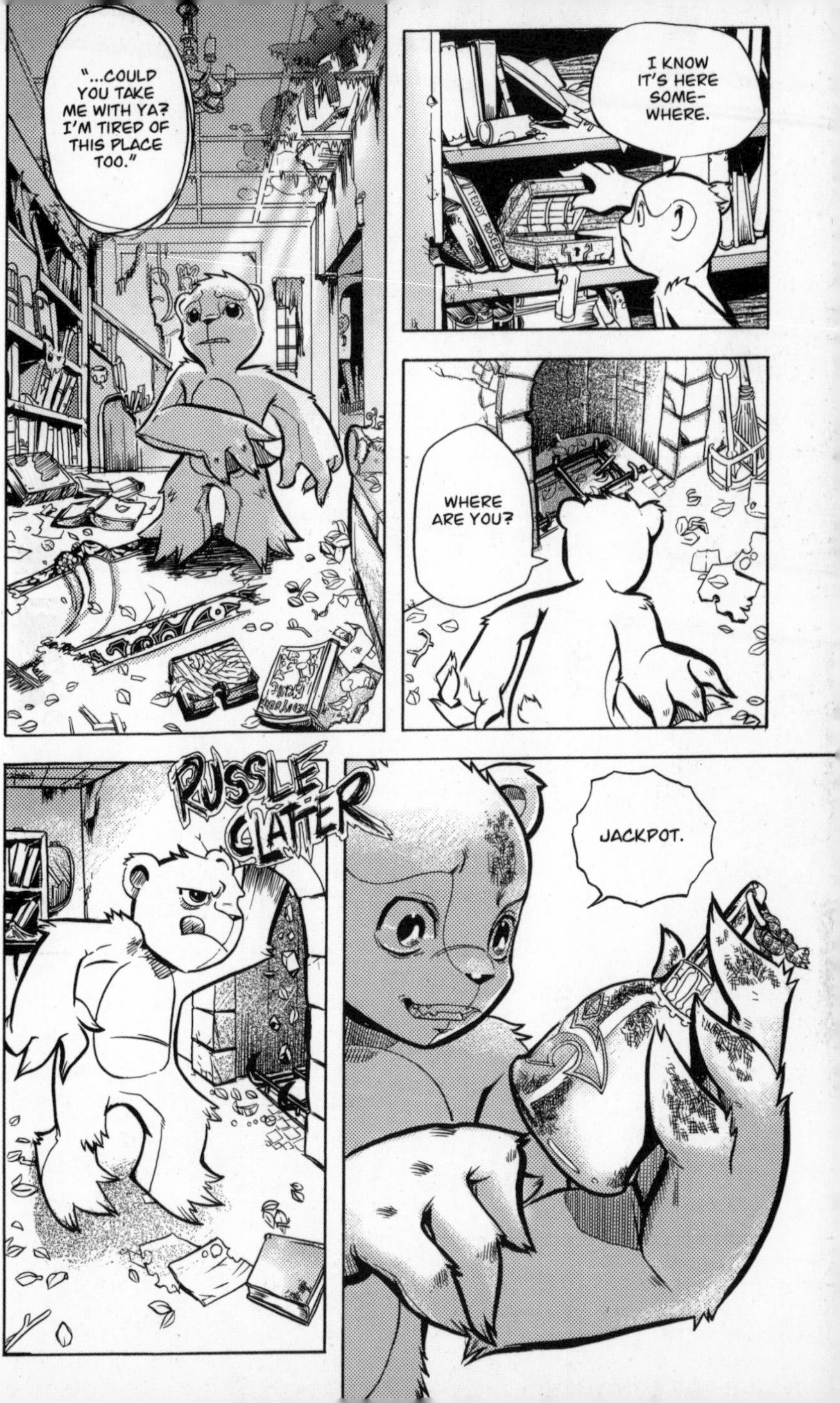
"...COULD YOU TAKE ME WITH YA? I'M TIRED OF THIS PLACE TOO."
TEDDY ROSEBELL
I KNOW IT'S HERE SOME-WHERE.
WHERE ARE YOU?
RUSSLE CLATTER
JACKPOT.

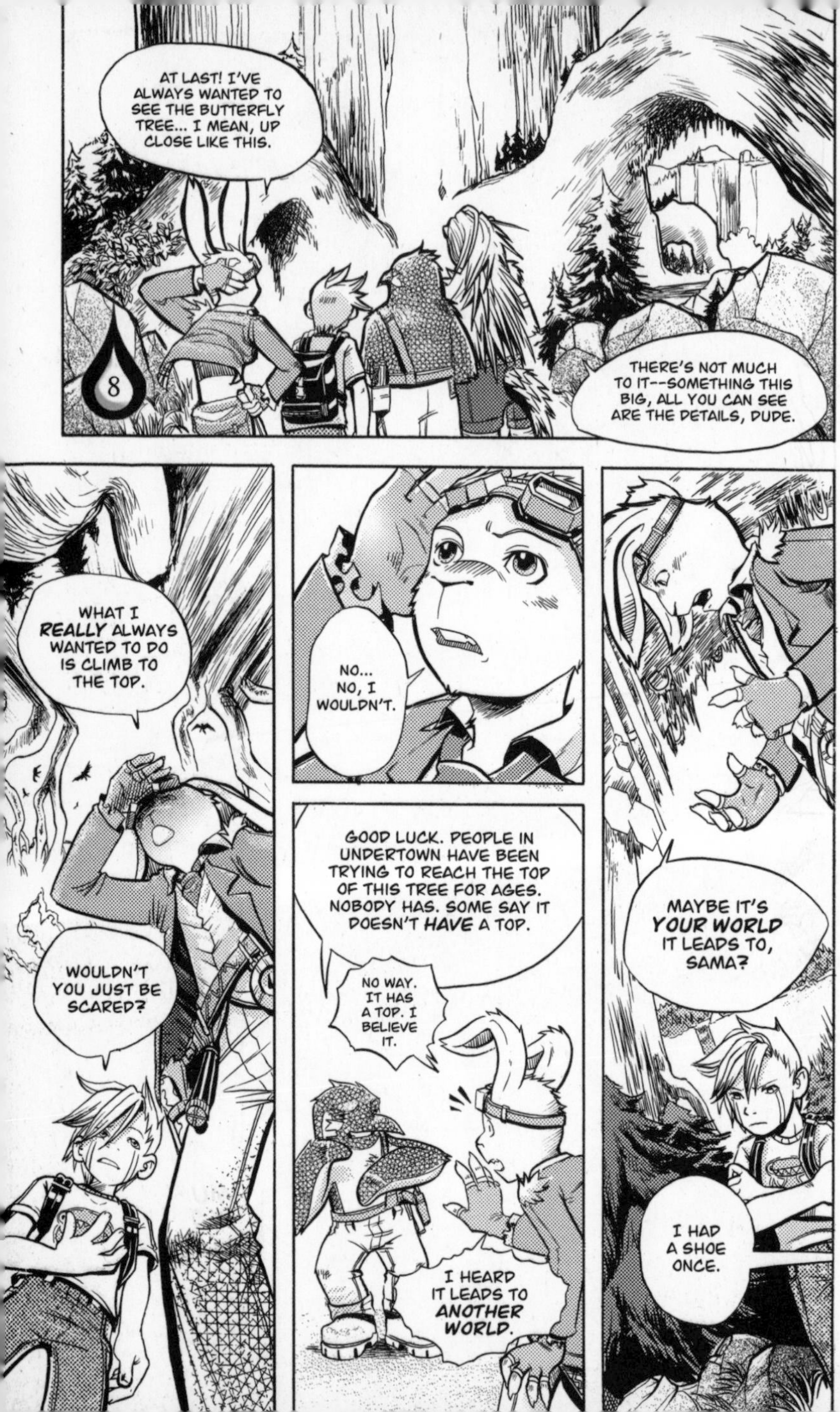
AT LAST! I'VE ALWAYS WANTED TO SEE THE BUTTERFLY TREE... I MEAN, UP CLOSE LIKE THIS.
8
THERE'S NOT MUCH TO IT--SOMETHING THIS BIG, ALL YOU CAN SEE ARE THE DETAILS, DUDE.
WHAT I *REALLY* ALWAYS WANTED TO DO IS CLIMB TO THE TOP.
WOULDN'T YOU JUST BE SCARED?
NO... NO, I WOULDN'T.
GOOD LUCK. PEOPLE IN UNDERTOWN HAVE BEEN TRYING TO REACH THE TOP OF THIS TREE FOR AGES. NOBODY HAS. SOME SAY IT DOESN'T *HAVE* A TOP.
NO WAY. IT HAS A TOP. I BELIEVE IT.
I HEARD IT LEADS TO *ANOTHER WORLD*.
MAYBE IT'S *YOUR WORLD* IT LEADS TO, SAMA?
I HAD A SHOE ONCE.

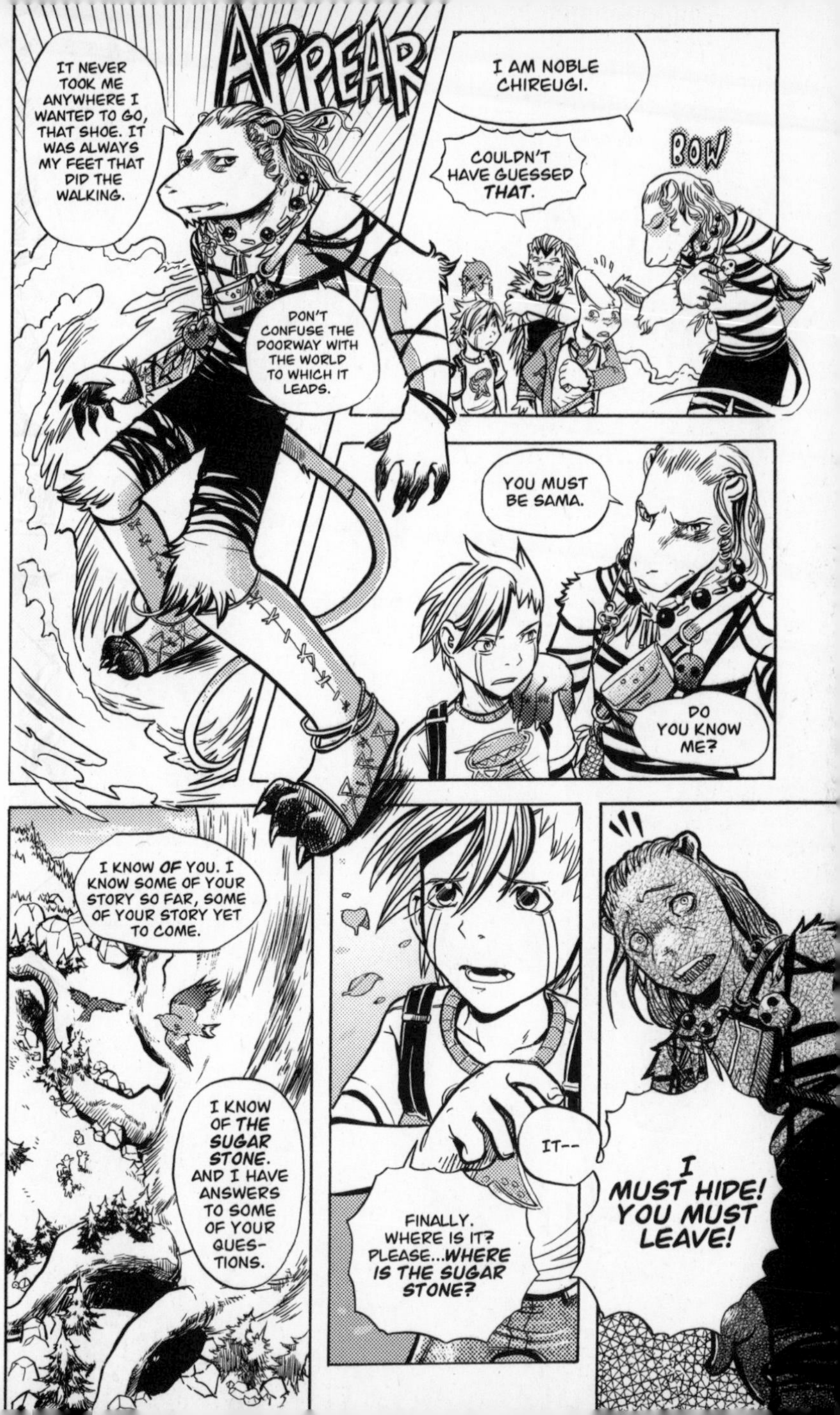
APPEAR
IT NEVER TOOK ME ANYWHERE I WANTED TO GO, THAT SHOE. IT WAS ALWAYS MY FEET THAT DID THE WALKING.
DON'T CONFUSE THE DOORWAY WITH THE WORLD TO WHICH IT LEADS.
I AM NOBLE CHIREUGI.
COULDN'T HAVE GUESSED THAT.
BOW
YOU MUST BE SAMA.
DO YOU KNOW ME?
I KNOW OF YOU. I KNOW SOME OF YOUR STORY SO FAR, SOME OF YOUR STORY YET TO COME.
I KNOW OF THE SUGAR STONE. AND I HAVE ANSWERS TO SOME OF YOUR QUES-TIONS.
FINALLY. WHERE IS IT? PLEASE...WHERE IS THE SUGAR STONE?
IT--
I MUST HIDE! YOU MUST LEAVE!

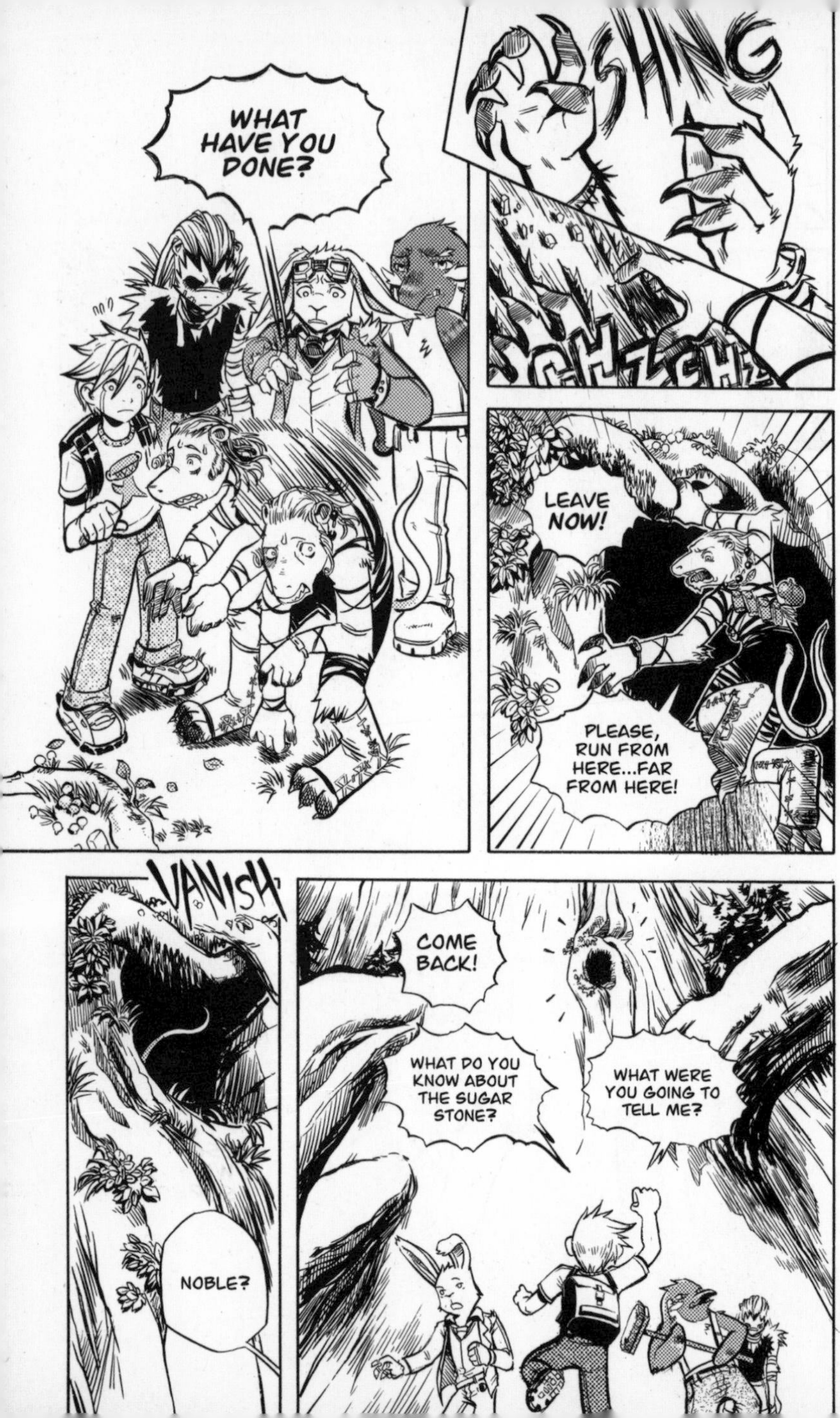
WHAT HAVE YOU DONE?
SHING
LEAVE NOW!
PLEASE, RUN FROM HERE...FAR FROM HERE!
VANISH
NOBLE?
COME BACK!
WHAT DO YOU KNOW ABOUT THE SUGAR STONE?
WHAT WERE YOU GOING TO TELL ME?

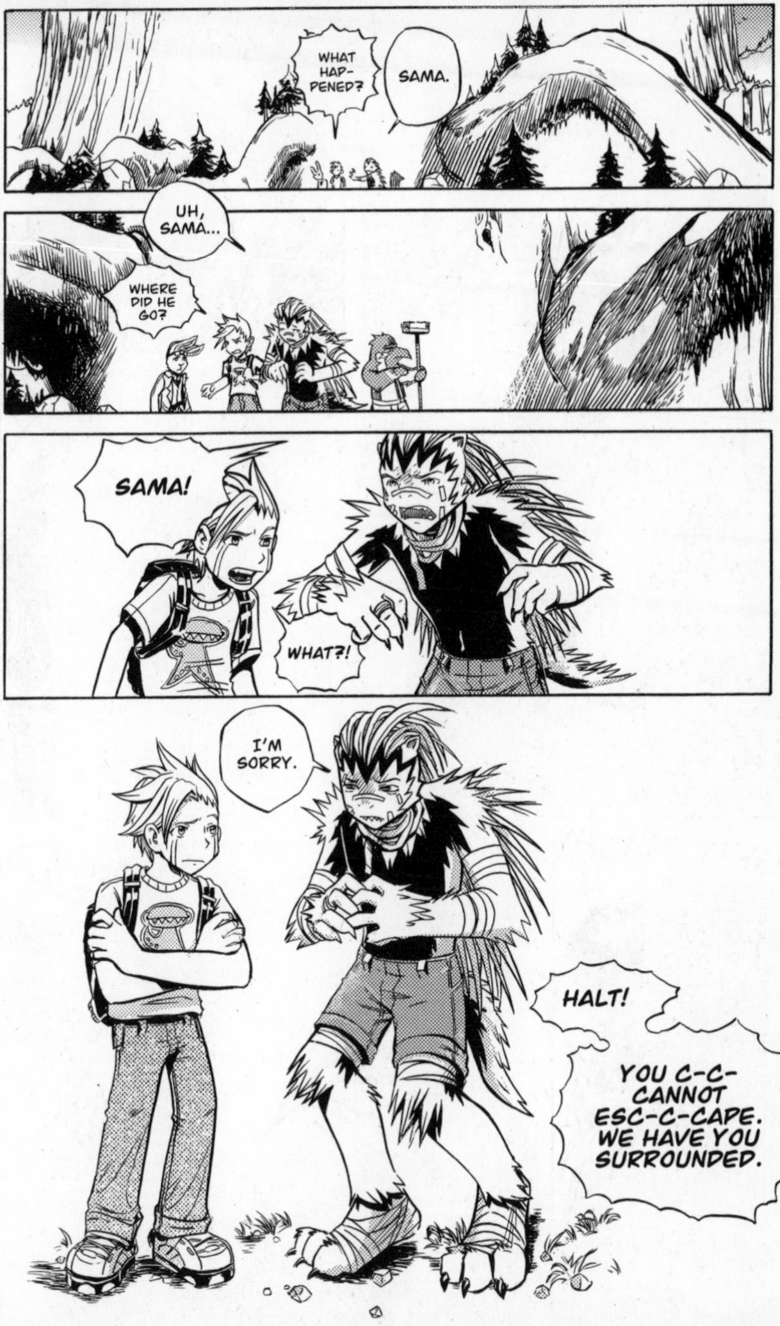
WHAT HAP-PENED?
SAMA.
UH, SAMA...
WHERE DID HE GO?
SAMA!
WHAT?!
I'M SORRY.
HALT!
YOU C-C-CANNOT ESC-C-CAPE. WE HAVE YOU SURROUNDED.

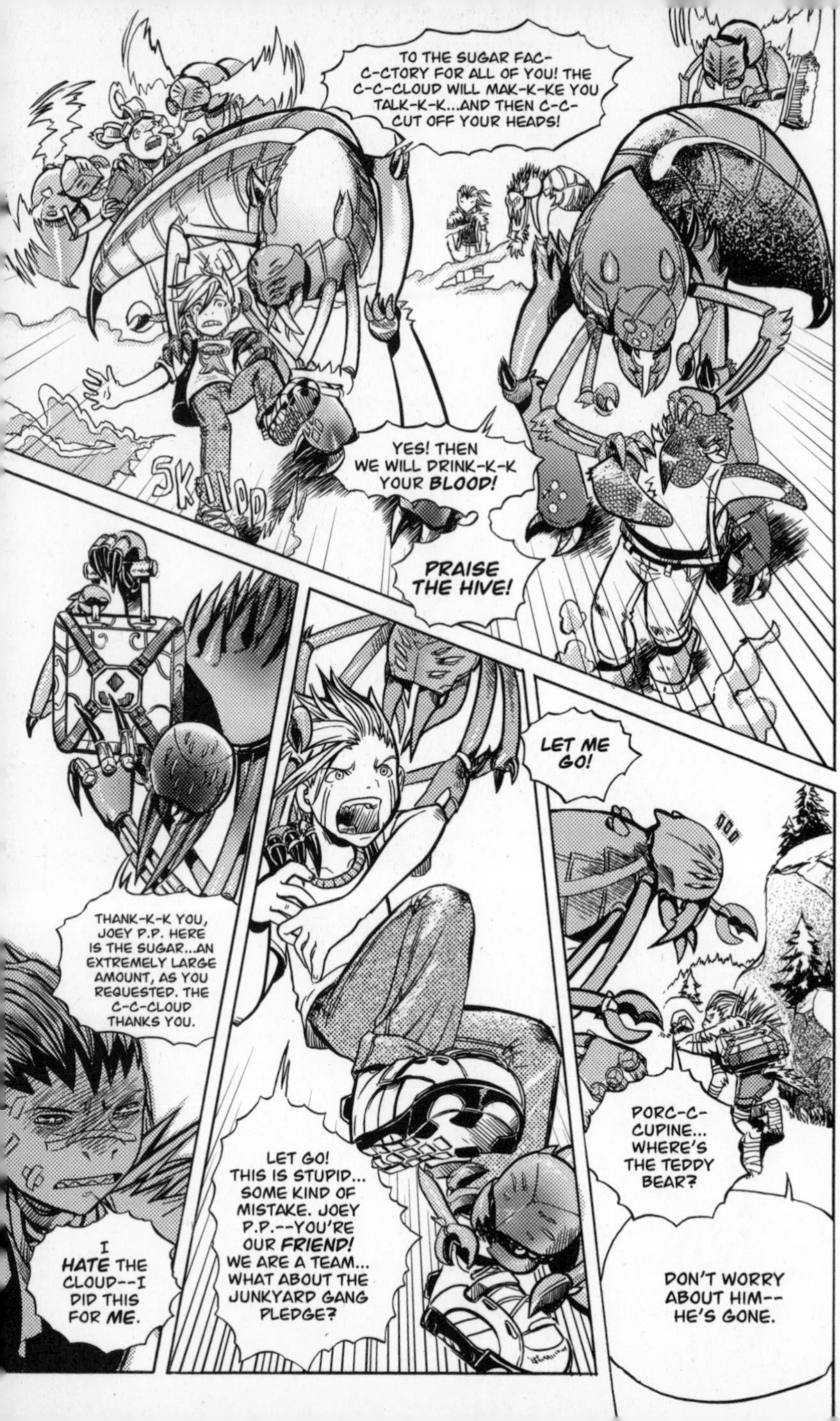
TO THE SUGAR FAC-C-CTORY FOR ALL OF YOU! THE C-C-CLOUD WILL MAK-K-KE YOU TALK-K-K...AND THEN C-C-CUT OFF YOUR HEADS!
SKIIDD
YES! THEN WE WILL DRINK-K-K YOUR BLOOD!
PRAISE THE HIVE!
THANK-K-K YOU, JOEY P.P. HERE IS THE SUGAR...AN EXTREMELY LARGE AMOUNT, AS YOU REQUESTED. THE C-C-CLOUD THANKS YOU.
I HATE THE CLOUD--I DID THIS FOR ME.
LET GO! THIS IS STUPID... SOME KIND OF MISTAKE. JOEY P.P.--YOU'RE OUR FRIEND! WE ARE A TEAM... WHAT ABOUT THE JUNKYARD GANG PLEDGE?
LET ME GO!
PORC-C-CUPINE... WHERE'S THE TEDDY BEAR?
DON'T WORRY ABOUT HIM--HE'S GONE.

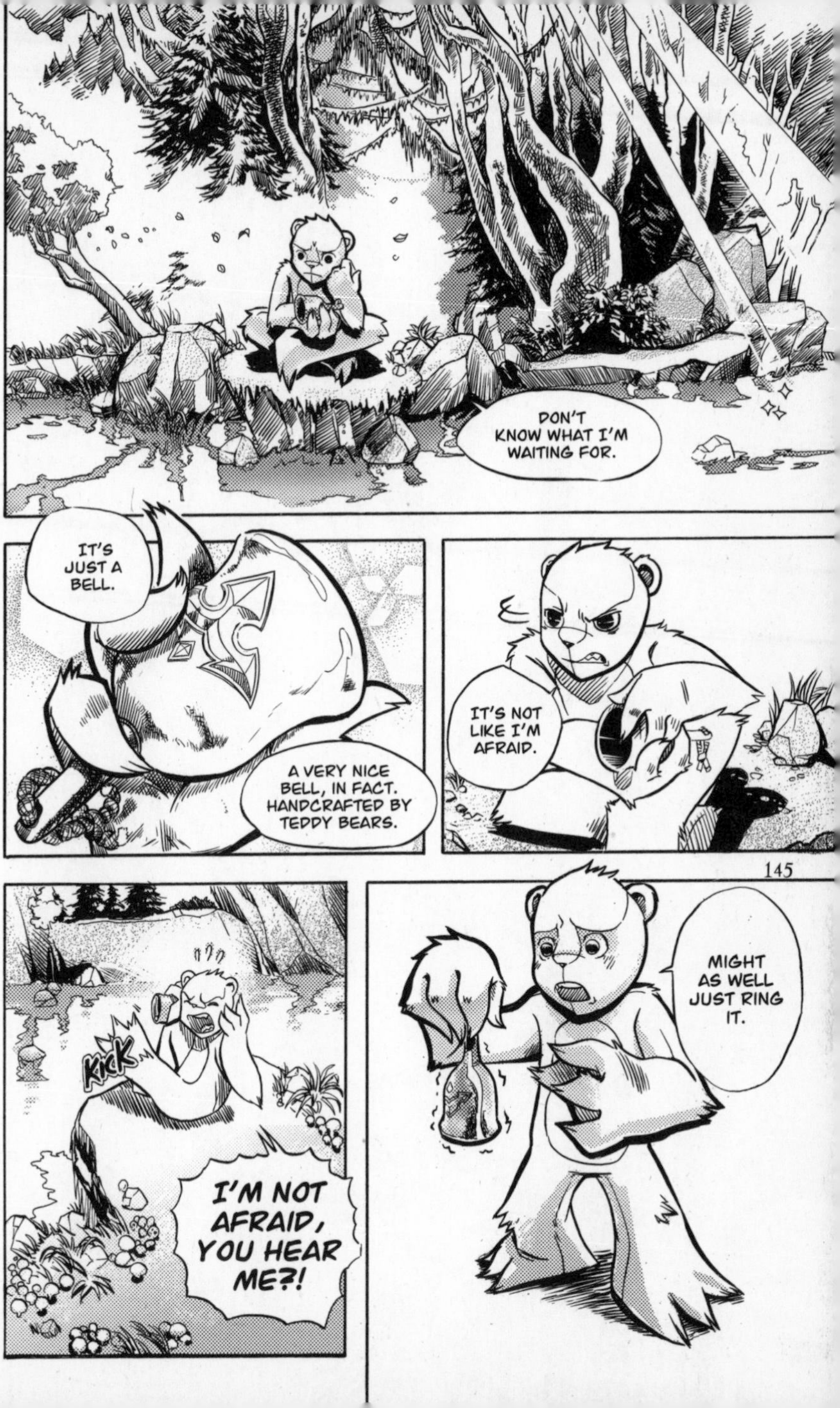
DON'T KNOW WHAT I'M WAITING FOR.
IT'S JUST A BELL.
A VERY NICE BELL, IN FACT. HANDCRAFTED BY TEDDY BEARS.
IT'S NOT LIKE I'M AFRAID.
KICK
I'M NOT AFRAID, YOU HEAR ME?!
MIGHT AS WELL JUST RING IT.

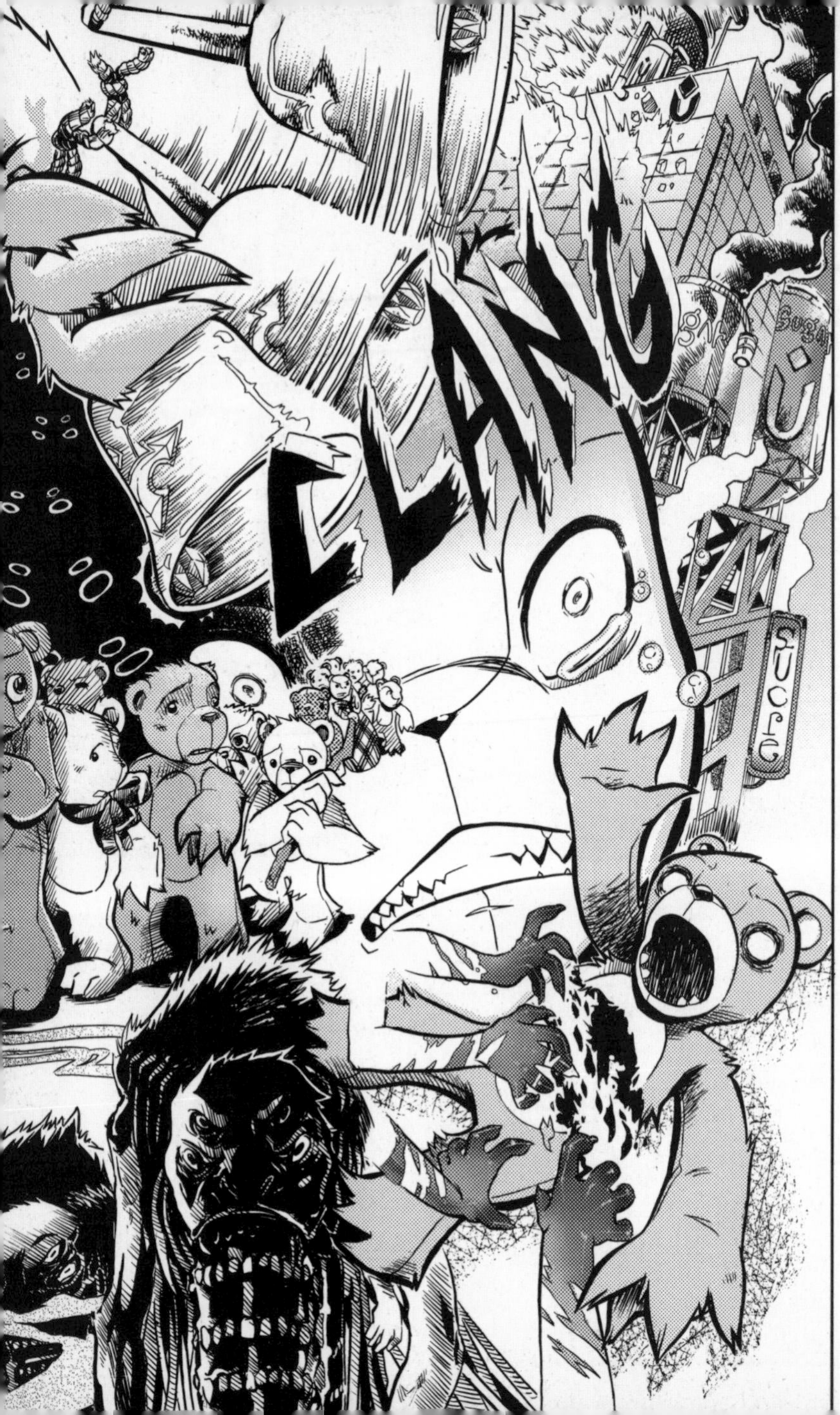
CLANG
Sucre

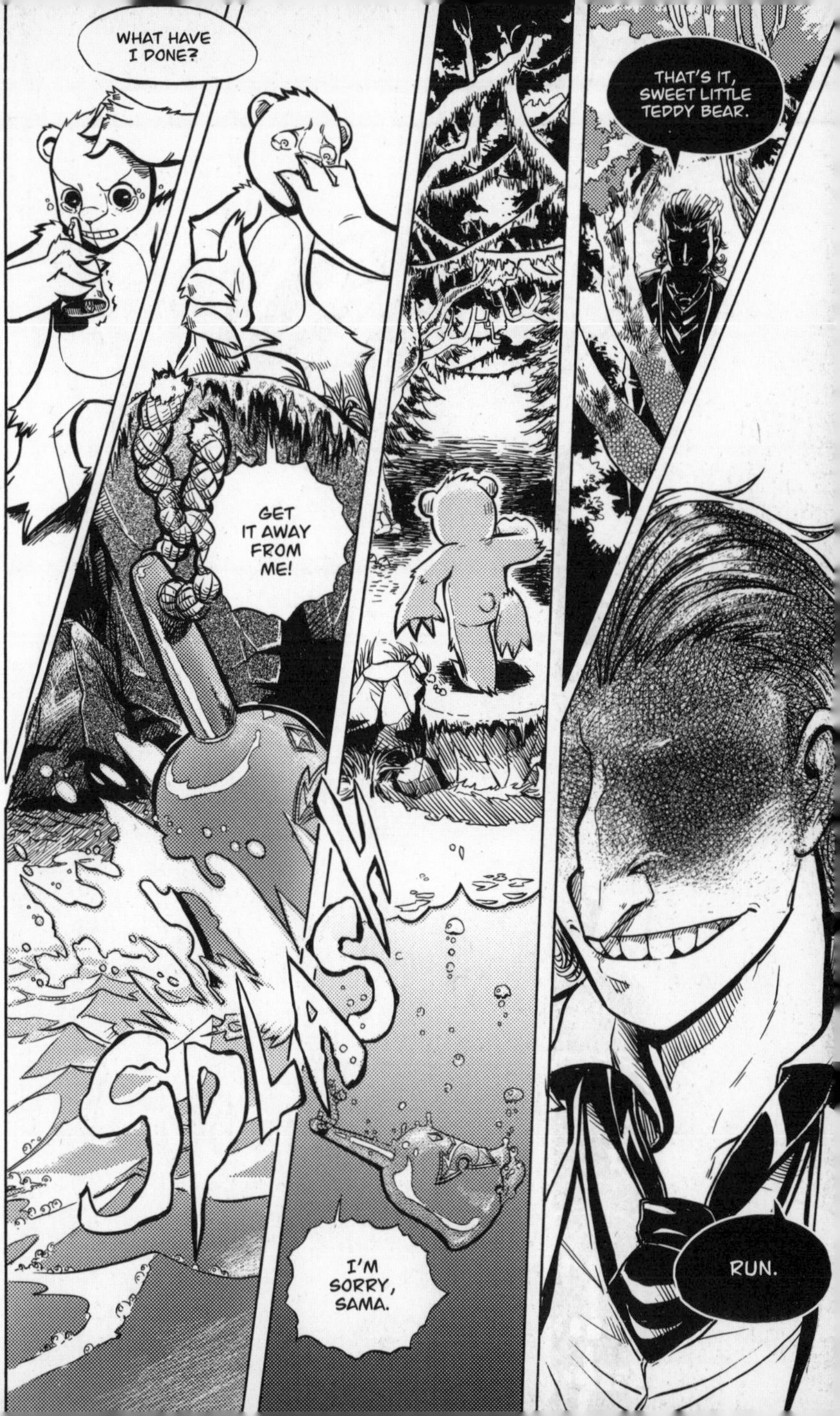
WHAT HAVE I DONE?
GET IT AWAY FROM ME!
THAT'S IT, SWEET LITTLE TEDDY BEAR.
SPLASH
I'M SORRY, SAMA.
RUN.

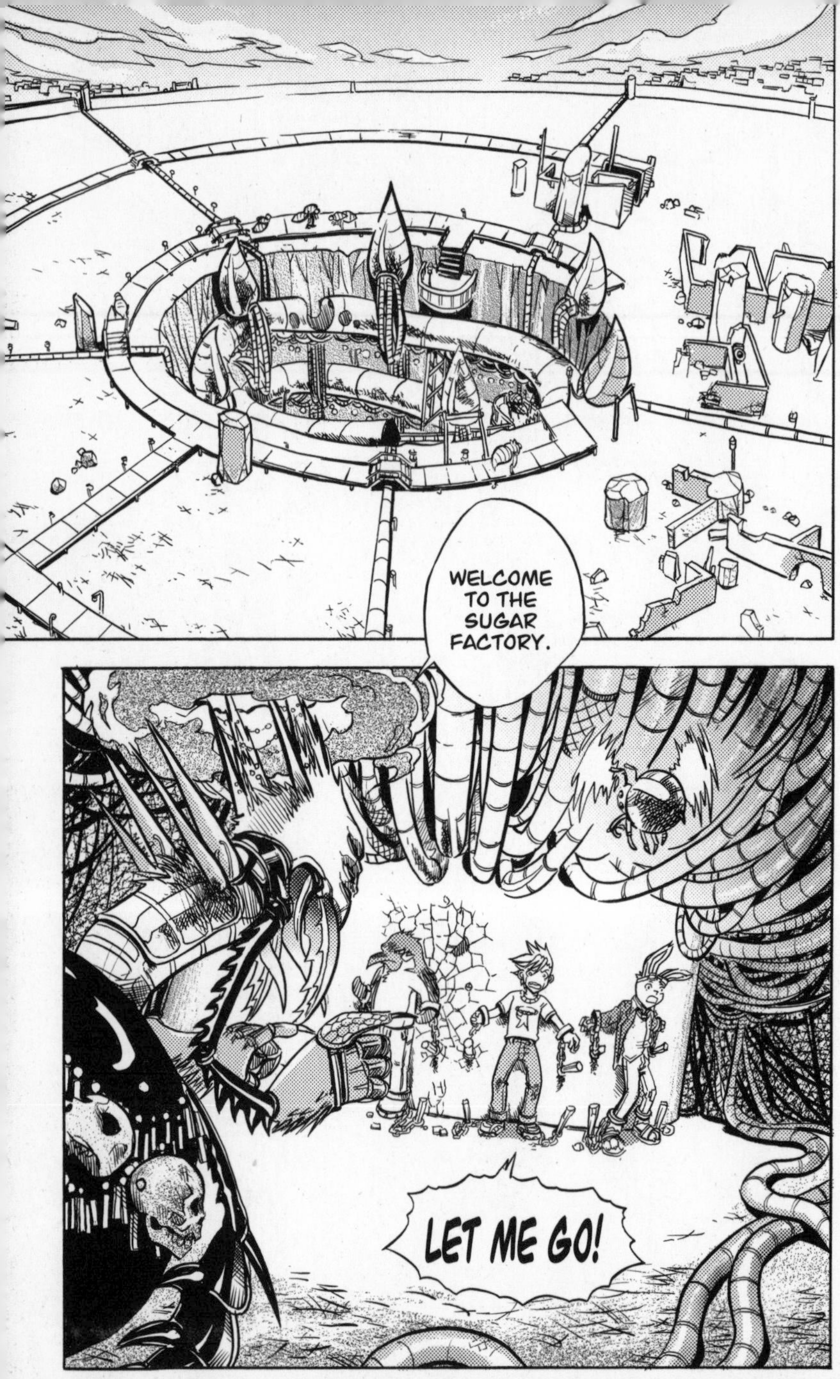
WELCOME TO THE SUGAR FACTORY.
LET ME GO!

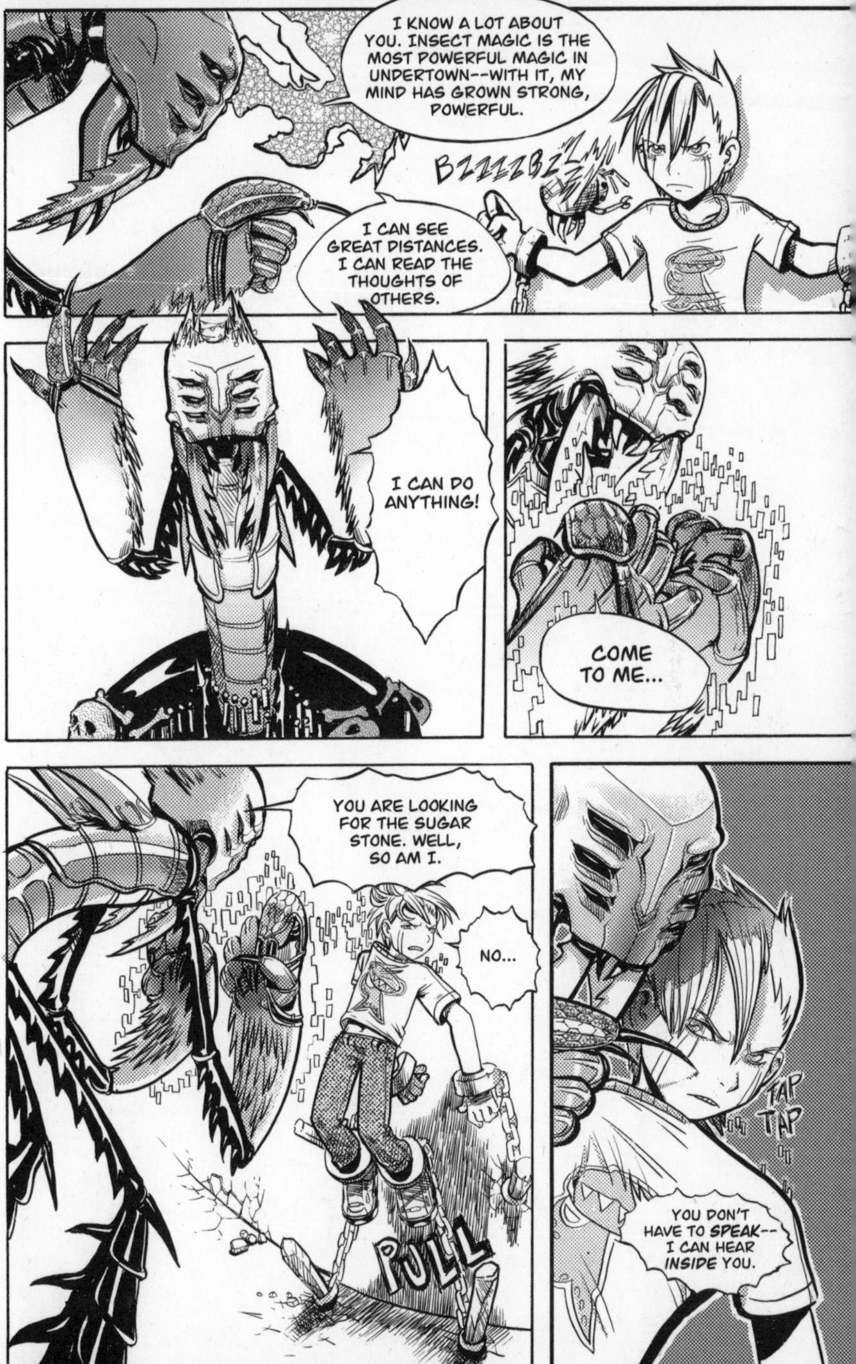
I KNOW A LOT ABOUT YOU. INSECT MAGIC IS THE MOST POWERFUL MAGIC IN UNDERTOWN--WITH IT, MY MIND HAS GROWN STRONG, POWERFUL.
BZZZZBZZZ
I CAN SEE GREAT DISTANCES. I CAN READ THE THOUGHTS OF OTHERS.
I CAN DO ANYTHING!
COME TO ME...
YOU ARE LOOKING FOR THE SUGAR STONE. WELL, SO AM I.
NO...
PULL
TAP TAP
YOU DON'T HAVE TO SPEAK-- I CAN HEAR INSIDE YOU.

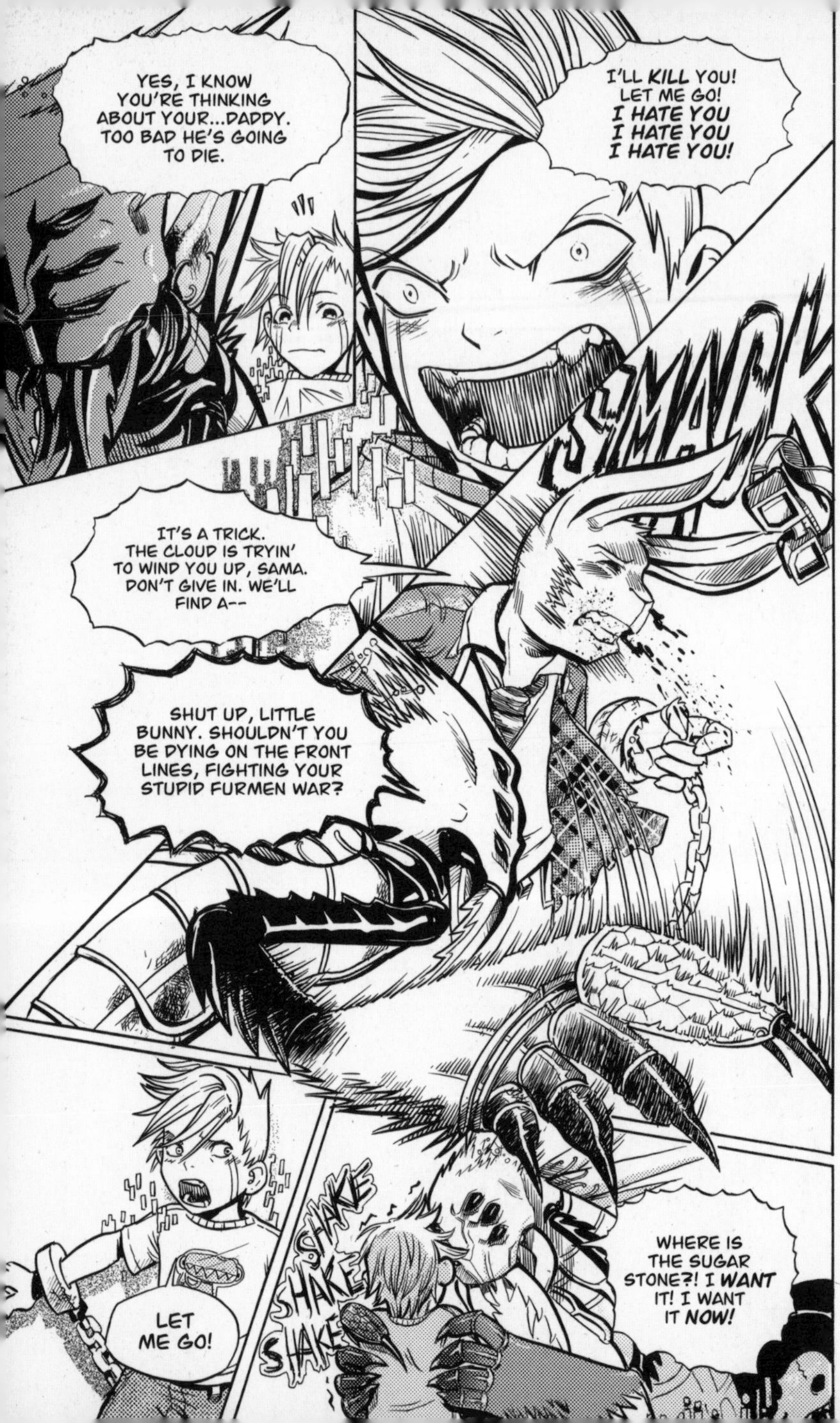
YES, I KNOW YOU'RE THINKING ABOUT YOUR...DADDY. TOO BAD HE'S GOING TO DIE.
I'LL KILL YOU! LET ME GO! I HATE YOU I HATE YOU I HATE YOU!
SMACK
IT'S A TRICK. THE CLOUD IS TRYIN' TO WIND YOU UP, SAMA. DON'T GIVE IN. WE'LL FIND A--
SHUT UP, LITTLE BUNNY. SHOULDN'T YOU BE DYING ON THE FRONT LINES, FIGHTING YOUR STUPID FURMEN WAR?
LET ME GO!
SHAKE
SHAKE
SHAKE
WHERE IS THE SUGAR STONE?! I WANT IT! I WANT IT NOW!

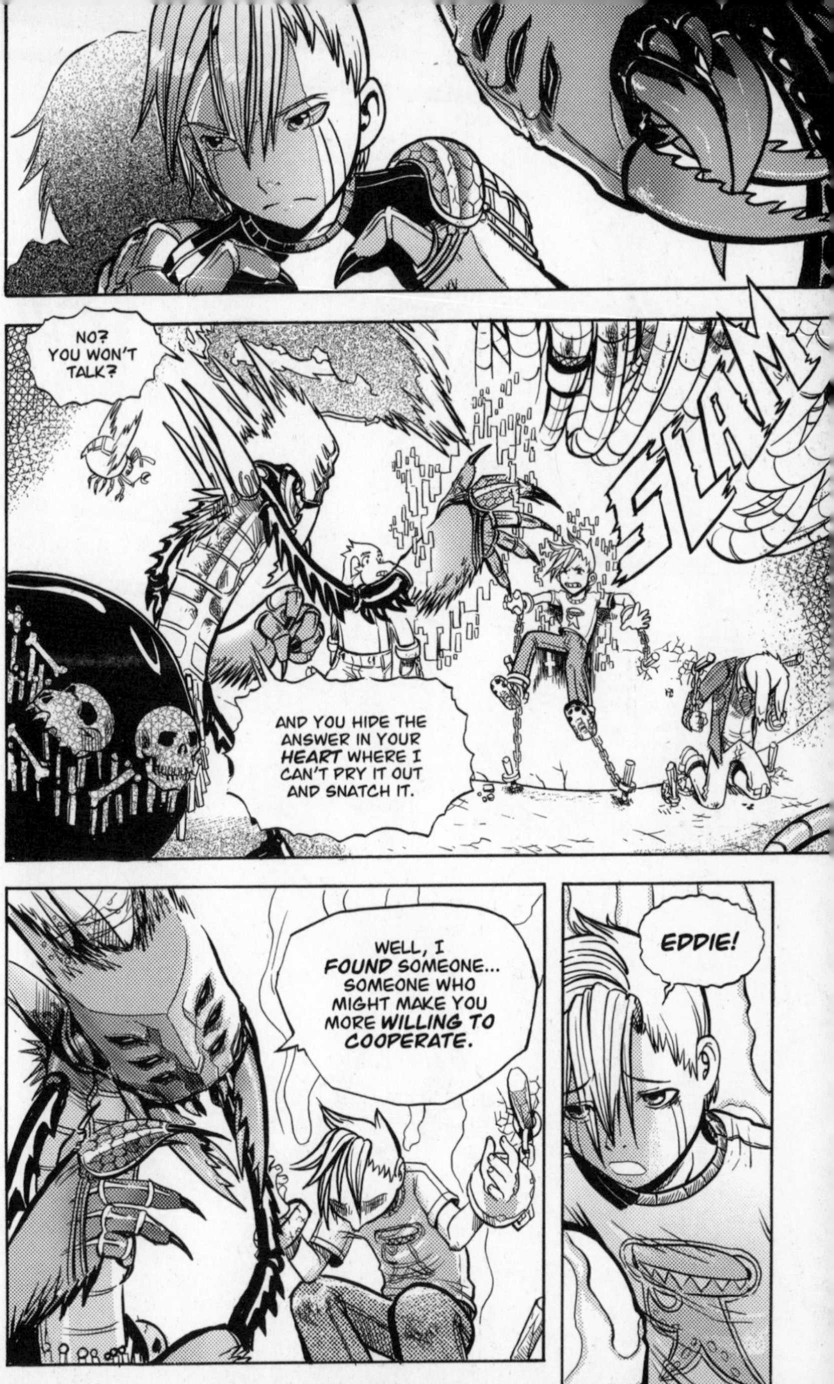
NO? YOU WON'T TALK?
SLAM
AND YOU HIDE THE ANSWER IN YOUR HEART WHERE I CAN'T PRY IT OUT AND SNATCH IT.
WELL, I FOUND SOMEONE... SOMEONE WHO MIGHT MAKE YOU MORE WILLING TO COOPERATE.
EDDIE!

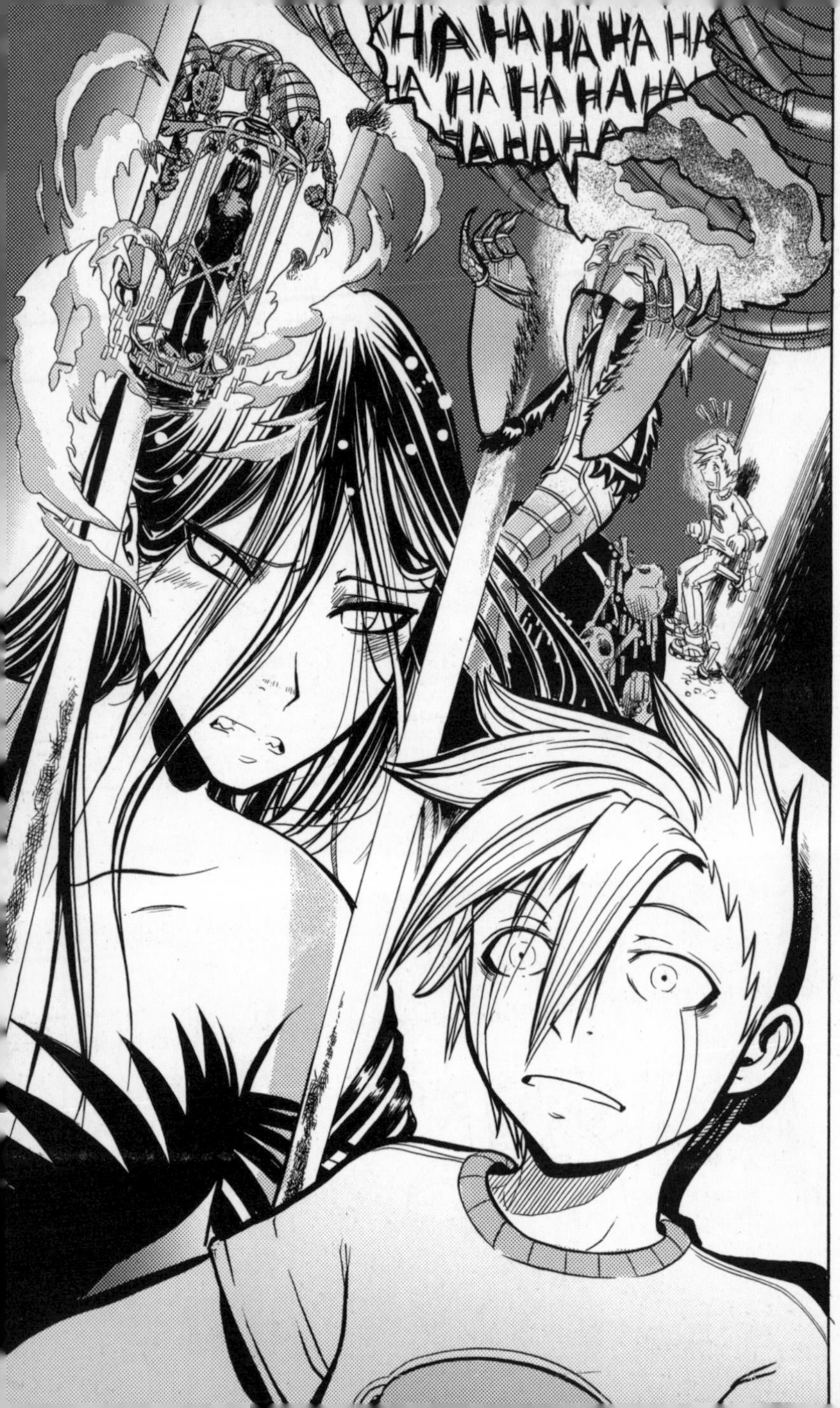
HA HA HA HA HA HA HA
HA HA HA HA HA HA
HA HA HA

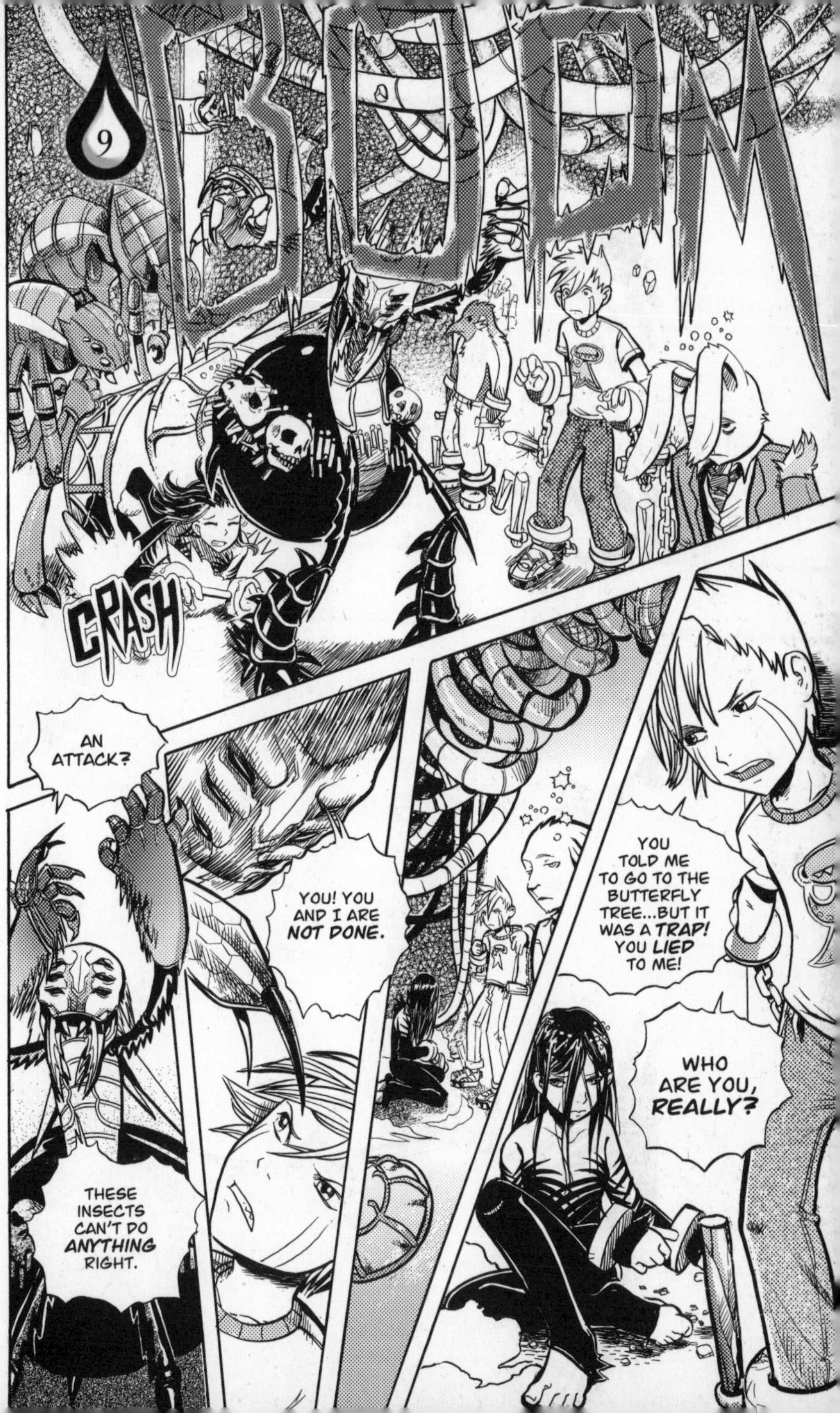
9
BOOM
CRASH
AN ATTACK?
THESE INSECTS CAN'T DO ANYTHING RIGHT.
YOU! YOU AND I ARE NOT DONE.
YOU TOLD ME TO GO TO THE BUTTERFLY TREE...BUT IT WAS A TRAP! YOU LIED TO ME!
WHO ARE YOU, REALLY?

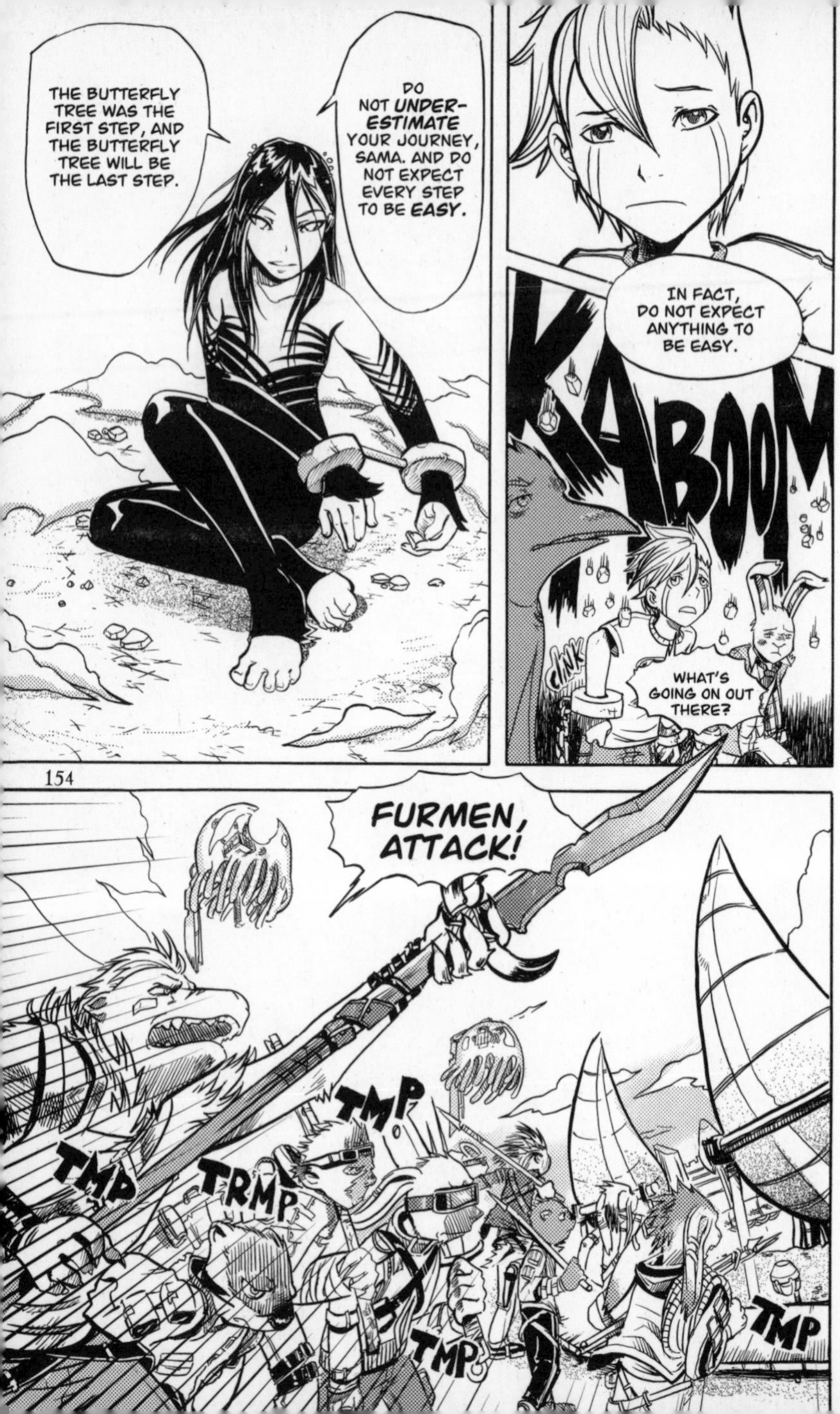
THE BUTTERFLY TREE WAS THE FIRST STEP, AND THE BUTTERFLY TREE WILL BE THE LAST STEP.
DO NOT UNDER-ESTIMATE YOUR JOURNEY, SAMA. AND DO NOT EXPECT EVERY STEP TO BE EASY.
IN FACT, DO NOT EXPECT ANYTHING TO BE EASY.
KABOOM
CLINK
WHAT'S GOING ON OUT THERE?
FURMEN, ATTACK!
TMP
TMP
TRMP
TMP
TMP

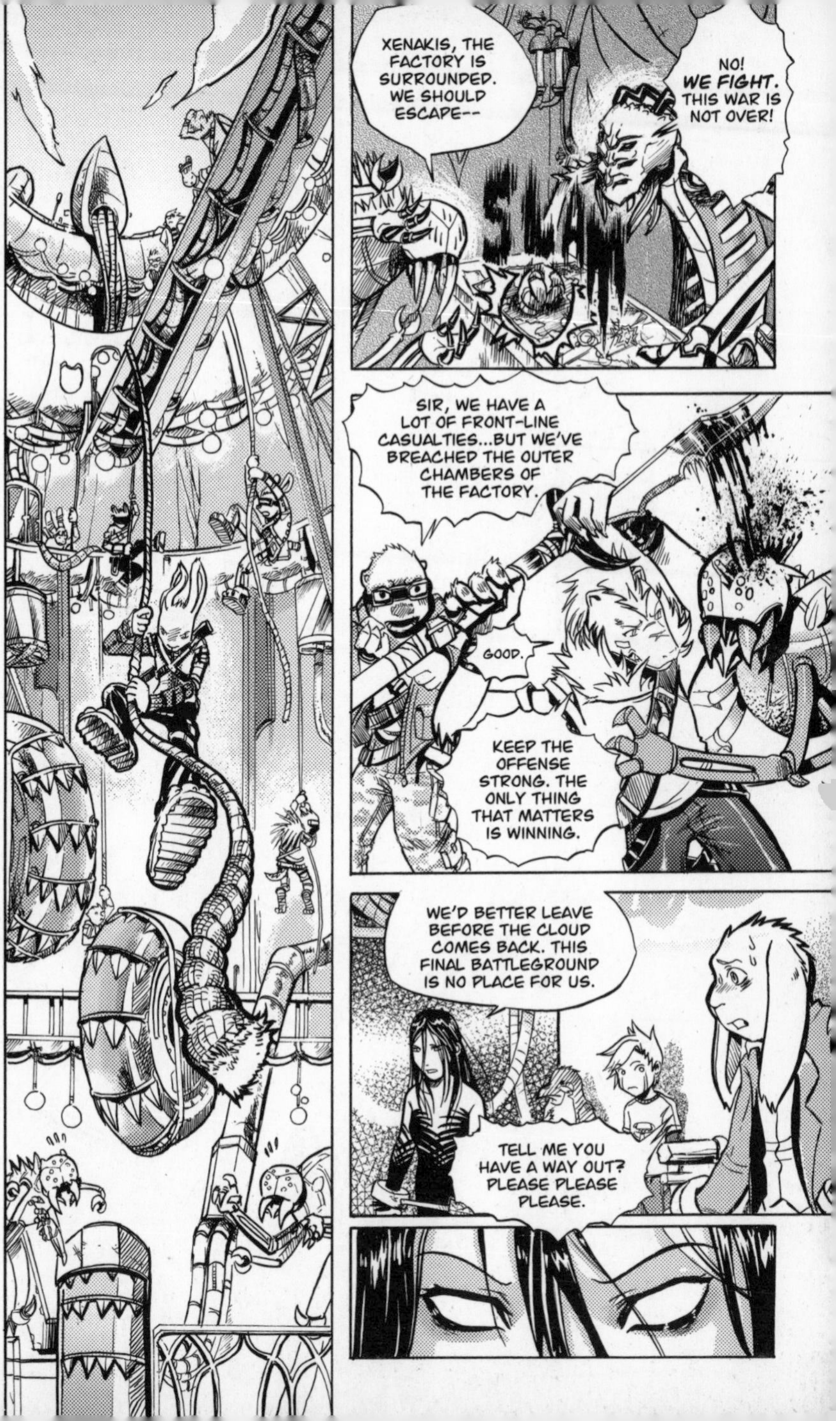
XENAKIS, THE FACTORY IS SURROUNDED. WE SHOULD ESCAPE--
NO! **WE FIGHT.** THIS WAR IS NOT OVER!
SLAM
SIR, WE HAVE A LOT OF FRONT-LINE CASUALTIES...BUT WE'VE BREACHED THE OUTER CHAMBERS OF THE FACTORY.
GOOD.
KEEP THE OFFENSE STRONG. THE ONLY THING THAT MATTERS IS WINNING.
WE'D BETTER LEAVE BEFORE THE CLOUD COMES BACK. THIS FINAL BATTLEGROUND IS NO PLACE FOR US.
TELL ME YOU HAVE A WAY OUT? PLEASE PLEASE PLEASE.

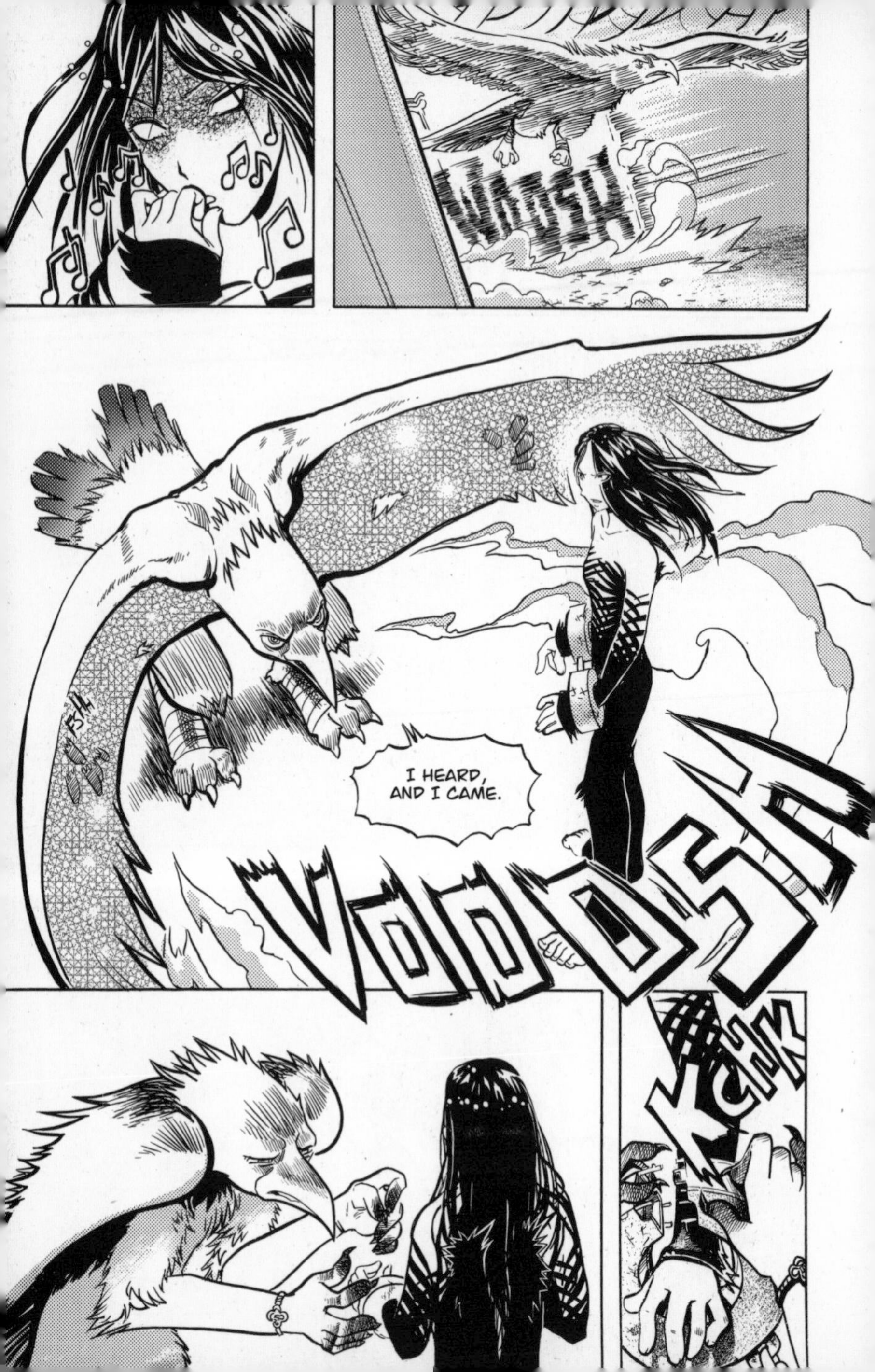
I HEARD, AND I CAME.

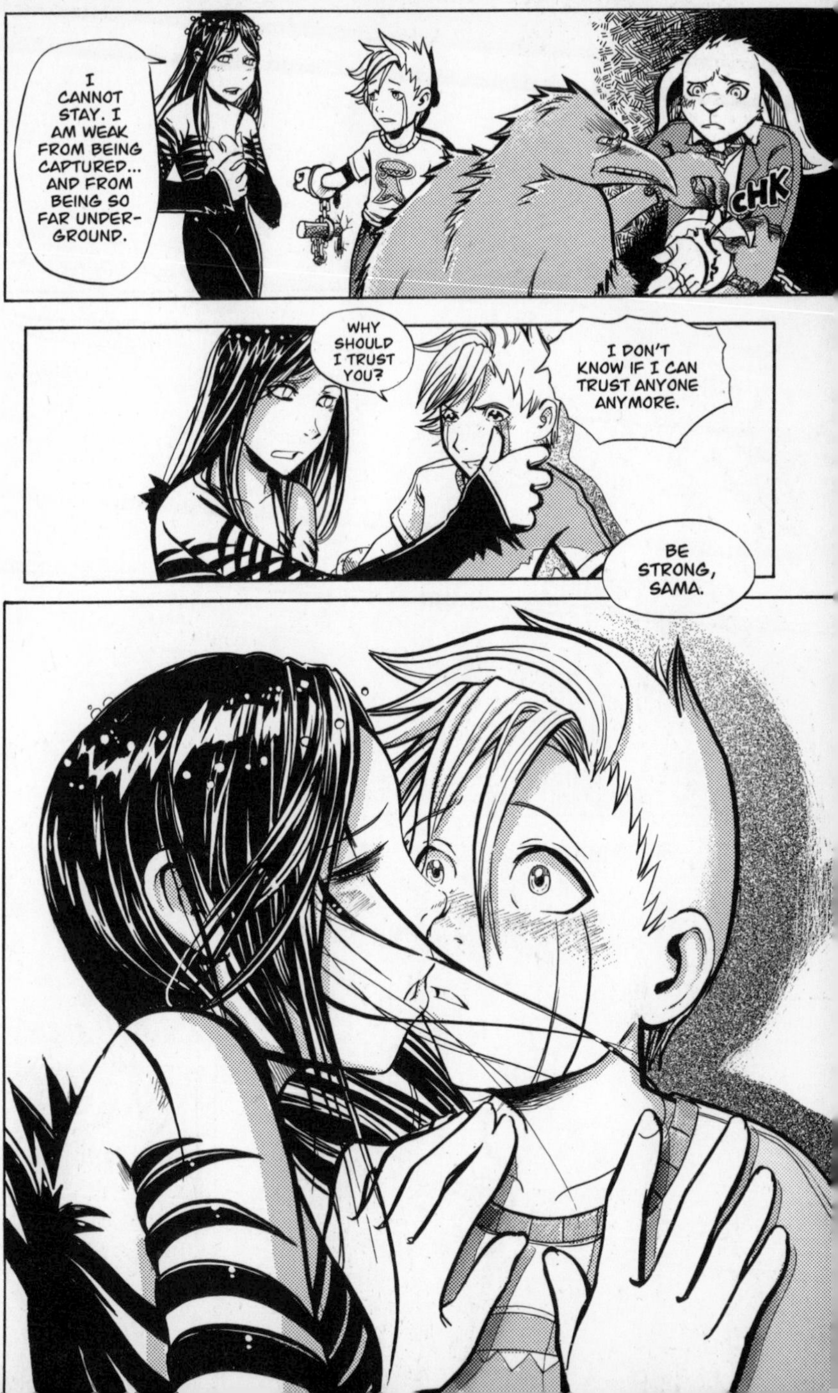
I CANNOT STAY. I AM WEAK FROM BEING CAPTURED... AND FROM BEING SO FAR UNDER-GROUND.
CHK
WHY SHOULD I TRUST YOU?
I DON'T KNOW IF I CAN TRUST ANYONE ANYMORE.
BE STRONG, SAMA.

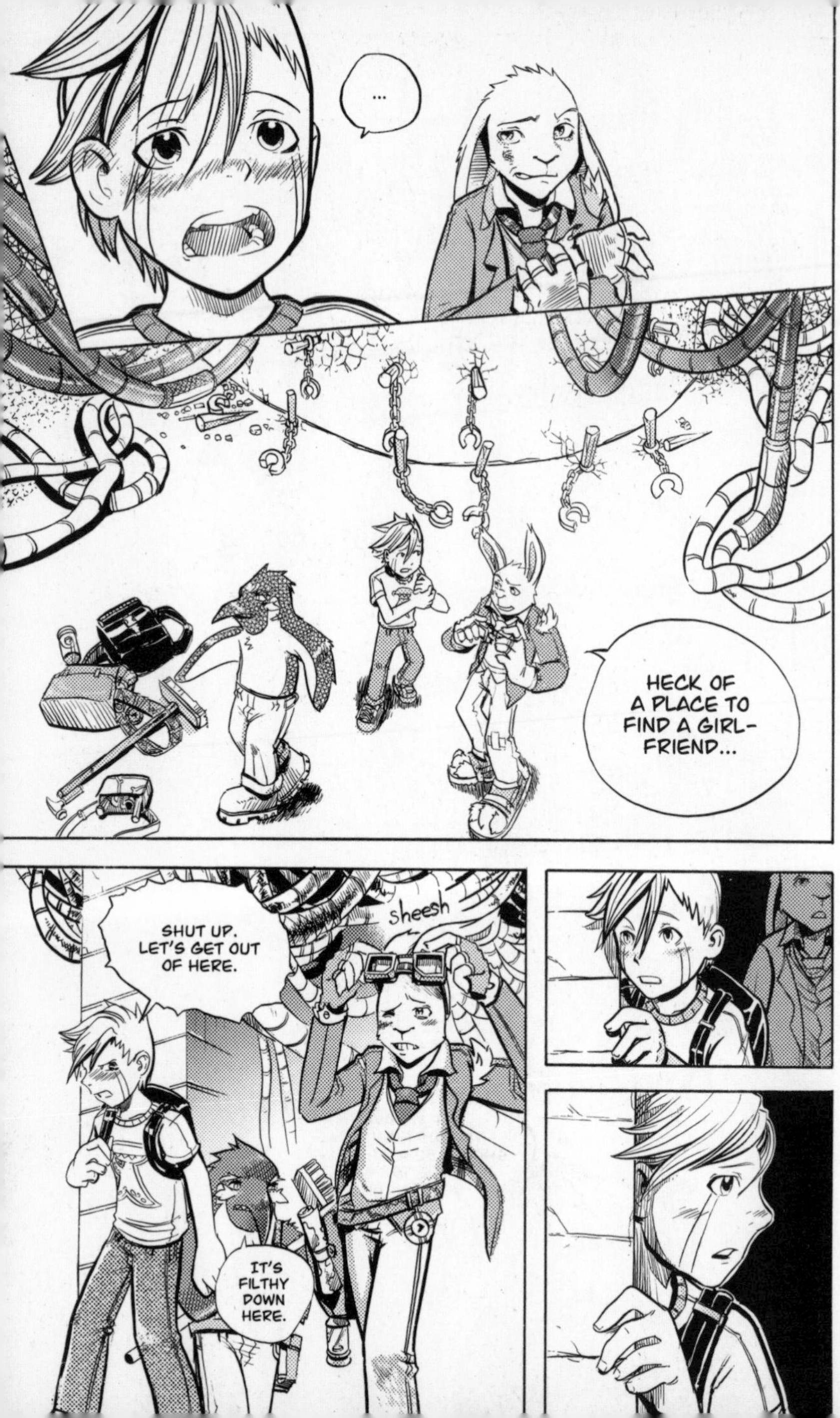

...
HECK OF A PLACE TO FIND A GIRL-FRIEND...
SHUT UP. LET'S GET OUT OF HERE.
sheesh
IT'S FILTHY DOWN HERE.

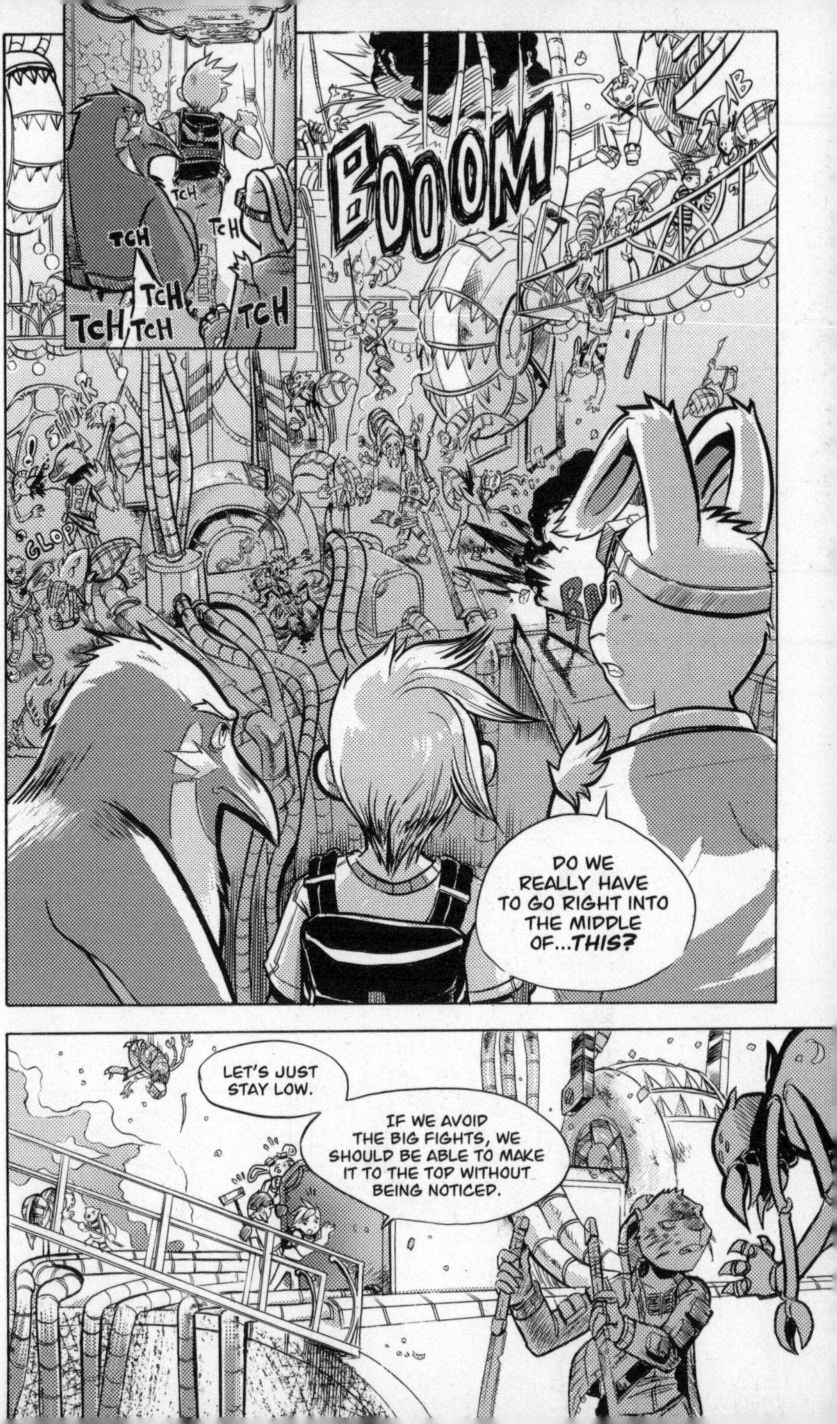
TCH
TCH
TCH
TCH
TCH
TCH
TCH
BOOOM
GLOP
DO WE REALLY HAVE TO GO RIGHT INTO THE MIDDLE OF...*THIS?*
LET'S JUST STAY LOW.
IF WE AVOID THE BIG FIGHTS, WE SHOULD BE ABLE TO MAKE IT TO THE TOP WITHOUT BEING NOTICED.

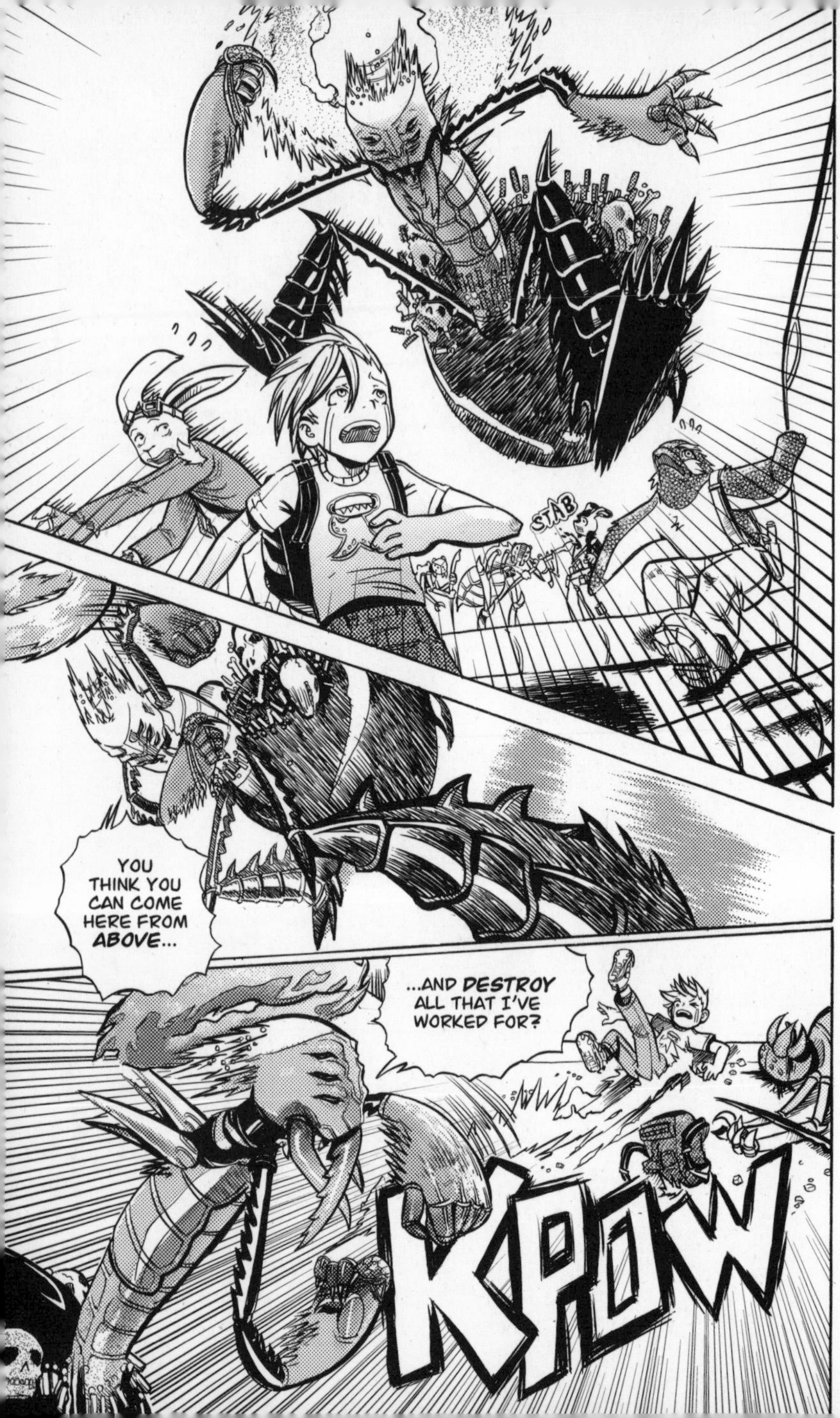
STAB
YOU THINK YOU CAN COME HERE FROM ABOVE...
...AND DESTROY ALL THAT I'VE WORKED FOR?
KPOW

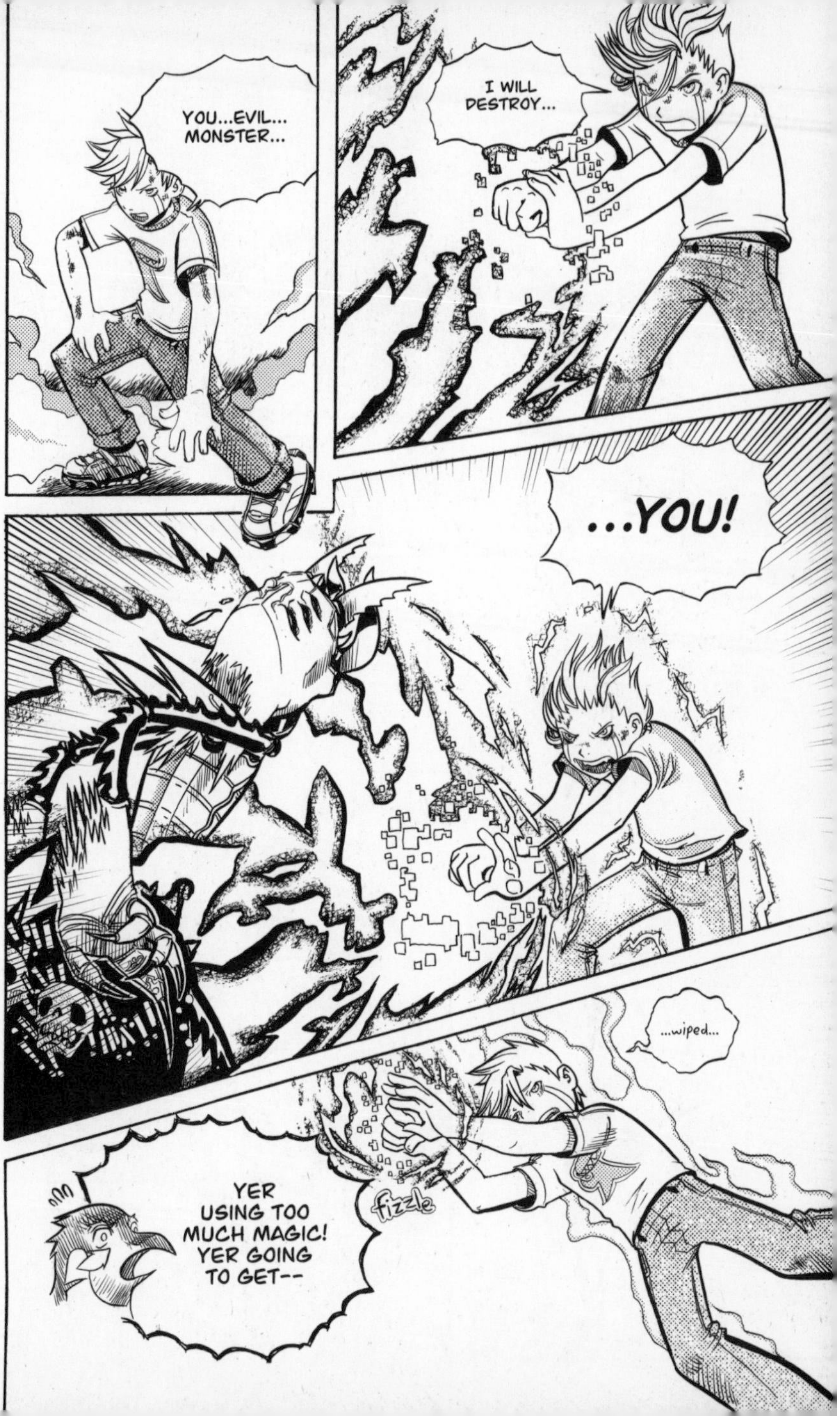
YOU...EVIL... MONSTER...
I WILL DESTROY...
...YOU!
...wiped...
YER USING TOO MUCH MAGIC! YER GOING TO GET--
fizzle

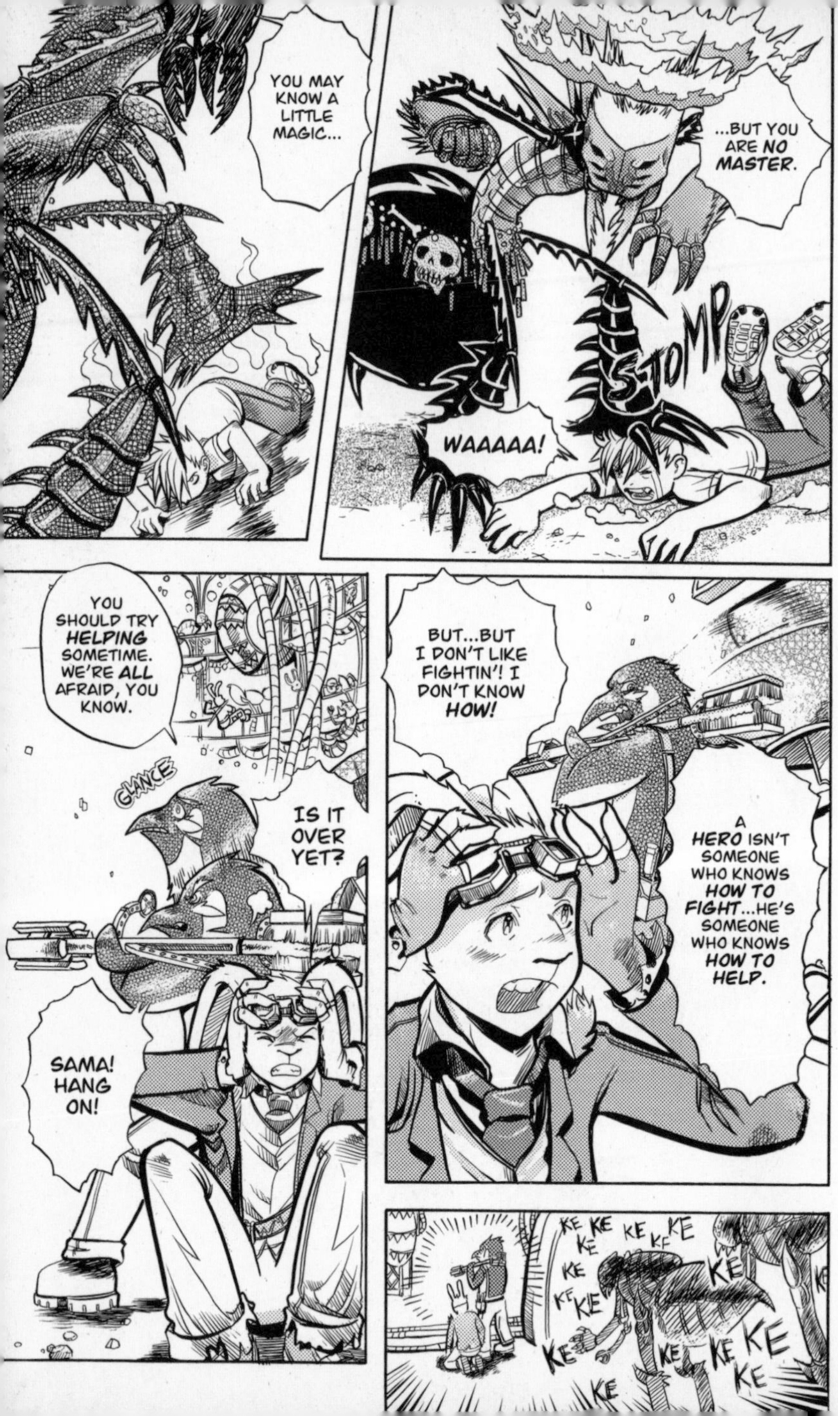
YOU MAY KNOW A LITTLE MAGIC...
...BUT YOU ARE NO MASTER.
STOMP
WAAAAA!
YOU SHOULD TRY HELPING SOMETIME. WE'RE ALL AFRAID, YOU KNOW.
GLANCE
IS IT OVER YET?
SAMA! HANG ON!
BUT...BUT I DON'T LIKE FIGHTIN'! I DON'T KNOW HOW!
A HERO ISN'T SOMEONE WHO KNOWS HOW TO FIGHT...HE'S SOMEONE WHO KNOWS HOW TO HELP.
KE KE KE KE KE KE KE KE KE KE KE KE KE KE KE KE KE

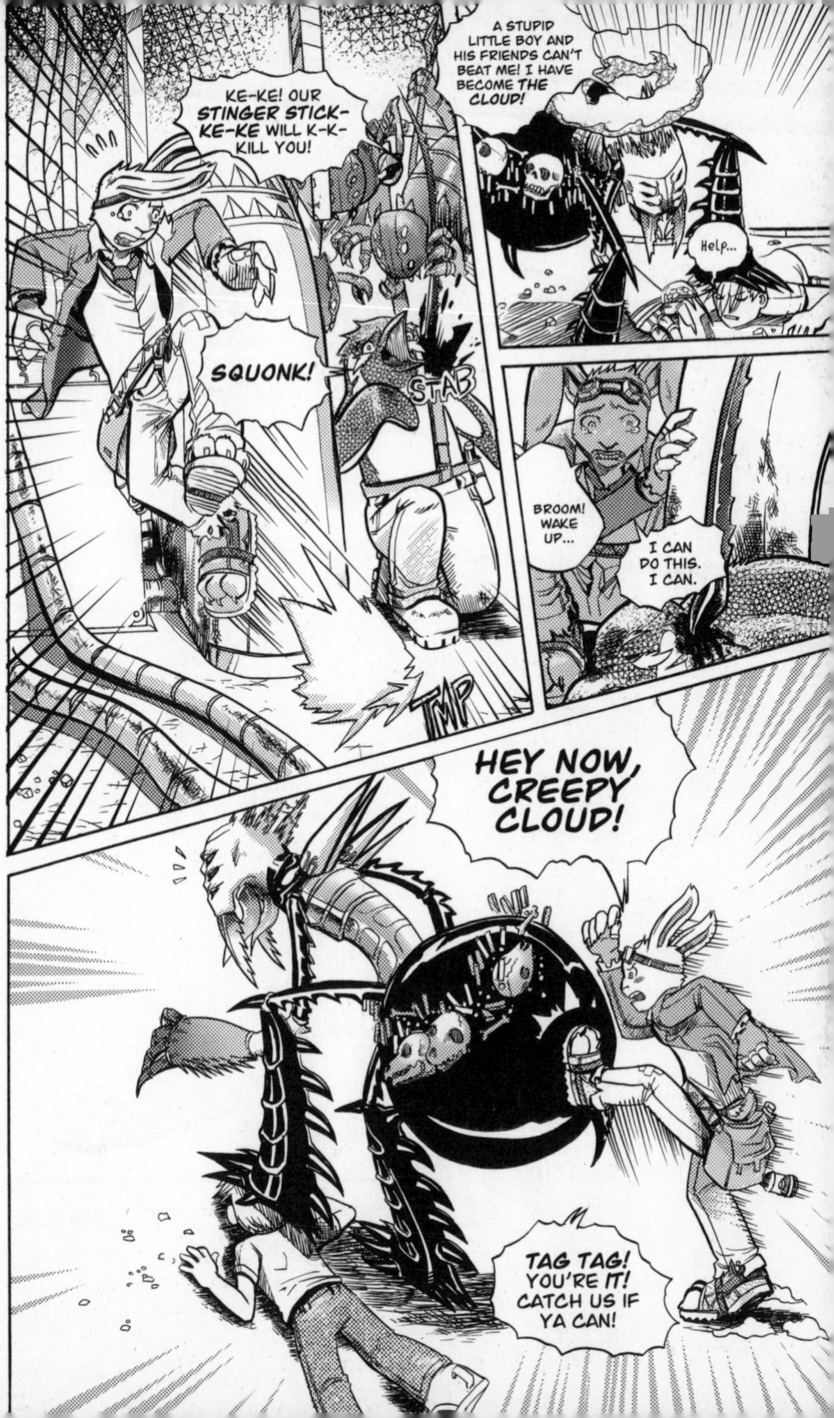

KE-KE! OUR STINGER STICK-KE-KE WILL K-K-KILL YOU!
SQUONK!
STAB
TMP
A STUPID LITTLE BOY AND HIS FRIENDS CAN'T BEAT ME! I HAVE BECOME THE CLOUD!
Help...
BROOM! WAKE UP...
I CAN DO THIS. I CAN.
HEY NOW, CREEPY CLOUD!
TAG TAG! YOU'RE IT! CATCH US IF YA CAN!

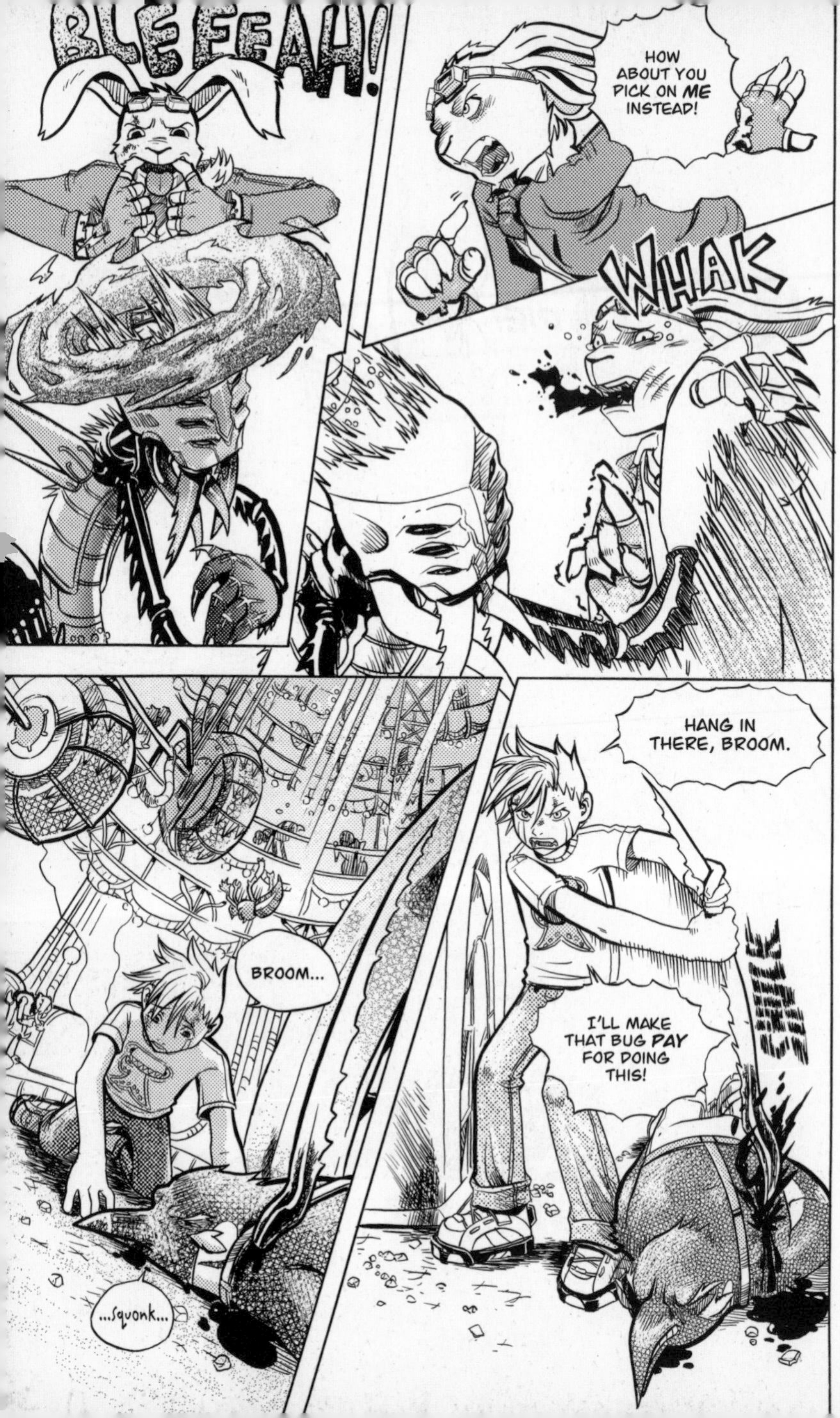
BLEEFAH!
HOW ABOUT YOU PICK ON ME INSTEAD!
WHAK
BROOM...
...squonk...
HANG IN THERE, BROOM.
I'LL MAKE THAT BUG PAY FOR DOING THIS!

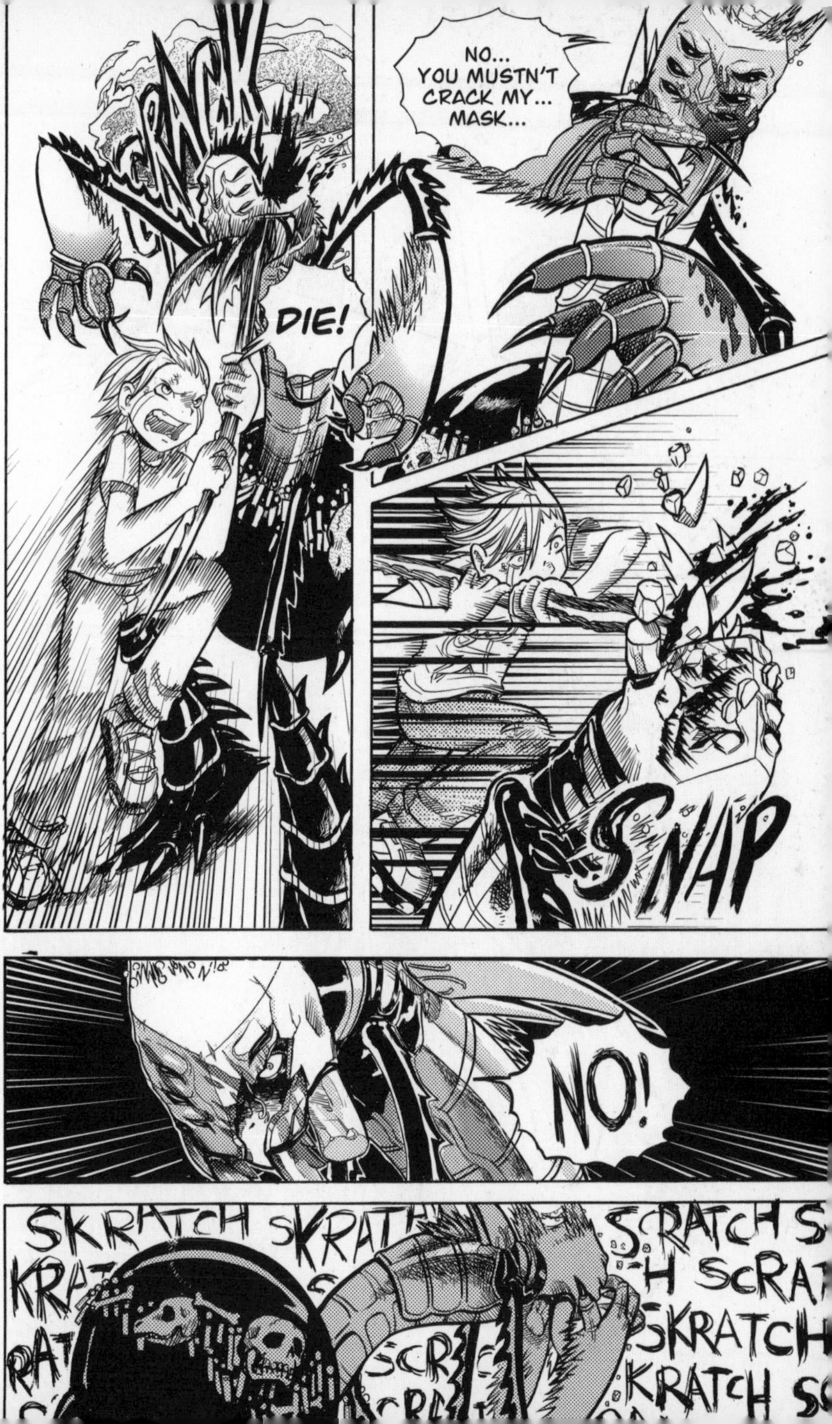
CRACK
DIE!
NO... YOU MUSTN'T CRACK MY... MASK...
SNAP
NO!
SKRATCH SKRATCH
SCRATCH
SKRATCH
KRATCH

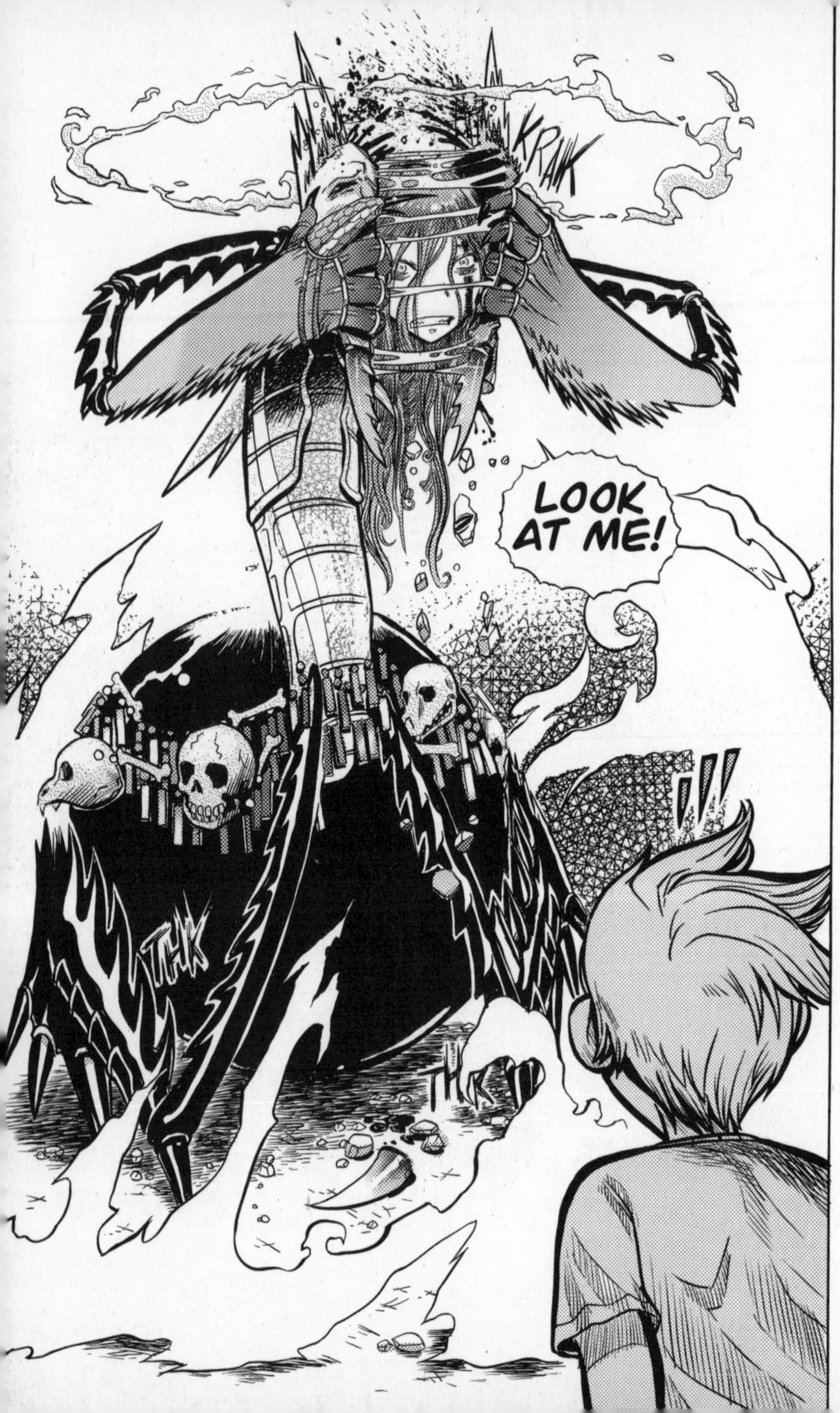
KRAK
LOOK AT ME!
THK
THK

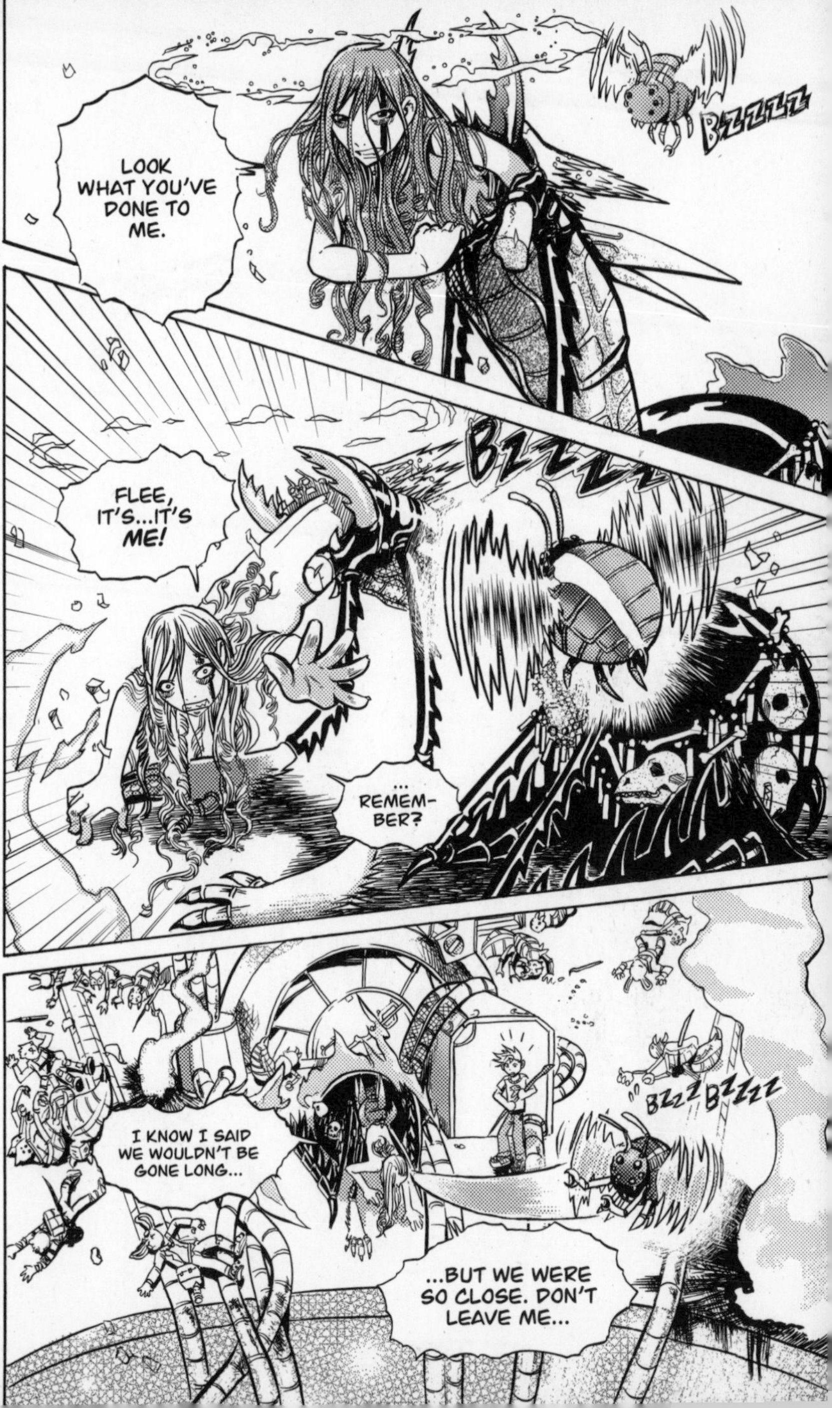
LOOK WHAT YOU'VE DONE TO ME.
BZZZZZ
FLEE, IT'S...IT'S ME!
BZZZZZ
...REMEMBER?
I KNOW I SAID WE WOULDN'T BE GONE LONG...
BZZZ BZZZZ
...BUT WE WERE SO CLOSE. DON'T LEAVE ME...

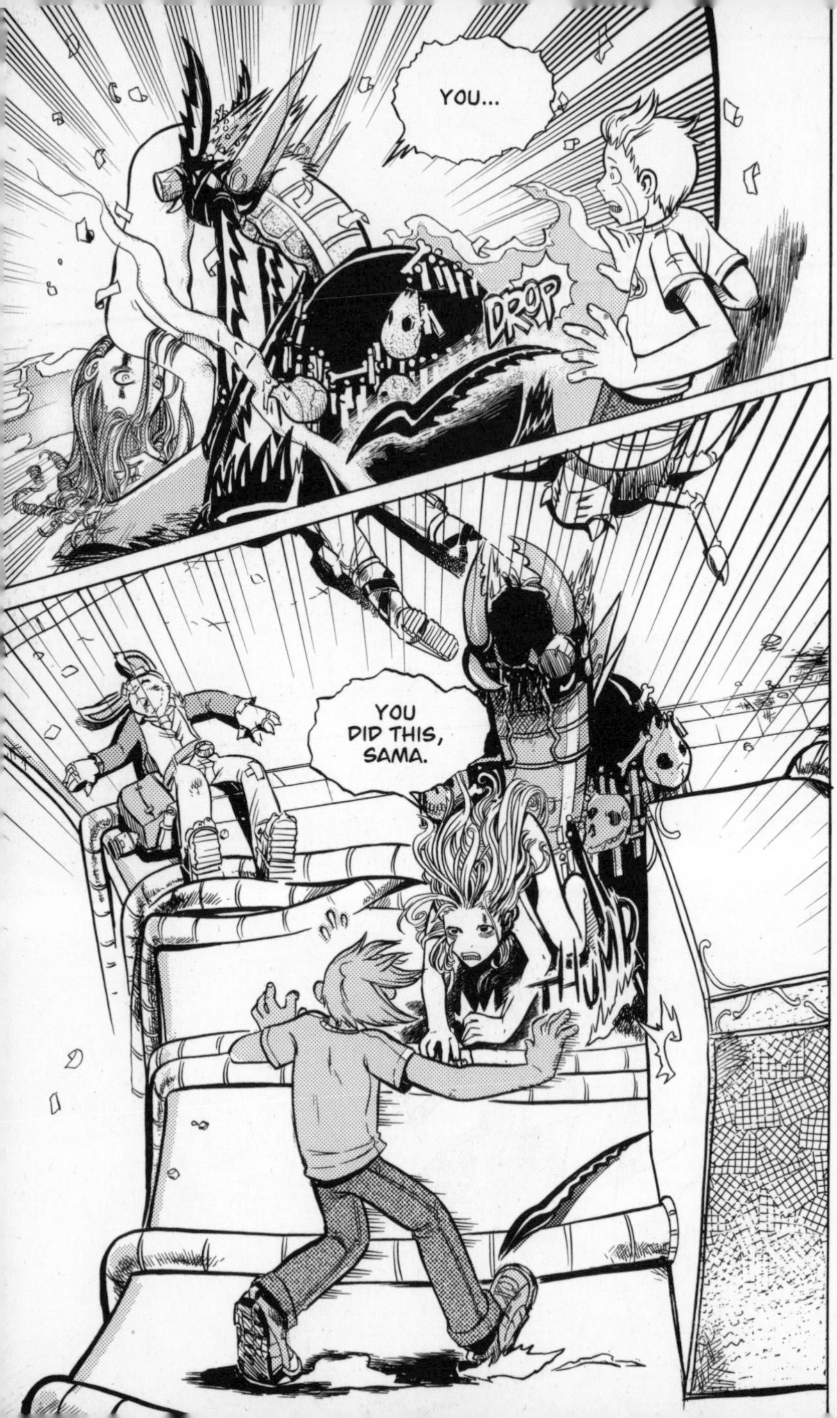
YOU...
DROP
YOU DID THIS, SAMA.
THUMP

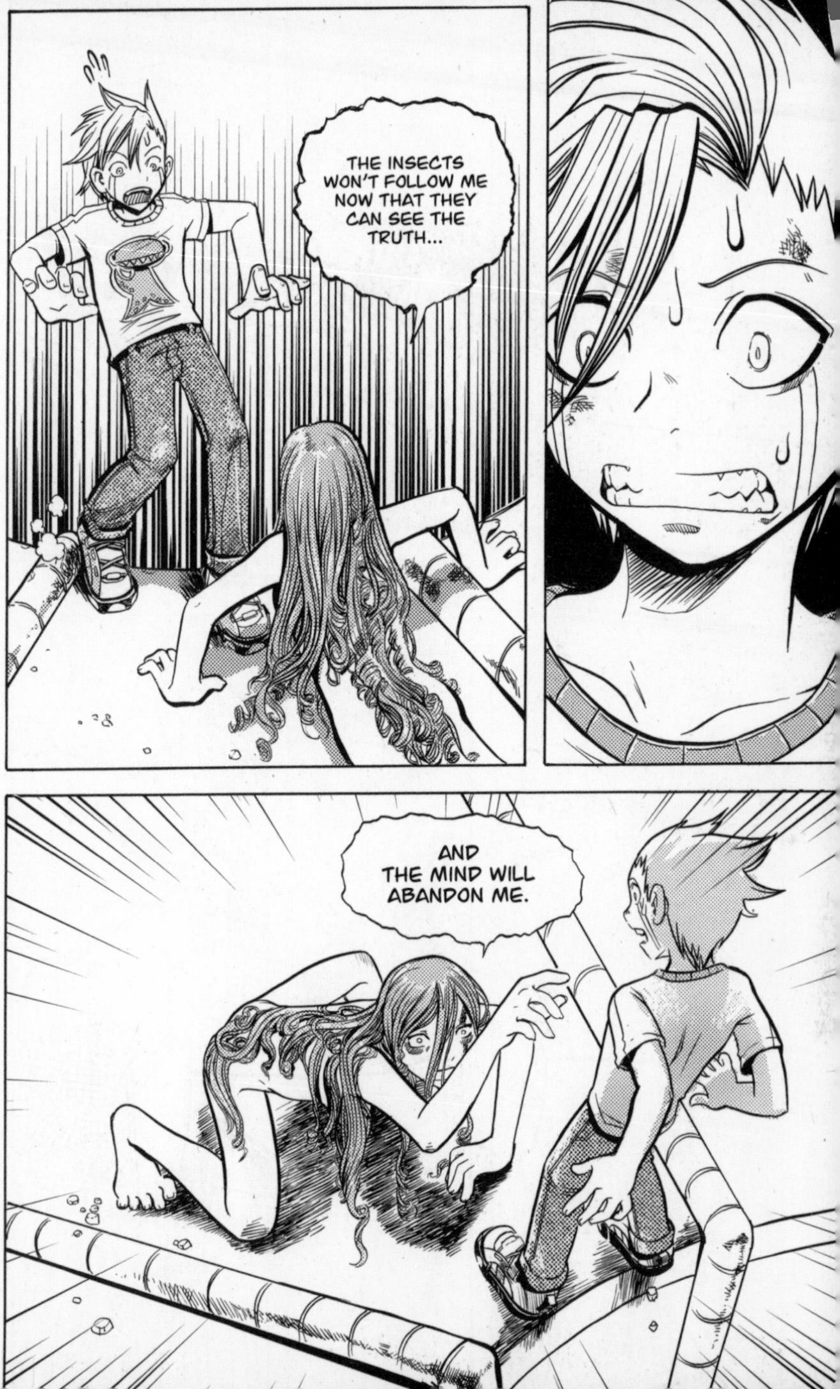
THE INSECTS WON'T FOLLOW ME NOW THAT THEY CAN SEE THE TRUTH...
AND THE MIND WILL ABANDON ME.

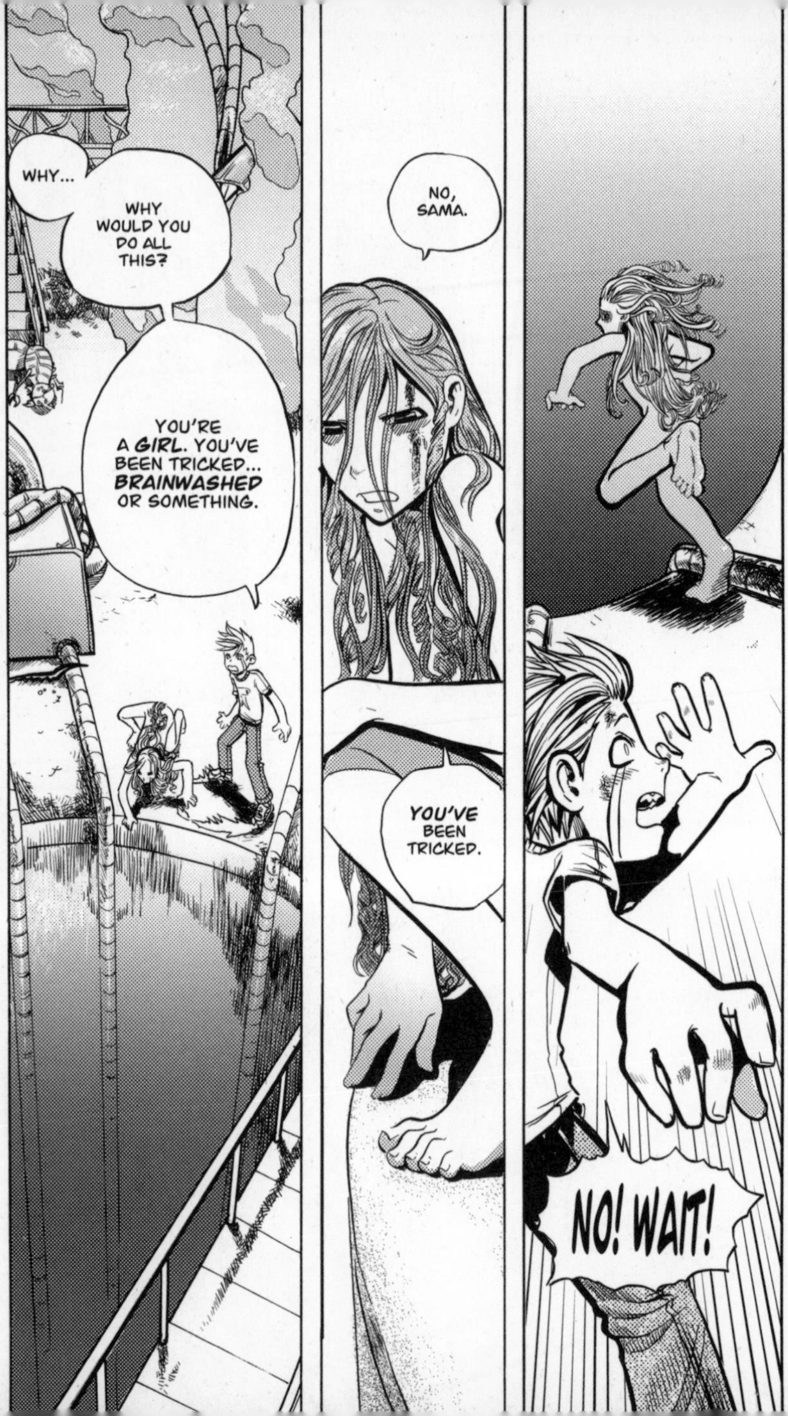
WHY...
WHY WOULD YOU DO ALL THIS?
YOU'RE A **GIRL**. YOU'VE BEEN TRICKED... **BRAINWASHED** OR SOMETHING.
NO, SAMA.
YOU'VE BEEN TRICKED.
NO! WAIT!

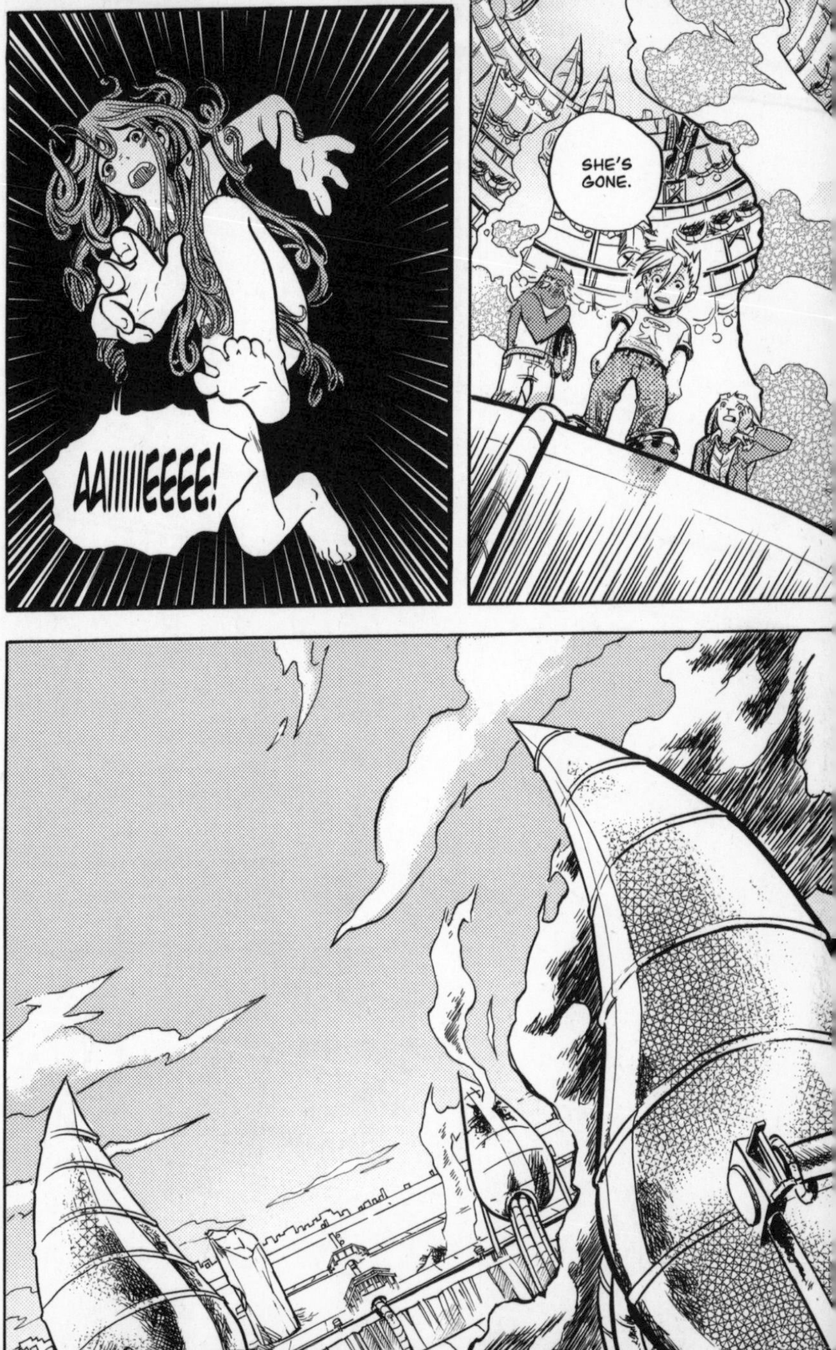
AAIIIIIIEEEE!
SHE'S GONE.

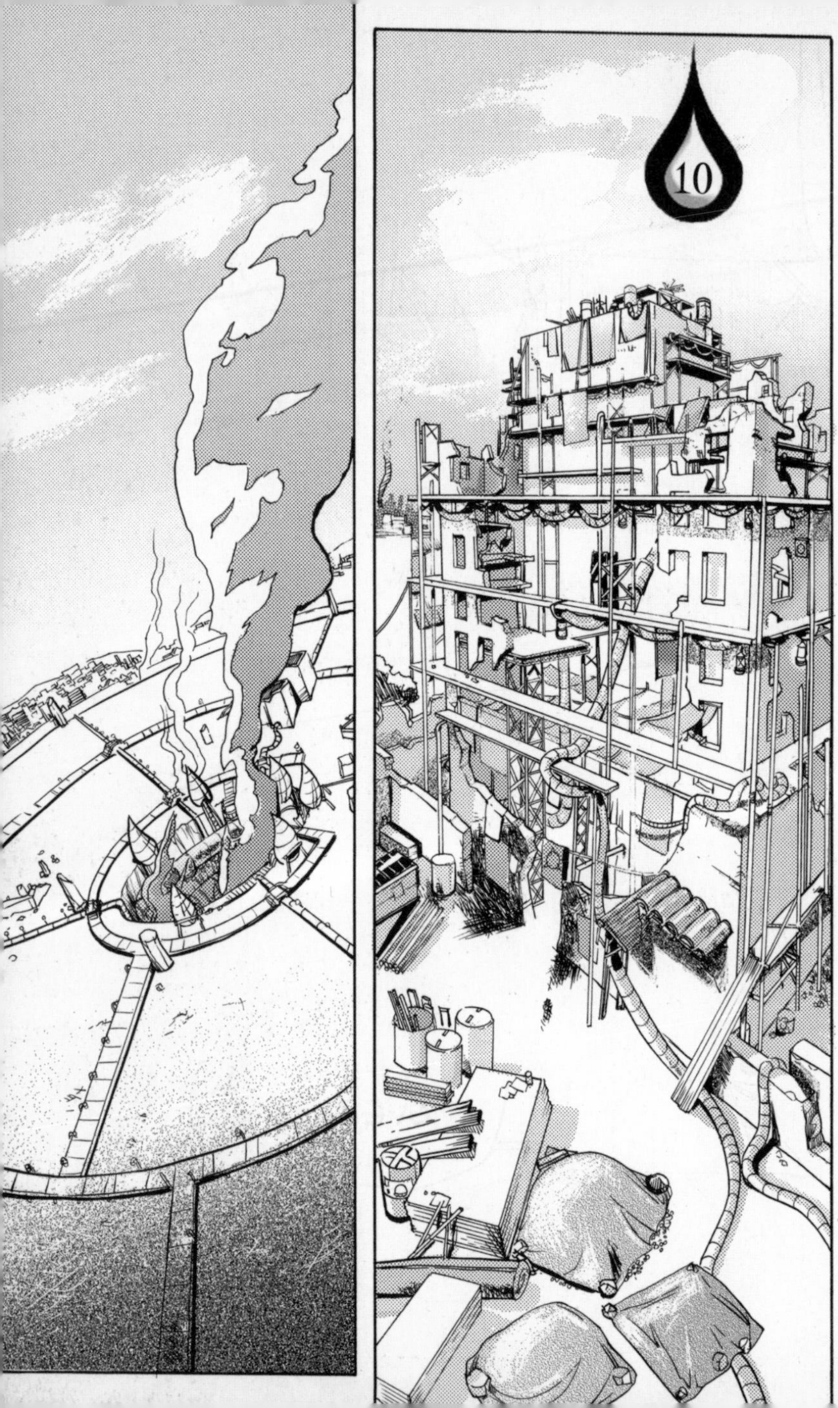
10

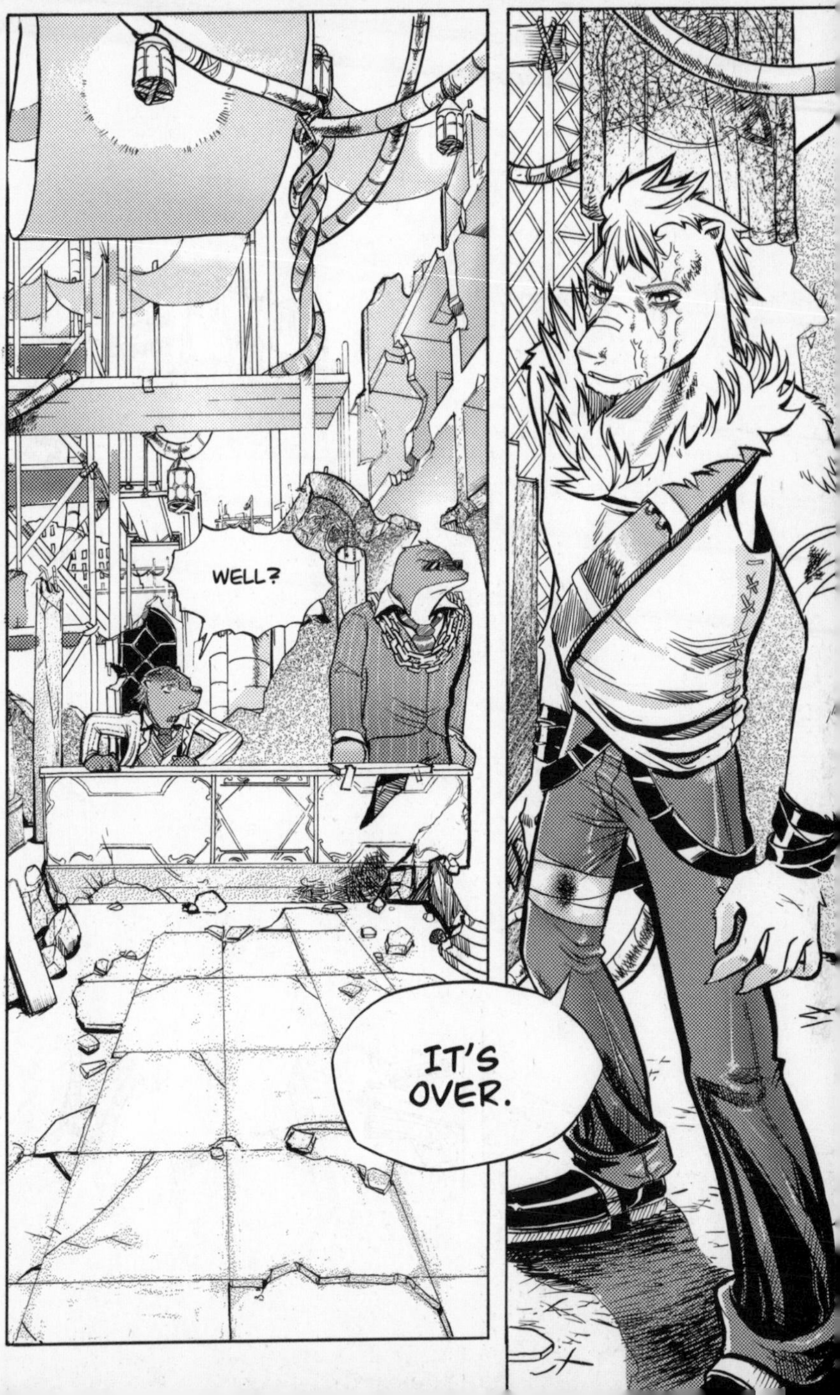
WELL?
IT'S OVER.

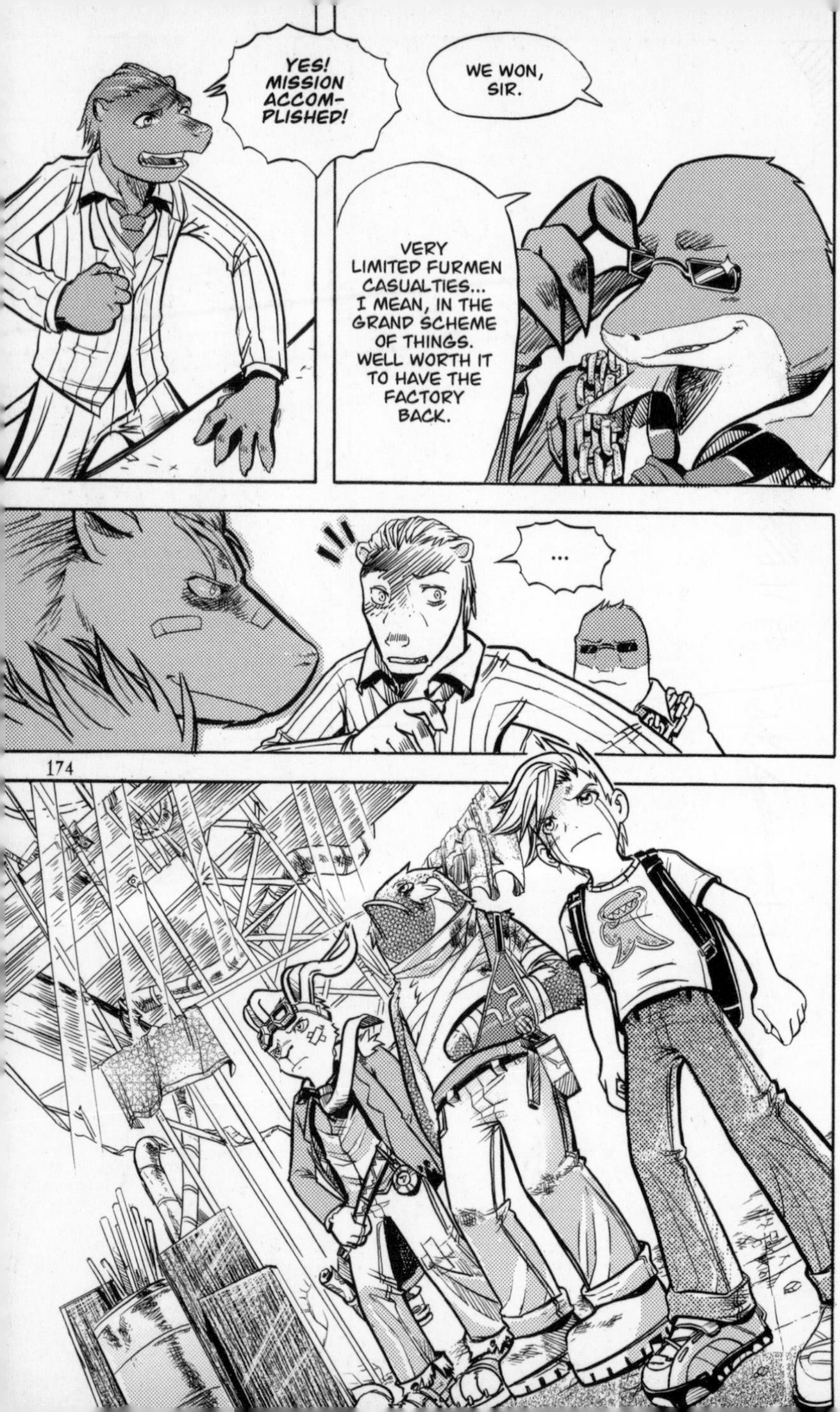
YES! MISSION ACCOMPLISHED!
WE WON, SIR.
VERY LIMITED FURMEN CASUALTIES... I MEAN, IN THE GRAND SCHEME OF THINGS. WELL WORTH IT TO HAVE THE FACTORY BACK.
...

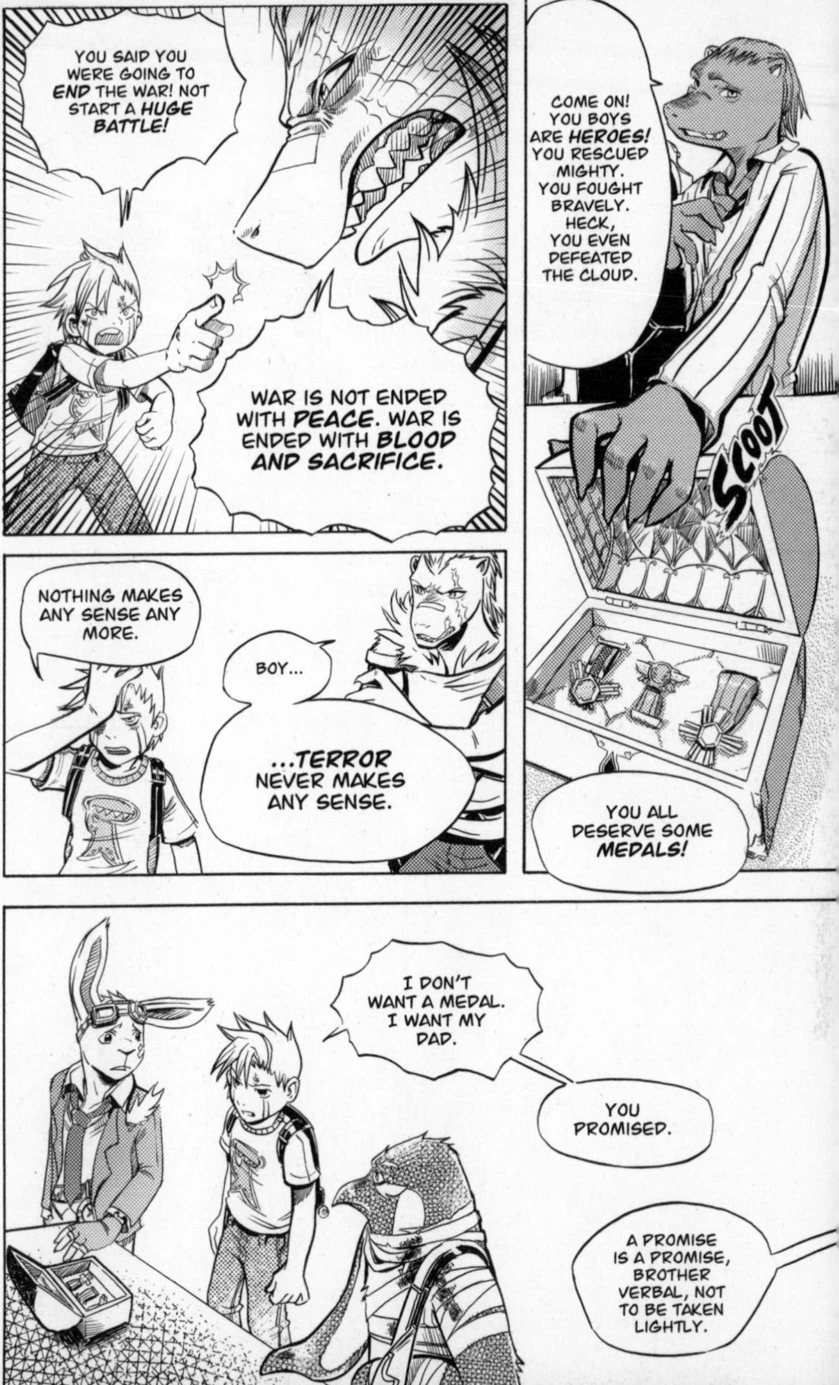
YOU SAID YOU WERE GOING TO END THE WAR! NOT START A HUGE BATTLE!
WAR IS NOT ENDED WITH PEACE. WAR IS ENDED WITH BLOOD AND SACRIFICE.
NOTHING MAKES ANY SENSE ANY MORE.
BOY...
...TERROR NEVER MAKES ANY SENSE.
COME ON! YOU BOYS ARE HEROES! YOU RESCUED MIGHTY. YOU FOUGHT BRAVELY. HECK, YOU EVEN DEFEATED THE CLOUD.
SCOOT
YOU ALL DESERVE SOME MEDALS!
I DON'T WANT A MEDAL. I WANT MY DAD.
YOU PROMISED.
A PROMISE IS A PROMISE, BROTHER VERBAL, NOT TO BE TAKEN LIGHTLY.

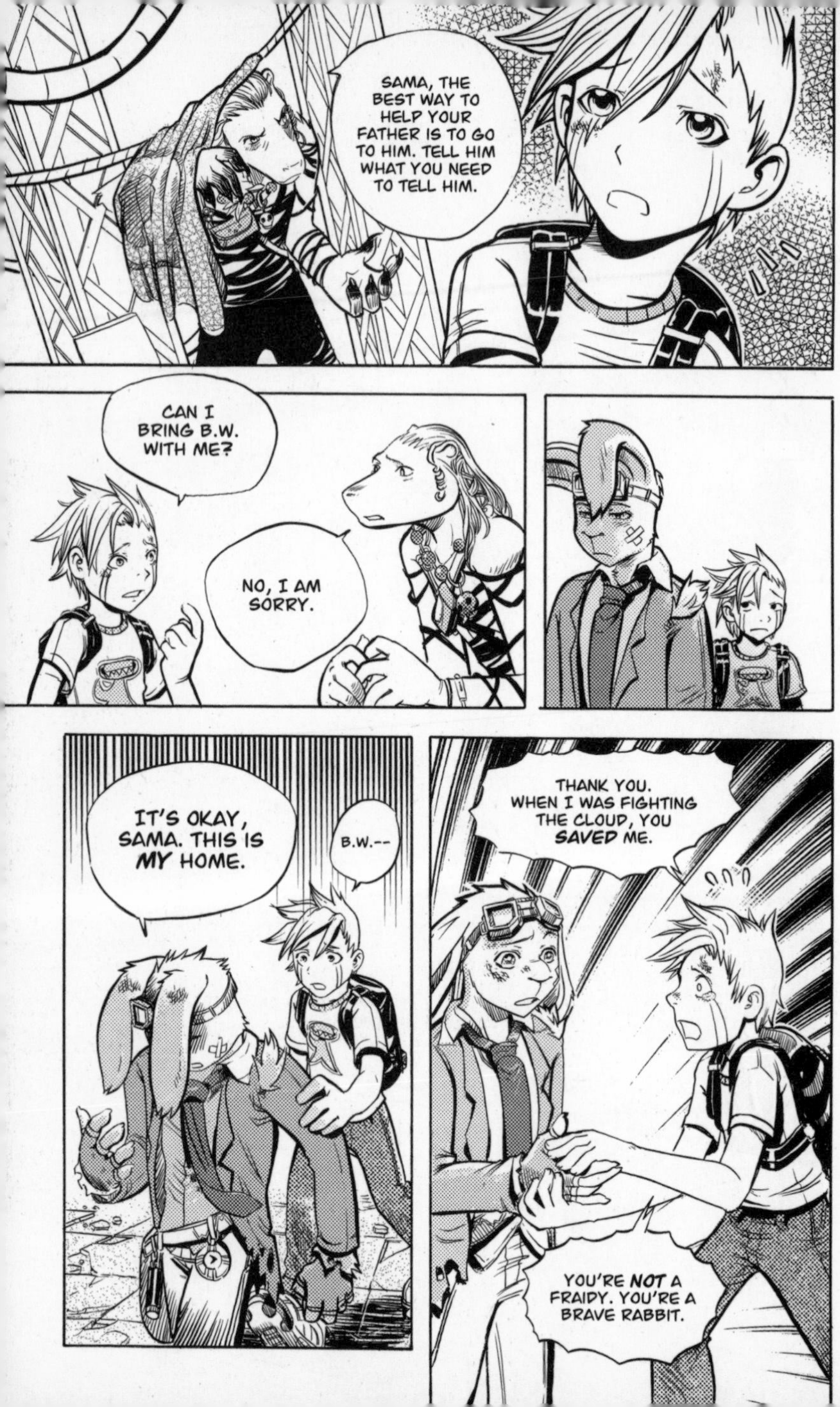

SAMA, THE BEST WAY TO HELP YOUR FATHER IS TO GO TO HIM. TELL HIM WHAT YOU NEED TO TELL HIM.
CAN I BRING B.W. WITH ME?
NO, I AM SORRY.
IT'S OKAY, SAMA. THIS IS MY HOME.
B.W.--
THANK YOU. WHEN I WAS FIGHTING THE CLOUD, YOU SAVED ME.
YOU'RE NOT A FRAIDY. YOU'RE A BRAVE RABBIT.

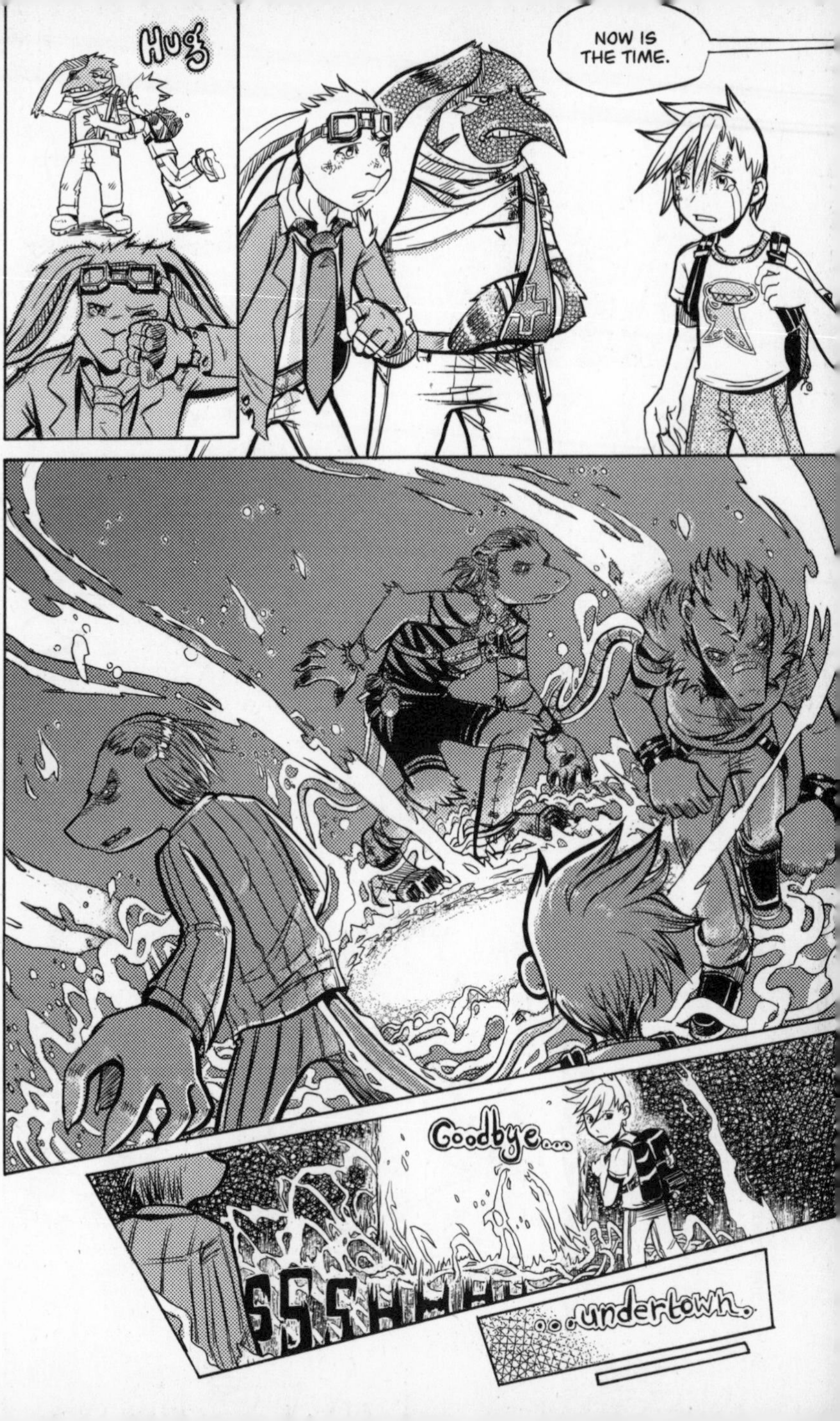
Hug
NOW IS THE TIME.
Goodbye...
...undertown.

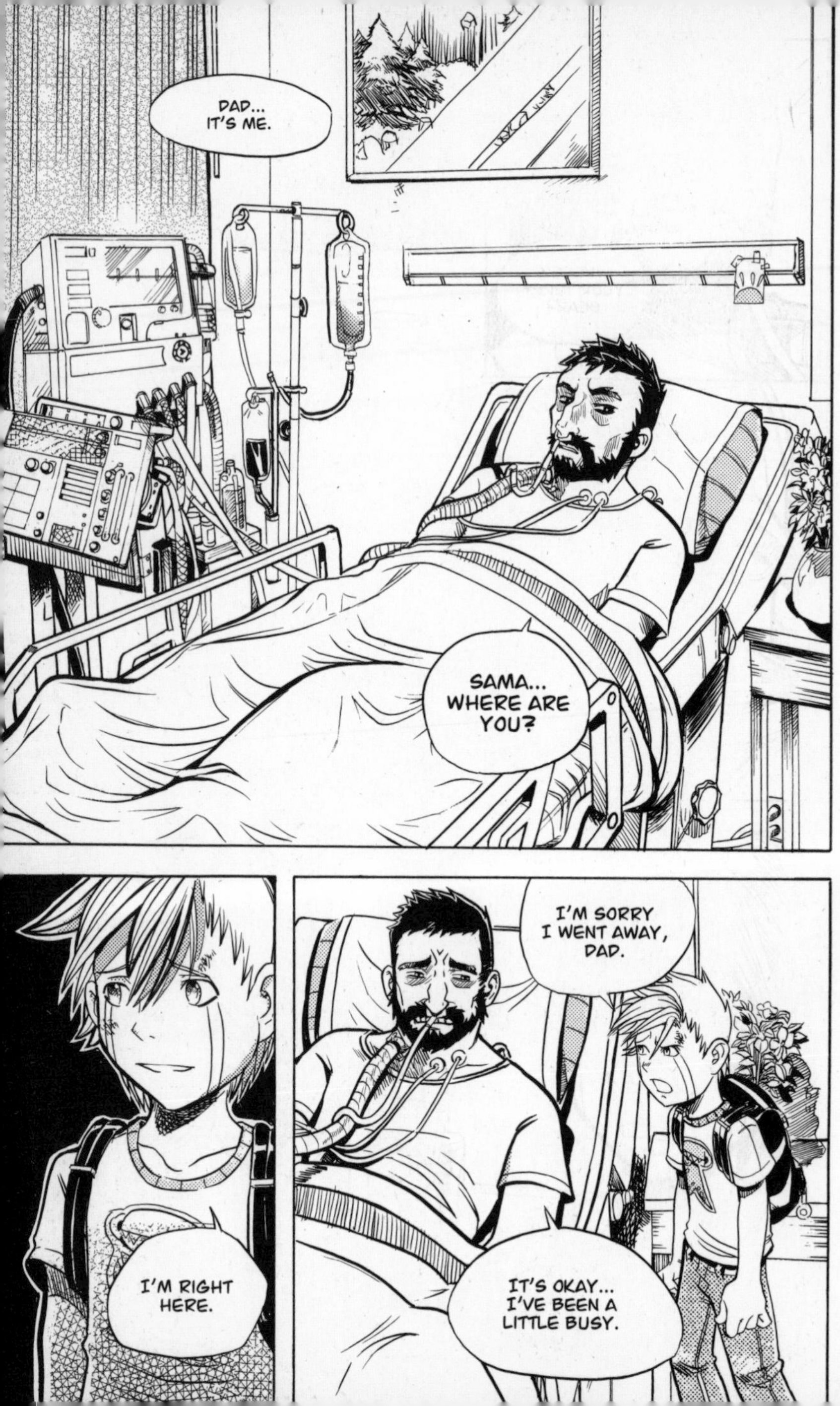
DAD... IT'S ME.
SAMA... WHERE ARE YOU?
I'M RIGHT HERE.
I'M SORRY I WENT AWAY, DAD.
IT'S OKAY... I'VE BEEN A LITTLE BUSY.

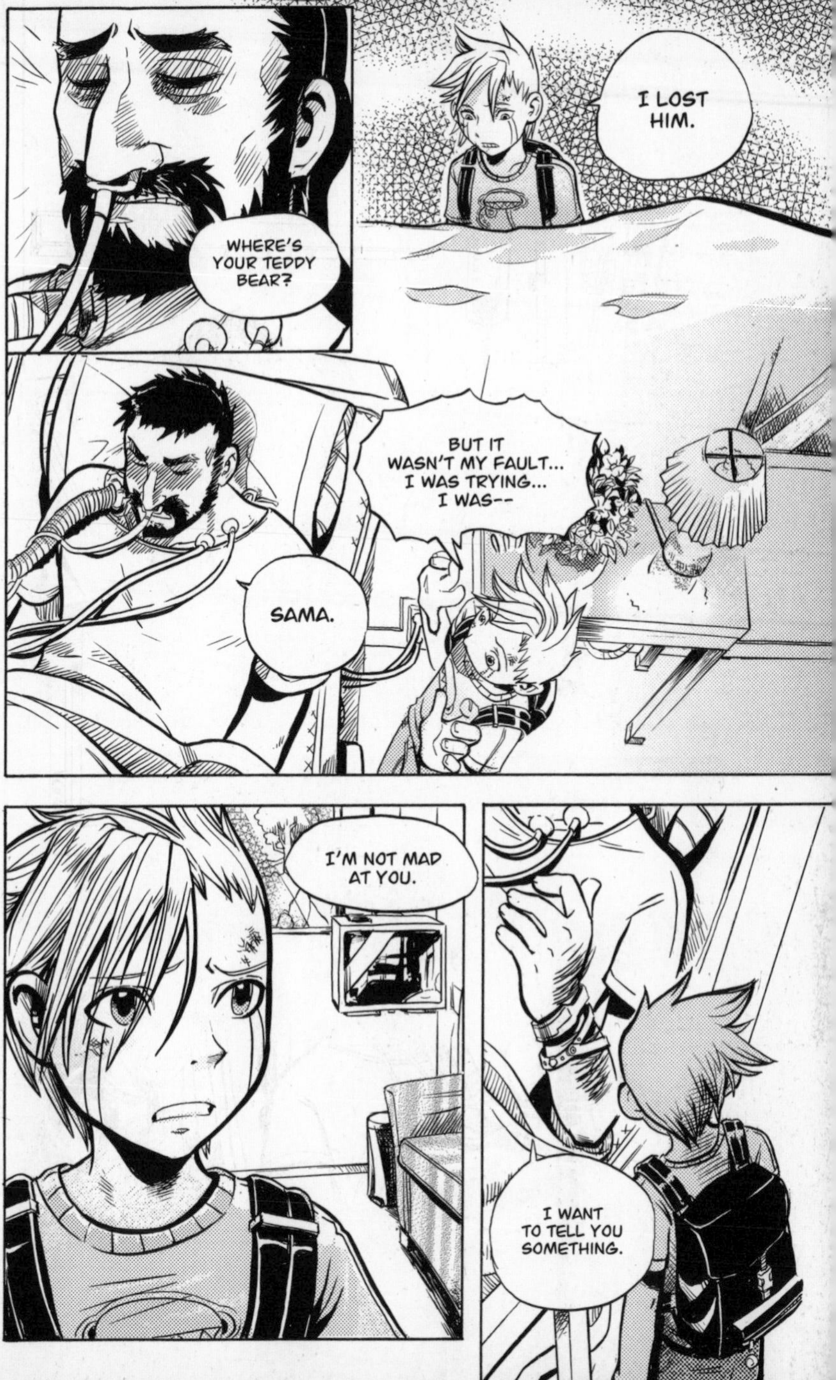
WHERE'S YOUR TEDDY BEAR?
I LOST HIM.
BUT IT WASN'T MY FAULT... I WAS TRYING... I WAS--
SAMA.
I'M NOT MAD AT YOU.
I WANT TO TELL YOU SOMETHING.

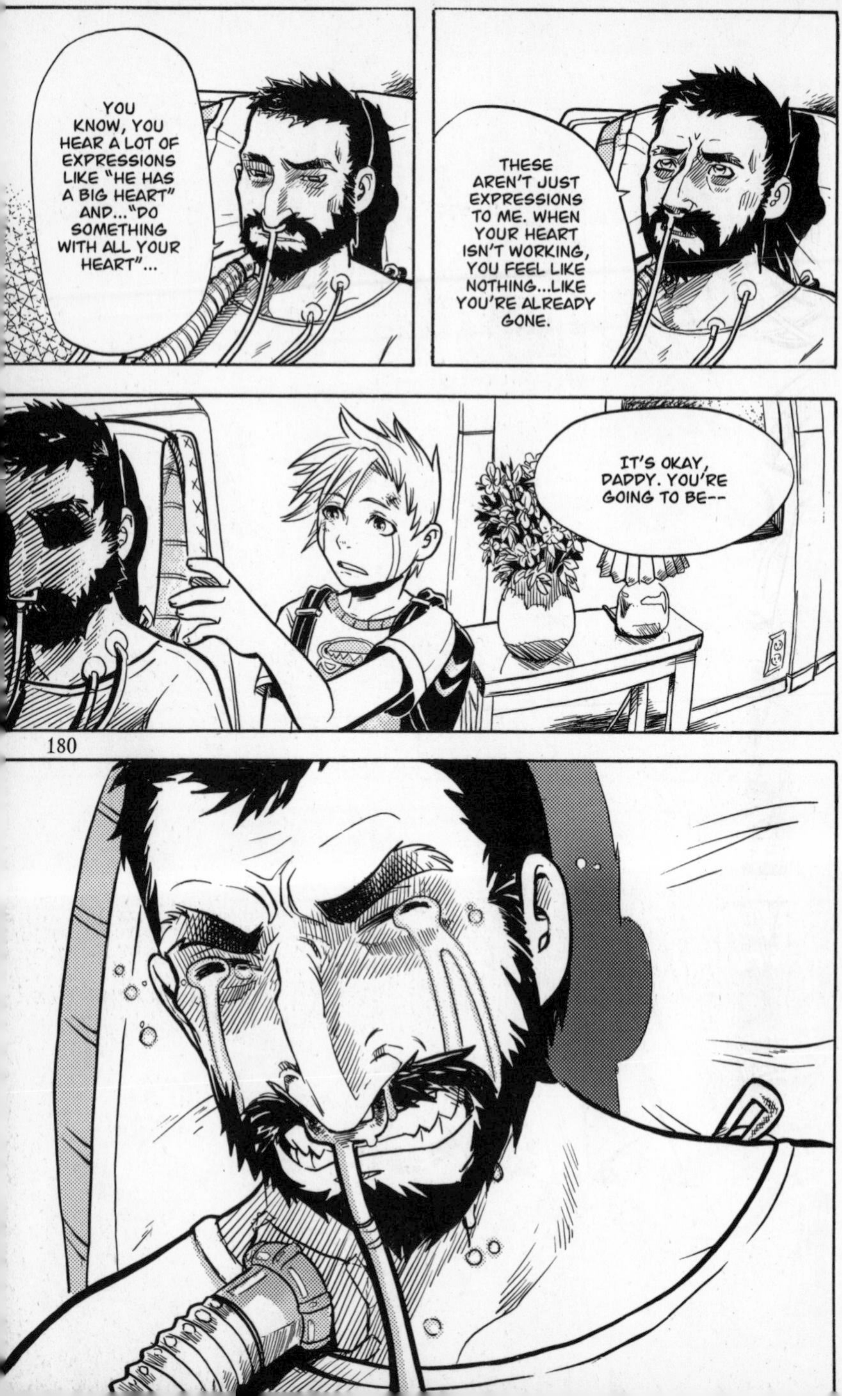
YOU KNOW, YOU HEAR A LOT OF EXPRESSIONS LIKE "HE HAS A BIG HEART" AND..."DO SOMETHING WITH ALL YOUR HEART"...
THESE AREN'T JUST EXPRESSIONS TO ME. WHEN YOUR HEART ISN'T WORKING, YOU FEEL LIKE NOTHING...LIKE YOU'RE ALREADY GONE.
IT'S OKAY, DADDY. YOU'RE GOING TO BE--

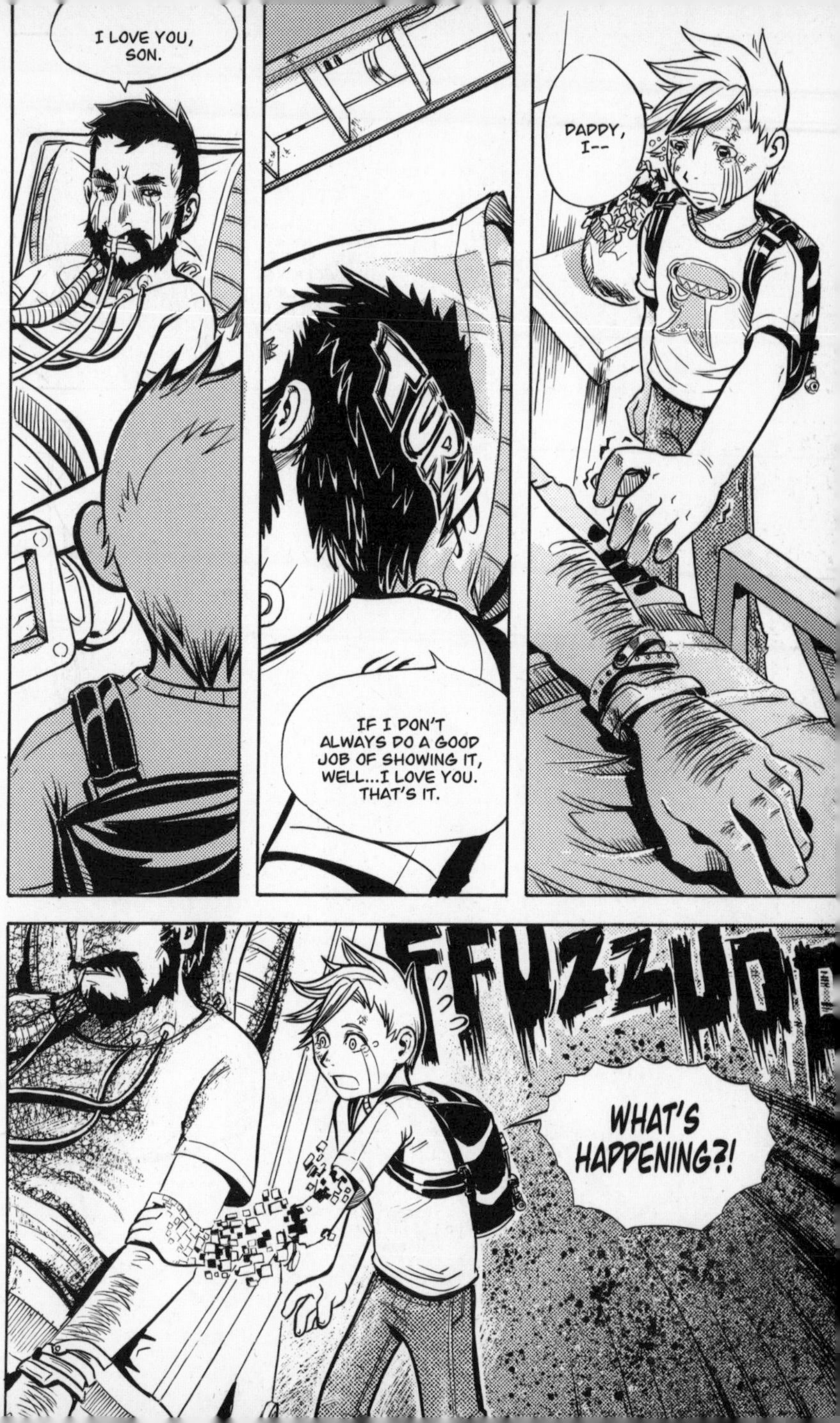
I LOVE YOU, SON.
IF I DON'T ALWAYS DO A GOOD JOB OF SHOWING IT, WELL...I LOVE YOU. THAT'S IT.
DADDY, I--
FFUZZUO
WHAT'S HAPPENING?!

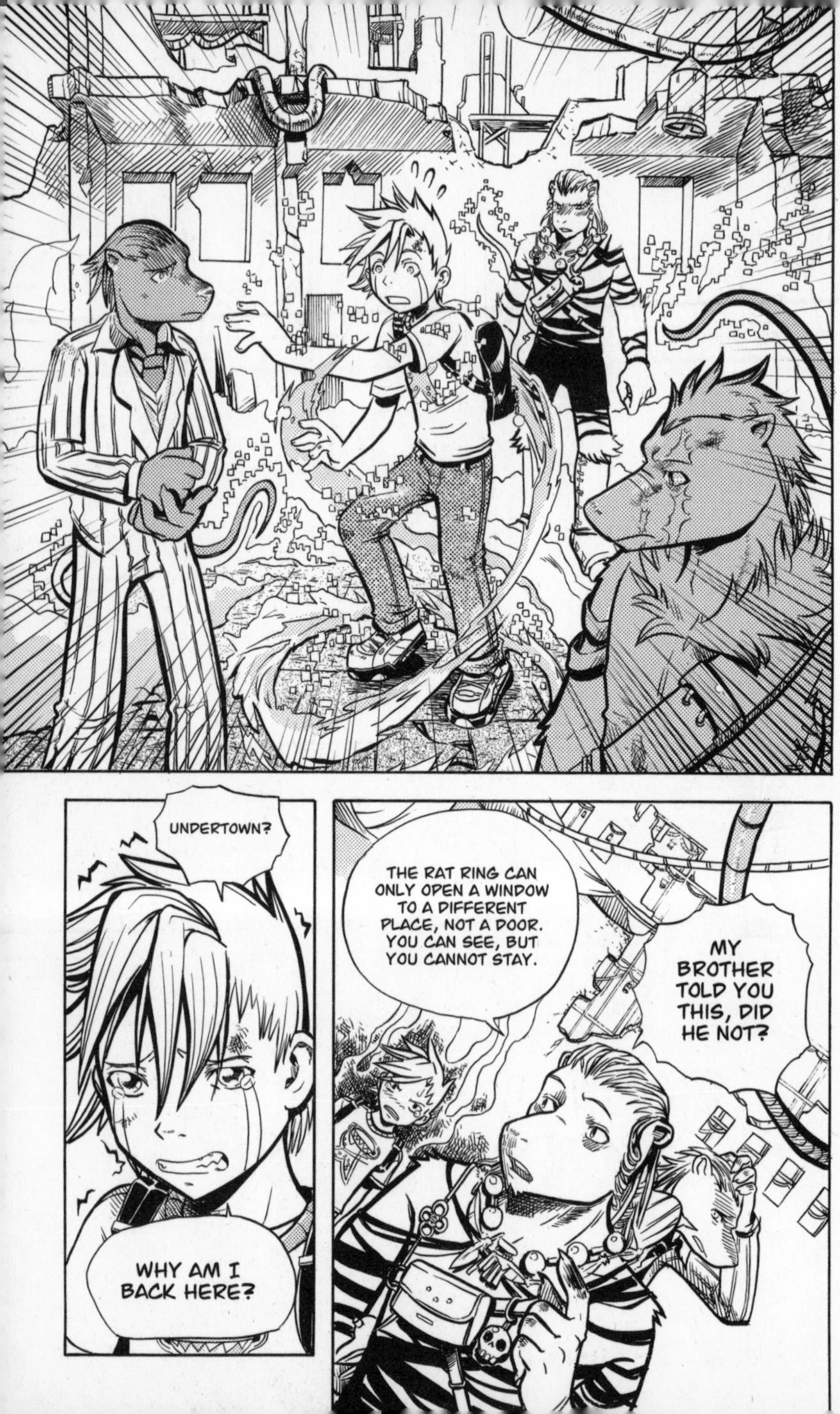
UNDERTOWN?
WHY AM I BACK HERE?
THE RAT RING CAN ONLY OPEN A WINDOW TO A DIFFERENT PLACE, NOT A DOOR. YOU CAN SEE, BUT YOU CANNOT STAY.
MY BROTHER TOLD YOU THIS, DID HE NOT?

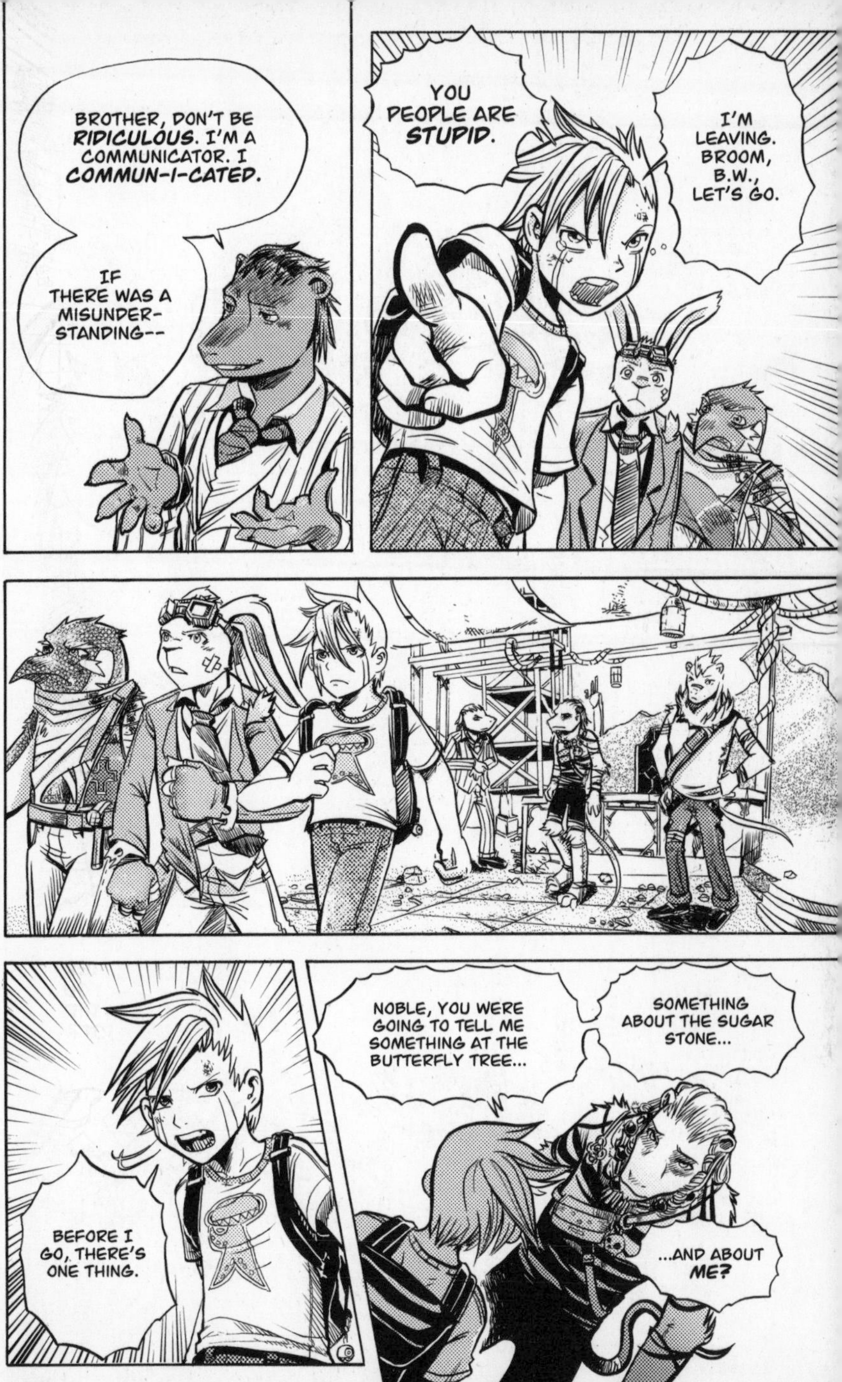
BROTHER, DON'T BE RIDICULOUS. I'M A COMMUNICATOR. I COMMUN-I-CATED.
IF THERE WAS A MISUNDER-STANDING--
YOU PEOPLE ARE STUPID.
I'M LEAVING. BROOM, B.W., LET'S GO.
BEFORE I GO, THERE'S ONE THING.
NOBLE, YOU WERE GOING TO TELL ME SOMETHING AT THE BUTTERFLY TREE...
SOMETHING ABOUT THE SUGAR STONE...
...AND ABOUT ME?

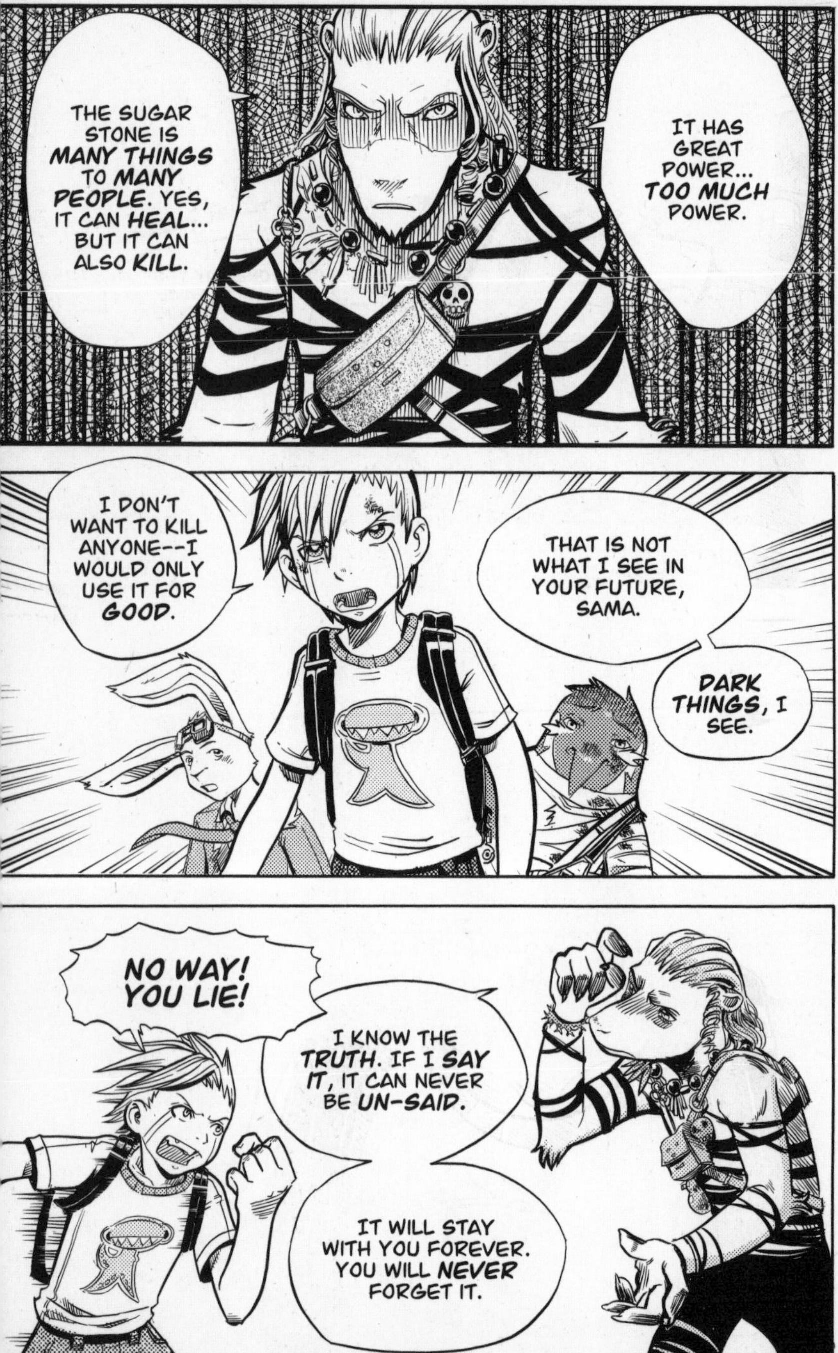
THE SUGAR STONE IS MANY THINGS TO MANY PEOPLE. YES, IT CAN HEAL... BUT IT CAN ALSO KILL.
IT HAS GREAT POWER... TOO MUCH POWER.
I DON'T WANT TO KILL ANYONE--I WOULD ONLY USE IT FOR GOOD.
THAT IS NOT WHAT I SEE IN YOUR FUTURE, SAMA.
DARK THINGS, I SEE.
NO WAY! YOU LIE!
I KNOW THE TRUTH. IF I SAY IT, IT CAN NEVER BE UN-SAID.
IT WILL STAY WITH YOU FOREVER. YOU WILL NEVER FORGET IT.

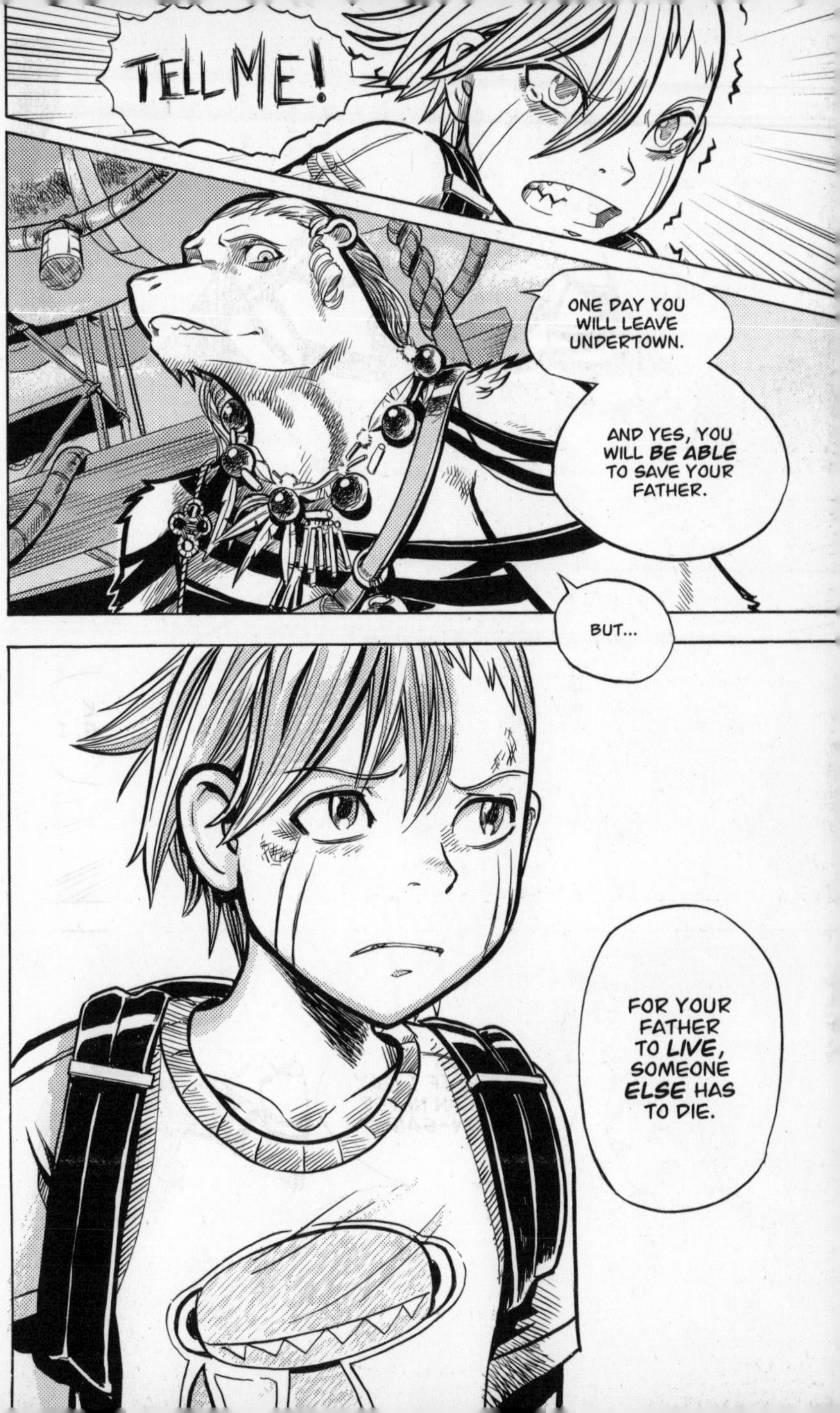
TELL ME!
ONE DAY YOU WILL LEAVE UNDERTOWN.
AND YES, YOU WILL BE ABLE TO SAVE YOUR FATHER.
BUT...
FOR YOUR FATHER TO LIVE, SOMEONE ELSE HAS TO DIE.

TO BE CONTINUED...

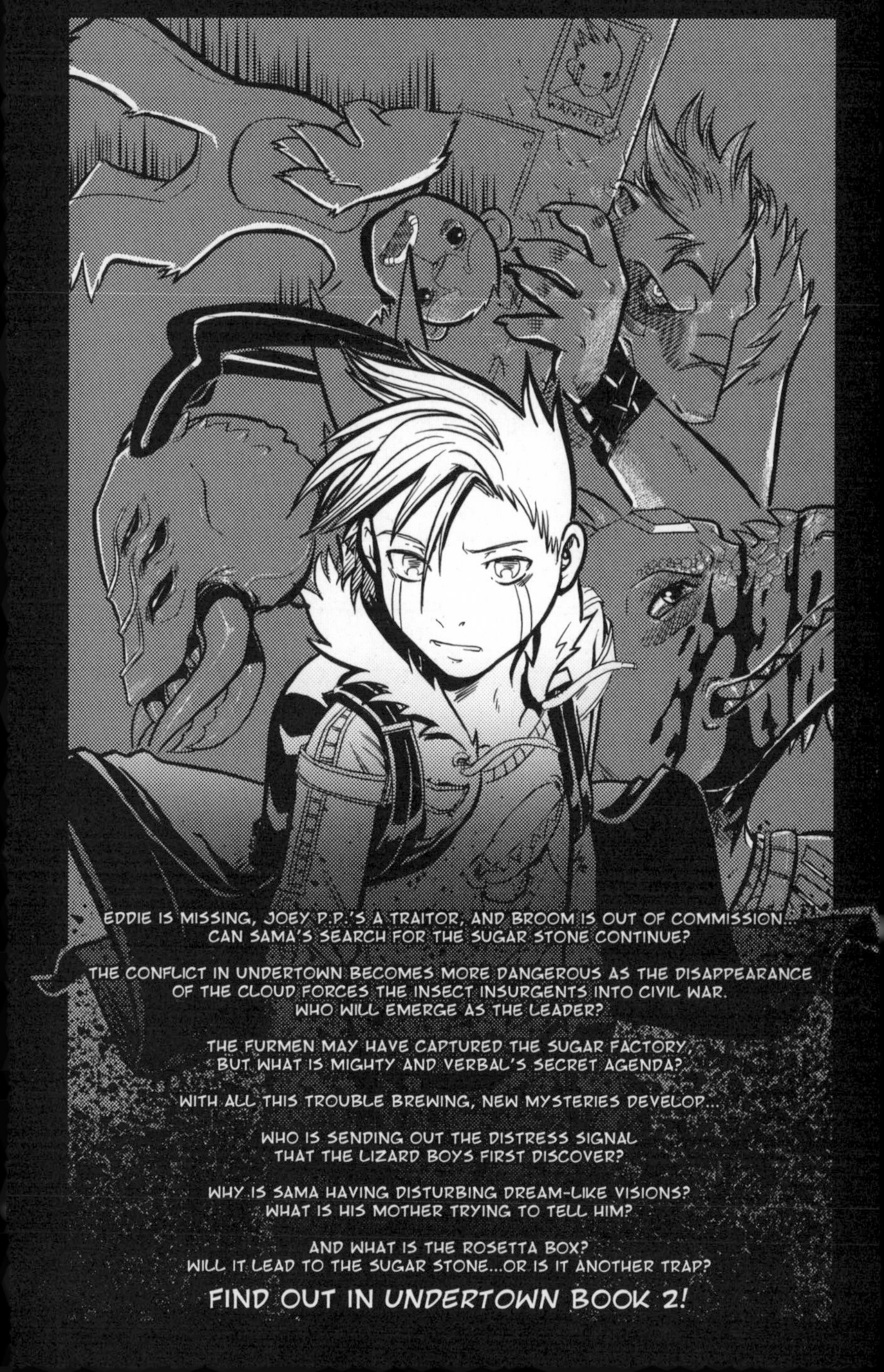

EDDIE IS MISSING, JOEY P.P.'S A TRAITOR, AND BROOM IS OUT OF COMMISSION...
CAN SAMA'S SEARCH FOR THE SUGAR STONE CONTINUE?

THE CONFLICT IN UNDERTOWN BECOMES MORE DANGEROUS AS THE DISAPPEARANCE
OF THE CLOUD FORCES THE INSECT INSURGENTS INTO CIVIL WAR.
WHO WILL EMERGE AS THE LEADER?

THE FURMEN MAY HAVE CAPTURED THE SUGAR FACTORY,
BUT WHAT IS MIGHTY AND VERBAL'S SECRET AGENDA?

WITH ALL THIS TROUBLE BREWING, NEW MYSTERIES DEVELOP...

WHO IS SENDING OUT THE DISTRESS SIGNAL
THAT THE LIZARD BOYS FIRST DISCOVER?

WHY IS SAMA HAVING DISTURBING DREAM-LIKE VISIONS?
WHAT IS HIS MOTHER TRYING TO TELL HIM?

AND WHAT IS THE ROSETTA BOX?
WILL IT LEAD TO THE SUGAR STONE...OR IS IT ANOTHER TRAP?

FIND OUT IN *UNDERTOWN* BOOK 2!

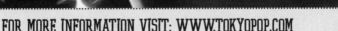

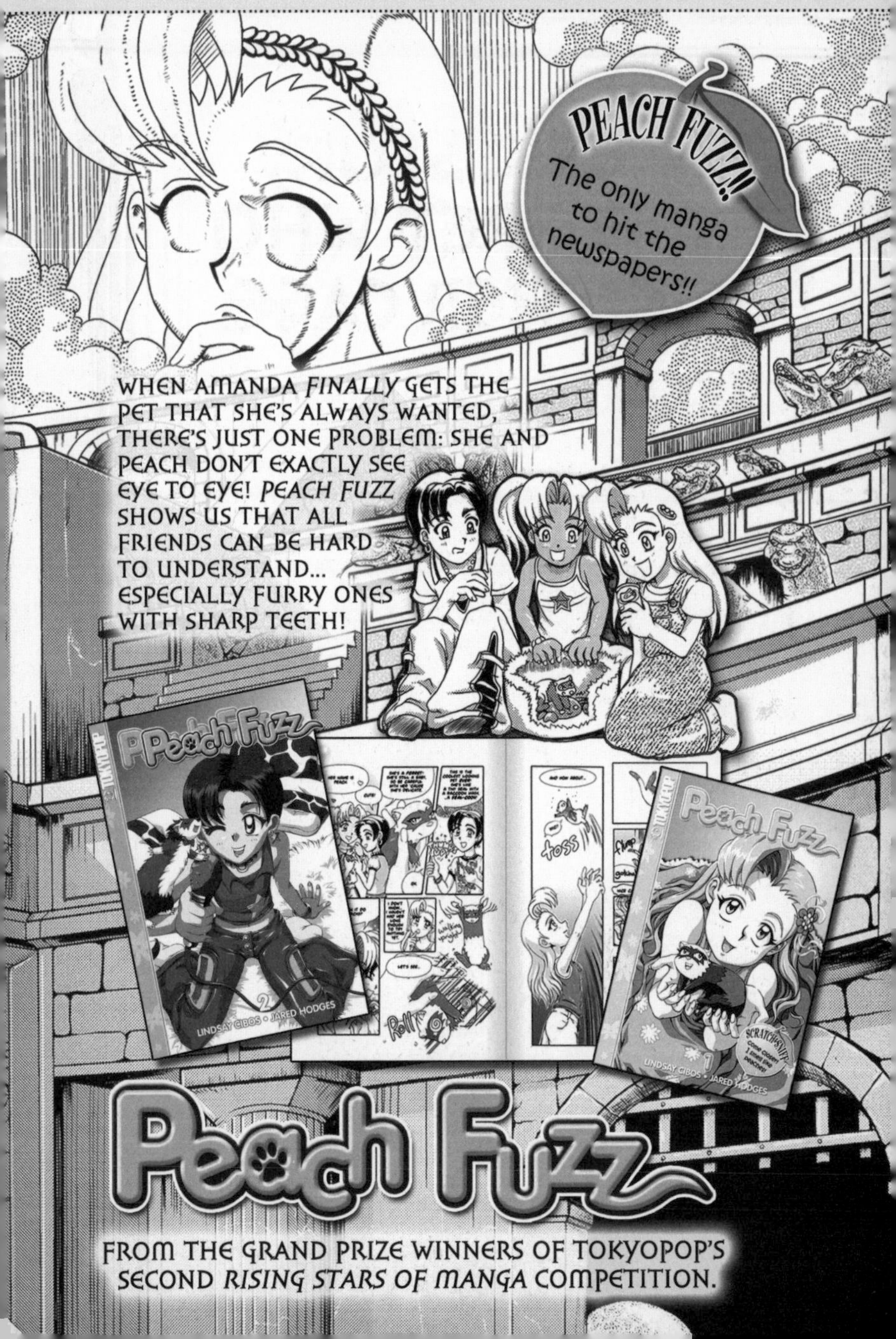
PEACH FUZZ!!
The only manga to hit the newspapers!!
WHEN AMANDA *FINALLY* GETS THE PET THAT SHE'S ALWAYS WANTED, THERE'S JUST ONE PROBLEM: SHE AND PEACH DON'T EXACTLY SEE EYE TO EYE! *PEACH FUZZ* SHOWS US THAT ALL FRIENDS CAN BE HARD TO UNDERSTAND... ESPECIALLY FURRY ONES WITH SHARP TEETH!
Peach Fuzz
TOKYOPOP
LINDSAY CIBOS • JARED HODGES
Peach Fuzz
LINDSAY CIBOS • JARED HODGES
Peach Fuzz
FROM THE GRAND PRIZE WINNERS OF TOKYOPOP'S SECOND *RISING STARS OF MANGA* COMPETITION.